MONTEREY BAY:
THE ULTIMATE GUIDE

MONTEREY BAY:
THE ULTIMATE GUIDE

FROM SANTA CRUZ TO SAN SIMEON

BY LUCINDA JACONETTE

CHRONICLE BOOKS
SAN FRANCISCO

For my mom, Joe, and Tim

Page 384 constitutes a continuation of the copyright page.

Printed in the United States of America

Library of Congress Cataloging-in-Publication Data:
Jaconette, Lucinda.
    Monterey Bay : the ultimate guide : from Santa Cruz to San Simeon / by Lucinda Jaconette.
p. cm.
Includes bibliographical references and index.
ISBN 0-8118-1925-6 (pbk.)
1. Monterey Bay Region (Calif.)—Guidebooks. 2. Pacific Coast
(Calif.)—Guidebooks. I. Title
F868.M7J325   1999   98-43451
917.94'7—dc21   CIP

Cover photograph: Larry Ulrich
Cover design: Pamela Geismar and Robin Lenowitz
Interior design: Amanda Bryan
Typesetting: Patrick David Barber
Interior illustrations: Jeff Siner and Wendy J. Wibbens
Maps: Ellen McElhinny

Distributed in Canada by Raincoast Books,
8680 Cambie Street, Vancouver, B.C. V6P 6M9

10 9 8 7 6 5 4 3 2 1

Chronicle Books
85 Second Street
San Francisco, CA 94105

www.chroniclebooks.com

CONTENTS

ACKNOWLEDGMENTS

I am truly grateful to the many people who contributed to this book. Not only have they enriched the pages with their knowledge and understanding, they have touched us all with their kindness.

For information about the Monterey Bay Aquarium, I am grateful to Julie Packard, Steven Webster, and Ken Peterson, as well as other members of the aquarium's staff and its cadre of volunteers, especially Sheila McMahon. They greatly deepened my understanding, and they continually work overtime to improve the future of our oceans. Gary Greene of the U.S. Geological Survey demystified the theories surrounding the origins of the Monterey Bay Canyon. I hope my words do his studies justice. Alan Baldridge, distinguished head librarian emeritus of the Hopkins Marine Laboratory, provided sources on the Monterey Bay Sanctuary and details on its natural history. Todd Bliss added knowledge of geologic formations. Paul Keel helped clarify elephant seal information. The staff at the Pacific Grove Museum of Natural History provided technical information.

For historical background of native peoples and cultures, David Breschini, Rob Edwards, Don Howard, Patrick Orozco, and Linda Yamane provided a strong foundation and much clarification. Elmer Lagorio, archivist at the Pebble Beach Company, along with others at the Pebble Beach Company, found answers to difficult questions. James McNaughton, command historian of the Defense Language Institute, provided information about the Presidio. Rohanna LoSchiavo walked me through the history of Cannery Row. Craig Barker recalled the spirit of Boulder Creek. Diane West-Bourke provided natural history information for the Waddell Creek area. Cole Weston shared his art and recollections, bringing Carmel and Big Sur into focus. Bill and Marilyn Fravel shared the community spirit and beauty of Davenport. Geoff Welch of the Pacific Grove Heritage Society read early drafts and provided insight into Pacific Grove history. Carol Robles offered information about John Steinbeck and Salinas. Polly Archer, Lisa Maddalena, and Marjory Cameron, Pacific Grove librarians, Helena Szczesiak, Harrison Memorial librarian and Doug Holtzman and Janice Rodman, Monterey City reference librarians, provided countless sources, often in record time. Pat Hathaway contributed data of the past from his museum-quality files. Annette Lindstrom shared in much of the early manuscript planning. Susan Retten read and clarified chapters.

This book is greatly enhanced by the fine eye and pen of Jeff Siner, whose landscape and architectural etchings convey the beauty of the area. Wendy J. Wibbens breathed life into the pages with her drawings of fauna and flora.

I am indebted also to the *Monterey County Herald* for permission to quote articles from its back issues. Adam Weiland, editor of the *Board and Batten,* newsletter of the Pacific Grove Heritage Society, offered his research and permission to use his compiled writings. Bill Bates allowed use of his quotes about Carmel. Joyce Krieg shared her public relations skills, radio expertise, and interviews.

Heartfelt thanks go to my family: To my husband Joe for his understanding, patience, humor, expertise, and company. To our son Tim for his insights, hugs, quotes, and additions to the Highlights for Kids sections. To my mom for her unconditional love, hours of help, and creative additions. To Florence and Paul Jaconette for their caring and enthusiasm. To my brothers Lincoln and Alfred "Chip" Olbrycht and their wives Lennie and Pam for encouragement and reading of numerous drafts.

I also want to thank my readers for their many letters of appreciation. Thank you also for helping the first edition make frequent appearances on the local best-seller list. And finally, I would like to thank the hundreds of people I interviewed for the stories they shared with me. Beyond a doubt, one of the greatest treasures on the Monterey Bay landscape is its remarkable people.

INTRODUCTION

This guidebook covers the stretch of California's Central Coast bounded by the Monterey Bay National Marine Sanctuary. Created by the hard work and determination of Central Coast residents and formally established by Congress in 1992, the sanctuary is the largest protected marine area in the lower forty-eight states. Encompassing five thousand square miles of open water (4,024 nautical miles), its boundaries range from the shore to deep ocean habitats, extending from the high tide mark to as far as fifty-three miles offshore. Rich biological and cultural resources are protected by this designation. A balanced description is given by renowned oceanographer Dr. Sylvia Earle: "Today, Marine sanctuaries are places in the sea, as elusive as a sea breeze, as tangible as a singing whale. They are beautiful, or priceless, or rare bargains, or long-term assets, or fun, or all of these and more. Above all, sanctuaries are now and with care will continue to be 'special places.' Each of us can have the pleasures of defining what that means." The coastal stretch covered in this book extends through the natural range of the Monterey pine tree north and south through five counties, from Año Nuevo, just beyond the northern coastal borderline of Santa Cruz County south to Cambria near the southern boundary of the marine sanctuary. Moving inland, this area stretches east through the coastal range, the Carmel and Salinas Valleys, and the outskirts of the rolling Gabilan Mountains.

Along the Central Coast of California, the Pacific Ocean curves into the beautiful crescent of the Monterey Bay, core of the marine sanctuary. Gliding above, pelicans ride the winds alongside hang gliders who seek out the seaside updrafts. At the surface a whale salutes with the whack of his flukes, while relentless waves crash to foam against rocks a hundred million years old. Hidden beneath the surface is the deepest marine canyon gouged from the ocean bottom off the mainland of the United States. Within and beyond Monterey Bay, more marine canyons reach into the sanctuary's waters where wrecked ships and a dirigible share the Central Coast ocean floor with one of the most diverse marine habitats in the world.

What creatures are at this moment floating on the waves or treading inland forests? Why is that volcano severed in half? Who were the first people here, and where are their descendants? Where can I see the best views, the definitive architecture? Where can I try out a hang glider or a kayak, or learn to cook with regional masters? Where can I find a serene cove, Victorian garden, or forested glen? And what, to echo the most important question of any traveler, is there to eat?

You will find the answers here. Not just in a see this, go here manner, but with an invitation to really know the layers and intricacies of each place. The visitor capital of this area is the Monterey Peninsula, one of the top five conference locations in the country. The city of Monterey is often referred to as the "Mother of the Western United States." Historic adobes serve as museums and business locations in this city of firsts in modern California history: first public building, first capital of California, site of the first official raising of an American flag in declaration of manifest destiny over seven Western states, first hotel, first theater, first billiard tables. The City of Monterey is located on the northern stretch of the Monterey peninsula within the County of Monterey and is itself a prime visitor destination. We'll take the City of Monterey as our first destination and the one from which all other travel radiates.

"To live much and without care, come to Monterey. This is the most peaceful and quiet country in the world; one lives better here than in the most cultured court of Europe. It is a great country with healthful climate, not too hot, not too cold, good bread, excellent meat, tolerable fish, and *bonne humeur* which is worth all the rest." Although this quote may sound like a chamber brochure it is ascribed to Diego de Borica, the Spanish governor of this region in 1794. Visitor surveys show that like governor Borica, people from other regions and states consider the areas in this book "Monterey." Most chambers, visitors, and residents would agree with Borica's words even as we enter the twenty-first century. However, many of the communities are geographically and culturally very different and treasure their individual identities.

"The greatest meeting of land and water in the world" is how artist Francis McComas described the lands around Point Lobos at the southern end of the peninsula. Four distinct communities, Pacific Grove, Pebble Beach, Carmel, and Big Sur, match this vision and are all lodging destinations for visitors to the Monterey Bay Aquarium.

The aquarium is the single greatest visitor destination in the area. Mysteries of the underwater world and new, deeper connections with life, such as those made during eye contact with a gentle octopus, attract visitors. Half of the aquarium is built in the City of Monterey and half in "The Last Hometown," Pacific Grove. Known for its love of the monarch butterfly and building preservation, this town boasts Victorian inns and a lovely scenic ocean border. Pebble Beach, the world-renowned golfing and forest resort and residential area, lies to the south between Pacific Grove and Carmel. Quaint homes, shops, artist studios, and galleries cluster in the one-mile-square village of Carmel, surrounded by little-known walking trails.

Beyond, to the south, the rugged Big Sur Coast extends the length of the Santa Lucia Mountains. South of Big Sur lie the opulent Hearst Castle and Cambria, an artists' colony and one of the few coastal small towns left south of the Monterey Peninsula.

Afternoon winds blow marine air that is cooled over the depths of the Monterey Bay Canyon into the Salinas and Carmel Valleys reminding inland dwellers of their connection with the sea. You can visit inland lakes via rural Carmel Valley Road or by horseback expeditions through the Ventana Wilderness Area. Other inland excursions bring you to the caves in the Pinnacles National Monument and to nearby San Juan Bautista, a town from another time with wooden sidewalks and a mission plaza.

A collage of communities (Seaside, Sand City, Marina, Moss Landing, Watsonville, Rio Del Mar, La Selva Beach, Seascape, Aptos, and Capitola) as well as the ecologically crucial Elkhorn Slough frame the journey from the City of Monterey north to Santa Cruz. In early summer, while standing under oak trees at the slough, you can see sharks' fins cut through the water.

In summer, a historic train carries visitors from the shade of thousand-year-old redwoods in the Santa Cruz Mountains to the Santa Cruz Beach Boardwalk. After nature tore out the heart of downtown in the 1989 earth-quake, the sometimes subtle and sometimes roaring rift between the students of the University of California at Santa Cruz and the town's population seemed to heal. Many former students are employed in the community. Frank Zwart came back to his alma mater as campus architect. When asked about his decision to return, Zwart echoed many of the residents' feelings: "The variety and liveliness attract me, hold me, and seem to be getting even better." Growth pressures from the "just over the hill" megalopolis of San Jose and the Silicon Valley continually raise the vigilance of local proponents of zero or controlled growth.

My own discoveries of the Central Coast began in my childhood, when the highlight of each summer was a trip to Santa Cruz. Today the redwoods are just as tall and the mountain air enlivens my body just as much. I still scream on the roller coaster, I just don't put my hands in the air. I had long thought this would be the ultimate place for me to live; when the opportunity presented itself more than twenty years ago, I accepted without hesitation. During those three decades I moved out of the area, staying away for a few years. Doing so allowed me the perspective to offer an insider's guide and also point out the uniqueness of what some residents overlook as ordinary.

"Tell them it changed overnight," was the advice from a surfer friend when I announced I was compiling this revised edition. "I went out to the waves at Asilomar one morning and I didn't recognize a single face. They were all new hot doggers. I've moved to the inner bay." A member of the Monterey History and Art Association echoed the surfer's views. "I've lived here thirty years and it's all been pretty much the same, and now it's changing before our eyes."

A variety of changes to the area are included in this edition. Some longtime favorite restaurants have closed doors. Readers will also find many additions to the Lodging and Restaurants sections. New text also describes the Outer Bay Wing and one additional floor at the Monterey Bay Aquarium as well as recent exhibits that feature behind-the-scenes action. New sections add opportunities for visitor interaction with the inner workings of the aquarium, explain changes in the surrounding marine reserve, and provide wildlife observation opportunities.

There have been dramatic changes in the inner Monterey Bay land loop. Fort Ord closed as a major military base. Thousands of acres of the land here opened to the public for recreational use. The prototype California University of the new century also opened on the former base; 80 percent of the holdings in the library are on disks rather than books. The sandpit of neighboring Sand City was replaced by high-volume discount stores, while surrounding industrial areas are developing distinctive specialty shops. Seaside added golf courses and new visitor accommodations. Marina gained a new aero sports complex and sculpture center.

California's growth economy has brought new life to places hit hard by the 1989 quake and the economic recession of the 1990s. Santa Cruz, Cannery Row, and Pacific Grove have changed notably. Major donations have opened new museums and expanded existing museums in Monterey.

El Niño weather was credited for creating bumper grape harvests. Monterey County and Santa Cruz County wineries are receiving the national and international recognition they deserve, and new wine tasting information has been added to this edition.

The new, highly acclaimed Steinbeck Center is changing the face of Salinas. Oldtown is drawing new restaurants, adding to the revitalization. In response to readers' requests for "true West" experiences, I've included information for authentic working-ranch stays.

To reflect the region's commitment to families, I've added sections about activities especially enjoyed by kids. From amusement parks to newly opened hikes and campgrounds, the book includes more family pleasures.

Slides, thanks to El Niño storms, closed Highway 1 in both directions through Big Sur for a record number of days in 1998 and brought new alignments to the route. Another campground and more hiking trails opened in Big Sur. Further south, the elephant seal population boomed at a newly populated birthing beach. Record numbers of wildlife viewers swarmed to the area around Piedras Blancas. Nearby Hearst Castle added a new dimension in cinematography.

Near Año Nuevo, the northern elephant seal reserve, the town of Davenport is determined to keep its identity as thousands of acres of potential park land surrounds it. New galleries are opening to showcase the many artists who call this area home. Still, the soup at the Cash Store is as hearty as always.

While there have been notable changes to this region, the core has stayed the same: A historic haven rooted in an incredibly beautiful environment. Now there are challenges for us to maintain this haven.

The format of the book has also remained basically the same. Each chapter begins with a short overview of the area visited followed by a Getting Ready section, which tells you what to expect. Prior planning will help you create glorious days. When times, prices, and buying information are included they are guides only; remember they change over time. Call first for the latest information, especially for dining and lodging.

The Directions section in each chapter guides you from major highways and from the aquarium. With these directions you can start your trip from any point in the area.

GETTING READY

BEST TIMES TO VISIT AND SPECIAL EVENTS

Most people visit the Central Coast during weekends in summer and on three-day holiday weekends throughout the year. The area attracts international, national, and statewide visitors, plus people from nearby metropolitan areas who escape here for the weekend. Make reservations before you visit in summer or on holiday weekends—well in advance if you have a special place mind. The Friday evening incoming and Sunday outgoing traffic can be quite heavy. No segment of the Central Coast is a metropolis, so even when the crowds are shoulder to shoulder in top tourist locations you can still find a secluded beach or wooded glen, sometimes just a few blocks away.

Some visitors prefer the warm days of spring and autumn, when the crowds are few. In addition, many hotels, motels, and resorts have special off-season rates (November through March), sometimes called winter specials, advertised in *Sunset Magazine* and the *San Francisco Chronicle.*

When you are in the mood to celebrate, this is the place: the festival capital of California. Steinbeck's birthday, the Monterey Jazz Festival, a calamari festival, a welcome-to-the-monarchs butterfly parade, a begonia festival, an unbirthday party, a migration festival, and a garlic extravaganza are just a few. (The unbirthday? Robert Louis Stevenson, who lived and wrote here many years ago, gave his away to a little girl who was born on Christmas and wanted a birthday of her own.) For private celebrations, the area excels in quantity and quality of restaurants as well as private beaches and wooded nooks for the most romantic of candlelit dinners. A Calendar of Events is included at the back of this book to aid your planning.

CLIMATE AND CLOTHING

The Central Coast is one of the few places where you can experience four seasons on the same beach in any one day, sometimes in less than an hour. Ten minutes' drive from the beach, or from anyplace else in the area, you may find temperatures very different from where you started. When Pebble Beach is cool and foggy, the Carmel Valley may be sunny and hot. Notes below, expanded in each chapter under this heading, describe three basic climate types by region. Remember that these notes are generalities and that heat waves do occur in cool coastal environs, usually a few times each summer, and sometimes with more regularity. In other words, be prepared for anything, weather-wise.

COASTAL AREAS. Spring and autumn are usually the sunniest seasons. When California's inland valleys heat up in July and August, the trees and dunes along the coast disappear in fog. Pack suntan lotion, a hat, and a jacket. During any season, winds pick up quickly and moist fog can blow in almost as fast as you can get out of your car. By the time you put your jacket on, the bright sun may burn the fog away for the day.

The Big Sur Coast generally follows coastal weather patterns but has its own small bays and microclimates that create variable conditions. On Monterey Bay, the central section around Moss Landing and Castroville is historically the foggiest. Usually, the warmest stretch of beach is in the northern arc of the bay from Seacliff up through Santa Cruz. In the middle of this arc an eddy effect creates a shelter from northwesterly winds and attracts warmer inland air with less fog. Monterey, Seaside, Marina, and the eastern half of Pacific Grove are generally the sunniest stretches of beach along the southern arc. Even farther south, however, when everywhere else is foggy, Carmel is sometimes gloriously sunny.

Winter is the cooler, unpredictable rainy season. Storms can follow blissful seventy-degree days. Snow and heavy frost are extremely rare, although snow did blanket the Pebble Beach "Crosby" golf tournament in 1962.

Ocean water temperatures have historically sent swimmers diving into wetsuits. In summer 1997 the waters were so warm thanks to El Niño that water lovers wore swimsuits only.

INLAND VALLEYS. Spring is balmy, at an average seventy degrees with occasional rain. Wildflowers are abundant. In summer, fogbound coastside residents head into nearby valleys to swim at resort and club pools or river beaches. The farther inland you go, the hotter it gets, with some ninety- and one hundred–degree afternoons. The southern lake regions are much hotter; ninety- to one hundred–degree temperatures are common.

Winters are mild and sometimes wild. Flooding can occur during heavy rains. Snow blankets the hills occasionally. Call ahead about conditions if you are entering Los Padres National Forest on routes that lead from Carmel Valley Road or traverse the Santa Lucia Mountains, such as the Nacimiento-Fergusson Road. These may be flooded.

MOUNTAINS. The mountains can reach ninety and even one hundred degrees during summer months. The evenings cool down, so bring a jacket with you. Summer extends through October. In many years the kids go trick-or-treating before days feel crisp. Winter storms can be treacherous. Use extreme caution when driving a mountain road in a storm.

CLOTHING. Comfortable, casual attire is the norm for the Central Coast. Bring shorts, long pants, short sleeves, and long sleeves. Capitola Beach and the Santa Cruz Beach Boardwalk are the most casual places; the Pebble Beach lodges are the most formal. Prepare for all types of weather and recreation possibilities. Layer your clothes, so when a cold, drizzly, foggy morning turns gloriously sunny you can enjoy it in short sleeves. Most visitors say the summers are cooler than they expected. Every location offers pleasant walks, so wear or bring a good pair of hiking shoes with you.

TOUR LENGTHS

The geographical area of each chapter is close enough to the rest to enjoy as a day trip from a central location along the Monterey Bay. You might also want to read through this guidebook, pick your favorite places, and stay a couple of nights in each. To explore the Central Coast well you need at least a week.

HIGHLIGHTS FOR KIDS

For this second edition, I have added a section on Highlights for Kids at the beginning of most chapters. Most adults will also enjoy the activities for kids. The ultimate highlight for kids in this area is the connection they are able to make with an incredibly beautiful and important natural environment. The activities in these sections are most appropriate for ages four to sixteen.

Poison Oak

Blacklegged Tick

WILDLIFE WISDOM

The Central Coast abounds with opportunities for getting close to nature. Every town and city in the area has walking paths. Some, like Ocean View Boulevard in Pacific Grove, bombard your senses with nature's spectacular displays; others, like the Frog Pond Area in Del Rey Oaks, gently prod your soul. This is Ansel Adams and Weston country. Bring a camera. Bring binoculars. For the fossils in the cliffs and close-up looks at tidepool creatures, bring a hand lens.

The grizzly bears are gone from this section of the coast, but the outdoors still necessitates a few warnings. Almost every summer some young visitor (sometimes not so young) delivers a beautiful bouquet of bright red "flowers" to the dinner table or tent site. The foliage turns out to be poison oak, and the visitor spends a miserable two weeks slathered in anti-itch cream. (The itch from poison oak is caused by the plants' irritating oil.) Poison oak, *Rhus diversiloba*, is very common along hiking trails throughout the Central Coast. It is identified by its clusters of three shiny leaves in the spring and early summer, bright red foliage in late summer and autumn. When its leaves are gone in winter, the barely noticeable twigs are still potent. Nature couldn't have provided a better watchdog for tree seedlings and easily trampled flowers than the poison oak that keeps hikers on the paths. Ask a ranger or a local to help you identify this plant if you are not familiar with it.

When hiking in grasslands be aware of the Western blacklegged tick, *Ixodes pacifica*, which carries Lyme disease. In its adolescent stage the dark tick is the size of the head of a common pin. A fully engorged adult is no bigger than a small kernel of corn. California's Western fence lizards, commonly known as blue belly lizards, can stop the spread of the disease by inhibiting it in their blood. But lizard populations have dropped, and the disease has begun to spread in California, although it is still uncommon.

Two-thirds of Lyme disease victims develop a ringlike rash on the skin where the tick attached. Other early signs include low-grade fever, fatigue, and muscle aches. The second stage of symptoms occurs weeks or months later and can include paralysis of facial muscles, severe headaches, and abnormal heartbeat. Call your doctor if you notice any of these symptoms.

The best way to avoid Lyme disease is to avoid ticks. Stay on trails. Tuck your pant legs into your socks. Wear light-colored clothing so you'll spot ticks. Apply insect repellent, and check your body frequently to stop ticks before they attach to your skin.

VISITOR INFORMATION

Each chapter includes phone numbers of major visitor services. Resources in local newspapers are also recommended. For area-wide listings of specialized tours, sports facilities, wineries, and other particular interests, see the Resource Guide.

PARKING AND RESTROOMS

The more densely visited and exclusive an area is, the more troublesome it is to find a reasonable parking place and a rest room. With this in mind, recommendations are given for only the more populated coastal towns and problematic areas. (Parking rates are current as of this writing.)

ALTERNATE TRANSPORTATION

One of my favorite ways to travel is by train. I love destinations where, after arriving, I can walk to the places I want to visit. Although the Amtrak's rail service to the hub city of Monterey is by way of connecting buses from rail stations in San Jose, Gilroy, and Salinas, the connections are quite good. Work is now underway to extend rail service. Railroad depots are being spruced up in Watsonville, Seaside, and Salinas in anticipation of final funding for passenger rail service.

The transit plaza in Monterey is not a building but does have a covered area. It is located at triangular Jules Simoneau Plaza bounded by Munras Avenue and Pearl and Tyler streets in the pleasant center of the city's revitalized historic downtown. Several hotels are within easy walking distance. At the plaza you can catch local bus service (Monterey-Salinas Transit, MST, 831/424-7695 or 831/899-2555) to other downtown locations, Fisherman's

Wharf, Pacific Grove, and Carmel. The plaza flies the flags of the United States, Mexico, and Spain plus the California Bear Flag and pennant of the downtown association. These can serve as landmarks for travelers in the downtown.

Bike rentals are available nearby. You can bike along the entire coastline from north of Monterey to Cambria. In summer, for a very reasonable price, MST buses service Highway 1 south along the coast to the community of Big Sur. Several tour companies, most notably Otter-Mobile Tours & Charters on the Monterey Peninsula (831/649-4523), provide any extra sightseeing you might desire. Pebble Beach cannot be reached by regular transit bus service.

PLACES TO STAY

Listings provide a variety of accommodations, including bed and breakfasts, resorts, hotels and motels, and campsites (when especially appropriate). The rates cited are for summer weekends. Some places maintain the same rates all year; others offer rates based on the day, season, or special event. Weekday rates are sometimes less than weekend rates. Whenever you call to make reservations, ask about special rates.

Where should you stay? It is always frustrating to spend any vacation time changing your reserved location. As you read the chapters in this book decide which areas especially appeal to you.

RESTAURANTS

This region abounds with fabulous restaurants, far too many to include them all. I have selected restaurants to provide a variety of choices and to honor particular restaurants' commitment to quality and service. Most here are recommended by my readers and verified through local "Best" surveys and awards. Dividing restaurants into geographical areas presents a problem when one good choice is also in other areas. I will recommend the Bagel Bakery in Monterey County in this introduction as it is a locally created and owned chain of bagelries found throughout the county. The Bagel Bakery consistently wins local nods of approval for best inexpensive eats and "best food on the go."

The abbreviations for credit cards are: AX, American Express; D, Discover; MC, Master Card; V, Visa.

HISTORICAL HIGHLIGHTS

Historical background in the introduction to the tours offers extra dimensions to the places you visit. A beach feels different when you realize it was once a Chinese abalone village and later a rum-runners hide-out. Along with harboring a history, the Central Coast is continually making its future; it changes every day.

TOUR: POINT OF WELCOME

The tours are the heart of the book. Before there was a book, I led school field trips, city recreation department walks and hikes, and countless excursions for friends and companies in this region. Instead of just providing descriptions and locations, I've organized the information geographically in the tours. You'll also hear the voices of locals and find the significance of places you might otherwise miss.

Each chapter includes walking tours. Each of these tours introduces you to a number of different places or provides in-depth information. Two of the book's tours are suitable for either walking, biking, or driving. Seven scenic driving tours are included.

When I visit a place for the first time, I like to head for the spot with the best view. Some locations where you can experience breathtaking overviews of the Monterey Peninsula include: the summit of Highway 17 for those traveling south from the San Jose area; the summit of Highway 152, west of Gilroy, an alternate crossover for those traveling south on 101; from Jacks Peak, for those traveling north on Highway 68; the Sloat Monument area on the Presidio Hill, for those who have already arrived in the Monterey Peninsula; Shepherd's Knoll and Huckleberry Hill, for Pebble Beach visitors; and Pogonip Park, accessible from Highway 9 or High Street, for those on the Santa Cruz side of the Monterey Bay.

CHAPTER 1

THE MONTEREY BAY AQUARIUM AND THE MONTEREY BAY NATIONAL MARINE SANCTUARY

A PARTNERSHIP

The Monterey Bay National Marine Sanctuary stretches three hundred miles, from the Farallon Islands off the coast of San Francisco south along the enclaves of Monterey Bay and, farther south, along the Big Sur Coast, to Cambria. Located on the border of the cities of Pacific Grove and Monterey, the Monterey Bay Aquarium provides visitors with a close-up view of the life and wonders of the sanctuary.

GETTING READY

This chapter provides an overview of the sanctuary and highlights the wildlife visitors may encounter at the destinations in any of the chapters. The tour for this chapter is of the Monterey Bay Aquarium.

BEST TIMES TO VISIT AND SPECIAL EVENTS

THE MONTEREY BAY NATIONAL MARINE SANCTUARY
Every day is memorable here. Some of the migration cycles and natural cycles that take place are among the most special events in nature.

In the last two weeks of February, art, science, literature, and great fun combine at the Monterey County Whalefest (831/644-7588). Gray whales begin passing through the sanctuary's waters in late November or December on their way to birthing lagoons in Baja California. The peak month for observing these whales is January. Seeing sixty whales on a three-hour off-shore expedition is common. You may even be extremely lucky and witness a birth in the ocean. From February to mid-March you might observe mating

MONTEREY BAY NATIONAL MARINE SANCTUARY

Gulf of the Farallones National Marine Sanctuary

OAKLAND

SAN FRANCISCO

San Francisco Bay

PACIFICA

Pillar Point

PALO ALTO

SAN JOSE

Pescadero Point

Pigeon Point

BOULDER CREEK

Año Nuevo Point

SANTA CRUZ

GILROY

WATSONVILLE

Elkhorn Slough

MOSS LANDING

CASTROVILLE

SAN JUAN BAUTISTA

PACIFIC GROVE

PEBBLE BEACH

MONTEREY

SALINAS

CARMEL

Point Lobos

Carmel Valley Rd.

Carmel River

SOLEDAD

Point Sur

BIG SUR

Pfeiffer Point

GREENFIELD

KING CITY

LUCIA

GORDA

Salinas River

Point Piedras Blancas

SAN SIMEON

CAMBRIA

PASO ROBLES

Monterey Bay National Marine Sanctuary

Pacific Ocean

N
W   E
S

activity. From March to May, mother whales return with their calves for summer krill feeding in the Arctic. Orcas are spotted most often in autumn and spring, when they feed on young gray whales and elephant seals. Tour boat and fishing excursions occasionally witness orca and gray whale battles. Humpback whales feed in the sanctuary's waters from May through June. Unpredictable but memorable blue whale sightings begin around July.

In late November and December, male elephant seals, the largest of all pinnipeds, haul themselves out of their ocean domain onto the beaches of Año Nuevo north of Santa Cruz and also near Piedras Blancas north of San Simeon. To establish a dominance hierarchy the fourteen- to sixteen-foot bulls weighing up to 5,000 pounds engage in violent, bloody battles. The bulls who rank at the top of the battles will collect the most breeding females. A few females arrive but the bulk of the female population swims ashore in January. Within five days after arriving they give birth to seventy plus–pound pups. Pups suckle mom for up to four weeks and increase their weight to between two hundred and four hundred pounds. Females mate close to the time they wean their pups. After breeding, adult elephant seals abandon the beaches and return to their northern feeding waters where they remain as ocean-dwelling mammals for several months. As the chubby pups begin to hunger they enter the ocean, seeking food. In April and May, the females return to the beach for catastrophic molting of all their fur, losing their complete outer layer of skin. They then return to the northern waters far off shore from Washington. Males molt in July and August then also swim to the open ocean, as far north as Alaska.

Usually in February, at the time of the big rains, when the waters rise and roar in rivers and streams, female steelhead trout, followed by up to twenty males in pursuit, swim up selected streams to spawn in gravel sandbars. The oldest and most ragged-looking of the females die in the river but the young females return to the ocean after spawning. With the flow of the tides and phases of the moon, this action continues until summer.

Sharks pup in Elkhorn Slough in June. Watch for shark fins passing through waters shaded by oaks.

Otters swim year-round throughout the range of the ocean waters described in this book. Most pups are born between February and March or between August and September. You may spot mothers sculling along, each with a small furry pup resting on her stomach.

THE AQUARIUM

The aquarium is open daily (except Christmas) from 10 a.m. to 6 p.m. Crowds are smallest on weekdays and either first thing in the morning or late afternoon. Weekends usually offer a wider variety of free shows. Special

shows such as Otter Feeding and Kelp Forest Fish Feeding and Tidepool
Divers take place throughout each day. Call before you arrive for show times:
831/648-4888. During summer more interpretive programs are offered. The
Monterey Bay Aquarium Research Institute's (MBARI) remotely operated
vehicles (ROVs), submersible crafts that travel to the depths of the sanctuary,
broadcast live shows daily as weather and exploration permit. Throughout
the year special evenings are reserved for all-night sleepovers for aquarium
members.

The aquarium offers educational classes all year long. Weddings and other
private social and business gatherings can be arranged before 10 a.m. and
after 6 p.m. On-site catering is available through the Portola Cafe. To
arrange a private event call 831/648-4888.

TICKET INFORMATION

THE MONTEREY BAY NATIONAL MARINE SANCTUARY
Check the appendix for specific whale and wildlife tours.

THE AQUARIUM
Tickets currently are $14.95, adults; $11.95, seniors, students, and military
personnel; $6.95, children ages three to twelve. Children under three are free.
Groups of twenty or more qualify for group rates. During peak hours in summer and on major holiday weekends, you may stand in line an hour before
you can enter the aquarium. Advance ticket sales allow you to enter with no
waiting.

Memberships support ongoing aquarium programs, educational services,
and new exhibits. Memberships are especially recommended for those who
visit the aquarium more than once a year. Membership rates range from $75.
If you are purchasing a membership onsite, go directly to the membership
express entrance. There are a variety of membership options available.
Memberships entitle guests to unlimited express-entry visits, guest passes,
admission to special evening and event programs throughout the year, a 10
percent discount on purchases, and the opportunity to participate in aquarium travel excursions.

Order tickets and memberships by calling the aquarium: 800/756-3737
(within California) or 831/648-4888. Tickets and memberships are also available at all Northern California BASS outlets (Wherehouse and Tower record
stores), by phone at 510/762-BASS, outside California, 800/225-2277; and
online through TicketWeb on the aquarium's Web site, www.mbayaq.org.
Many Monterey Peninsula hotels sell advance tickets to their guests (with no
fee). Visitors to the Monterey Peninsula can also book hotel rooms and get special value aquarium coupon packages by calling 800/555-WAVE (555-9283).

CLIMATE AND CLOTHING

THE MONTEREY BAY NATIONAL MARINE SANCTUARY

Although shoreline water temperatures have risen an alarming 2 degrees over the last ten years, wetsuits are still necessary for water play in the ocean. Wear layered clothing for any expeditions on or near the water.

THE AQUARIUM

Wear comfortable walking shoes and casual clothes. You may need to sit on the floor during crowded shows and get wet up to your elbows at the touch tanks. Indoor exhibits extend to several outdoor areas, so you might need a jacket on cool or foggy days.

TOUR LENGTHS

THE AQUARIUM

Allow at least three hours to explore the aquarium. If you need a break, the aquarium will stamp your hand so you can return any time during the day.

VISITOR INFORMATION

THE MONTEREY BAY NATIONAL MARINE SANCTUARY

For brochures outlining recreational opportunities and ocean-use regulations and for details about research and education symposiums, contact the Monterey Bay Sanctuary Program: 831/647-4255. To contact the Office of the National Marine Sanctuary, call 831/647-4201.

With the designation of the sanctuary in 1992 came a longterm commitment to honor and protect these waters and wildlife for future generations. Local citizen volunteers are trained for BAY NET, the Monterey Bay National Marine Sanctuary Volunteer Network 831/375-4509. Some set up spotting binoculars and answer questions along the waterfront in Monterey and Pacific Grove, and others work as docents at the elephant seal viewing areas north of San Simeon. Look for the volunteers' blue jackets.

THE AQUARIUM

The main aquarium information number is 831/648-4888. An information booth is set up inside the entrance. Volunteer docents are stationed at exhibits throughout to answer your questions; those with orange jackets have finished a series of training courses. Many volunteers with and without the orange jackets have backgrounds in oceanography, diving, or teaching. The aquarium's education division provides a rich grounding of information in various topics related to the Monterey Bay National Marine Sanctuary.

Still and video cameras are welcome. Flashbulbs can be used except at posted exhibits where they would disturb the animals. Visitors can also borrow a camera from the information desk. Commercial photography must be arranged in advance through the public relations department, 831/648-4800.

PARKING

THE AQUARIUM

A city-owned parking garage on Foam Street off Prescott Avenue and Wave Street, about three blocks from the aquarium, offers twenty-four hour parking, at a fee of $1 per hour. A city-owned lot located on David Avenue, within a half-block of the aquarium, offers parking at $1 per half hour. Metered parking is available on the street for twenty-five cents for each twenty minutes, up to twelve hours. Some streets, such as David Avenue, offer free curbside spaces, but it's a rare day when a space is available.

ALTERNATE TRANSPORTATION

The WAVE shuttle bus, available from 9 a.m. to 9 p.m. daily, every fifteen minutes during summer and on selected year-round weekends, links the aquarium with downtown Monterey, the Monterey Simoneau Transit Plaza, and waterfront locations. One fee covers unlimited rides all day (831/899-2555).

For pedestrians and bicycles, the Monterey Peninsula Recreation Trail passes beside the aquarium. Bike rentals are available in the Monterey Plaza and at the Fisherman's Wharf area.

PLACES TO STAY

The Monterey Bay Aquarium's location is convenient to lodging in any of the surrounding areas. Monterey and Pacific Grove's lodgings (pages 57 and 88) are only steps away, as these towns border the aquarium. Santa Cruz is a forty-five minute drive. Many visitors stay in the community of Big Sur, which is a little more than an hour south.

RESTAURANTS

Cannery Row restaurants are within a short walking distance of the aquarium. The aquarium also offers on-site dining at the Portola Cafe.

PORTOLA CAFE (on the first floor of the aquarium). At this beautiful location overlooking the bay, diners have choices. Dine in a quiet full-service restaurant with linens and flowers; in a self-service cafeteria with a selection of fish, burgers, soup, and salads; or at an espresso, drinks, and oyster bar with menu selections.

Reservations are suggested for the full-service restaurant, as its pasta and fresh fish selections as well as friendly service and ocean views make it a popular choice for aquarium visitors and locals alike. The full restaurant serves from 11 a.m. to 3 p.m.; the oyster bar and cafeteria remain open until 5:30 p.m. 831/648-4870. AX, MC, V. A la carte cafeteria selections, mostly under $5. Entrees in restaurant mostly under $15.

INTRODUCTION WITH HISTORICAL HIGHLIGHTS

"When that little ball of fur tentatively pats my face and sniffs at me with its fresh squid breath I just melt." Sheila McMahon, a sea otter rescue volunteer at the Monterey Bay Aquarium, watches as a scuba diver swims underwater in a shallow tidal area nearby. A young southern sea otter whines like a puppy, twists and glides through the water, then slides on the diver's back as if she were its mother. The otter was orphaned in the ocean as a pup and brought to the aquarium for round-the-clock care by aquarium staff and a group of volunteer adoptive mothers like Sheila McMahon. They nurse the baby otter with a rich formula of clams, squid, half-and-half, fish oil, and vitamins and minerals. To keep the pup clean and buoyant, volunteers constantly comb and brush its hair. Now the diver is helping the pup to acclimate to life on its own in the ocean by teaching it to forage for its food. The aquarium staff keeps the otter's name secret so that any divers and anglers with the wrong intentions will not take advantage when it finally cuts its bonds with humans and swims free. The otter is tagged for electronic tracking and observational identification.

Just as the Monterey Bay Aquarium diver introduces the young otter to its place in the vast ocean, the aquarium introduces nearly two million visitors each year to the wonders of the Monterey Bay National Marine Sanctuary. On any afternoon several hundred of these visitors sit in a dark auditorium at the aquarium and gasp as they watch broadcasts of *Live from Monterey Canyon*, such as a rare vampire squid getting sucked into a transparent cylinder—the catch of the MBARI ROV, the submersible remotely operated vehicle.

The aquarium sits on the rocky shores on the southern side of Monterey Bay. Right offshore, the ocean bottom drops into the twisting and branching abyss of the Monterey Canyon. Imagine the Grand Canyon of the Southwest flooded with seawater and toured by hundreds of types of fish, assorted sea mammals, and bouquets of sea plants. Imagine sharks, mackerel, whales, giant kelp, and red algae. Sea stars cling to crevices, and colorful sea anemones hold fast to sheared cliffs. Your mental vista of all this would resemble the thirteen mile–wide, mile-deep canyon off the coast of Monterey.

DIRECTIONS

The aquarium looks like an industrial building, with two tall smokestacks. Use these smokestacks as landmarks when you are in the Cannery Row area.

From the Central Valley, Highway 156 connects to 101 just west of San Juan Bautista, leading to the continuation of 156 west to Highway 1. Take 1 south to Monterey. **For southbound travelers,** travel scenic Highway 1 from the San Francisco Bay Area, or take Highway 17 to Highway 1 from the San Jose area. Also, Highways 101 and 280 from San Francisco (through the south bay and San Jose areas) connect to 17 and then 1 at Santa Cruz. Highway 17 is a curvy mountain route; circumvent it by taking 101 from the San Francisco and San Jose areas farther south to Prunedale (which is twenty minutes south of Gilroy and ten minutes south of the San Juan Bautista exit). From Prunedale take Highway 156 (the Monterey Peninsula exit) west to Highway 1, and continue south to Monterey.

Exit Highway 1 at Del Monte Avenue/Pacific Grove and go straight, following the brown signs. (For the Monterey Visitor's Center, turn left at Camino El Estero.) Beyond Fisherman's Wharf veer right, and continue through the tunnel. Past the tunnel, turn right at the first street to follow historic Cannery Row to the aquarium. After five blocks you may want to turn left at Hoffman Avenue, then right on Foam Street for the parking garage entrance.

From Southern California, travel northbound on Highway 101 or coastal route Highway 1. Most people who take Highway 1 as part of a loop with Highway 101 prefer to drive Highway 101 north, then travel the ocean side of Highway 1 on the southbound return trip.

From northbound Highway 101, take the Monterey Peninsula exit in Salinas to Highway 68. (For a more scenic parallel route see the Inland Excursions chapter, page 213.) Follow Highway 68 west to Highway 1 south and exit immediately at Fremont Street. Turn right on Camino El Estero (the Monterey Visitor's Center will be on your right in the second block) and travel to Del Monte

Avenue. Then turn left and follow the brown signs through the tunnel. Past the tunnel, take the first right turn to follow historic Cannery Row to the aquarium. After five blocks, you may want to turn left at Hoffman Avenue, then right on Foam Street for the parking garage entrance.

From northbound Highway 1, take the Munras Avenue exit in Monterey. Turn left at Soledad Drive and then right at Pacific Street. Continue on Pacific Street until it becomes Lighthouse Avenue. Turn right on Cannery Row, which leads to the aquarium.

Highway 1 north or southbound travelers can also take the Highway 68/Pacific Grove exit, then travel ten minutes north to the second traffic light in Pacific Grove. Turn right at David Avenue. David Avenue merges with Wave Street in front of the aquarium.

THE ORIGINS OF THE CANYON AND THE SANCTUARY

The canyon is the largest of several canyon systems that cut the ocean floor along the Central Coast. Just south of Carmel at the beach off San Jose Creek, the head of the Carmel Canyon is so close to shore that you can wade into it at low tide. (However easy wading there appears, the force of the water through the canyon often sends large sneaker waves against the shore, sweeping away anyone or anything it meets.) According to Gary Greene, a geologist with the U.S. Geological Survey, rock types from the various canyons match. This matching shows that many of the separate canyons in the area may be severed parts of the greater Monterey Canyon.

What caused the canyon? In the words of Greene, "The answer to that question is not straight facts but involves complex processes, and still perplexes us." Scientists have searched for clues ever since the canyon was discovered in 1890 by pioneer scientist George Davidson, who was astonished to find it while taking soundings with a hand line and lead weights. For many years scientists theorized the canyon was carved when it was above the surface, perhaps as a former drainage of the San Joaquin–Sacramento River Basin, thus making Monterey Bay the original repository of the waters now forming San Francisco Bay.

Monterey Bay Aquarium

Turbidity currents provide an additional answer to the canyon's puzzle. Rocks, mud, and sand are continually washed from the land almost to the continental shelf. When the weight of these accumulating sediments reaches a critical mass—whoosh! The seaward edge of the mass sags and the mass slides over the brink. The sudden precipitous movement forms the turbidity current. Depressions that form along the continental shelf in areas of more frequent sliding become the heads of turbidity-charged underground canyons. Undersea landslides then continue to widen and deepen the canyons.

Since the 1960s the plate tectonics theory has convincingly portrayed the Pacific plate of the Earth's crust as colliding with the North American plate. California's Central Coast is located on the Pacific plate. Massive collisions, with the Pacific plate caving beneath the North American plate and causing its uplift, created volcanoes along the the edge of the continent to form the arc of the Sierra Nevada. About twenty million years ago the Pacific plate off Central California stopped diving beneath the North American plate and started to inch its way northwest, along the fracture now known as the San Andreas fault system, an eight-hundred-mile-long network of faults.

Name your left hand the North American plate and your right hand the Pacific Plate. Now press your fingertips together and push hard; your fingers will rise from the conflicting pressures. The Santa Lucia mountain range along the Pacific Coast is still growing upward by a similar impingement of the Pacific plate against the North American plate. Continue pressing your fingers together as you move your right hand sideways, and fold it slightly beneath your left. A model of land movement along the Central Coast is at your fingertips.

Geologists named the land west of the fault in Northern California "Salinia." Granite composes its basement rock, as contrasted with the metamorphic and sedimentary rocks on the east side known as the Franciscan Formation. Although the movement of the fault is now primarily horizontal, over millions of years the movement has alternately been vertical, thrusting the land higher than sea level—which accounts for the sharks' teeth fossils people find around Boulder Creek, a thousand feet high in the Santa Cruz Mountains. Gary Greene cited the vertical movement as the possible and well-accepted explanation for how a canyon could have been cut hundreds of feet in depth near or above sea level, by streams or submarine currents, but also have been dropped well below the surface and cut as well by turbidity forces.

People still ask, however, "What river cut the canyon?" Upon seeing the resemblance of the Monterey Bay Canyon to the southwestern Grand Canyon, Robert Lloyd Allen, a navy officer attending the Naval Postgraduate School in Monterey in the early 1980s, hypothesized that the entire Monterey Canyon had moved north from the Colorado River Basin. He used a computer to simulate the movement of the Monterey Canyon and the San Andreas fault and found that twenty million years ago the site of the Monterey Bay would have been west of Bakersfield. The Gulf of California, where the Colorado River now empties, is relatively new, geologically speaking, and did not exist twenty million years ago. Allen theorized the Colorado River may have once followed a more northwesterly course and carved a southern end to the Grand Canyon through uplifted Salinian landscape.

Greene and other geologists place the origin of the Monterey Canyon near present-day Santa Barbara. Most geologists reject the Colorado River hypothesis because of the mountain ranges it would have needed to cross and the geologic time sequence, among other factors. In fact, I was told by one geologist, who wishes to be left anonymous, that he'd rip this page from the book if I printed such hogwash. The most accepted theory claims that the major carver of the canyon's walls and depths was probably turbidity currents rather than any one powerful river.

The Monterey Bay Aquarium Research Institute (MBARI) submersible research vehicles make modern exploration of the canyon possible. About the size of a Volkswagen bug, each sub has an array of cameras, sampling devices, and instruments that record temperature, depth, and other conditions. Officially called Remotely Operated Vehicles (ROVs), the unmanned subs are tethered to a research vessel from which scientists operate them by remote control to depths of four thousand meters in waters that brim with creatures as small as microscopic plankton, as large as blue whales, and as exotic as the predacious siphonophore, a shimmering string of gelatinous beads measuring 120 feet long that devours any organism in its path (www.mbari.org).

The canyon is the centerpiece of the Monterey Bay National Marine Sanctuary, the nation's largest marine preserve. The range of the species and underwater environments it hosts makes it one of the richest, most varied aquatic communities in the world. Extending along more than 300 miles of coast south from the Farallons, by San Francisco, and ending near Cambria, the sanctuary boundary encompasses an area the size of the state of Connecticut. Different zones of the 5,300-square-mile sanctuary contain the deepest and largest underwater canyons on the West Coast, 10,663 feet below the surface at the sanctuary's deepest point. Expansive ocean waters with a sandy and muddy floor, kelp forests that support an abundance of life, rocky shores dotted with tidepools, miles of beaches, and fragile wetlands fill the sanctuary.

"Folks here feel passionately about their environment and where they live. The government established the sanctuary in 1992, not because the national government wanted it, but because the people fought for it for fifteen years," says Milos Radakovich, volunteer coordinator for BAY NET. A marine sanctuary is similar to a park, in that its natural beauty is protected by the federal government and that conservation of its resources is balanced with research, recreational, and commercial uses. Numerous endangered species find refuge in its waters and along its shore. The sanctuary is home to 26 species of marine mammals, 94 seabird species, at least 345 fish species, 4 species of turtles, 450 species of marine algae, and thousands of invertebrate animal species. With new discoveries, the numbers of known species keep growing.

The pristine coast also supports thousands of people who are employed in marine research, coastal agriculture, and fisheries. In addition to MBARI, eight other key research facilities are located in the Monterey Bay region. Millions of people use the sanctuary waters as a place for recreation. Swimming, diving, sailing, surfing, kayaking, birding, sport fishing, whale-watching, tidepooling, and beachwalking are among the pleasures enjoyed by residents and visitors alike. Winter waters are the clearest for diving. No spearfishing is permitted in designated Doc Ricketts Park Underwater Park, the waters from the breakwater to Lover's Point.

The indigenous populations that lived in California before European contact are estimated to have been nearly a third of the inhabitants of the Americas north of Mexico. More than three hundred languages and dialects were chronicled by Spanish and later settlers. The first groups who settled along the Central Coast relied on the ocean for a major part of their food supply. They discarded shells and bones in mounds that remain as the primary evidence of their use of the environment. On trips to beaches throughout the sanctuary you might sit near one of these shell middens, with layers of chipped shells and stones interspersed in the sand. Most middens, even though they have been disturbed, are not roped off from the rest of the beach. Overall, mussels are the most abundant shells found. Abalone, too, was especially important along the Monterey Peninsula.

Several major tribes and numerous smaller groups of the Hokan, Penutian, and Chumashan (southern coastal region) language groups inhabited the land areas around the present sanctuary. Natural resources were abundant and there was little intertribal conflict. Artifacts unearthed in Scotts Valley, north of Santa Cruz, show that people possibly lived there 10,000 years ago when a now-dry lake covered the valley floor. Farther south, the earliest archaeological evidence shows that ancestors of the Hokan-speaking Esselen tribe lived near Moss Landing 9,500 years ago. By 4,500 years ago the Esselen had moved to the south, along the Big Sur coast, and inland, to the present-day town of Soledad. New tribes moved into the area and climatic changes are thought to be the reasons for the shift in the tribe's location. In the 1700s some thirty groups of Penutian-speaking people lived north of Big Sur. Tribes and groups such as the Rumsien, Mutsun, and Kalendaruc were grouped by European settlers and later archaeologists as the "Costanoan," derived from the Spanish for "of the coast." The descendants of the tribal groups sometimes prefer the encompassing tribal name "Ohlone."

Baskets and arrow points are the most commonly found artifacts. The largest "quarry" and stoneworking area was located at Año Nuevo Point. Although few completed arrow points are still found, purposely chipped rock is found in the middens throughout the dunes of the area. The Penutian groups were gatherers of acorns and seeds. They cooked by dropping heated stones into watertight baskets. The groups sailed the bay and river areas on reed rafts. They also ate sea mammals such as otters, seals, and sea lions, as well as inland mammals.

The cultures and populations of these tribes were largely wiped out, directly and indirectly, by Spanish missions and later settlements of the area. The cultures of the first peoples were often dissimilar from each other, but they practiced a common stewardship of the land. Archaeological evidence continues to be studied, redefining which tribes lived where and brought what customs to the lands. Awareness of the old ways is growing among descendants, who continue the stories and traditions of tribes who lived for more than two hundred generations in harmony with each other, the land, and the ocean.

Human imprints from a wider range of the world's cultures began with Spanish explorer Juan Rodríguez Cabrillo, who led the first European expedition into Californian waters. English explorer Sir Francis Drake, who first sailed the sanctuary waters in 1579 aboard the ship the *Golden Hinde,* called the lands defined by cliffs such as those north of Santa Cruz "Nova Albion," meaning New England. This was forty years before the Pilgrims landed at Plymouth Rock, and so California was the first New England. Sebastian Vizcaino stepped ashore at Monterey and claimed the land for Spain in 1602. The land lay in the hands of the Esselen, the Rumsien, the Ohlone, and surrounding groups when the otter fur trade brought an influx of Russian sailors to sanctuary waters. In the late 1700s, as a reaction to the fur traders' use of Central Coast waters, the Spanish settled the area with a progression of missions and presidios. By 1773 there were two presidios and five missions but the total Spanish population was only about seventy. Juan Bautista de Anza led 198 emigrants north from New Spain in 1775.

Whaling, the fur trade, gold prospecting, and the opening of the Western frontier for settlement brought new people from diverse cultures to the sanctuary waters and surrounding lands. Chinese residents pioneered many of the fisheries, including those pulling in squid. Gennosuke Kodani, a Japanese immigrant, established the first abalone cannery at Point Lobos in 1898. Sicilians brought fishing techniques that helped Monterey become the world's busiest fishing port. Knut Hovden, a Norwegian, built the largest of the canneries, and Cannery Row boomed.

Diverse groups of immigrants and the needs of the United States continue to influence the uses of the sanctuary. By the 1960s most of the canneries had closed, due to diminishing sardine populations. Then and in the 1970s concern along the coast shifted from the economic impact of fishing to that of offshore oil wells. Citizens' efforts and federal scientific surveys provided the evidence of the rich biological diversity in the area and of the need for a sanctuary to protect marine life.

The National Oceanic and Atmospheric Administration (NOAA) manages the Monterey Bay National Marine Sanctuary and other national sanctuaries. For visitors, in general, rules prohibit the moving, injuring, or possession of historical resources and the taking, injuring, or harassing of marine mammals, turtles, or seabirds. As the Marine Mammal Protection Act specifies, people must stay one hundred yards from whales, fifty feet from otters, and must not approach harbor seals. Future regulations may change, and visitors are advised to consult information boards at beaches, marine attractions such as the aquarium, and harbor master's offices.

EVOLUTION OF AN AQUARIUM

Even before there was a designated sanctuary, nonswimmers and two-year-olds in strollers could explore the biodiversity of the kelp forests and the ocean floor, through the re-creation in the Monterey Bay Aquarium, which first opened its doors in 1984.

The largest window in the world becomes a passageway to the outer bay. A kelp forest beckons in a 335,000-gallon tank of water. Visitors pet the silky skin of bat rays, feel the tickle of sea star legs at the indoor tide pools, and visit eye to eye with sharks, giant octopi, and even human divers who clean exhibits and offer feeding demonstrations in the kelp forest.

No one remembers who first came up with the idea for the aquarium. In the 1970s, following decades of dwindling sardine catches, the closed and boarded up Hovden Cannery stood as a wooden ghost, at the west end of Cannery Row. In 1977 Nancy Burnett, her husband Robin, who taught at Stanford University's Hopkins Marine Laboratories—just a stone's throw west from the old cannery—and friends and fellow professors Chuck Baxter and Steven Webster brainstormed ideas for its future. "That boarded up cannery just caught our imaginations, and it was the topic of discussion at many a dinner," remembers Steven Webster, now education director at the aquarium. It wasn't just any aquarium they finally envisioned, but an aquarium that would showcase and educate people about the habitats of the local Monterey Bay, which were then visible only to divers or shrouded in unexplored depths.

At the same time the four scientists were drawing plans for the habitat-based aquarium, Nancy's parents, David and Lucile Packard, were searching for a focus to their family foundation. David Packard, with his partner William Hewlett, had built the Hewlett-Packard electronics giant in Northern California and had amassed fortunes. According to daughter Julie Packard, executive director of the aquarium, David Packard had challenged the foundation board members to come up with a substantial project. "The two ideas happened at the same time. It was a serendipitous event," Julie recalls.

Steven Webster smiled as he told me about the early plans. "We were naive with the first ideas we submitted for consideration. We thought we'd be able to wedge a series of aquariums in the old cannery." After a tour of every major aquarium in the country David and Lucile Packard offered a beginning one-time gift of $55 million from the family to the public for a top-notch facility. David Packard's vision and an extra gift from him of $13 million provided for the world-class Monterey Bay Aquarium Research Institute. Separate from the aquarium, its purpose is to design oceanic research technology and uncover the mysteries of the ocean. The nonprofit Monterey Bay Aquarium Foundation was created in 1978 to oversee aquarium operations and construction.

"Everyone wants to know how this project started," according to Julie Packard, who is also a marine botanist. "The final product was so much greater and richer than the original idea. What we have today is the result of all the ideas and work of all the creative people who have contributed through the years." She began working on the aquarium project with the four other scientists, as a volunteer, to prepare the proposal. She became more and more involved with the aquarium in the early days of slide shows and speaking engagements to gain community support, eventually turning her management skills to the executive directorship.

Many people ask why the aquarium looks so industrial. Most of the original cannery was dismantled; its walls and foundation too weak for the proposed aquarium—but there was a great desire that the feel and spirit of Cannery Row remain. For seven years, specialists transformed architectural blueprints into a system of complex seawater systems and giant exhibit tanks within 216,000 square feet of structures that complement the style of the old canneries. Towering fiberglass smokestacks were even added to give a complete feeling of authenticity.

As the buildings rose, exhibits were created. David Packard not only provided financial support but worked at his forge in Big Sur to create exhibits for the aquarium, including the gears and pulleys of a simulated tide machine. Sculpted off-site, a parade of life-size whale models saluted the old Cannery Row establishments, abandoned buildings, and onlookers as they were hoisted through aquarium doors to suspension cables above walkways. Local veterinarian Tom Williams cheered the completion of the thirty-foot otter exhibit. Prior to the aquarium's construction, he had kept orphan pups in his bathtub.

More than 300,000 animals and plants, representing more than 570 species of plants, fishes, invertebrates, mammals, reptiles, and birds of the region are housed in two wings of the aquarium. In the original wing your feet stay grounded, although you may sway a little when visiting the sixteen-foot-high kelp forest, sandy shores, and outer reef. The second floor houses rotating specialty exhibits such as the internationally recognized *Fishing for Solutions* and the crowd-pleasing *Behind the Scenes*. A third-floor observation deck overlooks the Monterey Bay. In the Outer Bay wing you feel suspended in another world as you glide through open waters with tuna, barracuda, and plodding sunfish. Children try on flukes and explore the environment in an interactive display room.

THE MONTEREY BAY SANCTUARY TODAY

You will probably first view the sanctuary waters from a high vantage point, whether it be an airplane window or the summit of Highway 17 in the Santa Cruz Mountains. It is the home of mammal species grouped in three orders: Cetacea, which includes whales, dolphins, and porpoises; Pinnipedia, which includes sea lions, fur seals, and true seals; and Carnivora, with the southern sea otter, a relative of minks, weasels, skunks, and badgers.

The sanctuary waters have long been noted for whales. "It is impossible either to describe the number of whales with which we were surrounded, or their familiarity. They blowed every half a minute within half a pistol shot from our frigates," wrote Jean Francois Galaup de La Perouse on a 1786 exploring expedition of the Monterey Bay area.

Biologists place the whales into two major categories: the Mysticeti (literally translated, "moustached") or baleen whales, and the Odontoceti, or toothed whales. Baleen whales, which are well represented in the ocean waters off the California coast, feed by filtering water containing shrimplike krill and other zooplankton into their mouths using brushlike strainers called baleen. The gray whale, *Eschrichtius robustus*, migrates farther than any mammal and is the best known to whalewatchers in the area. Roughly the size of ten elephants, the thirty-five- to fifty-foot-long, forty- to fifty-ton gray whale is marked by light gray splotches and a prominent midline ridge that melds to a series of bumps near its tail. The light splotches on the whale's skin are colonies of thousands of hitchhiking barnacles. Whale biologists often tell whales apart by their different patterns of barnacle clusters.

The gray whale feeds on bottom-dwelling amphipods in the Bering Sea from late spring until early autumn. Then some twenty-three thousand gray whales begin a ten-thousand-mile migration to Baja California, where the mother gray whales give birth to their young in the lagoons, the only whale known to do so in shallows. The migration travels in two overlapping pulses. First to swim south are the pregnant females, followed by the adult bulls. Immature bulls and cows come next. Gray whales are most often seen throughout the sanctuary in a southbound migration, from December to mid-February. Pods of gray whales most often swim in groups of four or five, but during the peak of migration, from early to mid-January, it is possible to see pods with up to fifteen individuals. Early birthings of calves in and near Monterey Bay have been reported each January. In 1997 the migration was later; some scientists relate this to El Niño's affect on warmer arctic waters.

The northbound migration spans mid-February to mid-May and peaks in early March. The whales return in the same order as the southern migration. Newly impregnated cows are the first to pass north. Mothers and slow-swimming calves are the last to pass north. They swim close to the shore, possibly as protection from pods of orcas. Sometimes the whales turn into the relatively calm waters of the Monterey Bay at the southern tip by Point Pinos. Some juvenile whales heading south do not complete the migration but turn and join groups heading north. Resident gray whales that do not migrate are also studied along the Central Coast. You can see pictures in movies and books, but nothing quite equals the close eye-to-baseball-size-eye contact you make with these barnacle-covered giants while standing on the deck of one of the whalewatching boats that you can arrange to take out of Santa Cruz or Monterey Harbors.

Some of the best places to view whales from shore include Davenport Cliffs, Asilomar Beach, Point Pinos, stretches of Pebble Beach including the Lone Cypress lookout, Point Lobos, highway pullouts located all along the Big Sur Coast, and the optimal view from atop the Big Sur Lighthouse. Gray whales can be seen close to shore at San Simeon Cove and along the Cambrian shore. Although they can be seen spouting and breaching with the naked eye, binoculars bring them closer.

The gray whale and humpback whales were the main prey of the "shore whaling" industry that had its beginnings in Monterey about 1854. They were harpooned from boats, towed ashore, rolled onto the beaches, and their blubber rendered into oil in kettles over open fire pits. Whaling stations were established up and down the coast, at Pigeon Point, Davenport, Santa Cruz, Moss Landing, Monterey, Point Lobos, Big Sur, and San Simeon. These whaling stations and the slaughter of mothers and calves in the southern lagoons brought the gray whales to near extinction. The passing of the whaling industry and the tightened government protection of the species has increased the gray whale numbers, making them the first California mammal to be removed from the endangered species list.

Other whales are spotted in the sanctuary's waters. Blue whales, *Balaenoptera musculus*, arrive in late June or July in most years, with frequent spottings through October. The largest animal ever to live on earth, the blue whale is blue-gray in color, long and sleek. Reaching lengths of a hundred feet, blue whales feed in the sanctuary on a diet of several tons of krill each day. Humpback whales are often seen in the sanctuary beginning in late April and early May. These are black or gray, with some white on the throat and belly. The flippers of the humpback whale are very long, approximately one-third of the whale's body length. Humpbacks are known for their dramatic breaches above water and for their songs.

Dolphins and porpoises are the smaller members of the toothed whale family. Dolphins are usually identified by their long beaks, whereas the shorter-beaked species are usually referred to as porpoises. The common dolphin, *Delphinus delphis*, and the Pacific white-sided dolphin, *Lagenorhynchus obliquidens*, are the most frequently sighted dolphins in the sanctuary. A resident population of bottlenose dolphins is often seen as it travels between Santa Cruz and Marina. If you sail about the bay, you will probably see dolphins leaping beside your boat. "I always feel happier when I see those fellers popping the waves alongside me," a local surfer told me. Surfers often

Gray Whale

feel that the presence of dolphins signals the absence of sharks.

Orcas, the largest members of the Odontoceti family, also frequent sanctuary waters. Adults grow to twenty-five feet in length, and they often hunt cooperatively in groups. Known commonly as "killer whales," the orcas are easily identified by their striking black and white markings, rounded flippers, and huge white dorsal fins.

As the Cetacea dominate ocean travelers' attention on the blue-green surface, colorful varieties of fish and invertebrates draw divers' attention around the granite outcroppings, shale reef, and any of 1,276 known shipwrecks that jut up here and there from the soft, flat sea floor. Rockfish are common year-round. Salmon arrive in summer to feed. Anchovies, albacore, squid, and flatfish are among the other main types found offshore. The waters of the sanctuary encompass much of the "red triangle," the section of California with the highest recorded number of white shark sightings and attacks. White sharks feed here on the seals, sea lions, and sea otters, among other sea mammals that fish the sanctuary waters.

The floating islands you see offshore are the tips of the kelp forest. Just as pyrite, "fools gold," tricked early miners into believing they had struck it rich, the bobbing bulbs of bull kelp, *Nereocystis*, fool many an otter seeker into thinking, even shouting, that they are viewing hundreds of bobbing heads offshore. The proper name indicates another comparison. *Nereo* means "sea nymph" or "mermaid." Wishful sailors may have seen the bulbs and surrounding leaflike blades as sea nymphs' heads with encircling hair. Otters do favor the kelp beds and often wrap themselves in the branches to keep from drifting with the currents. The bulbs of bull kelp, the most visible of the hundreds of sea plants in the sanctuary, are the "treetops" of underwater forests a hundred feet deep. The name comes from the hollow tapered stems, which resemble bull whips. Bull kelp is an annual that begins growing early in spring and reaches full size by autumn.

When conditions are right a different variety, giant kelp, *Macrocystis*, can grow up to ten inches a day—faster than any plant on earth. As you walk over kelp washed ashore in winter, the sand may pop under your feet. You've found the remains of gas-filled bulbs (the size and shape of Christmas tree lights) that form the base of the long, reddish-brown rippled blades that help the perennial giant kelp keep afloat. The kelp forests support a wide variety of sea life, including invertebrates and the larval and adult forms of many fish.

Green hillocks cover the beaches as large quantities of kelp wrack and varieties of sea plants wash ashore at Spanish Bay Beach in Pebble Beach (formerly known as Moss Beach) and along Asilomar Beach in Pacific Grove, especially by Jewell Avenue. Besides kelp, varieties include *Ulva*, or sea lettuce; *Laminaria*, shaped like a long-bladed oar; and *Egregia*, or feather boa.

Bull Kelp

Sea Palm

Sea Otter

Around the turn of the nineteenth century gathering sea plants for art was a favorite pastime of tourists. If you turn over the kelp on the shore you will see that it teams with life—particularly the insects called sandhoppers and small crustaceans. This provides an important food source for the shorebirds. The earliest inhabitants of these coastal regions used *Nereocystis* for food. The dried blades can be eaten like potato chips or pickled. Kelp is much more a part of your life, too, than you may realize, as it is used in toothpaste, some commercial ice cream, and pharmaceuticals. Many visitors perceive the local shores to be polluted because of foamy waves and shores. The foam is not pollution but a natural by-product of decomposing kelp and other organisms.

The southern sea otter floats about the kelp forest like a jester, somersaults, and dives deep to resurface nearby. Along Point Lobos and sections of the Big Sur coast you can spot "rafts" of twenty and more floating otters. When I kayak the bay, I grab onto the kelp if my arms are tired, if the current is too strong, or if I just want a special view of an otter to last a while. Looking a bit like floating logs, otters are distinguished from pinnipeds by their thick dark fur.

Red Abalone

They rely on their coats for warmth in the cold waters; unlike pinnipeds and whales, they do not have a thick protective layer of blubber. Otter fur may be as thick as a million hairs per square inch.

While swimming on their backs with hind webbed feet waving like flags, otters use tools such as rocks to pry abalone loose from rocks beneath the water's surface. You might see an otter tuck its favored prying rock in the body sac under its arm, dive repeatedly, then finally float on its back to stuff a shell's soft insides in its mouth. Otters also smash enclosed shellfish, most notably urchins, against rocks that are balanced on their stomachs to get at the soft morsels inside the shells. Just as ladybugs keep my roses from being devoured by aphids, otters keep the kelp forests from being devoured by sea urchins and abalones. When all populations are in balance, otters limit the growth of the grazing abalone and urchins, which allows for greater kelp growth, which in turn supports new abalone and urchins. When the otter population was at its lowest ebb in the late nineteenth and early twentieth centuries, the abalone population bloomed explosively. Vast reserves of abalone were harvested, first for their shell value and later as food. Ironically, some abalone harvesters now complain that otters limit their catches.

To distinguish female from male otters is not always easy. An especially rambunctious juvenile is likely to be a male. Females are often identified by their bloodied or scarred noses. As part of the mating ritual the male otter pulls the female's head back with his flipper and bites her nose severely.

Researchers at the aquarium have discovered that otter mothers pass food and tool preferences to their offspring. The grandchildren of one mother at Lover's Point in Pacific Grove are noted for their preference of beer bottle hammers. Another interesting fact: voracious eaters, otter fathers put their stomachs first and may even hold babies hostage for a share of a mother otter's food.

Although otters were noted as shore-dwelling animals in the early 1800s, they are now radically reduced in numbers and rarely seen onshore. Historically, the species numbered in the tens of thousands. With the invention of the samovar, Russians developed a great demand for tea. China's mandarins offered to trade the precious leaves for otter fur, used to trim ornate Chinese robes. In the late eighteenth and nineteenth centuries opportunist Russian traders forced Aleut hunters into hunting servitude. Two Boston sea captains, Jonathan Winship and James O'Cain, encouraged the Russian hunters south. Americans vied with Russians using Kanakas from Hawaii. John Rogers Cooper vowed to hunt down every otter to keep them from the Russians. The coastal settlement of Fort Ross in California was a Russian outpost of this trade from 1812 to 1841. The area from what is now Alaska through central California was stripped of its sea otters causing near extinction and a severely reduced gene pool. A few scientists were aware of

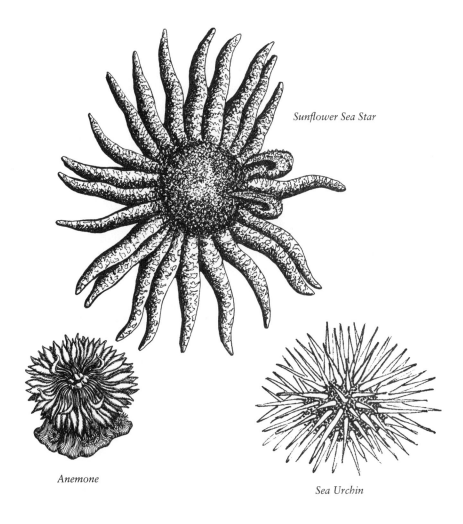

Sunflower Sea Star

Anemone

Sea Urchin

the otter's survival, but newspapers didn't believe a local restaurateur who reported he had "rediscovered" the California otter in a bed of kelp near Bixby Creek on the Big Sur Coast in 1938.

The range of the more than two thousand endangered otters now stretches from Año Nuevo Island north of the Monterey Bay to Point Purismo in Southern California. Some scientists are hoping the *San Francisco Chronicle*'s front-page reports of rare, isolated otter spottings in San Francisco Bay are indications of future growth of the species. "Actually, I'm really surprised that the sea otters seem to have stalled in population expansion in the last five years," reports Jack Ames, a marine biologist with the state Department of Fish and Game. "It could be that they won't grow in numbers until they can expand their range further." Otters remain extremely vulnerable to the effects of large oil spills because of their need for air insulation in their fluffy fur.

BAY NET docents point out otters to seekers. On days when docents are available, volunteers from Friends of the Sea Otter (see page 78), set up free viewing scopes at various locations along the bay from Cannery Row to Point Pinos.

The rugged rocky shores that surround the aquarium are made up of hundred-million-year-old exotic-terrain granites, possibly formed in the South Pacific. When the Pacific plate dipped under the North American plate, millions of years ago, the pressure melted the underlying rocks to form granite, which cooled slowly and floated northward on the magma on top of basalts. Large feldspar crystals can be found in the rock formations from the aquarium to the southern reaches of the Big Sur Coast. The granite results in the crystalline clearness of the water. More conglomerate rock foundations around Santa Cruz cause the water to be murkier on the north end of the bay.

After the high tide recedes from rocky outcroppings by the shore, water remains in depressions in the rocks: tidepools. Waves wash blankets of food over these tidepools, homes to colorful creatures including shore crabs, flowery sea anemones, sculpins, and spiny sea urchins. Barnacles open their shells and sweep the water with feathery legs to catch food. More species of sea stars are recorded within the sanctuary than any other place on earth. Limpet and chiton populations are also some of the most diverse in the world. An abundance of tidepools are located north of Santa Cruz in San Mateo County at Fitzgerald Marine Reserve, at Natural Bridges Park in Santa Cruz, along Ocean View Boulevard in Pacific Grove, along Seventeen Mile Drive in Pebble Beach, along Carmel beaches, at several park beaches along Big Sur, and near Point Piedras Blancas in the southern reaches of the sanctuary.

The first step in tidepooling is to locate a tide table to find the time of the lowest tide. Free booklets are available at the local Longs Drug stores, the concessions on Fisherman's Wharf in Monterey, and at many of the shops along the Big Sur Coast. Bring extra shoes—an old pair of tennis shoes is fine—to get close to the pools. Remember to be aware of the ocean; never turn your back on the waves while turning your attention to the creatures of the rocky shores. Sneaker waves can whisk tidepoolers off secure ledges. If you tug creatures off rocks just to look at them, you may tear their legs off. There is no harm in picking up creatures that release easily. They need frequent dips in water and like to return to their territory in the tidepools where you found them.

At first tidepooling sounds like a treasure hunt. "A purple sea star! Sea anemones—hundreds of them! A crab, over there, he's under that rock!" After the initial excitement you might want to choose any tidepool and observe it at leisure. Your reward will be a greater understanding of the creatures. Tidepools are the creatures' homes, so walk lightly, and let them stay, for the good of the sanctuary.

The kelp forests and rocky shores are also home base for many seals and sea lions. Eighty percent of the marine mammals in the northern Pacific spend all or part of each year in the sanctuary waters. The land shakes when the huge elephant seals drag their heavy bodies across their Año Nuevo reserve at the northern border of Santa Cruz County and in growing numbers along the shore north of San Simeon. Sea lions drape themselves on rocks along the coast. Harbor seals give birth in spring along the Cypress Point shore in Pebble Beach and the Big Sur coast. Elephant seals pup from December to March at Año Nuevo and on the sandy beaches north of San Simeon. Over the last twenty years the estimated populations in California of northern elephant seals, California sea lions, harbor seals, and northern fur seals have rebounded to numbers far greater than those of 1910, when the northern elephant seals numbered just two hundred. California sea lions are making harbor masters work overtime as they take over boat docks from Monterey to San Francisco and conservationists and representatives of fisheries are studying the effect of rising pinniped populations on the fishing industry.

To observe these playful mammals, bring binoculars and check tide tables. In general seals and sea lions will be out feeding during the highest tides and resting between tides and diving periods. All but the northern fur seal are commonly seen year-round. Several clues help viewers tell the difference between true seals and sea lions. Check for external ear flaps; sea lions have tiny ear flaps, seals don't. "Seals sink, sea lions dive" often holds true. True seals float in the water vertically, with only their heads sticking out, and submerge by sinking back tail first instead of diving like the sea lions. Sea lions often raft and hold their flippers straight up in the air. Networks of tiny veins in the flippers bring the warmth of the sun or the cooling air to their bodies. When the animals haul out on beaches or rocks their colorings, vocalizations, and flippers will help you identify them. If the mammal you're observing barks, it's the California sea lion that is used as the trained "seal" in circuses. Sea lions can walk on their hind legs and gather in noisy colonies. If it's bouncing and wriggling like an inchworm there's an excellent chance you've spotted the chunky harbor seal. Harbor seals have spotted silvery gray coats and large eyes. If you are walking along their beach they may follow you curiously from just offshore. Harbor seals groom with the long claws on their flexible fore flippers. To rest and sleep they balance their sausage shaped bodies on rocks just offshore and stay so still, their marbled bodies resemble sculptures above the rocks. Seals and sea lions both seek refuge on beaches during rough winter weather.

As the largest of the pinnipeds in this region, the male northern elephant seal is recognized for its large drooping snout and mammoth size, up to sixteen feet long and five thousand pounds. At UC Santa Cruz's Long Marine Laboratory, Burney Le Boeuf heads the world's longest-running study of elephant seals. One of his findings is that the elephant seal can dive the deepest of any mammal studied—to more than four thousand feet.

Miles and miles of sandy beaches in the sanctuary rise in places up to five hundred feet high. Waves deposit sand on beaches and in the mouths of man-made harbors, and westerly winds blow the sand inland, where it meets a drift line of coastal plants and forms a barrier of dunes. Over time the dunes themselves grow a mat of vegetation, which anchors the inland side. The dune system along the inner crescent of the Monterey Bay is one of the most extensive in the western United States. Many volunteers, ranging from preschoolers to community elders, are replanting native vegetation along dunes that have been trampled, mined, and planted with carpets of ice plant. Our family spent one Saturday morning planting sprigs of buckwheat and coastal daisy in the dunes along the Asilomar Beach in Pacific Grove. We had walked the ocean-view trail along Asilomar often and planted as a way to give back. Now when I walk the path I realize the gift was ultimately to us. We used to walk through stretches and stretches of quiet, monotonous ice

Sea Lion

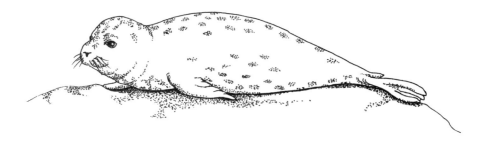

Harbor Seal

plant spikes and focus on the beauty of the crashing surf. Now the walk
includes butterflies flitting over small purple flowers, chirping birds, and grazing deer. Healthy dunes, planted in several varieties of native vegetation, support abundant wildlife that ranges from endangered butterflies, lizards, and
mice to songbirds, hawks, and deer. Many state beaches schedule nature
walks to help visitors and residents become more acquainted with dune life.
You might consider joining a volunteer dune restoration planting during a
coastal visit. Nature will water the planting, the deer will trim it, and on your
return visit you will get flowers at your feet.

The farthest inland reaches of the sanctuary habitats are the most fragile.
At the center of the coast along the Monterey Bay, Elkhorn Slough flows
inland for twelve miles. Rain-swollen creeks wash nutrients from inland to
the coastal wetlands; from offshore, the nutrients flow inland along the same
channels during high tide. Thus fed from both sides, sloughs and other wetlands are nurseries for many fish species, home to a variety of mud-dwelling
animals, and the food source and nesting habitat for millions of migratory
birds.

Numerous sea and shore birds roost in rocky outcroppings and dot sandy
beaches along the sanctuary. Endangered brown pelicans, cormorants, snowy
plovers, and common murres are among the ninety-four species of birds
found in the region.

On land the endangered brown pelican is one of the most comical birds
you can watch. It waddles along, balancing its huge scooped bill above its
neck. In flight, the pelican commands the skies. Pelicans fly singly and in long
gliding squadrons of up to thirty birds. When a hunting pelican spots food it
tips toward the water, wings bent in a V, and dives like a jet straight down
at rapid speed, then hits the water so hard the fish two yards beneath the

surface is stunned. The pelican swoops up the stunned fish, drains water from the sides of its bill, and stores the fish in its stomach. Abundant air sacs in its bill protect the pelican during its high-speed dives. In the 1960s and early 1970s high percentages of DDT in their diets caused pelican populations to drop dramatically. Today the pelicans are endangered but recovering.

A sea gull is just a sea gull until you begin to look closely at feather patterns and feet, bill, and eye colors. More than a dozen varieties of gulls visit the sanctuary. Western gulls are large and dark with long yellow beaks. Heerman's gulls have bright scarlet bills, white heads, and gray bodies. Juvenile gulls are usually lightly spotted. One of nature's designs for the gull's grabby nature became clear at the birth of a harbor seal along Cypress Point beach, in Pebble Beach. As the mother lay exhausted after the birth, the baby was nearby caught in a placental covering. Observers from a blind considered approaching to save the baby (though threatening the mother could have a counter effect) when a trio of gulls swooped down, gobbled up the placenta, freed the baby, and even snipped the umbilical cord—leaving mother and baby safe.

Whether you are a scientist, avid beachcomber, or occasional visitor, each moment in the sanctuary brings new discoveries. Available at dive shops, The Monterey Bay Marine Sanctuary Diver's Map published by Cooper Brothers Maps (P.O. Box 148, Pacific Grove, CA 93950), offers a detailed description of sanctuary waters from Monterey to Point Sur. The map is especially valuable for divers, kayakers, surfers, and boaters.

TOUR: THE AQUARIUM

The Monterey Bay Aquarium exhibits are a living extension of the Monterey Bay Sanctuary. In the original wing you feel you are observing the exhibits with a close-up lens. In the Outer Bay wing you almost feel you are one with those creatures of the sea that live without boundaries. Before you start your tour, check the visitor information board just inside the main entrance for special show times, such as Kelp Forest, Otter Feeding, Tidepool Divers, and Live Net. The shows are popular, informative, and will add to your enjoyment of the aquarium. Plan to get to their locations fifteen minutes early for good viewing spots. Aquarists often answer viewers' questions as part of the shows.

ORIGINAL WING

The three-story kelp forest marks the beginning of the habitats trail. The kelp forest looks so natural, many visitors believe they are looking through a window to the bay. Anchored to rocks by tangled holdfasts, the bladed strands of giant kelp grow through filtered sunlit water, spreading flat blades and bobbing bulbs. Sunlight pours through the roofless exhibit. Pumps propel up

Brown Pelican

to two thousand gallons of seawater a minute through jets to create natural currents. During 1997 El Niño depleted the water of nutrient-rich conditions, and Miracle-Gro was added to the kelp forest exhibit.

Sometimes Julie Packard takes a break from her office and enjoys the kelp forest. "These beautiful plants exhibit remarkable adaptations. At a hundred feet they are taller than most trees, but if they remained stiff like trees they would perish; instead they are flexible, they go with the flow. Different pigments capture sunlight in the various light changes at ocean depths. The exhibit represents a challenge met. We were the first to re-create the world of the kelp forest in an aquarium."

Dark turban snails and amber kelp crabs glide along the swaying branches. Pictures at the rim of the Kelp Forest exhibit help you identify some thirty-five species of fish circling about. You will certainly notice a flash of gold as senoritas dart by on their way to nibble tiny creatures from rocks and the backs of other fish. Like ocean opossums, kelp rockfish hang about, upside down and motionless. Leopard sharks glide by. These sharks aren't after anyone's arm. The electroreceptors in their snouts are searching for the single foot of the sea worm.

Red algae cover the rocky bottom, which also boasts a wide variety of sea

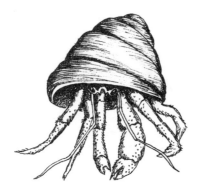

Hermit Crab

stars and sea anemones. If it weren't for volunteer divers like Patrick Malone and Gary Haas, all you would see is red algae. Brought in from the open sea by the pumps, the red algae attach to any hard surface, including windows. Patrick Malone waited for two years for his name to get to the top of a volunteer waiting list; now he drives more than a hundred miles from San Francisco to Monterey every other Saturday to clean windows by scrubbing the algae with suction cups and elbow grease. Haas leads diving tours in various locations around the world, but his favorite spot is the aquarium. "It's a thrill," he says. "Out in the bay the dives are spectacular, especially off Coral Beach in Pacific Grove, but you never get the opportunity to swim with so many species at one time. These fish are fed to keep them satisfied and prevent them from preying on each other. It's a fish Club Med. Out in the ocean the leopard sharks will spook at fifteen feet; here they brush against you. The best part, though, is picking a kid who is transfixed on your cleaning. You move very slowly, turning your body upside down. Suddenly the kid catches your upside-down grin and shrieks with laughter. The people are almost as fun to watch outside as the fish are in here." Divers like Malone and Haas enjoy the Kelp Forest exhibit most when they talk with the audience through an underwater microphone, during the twice-daily feeding shows.

In the adjacent Monterey Bay Habitats exhibit, leopard sharks, a large sevengill shark, and smaller sixgill sharks cruise a ninety-foot tank designed especially for their long glides. Leopard sharks and dogfish are fed smelt and other fish twice a day. The habitats meld together here as they do in the bay. Clouds of rockfish float over rocky reefs as flatfish lie half-buried in nearby patches of sand. To accentuate the Monterey Bay Aquarium's quest for authenticity, real shale reefs were brought from the bay, with clams, mussels, and other dwellers intact. Pilings from an old Monterey wharf, encrusted with decades-old anemones, barnacles, and tubeworms, anchor the far end of the habitats.

Hungry surfperches pick their meal of mollusks as they would in open water.

You may see an aquarist such as Andy Case vacuuming the bottom. When I asked him how he works alongside the sharks he replied, "I move slowly, just as you would in a field of cows. The important thing is to keep them from getting excited, so they don't panic and injure themselves."

Case's favorite tank is that of the curious octopus that seems to enjoy his gentle pats. Along the same wall with the octopus, exhibits highlight the deep reefs, the sandy sea floor, the shale reefs, and the slough.

The corridor of exhibits then opens to an interactive area, which is bordered by an aviary of shorebirds. Signboards identify the flowers of native dunes. Foraging sandpipers, avocets, plovers, and black-necked stilts probe the shore for food. My personal wish is that the aquarium double the size of this exhibit, as it is often crowded with people straining to view such treasures as the nests of ducks and marsh wrens.

Outside the aviary several bat rays flap through their shallow pool like giant birds. This is a place to roll up your sleeves. The spikes at the base of the bat rays' tails have been removed so that visitors can reach into the water to pet their silky backs as they glide by on their circular journey. Around 4 p.m. the bat rays hover near the sides of the pool and shake their wings. Lucky bystanders feed them a concoction of squid, clams, and shrimp.

A touch pool awaits visitors at the far corner of this floor. Sea stars, rock crabs, sea slugs, chitons, and various tidepool animals are available here for close tactile exploration. This is a helpful introduction to tidepooling, as you can ask the trained docents here questions.

Other highlights of the first floor include the great outdoor tidepool, a recreated coastal trout stream, and the otter exhibit. In the early days of the otter exhibit the otters were provided with live shellfish so visitors could watch them use rocks as tools to crack the shells. But playful otters used the rocks and discarded shells to pound and scrape against their see-through walls, making it necessary to feed them only the soft insides.

Upstairs, the aquarium features world-renowned special exhibits. *The Inside Story* takes you behind the scenes, where you can watch volunteers working with the orphaned otters, keeping them healthy and teaching them behaviors they would learn in the wild; scientists studying and feeding the aquarium's largest shark; and krill chefs preparing the daily entrees for 300,000 animals. Fourteen other "behind the scenes" views make this worthy of becoming a permanent display. It is scheduled to be open only through January 3, 2000.

Before you take the escalator to the Outer Bay gallery it may be time for a food break or a *Live from Monterey Canyon* viewing. Extensive gift selections and marine memorabilia at the gift shop may also tempt you.

NEW OUTER WING

As you step on the escalator to connect with the outer wing, imagine you are being pulled by a current beyond the ocean floor. For a while you seem close to the ceiling, among life-sized models of gray whales and white-sided dolphins. Curved walls and cushioned floors create a free-floating feeling. Light from a blue-domed ceiling shimmers as thousands of anchovies swim overhead in a huge 27-by-20-foot oval. This is your initiation to the deep.

I feel as if Robert Frost is asking "Are you a swimmer or a floater?" In the next tank the swimmers, torpedo-shaped mackerel, shoot by your face. Gracefully pulsating jellyfish drift by in a series of separate windows. Egg yolk jellies humor and comb jellies shimmer, but the orange sea nettle jellies drift in an incredibly blue tank that gives the feeling of forever. At this point you may want to trade shifts with your adult partner if young children are with you. Adults can take turns staring transfixed and learning with the children.

Flippers and Fins was created especially for children up to eight years of age. They can crawl through a "blubbery" whale and try their hands at several interactive exhibits. The leg flippers are especially fun. However, many children and adults do not quite understand the milk exhibit. Perhaps it will be revised.

In another gallery, large-scale models provide a magnified view of the tiny plankton that float in glass windows. Imagine a soup of these tiny giants of the food chain.

The ultimate exhibit beckons. The 1.2-million-gallon outer bay tank is the largest window on earth, two stories of serene depth. Schools of yellow-fin tuna roam around. Sharp barracuda cut through the vastness, and striped Pacific Bonito swim by, constantly moving—if they stop swimming they die. The sea turtle is the crowd favorite. Then there is the bulky ocean sunfish. It swims toward you, slowly propelling itself with two small side fins. Once it has arrived at the window's pane, it looks you in the eye, blows you a kiss, and disappears below.

A 7,000-square-foot exhibit of forty deepsea species carries a 1999 opening date. Some of the forty species for the display were collected from waters as deep as 1,000 meters. Most of the animals are part of an aquarium exhibit for the first time anywhere.

Outside the decks are waiting. Telescopes are set up to scan the horizon. Humans created the great tidepool in front of the deck's seating area; nature filled it with colorful sea stars, anemone, and other creatures. In summer, six-foot-tall shrimp and crabs may be part of the talented cast in a deck "learning through entertainment" show. But the top name on the marque is probably the otter off shore, cracking a shell on its belly rock.

WHAT ELSE TO SEE AND DO

After visiting the aquarium you may be asking yourself, now what? Other tours in this book begin right outside the front door. The aquarium is built half in Monterey and half in Pacific Grove; flip a coin. We next visit Monterey, California's most historic city. If your coin says Pacific Grove, skip ahead one chapter.

THE CITY OF MONTEREY

SHOWCASE OF HISTORY

Monterey's vibrant downtown has clusters of the most historic buildings in California. Cannery Row, Fisherman's Wharf, and sunny beaches front the open harbor.

GETTING READY

BEST TIMES TO VISIT AND SPECIAL EVENTS

Traffic to Monterey can be quite heavy during summer weekends and three-day-holiday weekends throughout the year. However, Monterey has so many visitor destinations, spread over so wide an area, that with two exceptions the city never seems crowded. Cannery Row and Fisherman's Wharf can get shoulder to shoulder with people during such weekends as Memorial Day and Labor Day, but the upbeat atmosphere of both places make them feel like big parties rather than crowded spots. Traffic does get unpleasantly congested there. Walk or from Memorial Day to Labor Day take the WAVE shuttle bus as often as possible.

Monterey offers a variety of special attractions and events throughout the year. For a year-round community party, visit the Old Monterey Farmer's Market and Market Place on Alvarado Street every Tuesday afternoon from 3 to 7 p.m., and the Certified Farmer's Market at Monterey Peninsula College every Thursday afternoon. Both markets feature the freshest fruits and vegetables, a selection of certified organic goods, baked goods, and more. On Alvarado Street, local musicians and clowns perform. Vendors sell a variety of crafts and street fair items, and restaurants serve menu items outdoors.

John Steinbeck's birthday is celebrated on February 27, with music, play excerpts, and readings. In March, musicians from across the county gather to play Dixieland (831/443-5260). On the last Saturday in April, the Monterey History and Art Association presents an annual tour of historic adobes (831/372-2608), led by local guides dressed in period costumes. Plays, music, and dances of the period enliven the adobes, some of which are opened at night. Funds raised support the Monterey History and Art Association. In June, Monterey plays the blues in a lively festival devoted to this quintessential American music. On July 4, one of the best Independence Day celebrations in

California begins with a parade, continues with a city picnic, and ends with spectacular fireworks over the water (831/646-3866). During the summer months, Monterey offers many special theater and music events, most of them centered near Fisherman's Wharf. The oldest continuous jazz festival in the United States returns to the city annually in September, bringing the biggest names on the scene and hot rising stars. Concerts are held outdoors under the fog, the stars, and the occasional jet from the nearby airport (831/373-3366).

CLIMATE AND CLOTHING

Monterey shares the typical coastal weather pattern. Due to its location on the bay, the city gets the sun earlier on foggy days and more often than communities to the south.

Dress in layers for the changeable temperatures. Casual clothing is the norm for this city. Good walking shoes are a must for the many excellent walking paths.

TOUR LENGTHS

Part of the downtown is a state historic park that features more than two dozen adobes, many of which are separate museums. To really appreciate Monterey and the history of California, plan to spend a whole day. You can walk to Cannery Row from downtown in thirty minutes by picking up the walking and bike path along the Custom House Plaza. Allow at least two hours for Cannery Row. Monterey is so rich in history, it really deserves at least a weekend; this is the cradle of the United States' government in the West.

HIGHLIGHTS FOR KIDS

The three tours in this chapter will be enjoyed by kids of all ages. The following attractions are especially kid-worthy.

The Monterey Recreation Department (831/646-3866) offers a catalog of activities and a summer camp program for residents and visitors. Check the Lyceum of Monterey County (831/372-6098) catalog for classes at a variety of local places of interest throughout the county, family field trips, and a summer- and winter-break program.

MY Museum, the Monterey County Youth Museum, 601 Wave Street (831/649-6444) was created by local parents and community volunteers to provide a place where play is learning and the "only limitation is your imagination!" Kids "fish" from a boat, "buy" supplies, and "cook" in an interactive version of Cannery Row. They can also make magnets dance, experiment with the latest communication computer technology, and create sculptures. The atmosphere is bright and airy and conducive to flights of imagination.

On the third level of the Wave Street parking garage, with a general admission of $4, it's a bargain at the price, and a hard place to get kids out of once they have begun to enjoy its many intriguing exhibits.

The Edgewater Packing Company, located across the street from MY Museum delights with whirling hoses on a merry-go-round, an amusement arcade, and laser tag center. Historic photo creations, popcorn, and candied apples add to the excitement.

Lake El Estero, located along Camino El Estero, includes the visitors center, a lake where you can rent paddleboats, two historic cemeteries, a walking path around the inland estuary, and the children's favorite, Dennis the Menace Park. If Dennis could have built a park this would be it. In fact, the park, was designed to be a place for "dos" rather than "don'ts" by its creator, Hank Ketchum. Children can climb on a real steam-train engine, board an old fishing boat, slide down an airplane, and run through a planted maze. At selected times of the year the lake is stocked with fish; and young anglers will enjoy lakeside fishing.

The Monterey Sports Center, 301 East Franklin (831/646-3700) features a clean, family atmosphere, while still meeting the needs of the serious athlete. Two indoor pools, a gymnasium, and the 112-foot water slide add to the fun. Children five years and under must be directly supervised at all times by someone at least sixteen years of age. Youth, thirteen–fifteen, who are accompanied by an adult may use the weight and fitness rooms. For out-of-city residents admission is adults (18–54), $5.50; youth (6–17), $3.50; children (5 and under), $1.25. Senior discounts and extended passes are available.

WILDLIFE WISDOM

Sea lions and pelicans hang out at the Municipal Wharf. In the winter, young male sea lions crowd the Coast Guard Wharf. Volunteers and paid staff have worked long hours swooshing sea lions from landward and wharf areas. Sea lions have been known to haul out on boats anchored in the harbor, causing them to sink. Don't try to pet or tease these gregarious animals. Otters are commonly seen in the waters off Cannery Row. You can rent kayaks for closer views of otters and sea lions at the beach north of Fisherman's Wharf and at the Custom House Plaza. Jacks Peak, a regional park located in the pines above Monterey, is a birders' favorite. The trails in Jacks Peak offer dramatic mountain-to-sea views. Jacks Peak is a day-use-only park. To reach it travel east on Highway 68 and turn right on Olmsted Road.

VISITOR INFORMATION

The Monterey Visitor's Center, 401 Camino El Estero, is open seven days a week for walk-in traffic. Visitor information can also be obtained at the

Monterey State Historic Park (831/649-7118), in the Stanton Center near the Custom House Plaza; the Monterey Peninsula Chamber of Commerce (831/649-1770), 380 Alvarado Street, and the Cannery Row Association (831/373-1902), in the green train car by the bike path near Prescott and Hawthorne streets, also provide visitor information. The visitor's center at the Monterey County Travel & Tourism Alliance (831/626-1424), 137 Crossroads Boulevard, Carmel, is a storehouse of information about the city of Monterey as well as about the entire county. Recorded visitor information can be obtained by calling 831/649-1770. Pick up a copy of the free *Coast Weekly* and a copy of the Thursday *Go!* published by the *Monterey County Herald* for theater listings, music, and special events.

PARKING

To cover all possibilities, pick up the city brochure "Smart Parking in Monterey." You may want to call or write the Monterey Chamber of Commerce for a copy of it before you visit. Parking in Monterey is available in lots, on metered streets, and along unmetered streets for limited time periods. You must have a residential permit to park for longer than one hour in certain residential sections; look for the signs that designate these.

Change for meters is available at the parking attendant booth in Fisherman's Wharf, the harbor master's office, and at lot 22, located between Cannery Row and Reeside Avenue. Usually the farther you are willing to walk, the less you will pay for parking. The most expensive lots charge $1 for each half hour. At the preferred downtown parking garage, on Washington Street between Franklin Street and Del Monte Avenue, parking is available at $3.50 for the full day with Sundays often free. At this writing the least expensive lot is located across from the Larkin House, on Calle Principal, where you can park for up to twelve hours, $.25 each hour.

During summer months, free aquarium parking is available at Del Monte Center with shuttle bus connections available.

ALTERNATE TRANSPORTATION

During the summer and at some peak visitor times the WAVE shuttle bus connects the downtown area with Cannery Row, Del Monte Shopping Center, and Pacific Grove for a nominal fee. The Simoneau Metro-Amtrak Plaza is located downtown across from the Cooper-Molera Complex. From here you can walk to all downtown locations, and the local bus service is convenient.

A scenic and convenient bike path connects Seaside with Monterey and continues on to Pacific Grove.

PLACES TO STAY

Monterey offers a variety of accommodations throughout the city. Cannery Row, New Monterey, the downtown area, and lower Munras Avenue are within walking distance of most locations of visitor interest. Some visitors to Monterey reserve rooms in neighboring Seaside, unaware that it is a separate city. See page 269 for Seaside area accommodations.

CANNERY ROW

MONTEREY PLAZA HOTEL, 400 Cannery Row. This formal hotel, known for its sweeping bay views and waterfront location, provides guests with high quality service and amenities. The hotel has two sought-after ocean-front sections as well as a section on the other side of Cannery Row, connected by one of the landmark Cannery Row bridges. Brazilian teak walls, marble finishes, and leather chairs grace the public areas. In the spacious bedrooms, floral fabrics and duvets complement the nineteenth-century Biedermeier furniture. Baths are Italian marble and many rooms on the bayside include balconies over the water. Access to a small beach is provided to hotel guests and the public through the plaza on the second level. The Duck Club, the hotel's flagship restaurant, features wood-roasted specialties. Schooners, a casual bistro with an outdoor plaza, is relaxing for breakfast, lunch, and dinner. The hotel has 285 rooms, seven suites, several banquet and meeting rooms, and a full fitness center. A full spa addition is planned. Rooms have minibars, VCRs, computer hook-ups, and terrycloth robes. 800/631-1339, 800/334-3999 in California, or 831/646-1700. Fax 831/646-0285. AX, D, MC, V. Parking $10. For two from $150 to $270; $405–$705 suite. Children seventeen and under stay free in parents' room.

SPINDRIFT INN, 652 Cannery Row. Situated along the bay, this elegant and romantic inn features feather beds (you can request a canopied one), wood-burning fireplaces, balconies or cushioned window seats, and panoramic bay views. Marble bathrooms with brass fixtures add to the luxurious ambiance. Accommodations include continental breakfast delivered to your door, afternoon wine and cheese, and nightly turndown with chocolate treat. Room service is also available from Paradiso Italian Restaurant next door. The hotel offers forty-one rooms with terrycloth robes, two telephones, refrigerators, minibars, VCRs, and valet parking. Special packages available. This is a lovely place for a honeymoon! 831/646-8900, 800/841-1879 (in California), or 800/232-4141. www.spindriftinn.com. AX, D, MC, V. For two from $149 to $209 streetside, and $309 to $409 oceanview. Winter rates available.

NEW MONTEREY

THE JABBERWOCK, 598 Laine Street. This bed and breakfast inn is located in a residential section just four blocks above Cannery Row and worlds removed from the hustle and bustle of the busy tourist areas. A brick driveway leads from the street seemingly to another time. Icelandic poppies, walk-through hedges, and a fruit-bearing lemon tree are part of the inn's one-half-acre garden oasis. The tile- and mosaic-floored and glassed-in porch on the first floor offers sweeping views of Cannery Row and the bay. A walkway of green carpet connects seven appropriately named rooms, each decorated in its own style, some more elegant than others. Four rooms have in-room private baths. The Toves features a hand-carved Queen Anne bed, nooks and crannies, and a claw-foot tub. Honeymooners and other romantically inclined guests will enjoy the large king bed and cozy fireplace in the ocean-view Borogove room. Make an unbreakable appointment for the day you need to leave, otherwise you may find yourself booking an extra night. Full breakfast and evening hors d'oeuvres. 831/372-4777 or 888/1-Burble. MC, V; two nights' stay required on weekends, three for holidays. For two from $105 to $190.

DEL MONTE BEACH

BEST WESTERN MONTEREY BEACH HOTEL (off Highway 1, Del Rey Oaks exit), 2600 Sand Dunes Drive. Your room is close to the sand and surf at this bright and airy beachfront hotel, which offers 196 rooms decorated tastefully in cool greens with floral decor. There are garden and poolside or oceanside rooms, twenty steps from an expansive sandy beach. The beach is inviting for beach walks, but the water does have riptides, so be careful. You can walk for miles along the beach, all the way to the wharves in Monterey. Restaurant, lounge, banquet rooms, pool, and spa. 831/394-3321 or 800/242-8627 or central Best Western number 800/528-1234. AX, MC, V; others also accepted. For two from $99 to $149.

DOWNTOWN

DOUBLETREE HOTEL (by Fisherman's Wharf), 2 Portola Plaza. A perfect plaza location for visiting historic downtown Monterey and Fisherman's Wharf. Beautiful atrium lobby. Large rooms with calming pastel decor, some with ocean views. Full service. Also the site of the Monterey Conference Center. Pool, restaurant, lounge. 831/649-4511 or 800/222-8733. www.doubletreemonterey.com. AX, MC, V; others also accepted. For two from $175 to $245.

HOTEL PACIFIC, 300 Pacific Street. In a garden setting, the feeling and adobe style of Old Monterey in a newer construction. All 105 accommodations are junior suites, each with a four-poster bed and sofa. They are available in sixteen buildings, clustered around courtyards and gardens graced with fountains. The rooms are cozy, decorated in a Spanish Old California style, some with private decks and fireplaces. A few suites have a view of the ocean or city. Each of the 105 suites has two TVs, three phones, gourmet coffee and tea, refrigerators, and wet bars. Some have whirlpools and there are two jacuzzis in the common area. Accommodations include continental breakfast and afternoon tea. Evening room service is available. 831/373-5700 or 800/554-5542. www.hotelpacific.com. AX, D, MC, V. For two from $190 to $249.

OLD MONTEREY INN, 500 Martin Street. Originally the family estate of the first mayor of Monterey, the inn is now a retreat from the bustle of the city. One acre of lovely gardens—with babbling brook, gnarled oaks, and blooming roses—surround the vine-clad country inn, which is located several gently curving blocks from downtown. Ten elegantly appointed rooms offer garden views. Several have fireplaces, jacuzzi baths, and feather beds. The Chawton and the Garden Cottage are secluded and offer whirlpool baths for two. Gourmet breakfast and afternoon wine and hors d'oeuvres. 831/375-8284 or 800/350-2344. www.oldmontereyinn.com. MC, V. For two from $200 to $280.

MUNRAS AVENUE

MARIPOSA INN, 1386 Munras Avenue. Though Munras Avenue is a busy street of motels and hotels leading from the freeway to downtown, every effort is made by the management to secure the quietest room possible for guests. Pastel walls, fireplaces, and newer facilities make this a pleasant place to stay. Beautiful gardens surround the best pool and spa location in the area. In-room coffee; complimentary breakfast in a sunny community room or on the garden deck. Most rooms with fireplaces, some are suites with private spas. 831/649-1414 or 800/824-2295. AX, MC, V; others also accepted. Winter specials offered. For two from $79 to $140.

EAST OF HIGHWAY 1

HYATT REGENCY MONTEREY, One Old Golf Course Road. When you step out the door from the main lobby, you are within footsteps of the Old Del Monte Golf Course, the oldest golf course in continuous operation west of the Mississippi. Beiges and subdued floral and leaf patterns set the room decor. Garden rooms and suites feature beam ceilings. Textured ceilings are also common throughout the hotel. Besides excellent golf packages, this 575-room hotel and conference center offers a variety of fitness facilities including two heated outdoor pools, championship tennis, a fully equipped fitness club, massage appointments, a game room, and bicycling. Camp Hyatt provides staff counselors and activities for kids. The Peninsula Restaurant has golf course views and quality cuisine, and Knuckles Historical Sports Bar features microbrews. On weekends, dancing and music fill one corner of the combination lounge and lobby, where a massive stone four-way fireplace warms a contented crowd. 831/372-1234 or 800/824-2196. www.montereyhyatt.com. AX, MC, V. For two from $98.

LONE OAK MOTEL, 2221 North Fremont Street. This reasonably priced motel offers comfortable rooms. Although Fremont is a busy street, the courtyard of the motel is set back from the noise. Some rooms have fireplaces and hot tubs. Satellite TV, fresh brewed coffee in the rooms, and a shared spa are available for all guests. 831/372-4924 or 800/283-5663. AX, MC, V; others also accepted. For two from $44 to $148.

RESTAURANTS

ABALONETTI, 57 Fisherman's Wharf. Enjoy casual dining in a bright dining room or outside on a private terrace. Oceanside views on the wharf. Fresh fish from the private loading dock; a dozen varieties of calamari dishes; excellent Caesar salad. Lunch and dinner. 831/373-1851. AX, MC, V. Entrees from $14 to $40.

CAFE FINA, 47 Fisherman's Wharf. Here find Fisherman's Wharf dining for formal occasions, with linen tablecloths, flowers, and ocean views, and for casual meals, with brick-oven pizzas and homemade fettucini and ravioli. Mesquite-grilled fresh fish, fresh abalone, meats, and chicken. Lunch and dinner. 831/372-5200. AX, MC, V; others also accepted. Entrees from $12 to $21, abalone at market price.

CIBO RESTORANTE ITALIANO, 301 Alvarado Street. Dark wood and patterned carpets add to the European ambiance of this Italian country-style restaurant. An elevated stage sets the bar apart from the dining room. Jazz is featured weeknights. After 9:30 p.m. on weekends, salsa, reggae, and rhythm and blues turn the establishment into a favorite weekend dance spot. More than a dozen appetizers, individual pizzas, and the freshest pastas. The *spiedini di pesce spada*, swordfish cut thin, rolled, and stuffed with bread crumbs, prosciutto, pine nuts, and currants is very special. 831/649-815l. AX, MC, V. Entrees from $9 to $20.

FRESH CREAM, 100 C Heritage Harbor, 99 Pacific and Scott Streets. This formal restaurant features understated elegance; there are early California impressionist prints, original oils depicting French chateaus, a spiral staircase to the lounge, and three private rooms for more intimate dining. The private rooms can be reserved for the 6 p.m. or 8:30 p.m. seatings. Floor-to-ceiling windows line four dining rooms offering expansive views of the Monterey Harbor. Consistently excellent French cuisine with a California flair. Impeccable service. Dinner. 831/375-9798. AX, MC, V; others also accepted. Entrees mostly under $40.

MONTRIO, 414 Calle Principal. Highly acclaimed chef Brian Whitmer launched this exciting pairing of great food and good vibes. Named Restaurant of the Year by *Esquire* magazine in 1995, Montrio continues to dazzle with imaginative combinations of fresh ingredients and wonderful attention to presentation, even though Whitmer has moved on to San Francisco. White clouds, constructed from sound-absorbing material, float above the tables. Dining here is upbeat. The front section and upstairs areas are somewhat quieter then other parts of the restaurant. Menu items include crispy Dungeness crab cakes with spicy remoulade, rotisserie selections, and a wonderful vegetarian risotto. 831/648-8880. AX, MC, V; others also accepted. Entrees $14.50 to $21.

PAPÀ CHANOS TAQUERIA, 462 Alvarado Street. This Mexican restaurant uses fresh ingredients to fill tasty huge burritos, chile rellenos, quesadillas, and a selection of *platillos especiales*. The rotisserie chickens are tender and juicy. Locals consistently give this restaurant five stars, as well as voting it "best inexpensive eats." The Taqueria is open until midnight. 831/646-9587. No credit cards. You can eat well for lunch and keep half a burrito for dinner for under $6.

SARDINE FACTORY, 701 Wave Street. The Captain's Room, with a fireplace and portraits of sea captains, is one of five rooms that each captures a mood or time in the history of Cannery Row. For small gatherings, guests can dine around a handcarved table in the wine cellar. The Baltino, fresh Monterey prawns sautéed with tomatoes, mushrooms, and garlic, glazed with vermouth, and the Monterey pasta dish, with Monterey prawns, baby lobster tail, scallops, linguini, roasted bell pepper, glazed onion, and brandy sauce, are two selections from the impressive menu featuring continental fare. Extensive "vault" of fine wines, including rare vintages. Dinner. 831/373-3775. AX, MC, V; others also accepted. Entrees from $17 to $30, fresh abalone at market price.

DIRECTIONS

All traffic to Monterey follows Highway I (see the directions to the Monterey Bay Aquarium, pages 26–27). The directions below serve as general guides to the Highway 1 freeway exits.

For southbound travelers *(exits are listed north to south):*
The Del Rey Oaks (218) exit leads west to Del Monte State Beach and inland to the town of Del Rey Oaks and farther to Highway 68.
The Del Monte Avenue/Pacific Grove exit leads to Del Monte Avenue, the main surface street that parallels the bay. It passes the Naval Postgraduate School and Fisherman's Wharf and continues to Cannery Row and Pacific Grove.
Casa Verde Way continues to the right (northwest) to Del Monte Avenue. It continues up the hill on the other side of Del Monte Avenue to Del Monte State Beach.
The Salinas Highway, 68, intersects with Olmsted Road, which leads to the airport and Jacks Peak. Highway 68 continues to Salinas.
The Central Monterey exit is one and one-half miles south of the Del Monte Avenue exit and leads to historic downtown Monterey and to Camino El Estero. Camino El Estero leads to the Monterey Visitor's Center, Dennis the Menace Park, and finally Del Monte Avenue. Brown directional signs along this route help you locate destinations.
The Soledad Drive/Munras Avenue exit leads to the downtown by way of Munras Avenue and the Del Monte Shopping Center. If you continue straight on Soledad Drive, then turn right at Pacific Avenue, brown directional signs will guide you to the downtown area and Cannery Row.

For northbound travelers *(exits are listed south to north):*
The Munras Avenue exit intersects with Soledad Avenue. Turn left at Soledad and right at Pacific Avenue, which leads to the downtown and, finally, to Cannery Row and the aquarium.

*Munras Avenue passes the Del Monte Shopping Center and a long
line of motels and ends in the historic downtown of Monterey.*
   *The Aguajito Road exit leads to Monterey Peninsula College,
the fairgrounds, and Del Monte Golf Course.*
   *The Salinas Highway, 68, Casa Verde Way, and Del Rey Oak
exit directions are the same as for southbound.*

INTRODUCTION TO MONTEREY
WITH HISTORICAL HIGHLIGHTS

Monterey is a historical highlight, a veritable open-air museum. Monterey
was the point where Sebastian Vizcaino landed in 1602 and claimed "the
Californias" for Spain. It was the site of the first Northern California mission
and the capital of the Spanish and Mexican regimes. The state's constitution
was drawn up in downtown's Colton Hall.

In 1997 and 1998 locals wrestled with the question of whether downtown
Monterey would remain tied to its historical past or welcome more fast food
and "chain" businesses. Petitions, buttons, and meetings centered around the
pros and cons of the two perspectives. As of this writing the city planning
commission is still studying the parameters of restaurants in historic
Monterey. "It's a great city," says Mayor Dan Albert. "When you think of
Monterey our historical past is very important. As we look at our future you
can't forget where we've come from. We've always been the center of the economic base of the peninsula." Behind it all, the historic buildings whisper
their stories from the past.

From two-thousand-year-old Rumsien village sites to the cutting edge of
modern marine-technology facilities, Monterey is like a layer cake of
California history. In fitting juxtaposition on any given day in the bay, the
tall ship *The Californian* may sail to port over the exploration zone of a
MBARI ROV submersible research vessel. Step ashore; most of the historic
parts of Monterey can be reached by interconnecting walking paths.

The city of Monterey extends from the bay on gentle hills to surrounding
upland forests. From Presidio Hill in the northwestern section of the city you
see the layout of the land, facilities, and population of Monterey as well as
enjoy incredible ocean views; they stretch from your vantage point across the
bay to the Gabilan Mountains. Once the site of a Rumsien village, the hill has
rested under four flags—serving as the location for gun encampments and
forts of Colonial Spain, Mexico, Argentina, and the United States. The hill is

now part of the Presidio of Monterey, home of the prestigious Defense Language Institute.

From Presidio Hill your gaze may focus on the ribbon of cars that flows along Lighthouse Avenue, separating the Presidio and its surrounding residential and visitor destination known as New Monterey from Cannery Row. You can pick out the two fiberglass faux smokestacks of the Monterey Bay Aquarium. Cannery Row, once a line of sardine factories, now hooks visitors with a selection of shops, restaurants, and motels, many of which are within original or rebuilt cannery buildings. The discerning eye finds many of the haunts John Steinbeck wrote about in *Cannery Row* and other books.

A walking and bike path, a former route of the Southern Pacific Railway, borders the Monterey waterfront, where three piers jut into the bay. The loud barking of sea lions may drift up to your vantage point from the Coast Guard Wharf, the first of these piers. Tourists and locals frequent fresh seafood restaurants and curio shops at Fisherman's Wharf, the second pier. Fishing boats unload their catch at the third, known as the Municipal Wharf.

The historic heart of Monterey lies in a confusing mishmash of downtown streets that fan out from the Fisherman's Wharf area. Unlike the East Coast, Monterey was not won from the colonial rule of the English. All of California and what are now seven adjacent states were under the rule of Spain at the time of the American Revolution. After Mexicans successfully revolted against colonial Spanish rule, these lands became part of the country of Mexico. U.S. rule of the seven-state area was first officially declared when land regiments under the command of Commodore Sloat raised the U.S. flag in a bloodless takeover at the Custom House, one of thirty-seven downtown historic adobes that now serve a multitude of uses, including museums, a restaurant, banks, and private residences. During the summer, and at select times during the year, actors and volunteers fill the shoes of notables from the city's history and roam the historic section in period dress, engaging in lively debates, pontificating their philosophies, and reminiscing about the life that was in Old Monterey. Where trade in hide and tallow occupied the streets a hundred years ago, coffee shops and bookstores now anchor a revitalized downtown, one that boasts the most historic buildings west of Williamsburg.

Lighthouse Drive continues south from the wharf and downtown areas to El Estero, once a marshy estuary, now a landlocked lake. Dennis the Menace Park, a circular lakeside path, and a historic cemetery surround the lower Lake Estero, while the tiny upper lake is alongside the newest part to the Monterey Peninsula Museum of Art, beautiful La Mirada.

As you view Monterey from Presidio Hill, the sunlit beaches and forests seem so inviting, and it is clear why Charles Crocker of the Southern Pacific Railway deemed Monterey the "most elegant seaside resort in the world."

Custom House in Monterey

Crocker directed the building of the historic Hotel Del Monte. The railroad was extended to Monterey in the late 1800s, and the Hotel Del Monte attracted trainloads of San Franciscans to the peninsula. The twice-rebuilt Hotel Del Monte, with surrounding grounds, houses the Naval Postgraduate School today. Plans are now being laid to once again extend rail service to the Monterey Peninsula for travelers.

Highway 1 cuts through the city limits with Del Monte Golf Course, Monterey Peninsula Community College, the county fairgrounds, and the airport lying on the highway's east side. Farther inland, on Highway 68, the newest business park is situated at Ryan Ranch. If you are driving north to the peninsula on Highway 68 you will pass the entrance for the highest mountain in the area, Jacks Peak. From Presidio Hill it can be spotted as the high peak just south of the airport.

In the late 1800s a land investor named David Jacks acquired most of the land that now encompasses Monterey, Seaside, Del Rey Oaks, Pacific Grove, and Pebble Beach, plus additional acreage. In 1859 David Ashley, a partner of Jacks, was employed by the city of Monterey to investigate the title it had received to thousands of acres of Mexican rancho lands. He presented the city with a $991 bill for his service. When the city leaders couldn't meet his wage from the empty treasury, Ashley convinced them to pass an act to sell off the Mexican rancho lands, more than thirty thousand acres, in order to pay the debt. A notice of the sale was then placed in an obscure Santa Cruz paper. On the day of the sale, Jacks was the only one who showed up, and he placed a lone bid of three cents an acre. Even the money he bid was basically worthless scrip. Upon learning of the transaction, city leaders and citizens were furious. They took the case to the U.S. Supreme Court, but Jacks prevailed.

TOURS

The first tour highlights the historic downtown. The Monterey waterfront, including Cannery Row and Fisherman's Wharf, is featured in the second tour.

HISTORIC DOWNTOWN TOUR

If you would like a historical perspective for this walk, begin at the Sloat Monument and on Presidio Hill, also known as Presidio Knoll. To reach the hill, enter the Presidio by turning inland on Artillery Street, off Pacific Street, just past Heritage Harbor. You can drive to park at the top by the monument. Parking is presently free and unlimited in this location. The hill is a microcosm of the many layers of Monterey. As of yet it has not been discovered by many tourists, or locals, for that matter, and you may be one of the few people there, or even alone.

A self-guided walking tour on the hill leads through the site of a Rumsien village, which some archaeologists pinpoint as the one called Tamotk in mission records. You'll see "rain rocks" with small mortar holes, believed to have been used by the Rumsien people in ceremonies for controlling rains. The Rumsien hunted and gathered their food. Larger mortar holes on the site were used for grinding acorns and other nuts.

The next layer in Monterey's history appears with the cross marking the grave of Alexo Niño, a black free man who died while traveling with Vizcaino in 1602. The oak under which Vizcaino, and later Portola, claimed the land for Spain grew at a point across from Artillery Street. The oak has since died, but you can see its preserved wood at the Cathedral San Carlos (Royal Presidio Chapel) on Church Street (see What Else to See and Do, page 80). The Spanish built their castillo (fort) on the hill, and its superior location gradually replaced the armament of the original Presidio by the chapel.

A memorial to Father Junipero Serra is found on the bayside foot of the hill, as is a monument to Hippolyte de Bouchard. Dreaded pirate Hippolyte de Bouchard and his crew sacked and looted Monterey in November 1818 and claimed the land for independent Buenos Aires, now Argentina—then sailed out of town a month later.

With the Presidio's sweeping views of the bay, you can see why it was used for encampments of the Spanish, Mexican, and successive U.S. armies. The Sloat Monument commemorates the taking over of California by the United States from Mexico without a shot being fired on July 7, 1846. If you look out to the ocean at the monument, then turn back in the direction of your right shoulder you will see the earthen fortifications of Fort Mervine, named after the commander who led the ground forces directed by Commodore Sloat. One of the five cannons on Fort Mervine dates to 1846. Fort Mervine operated until 1852. The other cannons date to the 1860s and may have been in use when Fort Mervine was reactivated in 1864 for the Civil War. After the Civil War, Fort Mervine was again abandoned and the Presidio was unused until 1902, when the Fifteenth Regiment moved in. The first U.S. vessel to land in Monterey Bay, *The Otter*, arrived in the 1790s.

The "Boston men" followed the hide and tallow trade to California and became entrepreneurs. To pick up the trail of the Boston men, and also begin the downtown tour, walk or drive to the Custom House Plaza.

You can pick up self-guided tour maps at the Monterey State Historic Park Visitor and Information Center, located in Stanton Center on the plaza across from Fisherman's Wharf. The guided walking tours led by state park personnel for a slight fee begin at this location. Three tours, each one to two hours in length, are offered daily (831/649-7118) and are heartily recommended. The park consists of eleven historic downtown buildings, which are marked with blue signs that give a short overview of the buildings' special qualities or history. For $5 you can purchase a pass that includes several guided tours and entrance to all buildings.

Stanton Center is a good starting point for a walking tour of downtown. The state park's information center, the Monterey Maritime Museum, a small theater, and a gift shop are located here. The theater presents a free twenty-minute movie about the history of the Monterey Peninsula. The movie stars local residents, and great care was taken to portray the history as accurately as possible. On some weekend afternoons, especially in the summer, live performers reenact special moments or cultural contributions from the past. Some performances feature impromptu roles for volunteers from the audience.

The Monterey Maritime Museum (831/375-2553), 5 Custom House Plaza, began as the private collection of Allen Knight and was formerly open free to the public, with fewer exhibits at an adobe on Calle Principal. In its current location the museum has been expanded and houses extensive exhibits that trace the cultural and nautical history of the Monterey area. There is an admission charge for adults and children. Rotating beams of light from the Big Sur Lighthouse Fresnel lens brighten the walls of the two-story building. Upstairs you can step beyond a re-created captain's room to view mementos such as whaling harpoons and the metal helmets of Japanese abalone divers. One room features scale models of various ships, including the *Savannah*, Commodore John Sloat's flagship.

During the summer, thanks to Monterey's commitment to theater in the open air, the plaza in front of the Stanton house is a lively, friendly place. Musicians and theater groups present performances that are free and first-rate. Arts and crafts shows often line the outer edges of the plaza. Frequent special events include the annual Greek celebration that features foods, music, and dancing. Along the other side of the plaza, players meet for friendly boccie ball games.

When you can tear yourself away from the plaza, cross to the Pacific House. This building was designed by Thomas Larkin, one of the enterprising Boston men who traded and built in Monterey in the 1830s. He first came to California at the request of his half-brother Captain Roger Cooper, who had come with the China trade. Captain Cooper had sold his ship the *Rover* to Arguello, the then governor of California, and at the governor's request stayed on to captain the ship. While in port Cooper stayed at Don Ignacio Vallejo's home. Vallejo was a wealthy member of the Mexican land-owning elite; Cooper married one of Vallejo's daughters, and became a Catholic and a Mexican citizen as well as a wealthy landowner himself. With his large cattle ranchos (one of which was located at what is now San Quentin Prison in Marin County) and shipping business Cooper wrote home for someone to come west and help manage his business affairs. Larkin sailed west to help Cooper, established his own businesses, and served as consul to the U.S. government and secret agent to the president.

Larkin worked for peaceful transmission of Mexican California to U.S. control. His buildings are examples of the Monterey style of architecture. Original homes in Monterey were constructed of adobe, a mixture of local mud and straw. Roofs extended over the sides to prevent the walls from melting in the rain. Monterey style designates two-story adobes with Yankee woodwork, such as doors, windows, tripped roofs, and second-floor balconies.

Larkin's original use of the Pacific House land was to sell its fresh well water to the ships at anchor in the bay. He later rented the building to the U.S. Quartermaster for offices and supplies. Crowds gathered behind the building for Sunday bull and bear fights. David Jacks bought the building in 1880 and it stayed in his family until it was given to the state in 1954. A museum of California history occupies the first floor, while the second floor houses the Monterey Museum of the American Indian, featuring interactive exhibits and an extensive collection of artifacts from the indigenous peoples of California and other regions of the United States.

The Custom House is the neighboring building. The Spanish government had forbidden international trade in California; the Mexican government welcomed trade as a source of revenue. Everything that came to port was taxed—sometimes at 100 percent of value. As Richard Henry Dana described the trade in *Two Years Before the Mast,* "Our cargo was an assorted one, that is it consisted of everything under the sun: we had in fact everything that can be imagined from Chinese fireworks to English cartwheels." On July 7, 1846, the U.S. flag was raised on the little flagpole at the north end of this building and the lands of seven present states became part of the Manifest Destiny policy of the United States.

From the Custom House you can easily walk to the first brick house in Monterey and the Old Whaling Station. Its name is a bit of a misnomer, as the "station" was actually the headquarters and employee residents' house. The whales were boiled down into fat on the beach in front of the house. Old photographs show whale bones scattered throughout the roads and yards of town. Look at the ground in front of the Whaling Station; the round dark disks are one of the few remaining whale vertebrae-sidewalks, which once stretched throughout Monterey. Behind the station sits a pot that was used to render the whale (and that always makes me a little sad).

As is the case with most of the public homes along this tour, the lovely gardens around the homes are open for your enjoyment. Almost every time I relax with a lunch in one of these gardens, I am visited by two companions, a squawking jay and a delicate hummingbird.

Walk to the Casa Del Oro & Garden, used as a general store by the nineteenth-century businessmen David Jacks and Joseph Boston. Here the nonprofit Historic Garden League operates the Boston Store. Next door this association tends the Picket Fence garden shop.

The general path of your walk leads next up Pacific Avenue, turns at Jefferson to include the old jail and Colton Hall, then crosses to the Larkin House and over to the Cooper-Molera complex. *Historic Monterey: Path of History Walking Tour,* published by the State of California and available for sale at shops along the way, offers short narratives about each of the historic adobes. The pamphlet does not replace the walking tours led by guides from the state parks department, which add detail and ambiance to the route. It is also fun to wander through the area and pick the ones that hold the most interest for you. When you see the little adobe houses remember that large families used to call these home. Some of the older children, especially those who worked as cowhands, would sleep on the front porches with their saddles for pillows.

California's First Theater (831/375-4916) is located at the corner of Pacific Avenue and Scott Street. It opened in February 1850 with performances by

U.S. Army officers, who produced some plays for the grand ticket price of $5. This is a great place to get a cool soda or sparkling water during the day. In the evening you can watch authentic nineteenth-century spirited melodramas.

"Clothing tells the human story," relates Marilyn McMorran of the Monterey History and Art Association. Around the corner at the Perry House, 201 Scott Street, costume designers ooh and ahh over the association's Historic Fashion Collection (831/375-9182). The ground floor features costumes from the 1770s to the present. After years of temporary lodgings, this museum has found a home in the Perry House, a historic whaling captain's house from the 1880s.

Farther along Pacific Avenue, the government complex has several notable buildings. The chunky adobe walls and metal doors of the jail hold many stories, including the escape of a suspected German spy in 1918. What is amazing to me is that the jail was used as recently as 1956.

Colton Hall was built in a New England style to house the city's first school and meeting hall. Rev. Walter Colton was the first American alcalde, or chief judge, of California and the hall was his brainchild. Erected from the labor of those found guilty of crimes and paid for with liquor and gambling taxes, it was completed just in time for the state's first constitutional convention. The second floor has been restored to look just the same as it did at that convention in 1850. Every year on October 13 local citizens reenact the signing of the constitution. The lower half of Colton Hall is presently used for city offices.

Although it is not a historic adobe, the Monterey Peninsula Museum of Art (831/372-7591), across the street at 559 Pacific Avenue, traces some of the early history of the area with its collection of early California artists. Asian and Pacific Rim art, ethnic and tribal arts, photography, and graphics are also featured. You can walk through the museum's sculpture garden to connect with Calle Principal.

The Larkin House, at the corner of Jefferson Street and Calle Principal, was one of the earliest two-story houses in California. Originally part store, as well as the house of the American consul Thomas Larkin, it is presently one of the best house museums in the United States. Larkin's granddaughter willed to the state the house and a number of furnishings, many of them original, in 1957. Guided walks are given, featuring a collection of antique English, American, and some Chinese furniture.

To step from another century to the cutting edge of modern architecture, walk through the Galerie Building, which fronts both Calle Principal and Alvarado Street. The adaptive reuse of the building exposes the timber trusses and concrete walls of the old Bank of America Building. With the addition of steel beams the entire building opens to a walkway of light. The building won a gold nugget award at the Pacific Coast Builders Conference for the Best Rehabilitated Commercial Building. "I take old bank buildings and recycle them," architect Stephen Eschler described the work to me.

As you exit on Alvarado Street you can turn left to visit the revitalized downtown or right to visit the Cooper-Molera complex. Whichever you choose first, be sure to come back for the other. The Cooper-Molera adobe is the site of the original Cooper home. As you walk in the store you will catch the fresh fragrance of a flower bouquet—some rose and lavender. The source is soaps handmade from the recipe of Alice Larkin Toulmin, granddaughter of Thomas Larkin. The items sold in the store support summer workshops for children who study California history here, the hands-on way. They make adobe brick, play nineteenth-century games, and help with the livestock and garden. Behind the Cooper store, behind walls of thick adobe, an eighteenth-century garden blooms in almost every season. Chickens scratch for feed and sheep ruminate. This is a very peaceful spot for writing letters or sharing lunch. The property also includes a museum of old wagons.

Pictures of the Coopers and Larkins as well as other early California settlers are displayed in a museum in one of the adobe rooms behind the store. An otter pelt to feel and samples of period china recovered from an excavation site are also displayed.

When you are ready to leave the urban sanctuary, venture onto Alvarado Street. Old brick sidewalks, the aromas of freshly brewed coffee, and a variety of shops fill this area. Farther down the street you can join a crowd of locals and visitors at Viva Monterey (831/646-1415) to catch the local band scene and share stories and drinks. The Monterey Victorian Hotel at 406 Alvarado Street is a remodeled William Weeks Hotel that features an ornate facade. A treasure is located just off Alvarado: the Old Monterey Book Company (831/372-3111) at 136 Bonifacio Place where the walls are lined with old and rare books, first editions, and prints. At the top of Alvarado Street, Bay Books (831/375-1855) offers a selection of books by local authors, an espresso bar, and a number of literary events. Each year for Steinbeck's birthday, a group of readers, including the mayor of Monterey and other community leaders, gather here to take turns delivering a dramatic reading of every chapter of *Cannery Row*.

WATERFRONT TOUR

"For quite a while Cannery Row crawled with frogs—was overrun with frogs." You may remember Mac and the boys bringing frogs to Doc's birthday party in John Steinbeck's *Cannery Row*. Local legend has it that descendants of those very frogs croak and ribbit today in echoing choruses from the construction sites up and down Cannery Row.

"Cannery Row in Monterey in California is a poem, a stink, a grating noise, a quality of light, a tone, a habit, a nostalgia, a dream," as John Steinbeck described it in *Cannery Row*, about 1945. It is still a poem. Nowadays, the only thing that really stinks in Cannery Row is the traffic. When you walk by the elegant oceanfront hotels, the waterfront restaurants, and the cornucopia of shops you'll notice the predominate aroma of chocolate, fresh-roasted coffee beans, and fresh sea air. In the evening, the frogs serenade and waves crash as stars light up "The Row."

Rohana LoSchiavo, who leads Historic Cannery Row Walking Tours (831/373-5571), brings some of the fascinating stories and colorful anecdotes of the past to life. "One of the first questions people ask me is, 'Where are the canneries?' The more you find out about the history of Cannery Row, the more you realize that many of the shops are housed in what were once canneries and factories."

The history of Cannery Row begins just north of the aquarium within the Pacific Grove city limits. Walk along the biking and walking path to a point just south of the building named Monterey Boat Works. All the buildings you see on the ocean side are part of the Hopkins Marine Station, a marine research school operated by Stanford University. As you look over the water you will see a grouping of white rocks. These same rocks may have been markers for groups of Chinese fishing families who, in the 1850s, loaded their belongings onto fifty-foot Chinese junks. They sailed north from their province of Canton, around the Bering Straits, down the wild West Coast, and into Monterey Bay. The rocks also mark the area where a Chinese fishing village flourished from the 1850s until it was burned by a fire of mysterious origins in 1906. The Chinese arrival in Monterey coincided with the abalone boom that was brought about by the overhunting of the southern sea otter. Abalone and later squid were dried for boat shipment to Chinese gold and railroad camps, as well as to Chinatown in San Francisco. The Chinese fished for squid by hanging lanterns over the bows of their boats in the dark of night. Attracted by the light, schools of squid would swim into the nets. If you are walking around the bay at night you might see bright lights gliding over the water. These are modern-day squid boats, the descendents of the Chinese lantern boats. But the scientific and fishing industries are talking about the overfishing of squid and the possibility the squid will meet the same demise as the sardine.

Some residents of the nearby community of Pacific Grove found the odor of dried fish and the site's shacks, as well as the accompanying opium dens, to be irksome. On a spring night the village burned, presumably set afire. Thereafter the village moved about a quarter-mile north, to the shores of McAbee Beach.

Sardine

As you walk back to Cannery Row you'll see a large wooden square resting on the grassy slope. This hopper was one of many that held fish just offshore before pumps from atop the canneries would suck the fish inside through long tubes. As you look back at the Monterey Bay Aquarium note the little square re-created pumphouse atop the roof.

On the side of the aquarium you'll see the red sign "Portola Brand." Many buildings along the row have similar signs, which denote the canneries that operated at their spots. The aquarium occupies the site of the Hovden factory, the largest and longest-operating cannery on the wharf. Although Steinbeck captured its soul, its reigning royalty, "King of the Canneries," was the Norwegian Knut Hovden. Before Hovden, the sardine cans were hand-crimped; Hovden introduced the machine solderer. One of his employees, Pietro Ferrante, adapted the *lampara*, or "lightning net" from his native Sicily. Sicilian immigrants arrived to man and eventually own fleets of lampara boats. In 1926, Knut Hovden again increased the tonnage of sardine catches with the introduction of large purse seiners, vessels with nets as large as football fields. As you look north on Cannery Row you will see several "crossovers." The canneries were built at the waterfront to allow direct access to the ships. Across the street most of the buildings were storerooms, built next to the railroad (where the bike path is now) for easy shipping. Cans that started out empty would ride conveyor belts through the crossovers, be filled with sardines, which were cooked in the cans, and be shuttled back across to the warehouses for labeling and shipment. The northernmost crossover has been added for architectural integrity, but the Monterey Canning Company crossway and the Aneas crossway by the Monterey Plaza Hotel are authentic.

Cannery Row was published at the peak of the sardine fishing industry, when nineteen canneries and twenty reduction plants packed 250,000 tons of sardines a season. Sardines were canned for food and were pulverized in the reduction plants for their oil; the solids were sold for fertilizer. Many of the haunts of the book's characters—Doc, Eddie, Mack, Dora, and Lee Chong— are now visited by millions of visitors each year, many of whom are unaware of the stories hidden in the building's walls.

Kitty-corner from the aquarium, at 851 Cannery Row, a yellow stucco building houses Kalisa's La Ida Cafe (831/375-5328). Steinbeck's Eddie served bar here. Now children stop in to get ice cream and milk. For forty years the cafe has been owned by Kalisa Moore, respectfully known around here as The Queen of Cannery Row. Kalisa occasionally hosts magic shows and belly dancing on the second story, which was one of the three brothels in the Cannery Row of Steinbeck's time. She also finds time to organize the annual Steinbeck birthday party on February 27.

During the canneries' heyday the grocery store next to Kalisa's was the Wing Chong (loosely translated as Glorious-Prosperous) Market, 835 Cannery Row. This market was owned during Steinbeck's time by Won Lee, who was identified in *Cannery Row* as Lee Chong. The Lee family still owns the real estate of the old market that has lived up to its name. If you walk back behind the displays of the present tenant, the Cannery Row Shell Company, and look in the corner, you can open the door to the little freezer where Doc would pick up five quarts of beer when he had company.

Doc Ricketts, the real scientist and the fictional one, lived and worked across the street in Doc's Lab. The unpainted slat-board building looks much the same as when Ricketts worked in the back room, "dressed in a long rubber apron and rubber gloves." Both he and Steinbeck were avid tidepoolers. When Steinbeck was young he enjoyed beachcombing while visiting his parents' summer home in Pacific Grove. Doc and Steinbeck were good friends and traveled together by purse seiner to the Sea of Cortez, which resulted in their collaboration on the book *Sea of Cortez*. According to tour leader Rohanna LoSchiavo, "Ed Ricketts was the heart of Cannery Row in the 1940s, and even today you never hear an unkind word said about him." Ricketts worked in his lab to build one of the most comprehensive files of marine tidal animals attempted in his time. His book *Between Pacific Tides* has been widely used as a marine reference book.

Ricketts used to fry steaks and share beer with his friends at the lab. Since the late 1950s the lab has been the site of many a friendly dinner prepared by a club of local men who pooled their resources to buy it. The men sold the lab to the city in 1993 but retain use of it for occasional meetings over the next sixteen years. Currently, the lab opens for special events and select tours but is felt to be too fragile for daily visitors (831/373-1902).

If you want to view a special exhibit of Steinbeck memorabilia, walk to the back of the Wing Chong Market to Alicia's Antiques, a room filled with Americana. Alicia's opens the Steinbeck Memorial Room to the public daily from noon to 6 p.m. You can view family photos, handwritten letters, and some personal items of Steinbeck's.

Next you may choose to climb the Bruce Ariss Walkway. A companion of Ricketts and Steinbeck, Bruce Ariss was a beloved resident, artist, author, and community activist. The three white shacks along the walkway were moved here from another site. The stories of the Spanish, Japanese, and Filipino workers who lived in these shacks are recorded on exterior plaques.

The site of Flora Wood's (Dora Flood's in *Cannery Row*) Lone Star Cafe, 799 Cannery Row, looks nothing like the most famous of the Cannery Row houses of ill repute. Flora named her place the Lone Star after her home state of Texas. Steinbeck changed the name to the Bear Flag. After closing in the 1940s the house burned, and its generous madam died penniless. The site was next to the present-day Mackerel Jacks Trading Company where you can purchase such items as T-shirts and windsocks. If you eat up the street at Bullwacker's, 653 Cannery Row, in what is now called the Bear Flag Building, you will hear the claim that the restaurant site was the Lone Star Cafe.

On the next block a mural on what was intended to be a temporary construction has turned into a fixture of the neighborhood. Organized by Bruce Ariss, the mural painted by local artists depicts scenes from Monterey's culturally diverse history and holds some surprises. In 1998 many new paintings replaced some of the more weathered originals.

Farther up Cannery Row is an overview of the history of California, Monterey, and particularly Cannery Row at the Steinbeck's Spirit of Monterey Wax Museum (831/375-3770). This may be one of the few wax museums that features local history instead of a parade of waxed celebrities. Thirty businesses share this building at 700 Cannery Row, the site of the Monterey Canning Company. This cannery made huge profits when World War I cut off supplies of fish from Europe and domestic sales boomed. You can still see the original wood construction and rooftop pumphouse. A photographic essay of Monterey by journalist Tom Webber hangs on the rustic wooden interior slats. Upstairs you can visit several galleries, some of them working studios. The abstract art of John O. Thomson surrounds sculptor Frank Sunseri as you watch him create miniature seascapes of melded metal. In the background you can hear the voice of his wife Mary Lei singing. Carloads of children around the Monterey Peninsula listen to her tapes.

Samples of the wines of local vineyards can be savored as you overlook the bay at the Taste of Monterey (831/646-5446). More than one hundred wines from twenty-seven Monterey County wineries are showcased here. You are welcome to relax and enjoy the panoramic view from one of the window tables. You will probably spot some cavorting otters as you enjoy a glass of wine and sample appetizers, which may include local produce. This is a good choice as your first stop on a tour of Monterey County wineries. If you want to be able to taste Monterey when you are back in Los Angeles or Omaha, pack your suitcase with this nonprofit shop's wide selection of local gourmet food items. The room is also available for evening events.

In the same building is the tasting room for the family-owned Bargetto Winery (831/373-4053 or 800/422-7438), Monterey County's oldest tasting room. Bargetto is famous for unusual wines, including Dolcetto, pinot grigio, and dessert fruit wines. (See page 306.)

A bronze bust of Steinbeck faces Cannery Row at Steinbeck Plaza above McAbee Beach. A stairway leads down to the small sandy beach. You can also climb the stairs here to view the coast from the balcony of the T.G.I. Fridays Restaurant (831/656-0125).

Since Monterey had an ordinance to prohibit commercial fishing from the beach, the Chinese changed their economic base from fishing to small-business ownership. You can see this influence in the pagoda-style roof across the street from McAbee Beach.

Ed Ricketts's call for marine awareness and education continues at the Robert Lyn Nelson Studios (831/655-8500), in the Steinbeck Plaza at 660 Cannery Row. Before you enter the gallery take a moment to gaze over the ocean and imagine yourself sinking beneath the surface. In 1979 Robert Lyn Nelson created his landmark painting *Two Worlds* and his vision launched the modern marine art movement and inspired others to preserve life in the sea. In the studio, a mixed-media limited-edition print of three humpback whales in the above- and below-water worlds floats on the wall amid hundreds of originals and prints. Nelson was honored as official artist for the International Year of the Reef (1997) and the International Year of the Ocean (1998). Though he lives in Hawaii, Nelson periodically visits this, his only stateside gallery.

Continue to please your senses at the neighboring Ghirardelli Chocolate Shop and Soda Fountain (831/373-0997). There is no need to travel to San Francisco to enjoy the famous chocolate sundaes and selection of chocolate treats, or to see a huge vat of chocolate.

Farther along the sweets route a sidewalk fudge bear offers coupons and invitations for the Old Cannery Row Fudge Company (831/373-6672), 807 Cannery Row. Rocky Mountain Chocolate Factory of Monterey (831/372-1065), 647 Cannery Row, creates specialty chocolates and sauces as well as at least twenty varieties of candied apples and flavored truffles. You can fill up baskets and buy candy by the pound at the Candy Baron (831/372-4601), 601 Wave Street.

On the third level of 700 Cannery Row, where cans to be filled used to cross Cannery Row, the aerial crossover now marks a good point at which to digress and wander through the shops along and above the bay front. Behind the row of buildings that front Cannery Row you are likely to see three generations of families out for a bike ride—all on the same bike! Six-seater surrey bikes, touring bikes, and strollers pass you along a wide bike and walking path. The Del Monte Express of the Southern Pacific Railway chugged along here until the 1960s.

On the upper side of the bike trail The Edgewater Packing Company, a World War II–era venture located at Prescott and Cannery Row, shares a common wall with the brick building that was the area's first reduction plant. Nowadays inside the Packing Company, the noise at the main amusement arcade probably approaches the previous noise level of the cannery. But the whirling horses on the merry-go-round could out-race a conveyor belt any day. Across the street, on the third level of the parking structure, children are amused and imaginations sparked at the MY Museum (see page 54).

The Enterprise Packers Warehouse at 225 Cannery Row is a triple pleasure to visit: On the outside wall you can view the migration of whales in a wall mural by local marine artist John Jennings. Inside, the structure retains the industrial integrity from the time it was used as a warehouse, during World War II. And one of its tenants, the Monterey Bay Dive Center (831/656-0454), features its own boat and serves all divers' needs.

Before the canneries changed the waterfront from peaceful beach to full industrial center, a large mansion called the Trevis Estate was located at the north end of Cannery Row. The large shingle house across the street at 417 Cannery Row was built in conjunction with the turn-of-the-century estate. If the house looks a little familiar, maybe you saw the 1951 movie *Clash by Night*. The movie featured Barbara Stanwyck and fish-cutter Marilyn Monroe in her first costarring role.

Take a walk on Wave Street until you see the corrugated tin exterior of the Cannery Row Antique Mall, 471 Wave Street (831/655-0264). This building and Doc's Lab are the only two buildings with historic preservation status in Cannery Row. If you stand in front of the building for a few moments, you can be transported back in time to 1927, when this was Warehouse #2 of the Carmel Canning Company. When owner Steve Travaille was young, he loved collecting small old things: later he graduated with a degree in history, and for twenty years he restored derelict old buildings that someone else saw fit for bulldozing. In 1995 Travaille and his partners bought the building at 471 Wave Street and worked with "the very cooperative City of Monterey" to file for historic preservation status. Then Travaille worked with historic photos from photo historian Pat Hathaway to keep the building true to history. One hundred seventy art and antique dealers fill the 21,000-square-foot building. "We have the greatest variety of antiques on the Central Coast: antique fishing lures and poles, everything from rare Babylonian oil lamps to Elvis Presley lamps." When Travaille talks about his mall and "the value in history" you know this is the kind of mall that artists and historic preservationists dream about.

If you have taken advantage of ocean views along your walk, chances are you have spotted an otter rafting in the waves. Friends of the Sea Otter Education Retail Center (831/642-9037 or 800/279-3088), 381 Cannery Row, Web site: www.seaotters.org manages the only retail store and education center on the Central Coast devoted to otters as well as a twenty-four-hour-accessible kiosk full of information about otters, current marine events, otter and other ecological tours, and maps for otter spotting. One section of the center features museum displays and four cubicles for otter movies and Web site access. In the retail section you can choose among hand-carved sea otters or soft plush sea otters, greeting cards and fine art prints, otter ties, sea otter watches, sweatshirts, and more.

Across the street from the Friends of the Sea Otter at the corner of Drake Avenue and Wave Street, a bronze bust of Doc Ricketts holding a seastar in his hand seems to lecture anyone who pauses to rest on the benches facing him. Doc Ricketts was killed here by an evening Southern Pacific train on May 8, 1948. Passersby and old friends often add a flower to Doc's outstretched hand.

From Cannery Row, continue your waterfront tour by a very scenic stroll along the walking and bike trail. (If you have parked your car on the Row, you can take the shuttle back.)

The path continues to the Coast Guard Wharf. On special occasions the

Fisherman's Wharf in Monterey

Coast Guard opens its boats to tours. Sea lions bask on the wharf in great numbers during the winter. The private docks just to the south of the Coast Guard Wharf have a ten- to twelve-year waiting list, so sign up now. On your walk to Fisherman's Wharf you'll pass about 180 boats on private moorings, if they are not out enjoying the bay or the daylight-savings-time Wednesday night races.

When asked about her favorite part of her trip to California, Joan Hakun of Pennsylvania answered, "Eating all those delectable morsels of seafood they sell in the fresh air at the Monterey Fisherman's Wharf." Fresh-air seafood markets, casual and elegant seafood restaurants, some with their own boats, seashell shops and art galleries, ice cream cones and cotton candy stands make the wharf a lively destination. The Wharf Theater (831/649-2332) presents live performances featuring local actors and actresses.

The wharf is the pathway to adventures on the sea. The whalewatching excursions, tours of the sanctuary, and fishing expeditions you will see departing can be arranged by calling any of these: Chris's Fishing Expeditions (831/375-5951), Monterey Sport Fishing (831/372-2203), Randy's Fishing Trips (831/372-7440), or Sam's Fishing Fleet Inc. (831/372-0577). A glass-bottom boat ride (831/372-7150) around the harbor will give you an idea of how cloudy summer waters contrast with the crystal-clear waters of autumn. Cruises aboard the the seventy-foot sailboat *Chardonnay 11* (831/423-1213) and historic rides on the tall ship *The Californian* (800/432-2201) also board at Fisherman's Wharf. If you want the best view of the sanctuary try scuba diving. Monterey Bay Dive Center (831/656-0454), 225 Cannery Row offers instruction and a personalized dive service from their boat the *Silver Prince*. Extreme Adventures (408/871-3111, www.extreme-adventures.com) specializes in diving adventures along the reefs of the Monterey and Carmel Bays. Several other dive tours and shops provide quality guide service; see Resource Guide, page 359.

To see the local fishing industry at work visit the Municipal Wharf, just north of Fisherman's Wharf. A few processors continue to operate at the end of the wharf but business is not at all like it was in the heyday of fishing in the 1940s. Four hundred fifty berths share this wharf. Chances are good that the all-steel drag boats with the thick rolls of net in the back are bringing their catch to Tringali's wholesale fish market at the end of the wharf. You might see them unloading salmon, sole, or cod. Many of the colorful fishing boats you'll see are no longer in use. When one goes up for sale it is often bought by a local sailboat owner who resells the fishing boat and retains the slip for a pleasure craft.

Your walk can continue along the walking and bike trail or along the beach, or you may want to visit some of the other Monterey highlights below. If you opt for the beach, remember that rip currents and sneaker waves are common.

WHAT ELSE TO SEE AND DO

CALIFORNIA VIEWS PAT HATHAWAY COLLECTION, 469 Pacific Avenue (831/373-3811, www.caviews.com). More of a museum than a gallery, this is the home to more than 75,000 photographic images of California from Santa Barbara to Marin; 32,000 of the images are catalogued. Originals sell quickly. Historic prints of Cannery Row and the missions are the most popular. 11 a.m. to 5 p.m.; closed Sunday and Monday.

LAKE EL ESTERO, located along Camino El Estero. The Monterey Visitor's Center, Dennis the Menace Park, paddle boat rentals and two historic cemeteries flank this park. A walking path around the inland estuary is frequented by domestic geese and migratory water fowl.

LA MIRADA, 720 Via Mirada (831/372-3689). This is an elegant addition to the Monterey Peninsula Museum of Art. The historic house has been home to General Jose Castro, explorer John C. Fremont, and movie couple Elizabeth Taylor and Richard Burton when they were filming *The Sandpiper* in Monterey. The museum's galleries include the Jane and Justin Dart wing, which houses the Darts' extensive collection of Armin Hansen paintings, and the Virginia Klemme gallery of Asian art.

NEW MONTEREY. Stretching along Lighthouse Avenue from the Monterey Tunnel to Pacific Grove, this section of the city offers the Monterey Bay Sports Museum (831/655-2363), dining and lunch places, and an assortment of shops to wander through. It is often necessary to park on side streets.

SAN CARLOS DE BORROMEO DE MONTEREY CATHEDRAL / ROYAL PRESIDIO CHAPEL, on Church Street, opposite Figueroa (831/373-2628). This is the oldest church in continuous service in California. First built in 1770 under orders of Carlos III, King of Spain, to serve the first presidio in Monterey, the chapel was the worshipping place for the Spanish governors, the king's representatives in California, and was thus designated a royal chapel. Coats of arms are painted on the wall behind the altar: the shield of the Kingdom of Leon and Castile in Spain marks this as a royal chapel. The doorway and facade of the entrance are part of the original chapel, which was completed under the direction of Father Lasuen in 1794. Manual Ruiz, the stonemason who directed the building of the chapel and the Carmel Mission, is credited as the carver of the statue of Our Lady of Guadalupe on the facade. The fever to bring the Christian religion to the first peoples of California was fueled by devotion to the Lady of Guadalupe that arose with her visit to an Indian on Teypeyec Hill in Mexico City, as recorded by the Catholic Church in 1531.

In 1850 this church became the first cathedral in California. The sandstone for the construction was quarried near Carmel. The exterior of the building shows a neoclassical facade and a square bell tower. Transepts were added in 1858 to increase the size of the original chapel, which is now part of the cathedral. Hidden rooms, believed to be early confessionals, have only recently been discovered between overlapping walls. Some of the whale vertebrae used for sidewalks during Monterey's days as a whaling port can still be seen behind the church. Sections of the original oak that shaded the masses said at the Viscaino Landing in 1602 and the Serra Landing in 1770 are preserved in the entrance.

The office in the cathedral has a written guide to its many pictures and statues, several of which date from the eighteenth and nineteenth centuries. They include statues brought from the Philippines at the time of Serra and a statue of Mary that features gold work under the design of the garments and is regarded as California's finest statue of the Spanish era. The statue of Santa Rosalia, patron of Sicily, has been carried every year since 1935 in a procession through Monterey to the wharf for the blessing of the fishing fleet.

UNITED STATES NAVAL POSTGRADUATE SCHOOL, on University Circle off Del Monte Avenue (831/656-2441). The school's buildings and grounds are those of the lavish Hotel Del Monte. The first two hotels on this site were the acclaimed tourist destinations operated by the Pacific Improvement Company as the "most elegant seaside establishment in the world." After the first two burned, the present building was constructed by the next landholders, the Del Monte Properties Company, under the direction of Samuel F. B. Morse.

Visitors are welcome to walk the grounds and visit the main hall of the former hotel. First check in at the Quarterdeck Office at 220 Hermann Hall and ask at the desk for a key to the observation deck. The view from the tower is a beautiful overlook of Monterey. Outdoor concerts are presented on spring and summer holiday weekends by the Monterey Bay Symphony. Certain areas are restricted, but ample parking is available. The basement restaurant (831/656-2170) is open for dining. A popular full brunch is served on Sunday from 10 a.m. until 2 p.m.

VETERANS MEMORIAL PARK, on Jefferson Street and Skyline Drive (831/646-3865). This fifty-acre park offers picnic facilities, a playground, hiking trails, and campgrounds within the city limits in the skyline forest area of Monterey. Camping is allocated on a first-come, first-served basis.

CHAPTER 3

PACIFIC GROVE

THE LAST HOMETOWN

Monterey pines and Victorian houses crown the coastal community of Pacific Grove, which includes part of the Monterey Bay Aquarium within its city limits. A rugged coastline borders this "Piney Paradise" of 2.6 square miles with some sixteen thousand residents.

GETTING READY

BEST TIMES TO VISIT AND SPECIAL EVENTS

Pacific Grove is congenial at any time of day. This town does not feature the lively nightclubs of Monterey, but some restaurants and coffee houses offer late-night music.

Many special events add to the already attractive scenery. In spring the town celebrates its birthday during "Good Old Days" with a parade, old-time entertainment, a wildflower show, a quilt show, and an arts and crafts festival. In midsummer the very popular Feast of Lanterns draws crowds to the streets, ocean bluffs, and beach for an outdoor pageant and fireworks. As the summer winds down, the best days to walk the coastal route are when it closes to traffic during several 10K walk-run events along Ocean View Boulevard, sponsored by the nonprofit Beacon House and other organizations. In early October children parade through the downtown to welcome back the monarch butterflies, which return to winter in Pacific Grove just as local gardens and parks specially planted with the butterflies' favorite nectar plants begin to burst into winter blooms. Many people prefer to wait until January or February to see the monarchs at the peak of their winter population. Monarch mating season, usually during the first two weeks of February, is an especially popular time to visit. Vacations are actually planned around this event. On the same October weekend as the butterfly parade, the annual Victorian Home Tour takes place. Homes, inns, and churches—some of Pacific Grove's finest Victorians—open their doors to tours. Many pods of gray whales spout offshore along the coastal bluffs from late December through January, lessening through March. The Natural History Museum and the Pacific Grove Art Center offer special programs throughout the year.

CLIMATE AND CLOTHING

Pacific Grove offers a year-round temperate coastal climate. Spring and autumn are usually warm and sunny. The section of the town east of Forest Avenue is the summer sunbelt. When I think of Pacific Grove clothing I think of wheels almost as an accessory: kids (adults too) on rollerblades with bodyboards or surfboards tucked under their arms, parents pushing baby strollers, bicyclists pedaling along Sunset Drive. Comfortable clothes with athletic shoes are the best bet. Always bring a jacket and a bathing suit, since it can be in the seventies in January and in the sixties in August and vice-versa. Patrons of downtown restaurants and businesses look stylish; they take pride in the appearance of their town and themselves. Although El Niño weather conditions bring some warm surf days, the cold ocean waters around Pacific Grove usually require a wet suit for anything more than a quick dip or wading at Lovers Point.

TOUR LENGTHS

The complete coastal walking tour described below could take four to five hours round trip. Plan on a couple of hours for the other tours. As this is a small town, the best-bet weekend would include a visit to the Monterey Bay Aquarium, one special event, and parts of all three tours. I can remember visiting here for weekends and always thinking that I had to leave too soon. If you really want a relaxing trip, stay a week. A friend of mine from the San Francisco Bay Area comes here just to breathe the air and walk the coastal route; she swears it rejuvenates her better than a health spa.

HIGHLIGHTS FOR KIDS

Pacific Grove is a family town. The Pacific Grove Recreation Department, 515 Junipero Avenue (831/648-3130), offers a variety of programs for visitors and residents.

The Lovers Point Beach at the foot of Forest Avenue is the most protected area along the Central Coast for wading, swimming, and tidepooling. There are two sandy beaches, one on each side of a concrete pier accessible by stairs. The main beach is the safest. However, extreme care should always be taken. Additionally, the park has a volleyball court, a children's swimming pool (summer only), kayak instruction and rental, rest rooms, water faucets, picnic tables, and a snack bar.

The Museum of Natural History, 165 Forest Avenue (831/648-3116), offers a variety of hands-on exhibits and comprehensive monarch butterfly information. Walks in Washington Park and along Asilomar Beach offer children an opportunity for a beautiful connection with nature.

Several parks are especially made for fun. At George Washington Park, between Melrose and Alder Streets, a beautiful natural forest habitat is anchored at the Sinex Street side by a family area that includes barbecue grills, children's play areas, a baseball field, and rest rooms. Caledonia Park between Central and Jewell Avenues (behind the post office) contains a tot's play area and equipment for older kids, a picnic area, lawn area, basketball court, and rest rooms.

In July, the Feast of Lanterns brightens the sky with fireworks. Every child who enters the festival's sand-castle contest receives a prize, be it "Most Magical" or "Best Use of Kelp."

WILDLIFE WISDOM

Bison sold to the Pacific Improvement Company by a Wild West show, and native elk, too, roamed the streets here in the 1890s. The bison were rounded up and donated to Golden Gate Park in San Francisco, where their descendants live today. The elk are also gone, but the tradition of wild animals roaming the streets continues. Deer walk freely through the residential streets and gardens, especially near the Asilomar area. They can often be seen in herds on the golf courses or eating the flowers placed at the city cemetery. Fawns are born in late spring and early summer. Some residents equip their cars with high-frequency deer alarms to help warn the deer, especially fawns, that roam the streets. They are especially active and difficult to see around dusk. Drive slowly and keep a lookout for leaping deer.

Raccoons are also commonly seen crossing gutters or climbing trees in town. They seldom give up ground if challenged, so give them a wide berth. Red foxes are sometimes seen in the Asilomar and forest areas.

Butterfly-crossing signs have been installed along Grove Acre Avenue, near the town's Monarch Grove Sanctuary. Beginning in October and continuing throughout autumn, thousands of monarchs fly into this "Butterfly Town U.S.A." to winter here through March. The numbers vary from year to year, but as you drive through town you will see many gardens covered with flittering clouds of gold. You are most assured of seeing butterflies at the Monarch Grove Sanctuary. Washington Park was a mass of color in former years, and hopefully, with the new plantings that citizens of Pacific Grove are continuing to make, the butterflies will return in greater numbers to favored pines and nectar sources in the park.

More than fifty thousand of the four-inch orange-and-black butterflies may congregate in a single grove. They migrate to the groves to find relief from winter's cold. In cool and foggy weather or early in the morning they hang on branches in dense clusters, looking something like a bunch of dead leaves. When the sunshine warms the clusters, they burst apart and light up the sky with a flurry of orange and black.

You may want to bring binoculars to view the clustering butterflies up close. Be sure to watch your step, since butterflies are sometimes on the

Monarch Butterfly

ground. In January and February you can see the courtly mating ritual. The male butterfly chases the female in spirals through the air. When he catches her they drift to the ground together, too heavy to fly. On the ground they wrestle in dancelike movements, oblivious to the outer world for ten to fifteen minutes. The male strokes the female's head with his antenna. When she is calm, he stands on his head and flips her over. They attach abdomens and he lifts her through the air and carries her to the top of a pine or eucalyptus tree where they stay joined until the sun shines the next day.

The butterflies are slow-flying, especially during mating. For their protection, it is unlawful "to molest or interfere in any way with the peaceful occupancy of the monarch butterfly." The same ordinance asks citizens to "protect the butterflies in every way possible from serious harm and possible extinction by brutal and heartless people." And it's serious. The punishment for breaking the law is a $1,000 fine or a six-month prison term.

This coastline is abundant with sea life—otters, harbor seals, seal lions, pelicans, and tidepool animals. It is truly a remarkable place for the nature lover. Please help keep it that way. Take nothing from the beach or rocks (except perhaps trash, if you are inclined to help). Also, do not feed any animals—birds, squirrels, raccoons, deer, or other furry or feathered friends. Some species of wild animals are having serious overpopulation problems as a result of people feeding them.

VISITOR INFORMATION

The Pacific Grove Chamber of Commerce (Forest and Central Streets or P.O. Box 167, Pacific Grove, CA 93950; 831/373-3304) is very helpful. An excellent historical walking tour map and guide by Esther Trosow is available here. The Heritage Society of Pacific Grove (P.O. Box 1007, Pacific Grove,

CA 93950; 831/372-2898) operates the Barn Museum at Laurel Avenue and Seventeenth Street. On Saturdays from 1 to 4 p.m. you can pick up back issues of their pamphlet called "The Board and Batten," which highlights the town's history. Check with the Pacific Grove Museum of Natural History, at Forest and Central Streets, for answers to local natural history questions and information on the monarch butterfly migrations (831/648-3116). The free *Coast Weekly* and the *Monterey County Herald* (especially the Thursday "Go" section) available at newsstands offer information about restaurants and special events in town. For an older history of Pacific Grove, obtain a copy of *A Piney Paradise: A Pictorial Story of Monterey Peninsula* by Lucy Neely McLane.

ALTERNATE TRANSPORTATION

Monterey Salinas Transit (831/899-2555, www.mst.org) serves Pacific Grove with buses from the Monterey Simoneau Metro-Amtrak Plaza every thirty minutes. The Pacific Grove Asilomar Bus #1 route stops at the Monterey Aquarium, Cannery Row, downtown Pacific Grove via Lighthouse Avenue, and Asilomar. The WAVE bus operates from Memorial Day through Labor Day for a $1 full-day pass. WAVE buses connect Asilomar, Pacific Grove, the Monterey Bay Aquarium, and Monterey.

Golf carts are a legal but as of yet little-used means of street transportation. When driving through intersections and congested areas, look for the whip poles and red flags attached to carts to alert you of their presence.

PARKING

To really enjoy this small town, park your car and walk around the downtown area. You can park along the street on Lighthouse Avenue if you plan a short stay. Parking is limited to two hours, so if you plan to stay longer drive up to the public parking lot on Fountain Avenue, behind the Lighthouse Cinema.

PLACES TO STAY

Pacific Grove offers some truly elegant Victorian bed and breakfast inns as well as more conventional motels. These are just a few of the lodging possibilities that show the character of Pacific Grove. Contact the Pacific Grove Chamber of Commerce, P.O. Box 167, Pacific Grove, CA 93950 (831/373-3304) for more information.

COASTAL SETTING

BEACHCOMBER INN, 1996 Sunset Drive. A beach-style motel next to Asilomar Beach, the Beachcomber has a pool, sauna, complimentary bicycles, and barbecue facilities. Adjacent to the Fishwife Restaurant. 831/373-4769. AX, MC, V. For two from $69 to $110.

GREEN GABLES INN, 104 Fifth Street. This Queen Anne–style impeccably restored Victorian inn on Monterey Bay is divided between the main house and the carriage houses behind it. Families will be happier in the carriage house rooms, which have private baths. Teddy bears guard the comfortable parlor. Full breakfast and complimentary wine, tea, and hors d'oeuvres are served each afternoon. Eleven rooms, seven with bath; one suite. 831/375-2095. AX, MC, V; others also accepted. From Highway 1, take the Pacific Grove (Highway 68) exit and continue straight on Highway 68, merging into Forest Avenue. Continue straight on Forest Avenue to the Pacific Ocean; turn right on Ocean View Boulevard and drive half a mile to Fifth Street. For two from $110 to $225.

THE MARTINE INN, 255 Ocean View Boulevard. An ocean-front mansion built in the 1890s has elegant and gracious rooms. Two additional common areas include a small room downstairs overlooking the ocean and a larger library. Full breakfast. A player piano accompanies afternoon hors d'oeuvres. More expensive rooms have fireplaces and ocean views. All rooms have private showers or baths. Billiards table. Jacuzzi available. 831/373-3388. AX, MC, V. For two from $135 to $275.

SEVEN GABLES INN, 555 Ocean View Boulevard. A Mobil-rated four-star bed and breakfast, this Victorian mansion on the bay was constructed in 1886. Seven namesake gables cap the sprawling inn. A valuable collection of European antiques fills the interior. Rose-filled gardens weave between the main house, the cottages, and the guesthouse. All rooms offer stunning views of Lovers Point and the coastline. Your stay includes breakfast and afternoon tea. All rooms have private baths. Next door, the owners have also beautifully restored the Grand View Inn, once the home of Dr. Julia B. Platt, the town's first woman mayor. Reservations are taken at the same phone number. 831/372-4341. MC, V. For two from $155 to $295.

DOWNTOWN SETTING

CENTRELLA INN, 612 Central Avenue. This Victorian inn with garden cottages is more than a century old. The accommodations feature Victorian-style rooms with iron beds, antique armoires and clawfoot bathtubs. Several private cottages and suites offer living rooms with fireplaces, wet bars, TVs, and decks. Full breakfast, afternoon tea. Nineteen rooms, four suites, five cottages. 831/372-3372. AX, MC, V; others also accepted. For two, mostly from $139 to $219.

GOSBY HOUSE INN, 643 Lighthouse Avenue. This Queen Anne Victorian inn, listed in the National Register of Historic Buildings, has antique furnishings and unique decor in each room. Relax in rooms with floral-print wallpaper and lacy pillows. Full breakfast, afternoon tea. Twenty-two rooms, twenty with bath. From Highway 1 take the Pacific Grove (Highway 68) exit and continue straight on Highway 68 to merge into Forest Avenue. Continue straight on Forest Avenue to Lighthouse Avenue, turn left and travel three blocks. 831/375-1287. AX, MC, V. For two, mostly from $90 to $160.

WOODSY SETTING

ANDRIL FIREPLACE COTTAGES, 569 Asilomar Boulevard. Across from Asilomar Conference Center and an easy walk to the beach, these separate cottages and family houses include kitchens. There are knotty pine walls, fireplaces in all but two units, and many private patios. The largest family cottage includes five bedrooms with seven beds. The grounds include a meadow area where deer and butterflies join you. Spa. 831/375-0994. AX, MC, V. For two from $70 to $195.

BEST WESTERN LIGHTHOUSE LODGE AND SUITES, 150 Lighthouse Avenue. Thirty plush suites and sixty-six standard rooms share two different settings along Lighthouse Avenue. One standard section of rooms is located near the grounds of the cemetery, often visited by deer and raccoons. Towering pines and cypress add to the woodsy feel. Breakfast, afternoon wine, and hors d'oeuvres; jacuzzi, pool. AX, MC, V; others also accepted. 831/655-2111, 800/858-1249, www.lhls.com. For two, standard rooms from $89 and suites from $228.

BIDE-A-WEE, 221 Asilomar Boulevard. The Bide-A-Wee offers comfortable rooms and family units in a quiet setting near beach and golf. Rooms are decorated in a country-rustic style and some have ocean views. Coffeemakers in all rooms; a few have refrigerators. Pets allowed. 831/372-2330. MC, V. For two from $59 to $95.

BUTTERFLY GROVE INN, 1073 Lighthouse Avenue. This inn shares butterflies with the Monarch Grove Sanctuary grounds behind it. Pool, spa, and some kitchenettes and fireplaces. Suites in an old Victorian home. 831/373-

4921. AX, MC, V; others also accepted. For two from $99 to $149.

ROSEDALE INN LUXURY SUITES, 775 Asilomar Boulevard. These private units are nestled in the pines, across from the woods of the Asilomar Conference Center. All suites here feature cathedral ceilings, pine log furniture, fireplaces, and over-sized Jacuzzi tubs. Microwaves, VCRs, and wet bars add to the amenities. 831/655-1000. AX, MC, V; others also accepted. For two from $115.

ASILOMAR, 800 Asilomar Boulevard. You can also stay at Asilomar Conference Grounds, even if you are not attending a conference. The grounds are on 105 acres of pines and dunes, with breathtaking views of the sea. Here you can stay in the historic buildings, deluxe buildings, guest inn cottages, or the forest lodge. Advance reservations are recommended. 831/372-8016. MC, V. Rooms for two from $65 to $88.

RESTAURANTS

It's good there are so many great running and biking trails in this area. I would exercise four hours daily just to eat to my delight at the restaurants in Pacific Grove. The restaurants listed here are just the beginning. Those in the first list are ones we enjoy more if our young children are not with us.

FANDANGO RESTAURANT, 223 Seventeenth Street. A warm Mediterranean setting includes patio dining amid flowers cascading from window boxes; a window-lined terrace room; and a wine cellar, alcove, or private dining room for large parties. Romantic private nooks. Flavorful foods of Europe, including fresh seafood from the mesquite grill, rack of lamb, an array of paellas, and more. Full bar and extensive seventeen-page wine list. Fandango's won the Wine Spectator's "Best of" Award of Excellence in 1997. Lunch and dinner. 831/372-3456. AX, MC, V; others also accepted. Entrees from $11 to $24.

GERNOT'S VICTORIAN HOUSE, 649 Lighthouse Avenue. Situated in a century-old mansion, Gernot's offers Austrian specialties including breast of duck with raspberry sauce, local wild boar, fresh seafood, pasta, and wiener schnitzel. Private parties. Dinner. 831/646-1477. AX, MC, V. Entrees from $17 to $20.

THE OLD BATH HOUSE, 620 Ocean View Boulevard. For its beautiful ocean views, elegant Victorian interiors, and candlelight this restaurant is consistently voted most romantic in the county. New American fare. Specials include duck merlot, Monterey Bay abalone, roasted portobello mushrooms, and fresh mesquite-grilled seafood. Cocktails from 4 p.m., dinner from 5 p.m. 831/375-5195. AX, MC, V. Entrees from $19 to $33.

PASTA MIA TRATTORIA, 481 Lighthouse Avenue. Light-wood decor with cafe chairs and tables creates a casual atmosphere. Italian fare combines Northern and Southern Italian dishes with California touches and includes grilled fish, lasagna, gnocchi, and fresh pastas such as Linguini Marini with sun-dried tomatoes, spinach, and raisins. A fine wine list features Italian wines. Dinner. 831/375-7709. AX, MC, V. Entrees from $9 to $15.

TASTE CAFE & BISTRO, 1199 Forest Avenue. When I go to the county's freshest farmer's market I follow the chefs from this cafe around the stands; the farmers pull out boxes of their choicest produce for selection. An award-winning European restaurant, featuring the finest ingredients available. The menu features such items as herb-roasted chicken, escargots, fresh-made sausages, and daily soups. For dessert, the perfect bread pudding and crème brûlée. Dinner. 831/655-0324. No credit cards. Entrees from $10 to $14.

MORE CASUAL OPTIONS

ALLEGRO GOURMET PIZZERIA, 1184 Forest Avenue, Pacific Grove. In Carmel, 3770 The Barnyard, Carmel. In Pacific Grove, enjoy cozy indoor dining, patio seating, and a separate room for families. Adults will savor pesto calzones, seafood pastas, risotto dishes, garlic Caesar salads (voted the best in the county), and gourmet pizzas. Ten choices of large foccaccia sand-wiches include my favorite: eggplant with artichoke hearts, roasted sweet peppers, and aioli. The fresh mozzarella sandwich is also a local favorite. Recipes meet the standards of the American Heart Association, and whole wheat pizza crust is available. Kids get to watch the chefs toss dough made from scratch and take some dough to the table to sculpt. The kid's menu includes "rotelli to throw on the floor" for only $1 as well as six rotelli pasta kid-pleasers. Peanut butter and jelly pizza captures the young palates for sure. Lunch, dinner, and catering and take out-service. In Pacific Grove, 831/373-5656; in Carmel 831/626-5454. AX, MC, V. Entrees from $7 to $12.

BECHLER PATISSERIE, 1215 Forest Avenue. A large wall mural composed of favorite French postcard scenes greets you in the casual interior ordering and dining area, or you can savor your selection by the fountain in the glass-enclosed deck room. Light breakfasts and lunches of tasty quiches and sandwiches are served with delectable desserts. Famous as a place to choose scrumptious wedding cakes. Breakfast, lunch. 831/375-0846. Lunch entrees from $4.

FIFI'S CAFE & BAKERY, 1188 Forest Avenue. In a French home atmosphere with pastry shop seating, choose French bistro or healthy spa cuisine. Seafood, pasta, and chicken entrees, perfect French onion soup. Fruit tarts, chocolate chip cheesecake, and lemon mousse begin the delectable assortment of desserts to eat in or take out. Great cakes for birthdays. Lunch and dinner. 831/372-5325. AX, MC, V; others also accepted. Entrees from $11 to $16.

FIRST AWAKENINGS, at the American Tin Cannery, 125 Ocean View Boulevard. Especially for breakfast, brunch, and lunch, try the comfortable indoor booths or outdoor garden setting here. Pancakes of every variety, sandwiches that match ingredients to characteristics of local places, and Italian style frittatas are a few of the menu selections. 831/372-1125. AX, MC, V. Entrees mostly under $10.

FISHWIFE RESTAURANT (at Asilomar Beach), 1996 Sunset Drive. With fresh ocean breezes and Caribbean atmosphere, this is a heaven for fresh-fish and seafood lovers. Pastas smothered in seafood, prawns Belize, grilled fresh catch, and delicately cornmeal-battered calamari. Sensational key lime pie for dessert. Lunch and dinner. 831/375-7107. AX, MC, V; others also accepted. Entrees from $8 to $15.

MICHAEL'S GRILL & TAQUERIA, 197 Country Club Gate Center. Eat in on paper plates at comfortable booths, or take out. Grilled fare and Mexican and Cajun specialties that include blackened chicken burritos, fajitas, grilled chicken tacos, and charbroiled shrimp specialties. No animal fats used in cooking. Lunch and dinner. 831/647-8654. No credit cards. Entrees from $3 to $12.

PEPPERS MEXI CALI CAFE, 170 Forest Avenue. This "hot" local favorite features innovative Mexican and Latin American cuisine. Snapper Yucatan and homemade tamales are two favorites. Consistently voted by locals "Monterey Peninsula's Favorite Mexican Restaurant." Lunch and dinner. 831/373-6892. AX, MC, V; others also accepted. Entrees from $6 to $12.

THE TINNERY, 631 Ocean View Boulevard. Overlooking Lovers Point, the Tinnery has separate comfortable pub and formal dining rooms with fireplaces. Pasta, seafood, and steak. Breakfast, lunch, dinner; bar menu until midnight. Nightly entertainment in pub. 831/646-1040. AX, MC, V. Entrees from $9 to $18.

TOASTIE'S CAFE, 702 Lighthouse Avenue. A cozy restaurant that feels like a country home offers indoor or outdoor dining. Popular with locals and visitors. Pancakes, huevos rancheros, and omelettes lead off all-day breakfasts. Lunch is also served alfresco. Homestyle dinners have fresh-daily ingredients. 831/373-7543. AX, MC, V. Entrees from $8 to $15.

DIRECTIONS

Downtown Pacific Grove from the Aquarium. Drive west up David Avenue to Lighthouse Avenue, just past Central Avenue or one block up from the Nob Hill Super Market. (This is a bit tricky, as Lighthouse makes a jog at David Avenue. The old Lighthouse Avenue turns into Central Avenue and Hawthorne turns into Lighthouse Avenue.) Turn right on Lighthouse Avenue; this will become the main street through Pacific Grove. Travel along Lighthouse Avenue for about a half-mile and you will start to see the shops of Pacific Grove. The main town of Pacific Grove is along Lighthouse and Forest Avenues. The commercial area is just a few blocks long and most of the sights are within easy walking distance.

Downtown Pacific Grove from Highway 1. Take the Pacific Grove/Highway 68 West exit. Travel down this curving pine-forested road to the city limits of Pacific Grove. Stay in the right-hand lane. Highway 68 curves left to the Asilomar/Pebble Beach area. The fork of 68 that continues straight is called Forest Avenue and leads to the heart of Pacific Grove. You can turn right on Lighthouse Avenue or Central Avenue to backtrack to the aquarium.

INTRODUCTION TO PACIFIC GROVE
WITH HISTORICAL HIGHLIGHTS

Pacific Grove is known as America's "Last Hometown," and existed until 1969 as California's last dry town. It's a good place to find the best of small-town America along with a beautiful coastal setting and piney woods. Deer and raccoon wander through streets where kids bounce basketballs, baseballs thud in oiled mitts, and the high school band marches in hometown parades. Waves crash over the rocky coast while neighbors share news at Rocky Coast ice cream parlor. Monarch butterflies glide over church spires that dot the skies of this town which was originally founded as a Methodist retreat. "Pagrovians," residents of Pacific Grove have restored more than a thousand Victorian homes and cottages. Preservationists continue to cherish old-time values in Pacific Grove with an emphasis on preserving nature and nurturing families. They offer visitors their best: delectable restaurants, unique shops, specialty furniture stores, and Victorian inns.

Located next to Monterey, Pacific Grove could have melded into the larger town, losing its character and history just as many other little towns have in California. Instead Pagrovians have, over the years, fought to retain its small-town charm. Driving from Monterey into Pacific Grove produces an entirely different feel. A main street bordered by little shops and Victorian-style streetlamps, Lighthouse Avenue is reminiscent of early times when horse-drawn carriages bustled along dirt roads. Many grand old church buildings are visible, with greenbelt parks winding down to the shore. The older sea-side cottages and majestic turn-of-the-century houses still provide homes for many in the downtown area.

Pacific Grove was first developed in the 1800s as a dry coastal retreat for Methodist churchgoers, who came to worship in a quiet and beautiful natural environment. In 1875, land baron David Jacks donated one hundred acres of land to the Methodist Episcopal Church for a religious resort community. Reportedly, after the first minister, Reverend W. S. Ross spent a few months in a cabin along what is now Lighthouse Avenue to test the setting for its appropriateness as a resort, he was cured of an acute respiratory ailment. The next year he brought his brother and both their wives, who suffered from the same illness; they slept in hammocks under the trees and were restored to health. With high regard for the salubrious benefits of the area, the church formed the Pacific Grove Retreat Association. The West's first chautauqua (a religious camp meeting of sermons, educational lectures, family get-togethers, and psalm singing) was held in August of 1875. For the next ten years the meeting became an annual event. Sections of the retreat acreage were subdivided into thirty-by-sixty-foot lots to create hundreds of tent sites for seasonal visitors. At the end of the summer the visitors left, with only a caretaker remaining.

A series of "blue laws" were passed that dictated strict rules of behavior in the Grove. For example, one ordinance passed in the early 1900s stated: "It shall be unlawful for every person wearing a bathing suit or portion thereof, except children under the age of ten years, to appear in or upon the beach or in any place open to public—unless attired in a bathing suit or other clothing of opaque material, which shall be worn in such a manner as to preclude form. All such bath suits shall be provided with double crotches or with skirts of ample size to cover the buttocks."

Waltzing, playing the zither, reading the Sunday dailies, selling popcorn on the beach, and playing tenpins were similarly outlawed. A bell was rung each night to signal curfew. A fence was put up circling the retreat area, and the gate was locked after curfew. The fence also discouraged vehicular traffic. In 1880 Judge Langford, who had forgotten his key, finally became so enraged that he axed down the gate, thus opening Pacific Grove to the dangers of civilization.

Today, large Victorian mansions still grace hilltops while clusters of miniature Victorian cottages fill the grid of small-scale streets between Lighthouse Avenue and Ocean View Boulevard. Many lovely seaside cottages can still be found, in an area bordered roughly by First Street, Ocean View Boulevard, Pacific Street, and Lighthouse. Examples of a variety of architectural styles can be noted while walking around in this older part of Pacific Grove: Gothic Revival, Queen Anne, Stick/Eastlake, Colonial Revival, Spanish/Mediterranean, Shingle, American Foursquare, and Tudor.

Small green plaques on some five hundred of the older buildings, placed by the Pacific Grove Heritage Society, designate the year the houses were constructed. A building qualifies for a plaque if it was built in 1910 or earlier and still retains its original character and architectural style.

The result of preserving Victorians looks so fitting and elegant, the process of restoring them appears straightforward, even easy. It is, of course, hard work, and with a dilapidated Victorian, quite complex. When builder-artists Geoff and Joy Welch purchased a one-story board-and-batten house on Third Street featuring a tripped roof with gables, daylight could be seen through the walls. Ivy had made its way though the windows and into the house. Although they'd fixed up other homes, this was their first Victorian. They rebuilt the foundation to level the floors, installed new plumbing, heating, and electrical systems, and removed the suspended ceiling. They researched and incorporated "hardware from brass switch-plate covers to sash lifts, period wall paper, and reproduction plaster." Geoff milled Victorian door casings and kitchen cabinets to suit the architecture of that period. When the Welch family outgrew the little Victorian they constructed a new home at 1033 Bay View Avenue that drew from the style of Julia Morgan's Asilomar.

For their skill and care they won first place in the 1992 Heritage Society of Pacific Grove contest for "Best New Design," honoring construction that fits in with the historic design of the town.

In the first tour, the downtown area of Pacific Grove, there are many reminders of pleasures of the past. But if you walk slowly and ask a few questions along the way you'll also enjoy the town's true treasure, its people.

TOURS

The three tours in this chapter focus on different aspects of the town. The first is a tour of the historic main street and downtown area of Pacific Grove. This is meant to be a walking tour, with time to see some of the historic places and to do a bit of shopping along the way. The second is a tour of the coastline of Pacific Grove. This can be driven, but to really see the remarkable features I suggest walking or, if you are inclined, bike or kayak rental (see the Resource Guide for listings, pages 356–60). Finally, the third tour describes the butterfly groves, a short walk through the pine forests.

DOWNTOWN WALKING TOUR

This circular route through some of the downtown area is less than a mile in length, and can be done in parts. If there are young children in your group you may want to plan a play break at Caledonia Park. To make the tour more interesting for children, you might play such games along the way as "Who can find the smallest house?" "Who can find the house with the oldest plaque?" At 545 Lighthouse (831/375-3569), toward the top of the avenue, the Scotch Bakery, a Pacific Grove tradition for more than a hundred years, offers cookies, doughnuts, and milk for the trip and an assortment of baked goods for anytime.

Espresso, relaxing cups of tea, and chocolate fantasies could be sufficient incentive for me to climb the Alps. There are a number of small coffeehouses with coffee, tea, juices, and light fare. The Bookworks Bookshop & Coffee House is across from the post office at 677 Lighthouse Avenue (831/372-2242); Juice n' Java is at 599 Lighthouse (831/373-8652). The Red House Cafe (831/643-1060) at 662 Lighthouse offers porch or indoor seating and Caravali Coffee at 510 Lighthouse (831/655-5633) has indoor and outdoor seating across from the cinema. The Red House Cafe was narrowly saved from demolition and has been lovingly restored. The old yard and house basement is now Miss Trawick's Garden Shop (831/375-4605). Birdhouses, garden sculptures, and every gardening necessity are found here, even a serene bench for the weary walker.

Begin the tour at Lighthouse and Thirteenth Street. At this corner a three-story gray building etched with the name "The Grove" fills the footprint of a 1927 laundry building that was built solidly of twelve-inch-thick rein-forced concrete walls. Four weeks before the original building was scheduled to be demolished in 1994, Tom and Claude Finkling, together with sons Beau Finkling and Thompson Lane, purchased the dilapidated laundry and neighboring dirt hole, dug clean of toxic oil. Using old-fashioned construction techniques, they duplicated existing walls. They saved the old-growth red-wood roof trusses to mill 113 window casings and doorframes. Along the way they hit a spring and lifted and totally retrofit the building, which is now said to be the safest in Monterey County. Their ecologically based construction project houses the Grove Homescapes, (831/656-0864) on the street level and the Media Room in the basement. Antiques and art fill the staircased two-level interior, where the owners took the town's children and inquisitive adults on teaching tours during construction. Now people travel from great distances to visit the outdoor gazebo known for its incred-ible selection of orchids. Downstairs, the Media Room (831/655-2010, www.themediaroom.com) showcases the integration of electronics and home furnishings, home theaters, and a recording studio. Tickets are avail-able to live concerts and recording sessions.

"Come on over and make yourself comfortable" may well be the new motto in this "last hometown." Walking toward town you will pass a selec-tion of the many home furnishing businesses of Pacific Grove. Across the street from the Grove Homescapes, antiques and estates are auctioned on selected weekends at Hambrook's Auction Center (831/373-2101). At the corner of Fountain and Lighthouse, butterflies soar across the dramatic stained-glass window of Holman's Antique Plaza (831/646-0674), originally Holman's Store, once the largest department store in the county.

Walking on the south side of Lighthouse you will pass some of the oldest stores downtown. Those at 549 and 551 Lighthouse were built in 1888 and operated by the town's first druggist. A tobacco store was originally at 553. A restaurant, a bakery, and health food, clothing, and shoe stores are nestled together on the ground floor. Many people dine at the Victorian Corner (831/372-4641) at 541 Lighthouse Avenue to experience the feeling of old-time Pacific Grove. Historic photographs, friendly staff, and authentic sur-roundings make it a great place to complete your visit.

When I first moved to Pacific Grove and asked directions or said good morning to passersby, I found myself entering into discussions with strangers about the effects of El Niño on the weather, the new grandchildren, the latest show at the Pacific Grove Art Center, or the errant puppy. I was a little too hurried for the shopkeepers who conversed with and didn't just sell to their customers. As you discover Pacific Grove, rediscover the human warmth of yesteryear. Shopkeepers do have appropriate radar; if you're in a hurry they can get you on your way extra fast. But especially if you're from another country or have shopped primarily in malls, shop in Pacific Grove for an experience of hometown Americana.

When you reach Forest Avenue you will see the only example of Romanesque revival architecture on the Peninsula at 574 Lighthouse. Built in 1904 with simulated stone-block siding by architect W. H. Weeks, this was originally the Bank of Pacific Grove. Turn left up the hill. Along the way, the Pacific Grove Florist (831/375-9809) displays the artistic touch this community attracts. You can pick up a warm barbecued chicken or deli items for a picnic at Grove Market (831/375-9581). The butchers will probably know about the latest town event and sell you tickets for some worthy cause.

At the corner of Laurel and Forest you will see the Pacific Grove City Hall with its tall square clock tower. Here too are the chimes that can be heard every fifteen minutes throughout the town. During December chimes fill the air with seasonal tunes.

Turn right on Laurel. Next you see Ketchum's Barn, at Laurel and Seventeenth. Long after this barn was built by H. C. Ketchum in 1891 to house animals it was left vacant and became a refuge for a variety of "lost souls." Now it houses the Heritage Society of Pacific Grove Museum and administrative office. It is open to the public on Saturday from 1 to 4 p.m. all year. Inside you can ring the original chimes from city hall, wind up an old Victrola, and check out the goods and fashions of a re-created turn-of-the-century store. For a greater understanding of the town's heritage, view old photos and pick up previous copies of "The Board and Batten."

If you like, at this point you can take a one-block side trip up Seventeenth Street to the fire station at Pine Avenue. In front is the bell that was used to ring out curfew, when it was unlawful for any minor to be on public streets of Pacific Grove between 8 p.m. and daylight the following morning.

Going back down Seventeenth Street to Lighthouse Avenue you pass a number of Victorian cottages that now house shops and restaurants. Once at Lighthouse Avenue turn left and walk another four blocks, to Congress Avenue.

Here you'll find the Gosby House Inn, 643 Lighthouse, a Queen Anne–style home built in 1887 by J. F. Gosby, a shoemaker. Gosby added many more rooms over the years to accommodate overflowing guests. This house is listed on the National Register of Historic Places and California Historical Landmarks. Hart Mansion, next door to the Gosby House, is another Queen Anne–style building, constructed in 1892. Bookworks Bookshop & Coffee House (831/372-2242), on the corner, wafts the aromas of espresso and hot chocolate. Often the location for book signings and talks by writers, the store features a display of books by local authors.

Cross Lighthouse Avenue at Congress Avenue. The bronze *Butterfly Kids* statue of two monarch-parade participants, sculpted by the late Pacific Grove artist Christopher Bell, adds a quality of wonder to this usually bustling post office corner. Card tables are set up during local campaigns to introduce citizens to their candidates, and petition drives sometimes fill the sidewalks with avid debaters. A good selection of local papers and guides fills the newsstands here.

If you proceed down Congress Avenue, which becomes Caledonia Street, you will come to Caledonia Park at the corner of Caledonia Street and Central Avenue. Once a swamp, Caledonia Park now has a play area for children, benches, and picnic tables. As you walk down residential Central Avenue consider taking a detour on the 100 block of Seventeenth Street and back on the 100 block of Sixteenth Street, to enjoy the look of some of the cottages that were built on the tiny tent-size lots, which first sold for an average of fifty dollars each. When workers tear down interior wall coverings in these cottages while renovating, they often find the old tent frames still intact inside the walls.

B. C. Winston brought buffalo to Pacific Grove and built the Winston Hotel in 1904 at the corner of Sixteenth and Lighthouse. The friendly Lighthouse Cafe (831/372-7006) on the ground floor now fills the space that was originally the lobby.

Back on Central Avenue you will see the grand Centrella Inn. The Centrella Cottage was built in 1886. When it opened it was described as containing fifteen rooms fitted with all the conveniences of a first-class boarding and lodging house. It served as the headquarters for the Methodist ministers and their families in 1888. This is now a beautifully restored bed and breakfast inn.

Across the street is Chautauqua Hall, at the corner of Seventeenth Street and Central Avenue. This building is a state historic landmark, built in 1881. Chautauquas were the substance of a movement started in 1874 as an educational camp meeting on the shores of Lake Chautauqua in New York. The hall is still in use today. It frequently is used for community functions, including the schools' science fair, the quilt show, and exercise classes. Next to the hall on the south side is Elmarie H. Dyke Open Space, that has recently been built to offer a quiet corner for townspeople to rest or congregate. Educator, civic leader, and radio personality, Elmarie H. Dyke brought the Feast of Lanterns Festival to town and campaigned to see that Pacific Grove remained the last dry town in California. In 1969 the votes tallied against her cause and Pacific Grove was no longer dry.

Proceed down Central (heading north) and you see the small cottage that houses the Pacific Grove Chamber of Commerce. The Chamber, at the corner of Forest and Central, is open noon to 4 p.m., Monday to Friday. The people here offer helpful visitor information. Directional maps and event information are posted outside (831/373-3304).

Kitty-corner from the Chamber of Commerce you'll see a lifelike gray whale lying in the sand next to the sidewalk. Kids may be climbing all over this sculpture's back and sliding down the cement flukes. Named by the kids in town, *Sandy the Whale* welcomes visitors to the Pacific Grove Museum of Natural History at the corner of Forest and Central. The museum is open every day from 10 a.m. to 5 p.m., except Mondays and holidays. There is no charge, but a donation is always appreciated. The museum began as adults and children made excursions into the surrounding country and brought back specimens of flowers, shells, or anything that might be of instructive value. Prizes were awarded to encourage interest on the part of both adults and children. Over the years the museum has received many gifts, and today it has grown into an impressive array of native specimens. Extensive exhibits of native plants and animals and a grand exhibit of the monarch butterfly are housed here. You can find as well a relief map of Monterey Canyon that shows the steep drop of the ocean floor. Exhibits provide an introduction to the native Rumsien and Ohlone populations. The museum also has a small outside garden of native plants. In a special exhibit hall the rotating displays include the annual fungi exhibits in late winter and the wildflower show in April.

Jewell Park, across the street from the museum, hosts the town's annual birthday "Good Old Days" pancake breakfast. In the winter, machine-created snow blows in for one weekend and the park becomes a coastal winter wonderland.

The Pacific Grove City Library is across the street, on the corners of Grand, Central, and Fountain. Bulletin boards inside post information about community events. The Pacific Grove Public Library was established in December of 1905 and first opened to the public in 1908. This library is a great source of pride to the community.

After leaving the library you can either proceed down Central for a few more blocks and see some of the oldest churches in Pacific Grove or you might choose to head back up Fountain Avenue to your starting place. If you proceed down Central Avenue you see white, green, red, and brown spires rising above the homes. In the early days most of the sermons were preached outdoors in a quiet grove. The first building to be used solely for church services was built in 1877 near the Centrella Hotel. That building is no longer here, but others still are.

Saint Mary's by the Sea Episcopal Church at Twelfth and Central was built in 1887 and still has its original seventy-five-foot spire. Modeled after a

British church in Bath, it was designed in the Old English Gothic style. When the congregation outgrew the tiny chapel it was sliced in two, and three bays were added in the middle. Stained-glass windows include two signed Tiffany lilies.

THE COASTAL TOUR

Directions from the Aquarium. The aquarium sits on the border of Monterey and Pacific Grove, and the Monterey Peninsula Recreation Trail extends between the aquarium and Pacific Grove's Lovers Point. Located on the former Southern Pacific Railroad right-of-way, the trail has a separate walking and cycling path. So if you are at the aquarium you are ready to start this coastal tour route. If you decide to park your car check the signs, as most of the parking along this section of Ocean View Boulevard is limited to two hours.

Except for a few areas, all of the Pacific Grove shoreline is owned by the city or state. Hopkins Marine Station has a private section owned by Stanford University. Two parcels adjacent to Asilomar State Beach are also privately held. Otherwise all of the coastline is open to public use. In the section designated as the Pacific Grove Marine Gardens Fish Refuge from the aquarium to Point Pinos, fish, invertebrate life, crustaceans, mollusks, and plants cannot be taken or disturbed without proper permits or licenses.

Concern over public access to the beach is a part of the history of Pacific Grove. Unlike many other geographic areas, Pacific Grove has virtually unobstructed access to its coast.

The coastal tour described in this section extends approximately four miles along Ocean View Boulevard, which becomes Sunset Drive and follows the ocean all the way to Pebble Beach. If you leave your car you will need to double back on the same route, walk along the town's residential streets, or catch the MST #1 bus.

The coastal trip follows the coastline along the furthermost tip of the Monterey Peninsula. Be very careful next to the ocean. The water can be very cold, the rocks are slippery, and the waves can be unpredictably high. Pacific Grove is famous for its sneaker waves.

Begin at the Monterey Bay Aquarium, heading west. You soon see a building with a sign, "Monterey Boat Works." This is a part of Hopkins Marine Station of Stanford University. Farther on there is a gate, and there are many large classrooms and laboratories. Recently celebrating its one hundred-year birthday, Hopkins Marine Station is one of the world's foremost marine research institutes. The grounds are private and the beaches are protected to safeguard biological research.

The area near here was once a Chinatown. Several Chinese fish companies established a small village on what is now Marine Station Point. The properties between Chinatown and Lighthouse Avenue were used for drying squid. Hundreds of tons of it were dried on lattices, then tossed on the ground and turned with rakes.

Past the Hopkins Station the trail skirts the bay, offering breathtaking views of the blue-green waters, rocky outcroppings, and sea life. Sea otters float in offshore kelp beds, dive for sea urchins, and crack shells on the rocks they have balanced on their stomachs. Harbor seals stretch on rocks in unusual positions. They lie so still it seems as if a sculptor has molded them to the rocks. When the harbor seals are active their smooth heads bob in the waves, swimming so close with their eyes staring so directly at you it's as if they are trying to communicate some secret message. As you walk along you'll notice, on calm days, multicolored kayaks gliding over the glassy surface.

Berwick Park, on the coastal side of Ocean View Boulevard between Ninth Street and Carmel Avenue, south of the recreation trail, has a large, well-manicured lawn and a natural landscape area consisting of rocky outcrops and native plants. There are benches and plenty of areas for kids to run around in. This is also a favorite setting for outdoor weddings. We counted four, in one afternoon. As you travel along the path to Lovers Point you will see rows of Victorian houses on the inland side of the trail. Look for the namesake gables of the yellow Seven Gables Inn, 555 Ocean View Boulevard. The Grand View Inn next door was built in 1920 by Julia B. Platt. From her window she could see Lovers Point, the rocky arm of land you see jutting into the ocean. At one point the owner of the bathhouse that once stood near Lovers Point erected a barrier across her property to prevent access to the point and the beach. In 1932, Dr. Julia Platt challenged the owner to throw the gate wide open. The owner retaliated by padlocking the entrance. Dr. Platt filed the padlock. Then the gate was nailed shut. Dr. Platt, wielding an axe, chopped down the gate and the beach was opened to the public and has been open to this day. Dr. Platt was later elected the town's first woman mayor.

Scenes of early Pacific Grove painted by muralist John Ton with volunteers show you more about the town as you walk by a 344-square-foot section of retaining wall. On this *Mother Wall*, look for the Rumsien, the burning Chinese village, and the early Methodist retreat. Pacific Grove Arts Commission Chairperson Les Reed explains, "This is the first of six to eight murals planned in the Irene Masteller Mural Project. All will depict the history of Pacific Grove." The best view is from a kayak, fifty feet off shore.

Lovers Point is the next park on the trail. The name of this park is often attributed to its amorous history, but many accounts describe it as a derivative of "Lovers of Jesus Point." Located at the end of Seventeenth Street, this is a

Pacific Grove Lighthouse

landscaped community park of 4.4 acres. Here windswept cypresses arch over sculpted rock. Families enjoy the two sandy beaches here. The waves offshore are favorites of surfers. The prodigious kelp beds are favorites of otters and scuba divers.

Currently an elegant restaurant, the Bath House sits high above the beach here. It takes its name from the early bathhouses at this location; in 1875 a little brown frame shack that was used for saltwater bathing, and in 1882 a rambling structure with twenty-two dressing rooms and eight private saltwater baths.

William Smith acquired the land at Lovers Point in 1904 when it was mainly a pile of stones and cliffs of solid rock. At the time he acquired it, Pacific Grove was still a Methodist camp meeting ground, and there were objections to a beach where people could go on Sunday. Despite opposition, Smith blasted in the cove and set up a new bathhouse, bathing resort, and boathouse. With the rock he blasted loose he constructed the stone wall that stands today.

Glass-bottom boats bedecked with swan heads used to glide across the waters here. After reading about the original William Smith, I asked the present-day William Smith, owner of local Pacific Bay Real Estate, if he was a relation. William responded, "No, but I used to row the glass-bottom boats, and I have one of the last ones." Geoff Welch, president of the Heritage Society, my son Tim, and I rode out to a Carmel Valley field and found the boat with swan heads peering out of tall pasture grass. William donated the boat to the Heritage Society. Frank Sinno from Monterey Boat Works worked to restore the boat. The original boat broke in half, but he worked with the Monterey Bay Boat Works to build a complete replica, keeping the original swan heads. "I did it as a payback to the city of Pacific Grove. My family operated the Monterey Boat Works at what is now Standford University's Research Center. And I did it mostly in memoriam to my close friend Russel Sprague whose family had the swan boat concession." The swan boat may return to Lovers Point for permanent display.

Once past Lovers Point the separated bike trail ends. The walking trail continues. If you are on a bike you will need to ride on the street for about a mile until a painted bike lane reappears.

On any Sunday in April the billowing sails of rainbow catamarans race offshore behind rolling waves that build to snow-white pillowy hills. The waves crash on ancient rocks just beyond a shoreline draped in a phosphorescent magic pink carpet of ice plant, *Mesembryanthemum floribundum*. This area beyond Lovers Point is known as Perkins Park, named after Hayes Perkins, a landscaper, who laid out gardens in Africa and other countries. Perkins singlehandedly planted this beautiful shoreline park.

If you travel on along Ocean View Boulevard you encounter the wilder part of the trail. The path winds on until there are fewer houses and the ocean and bay waters meet. At Ocean View Boulevard and Asilomar Avenue you come to the edge of the Municipal Golf Course. In 1997, John Denver's light plane crashed into the ocean off the rocky shore just south of here. As of yet there is no official marker, but flowers are often draped over rocks on the shore. Crespi Pond is off to your left, on the inland side of Ocean View Boulevard; this is a tiny freshwater pond named for Father Crespi, chronicler of the Portola expedition, who noted the pond in his annals in 1770. Just beyond the pond, the stone shelter offers the only bathrooms available for the next mile, until the conference grounds. It is possible to walk a couple of blocks up Asilomar Boulevard to the Pacific Grove Golf Course Clubhouse for breakfast or, at lunch, sandwiches.

Across from Crespi Pond is Point Pinos, "the Point of Pines," named by the Spanish explorer Sebastian Vizcaino in 1602. The outreaching point marks the meeting of the southernmost tip of the Monterey Bay and the greater Pacific Ocean. The one-mile stretch around Point Pinos is owned today by the U.S. Coast Guard and maintained by the city of Pacific Grove. Presently, during low tide you can climb out on the rocks and have a panoramic view both out to sea and back to the lighthouse that is perched on the grassy knoll. Because of the 1993 identification of a variety of endangered plant species, the city has requested that the state park system restrict entrance to the area, with boardwalks, fences, and trails.

Be very careful when close to the ocean here. The waves can be unexpectedly high, and this is not a good place to swim or even wade.

The Point Pinos Light Station can be entered from Asilomar Avenue, across from the El Carmelo Cemetery. This is the oldest continuously operating lighthouse on the West Coast. Its beacon has flashed nightly since February 1855. The first light source was a sperm whale oil lantern. Later, lard oil replaced the sperm whale oil, then kerosene, then incandescent vapor, and finally electricity in 1915.

The light source is now a 1,000-watt bulb, amplified by lenses and prisms to produce a 50,000-candlepower beam, which is visible under favorable conditions up to fifteen miles out at sea. The light flashes in a simple on-off arrangement. In addition there is a horn that is used to blast warnings to fog-bound travelers. On a foggy day or night you might hear the foghorn even if you are a long way away. Robert Louis Stevenson visited keeper Allen Luce in 1879, after a walk through the woods from Monterey, and praised Luce's hospitality, piano playing, ship models, and oil paintings. The lighthouse is open to the public on Saturdays and Sundays from 1 to 4 p.m. Inside you will find some of the early records, including descriptions of ships that wrecked nearby. You can tour the ground floor of the building, but the light itself is not open to the public since it is still in use. If you take the Pebble Beach tour, look back this way from Spanish Bay Beach to see the light flashing.

If you go back to Ocean View Boulevard and continue with the tour you will encounter even wilder coastline. There are benches to rest on and tide-pools to explore. Be very careful here, though, as the waves have taken away the unwary who have ventured too far.

The Lighthouse Avenue Extension is the old line between city and county limits. Here Ocean View Boulevard changes names to become Sunset Drive. Asilomar State Beach and Conference Grounds are located on Sunset Drive between Jewell Avenue on the north and Spanish Bay, the northernmost section of Pebble Beach, on the south. Asilomar State Beach consists of rocky coastlines, tidepools, sand dunes, and a large white crescent of sand. In addition to the beach area, Asilomar Conference Grounds has pine forest and dunes that provide a natural setting for deer, raccoons, and a variety of other wildlife. In all, Asilomar covers one hundred three acres. Asilomar State Beach is a part of the California State Park system; the conference facilities are operated by a nonprofit corporation.

Asilomar, a combination of the Greek *asilo* ("haven") and the Spanish *mar* ("sea"), was first established in 1913 as a YWCA retreat. The architect of

Hearst Castle, Julia Morgan, designed the original buildings, which are listed as a State Historic Landmark, a National Historic Landmark, and are on the National Register of Historic Places. One can observe Morgan's informal wood Craftsman-style architecture at the entrance gates (built in 1913), the administration building (1913), the chapel (1915), Crocker Hall (1927), Scripps Hall (1927), and Merrill Hall (1928).

In recent years there has been extensive restoration work on the beach to replant the area with native plants and preserve the dunes. You can view a native plant nursery on the Asilomar property and participate in dune-planting days.

If you forgo food during your walk, you may enjoy the fish and pastas at the Fishwife Restaurant located at the end of Asilomar Beach. Up the road the Korean Sunset View Restaurant offers light and fluffy tempura and other authentic specialties for lunch or dinner. It also has chocolate and strawberry stick treats for any young troopers with you.

Farther on, Sunset Drive becomes Highway 68, which continues to Highway 1. You can drive back to the business center of Pacific Grove by turning left on Seventeen Mile Drive. If you are walking you might choose Asilomar Boulevard. If you walk back along Grove Acre Avenue you will get to the butterfly sanctuary in about twenty minutes.

To Connect with the Pebble Beach Tour. If you are driving or biking turn right off Sunset Drive at Seventeen Mile Drive. Drivers need to pay a fee to continue. If you would like to walk on into Pebble Beach, you can choose either of two routes. Walk along the beach to the south end of the sand. From here a slat-board walkway continues to Spanish Bay. Or you can take the other entrance to Pebble Beach located off Sunset Drive; just past the Beachcomber Motel turn right at a dirt pathway. This leads behind a gravel yard to the outskirts of the Links at Spanish Bay. The path leads to the top of a small scenic knoll before descending to a rest area with rest rooms and water. (See the Pebble Beach chapter, page 111.)

Before you leave the Pacific Grove area, come back to this coastline route at sunset. The ocean often glows silver and gold beneath crimson skies as the sun melts into the horizon beyond.

THE BUTTERFLY TOUR: THE MONARCH GROVE SANCTUARY AND WASHINGTON PARK

Washington Park is the largest of Pacific Grove's city parks, with approximately twenty acres. It is six blocks long and is bordered by Short, Alder, Sinex, and Melrose streets. The park has been left as natural acreage with large Monterey pines and oaks towering above the ground. It is an important wildlife habitat and is a wintering area of the monarch. To find the butterfly groves, follow the wood-chip trails into the center of the forest. The butterflies move around from tree to tree, so you will need to look carefully. Look for large clusters hanging from branches in the taller trees.

With the exception of 1996, in recent years few butterflies have been found in Washington Park. No one knows what caused the monarchs to return to the park in 1996. To help bring back the large masses of monarchs that formerly congregated here the city of Pacific Grove is in the process of reworking it to suit them. Volunteer work forces have been laying trails and planting new Monterey pines and native understory. Though the trails are obviously for humans, the overall aim of the work is to achieve a balance of shade and wind-breaking capacity with full sun hitting the trees during the day. Butterflies need direct sun for at least thirty minutes during the late morning to early afternoon, so that they can warm up and fly to locate water and nectar sources. Of course, the paths also keep humans from tamping down the soil around the roots of the trees.

DIRECTIONS

Directions to the Monarch Grove Sanctuary from the Monterey Bay Aquarium. Take David Avenue up to Lighthouse Avenue. Turn right. Take Lighthouse past downtown Pacific Grove for one-half mile. Turn left on Ridge Road and continue to just past the Butterfly Grove Inn. The Monarch Grove Sanctuary will be on your right.

Directions to the Monarch Grove Sanctuary from Highway 1. Take Highway 68 to Pacific Grove. Highway 68 becomes Forest Avenue; continue on to Lighthouse Avenue and turn left. Take Lighthouse through downtown Pacific Grove for one-half mile. Turn left on Ridge Road and continue to just past the Butterfly Grove Inn. The Monarch Grove Sanctuary will be on your right.

You can plan to spend a few minutes or many hours looking at and enjoying the butterflies and relaxing in the pines. The forested park offers a glimpse at the way Pacific Grove looked before settlement. Reportedly, the pines were so thick that people were frequently lost.

The Monarch Grove Sanctuary is wheelchair accessible. A wide pathway leads to a stand of eucalyptus trees where the butterflies congregate. Docents will occasionally set up spotting scopes here for closer viewing opportunities. The path continues past a former residence, presently vacated. In winter, a natural spring occasionally flows on the far side of the building. Often in memory of a loved one, citizens have planted trees here and donations have been made for their continual care.

While there are no facilities at the sanctuary, bathrooms and water are available at Washington Park. There are also picnic tables and benches and a play area for children at the far south section of the park.

WHAT ELSE TO SEE AND DO

CAMERON & SMITH HIGHLAND FLY FISHING OUTFITTERS. Brake here for trout. The store is at 215 Grand Avenue (831/657-0931) but the thrill and beauty are found at the limestone and spring creeks where trout gather. The store owner here is Brett Smith, a biologist and director of the Big Sur Wild Trout Project. Smith and highly qualified guides lead catch-and-release trips into exclusive areas of the Big Sur Ventana Wilderness Area. The store carries Smith's own rods, flies, products for building flies, and an assortment of other fly-fishing goods. If you have even the slightest interest in trout talk to Brett Smith about the legendary rare black trout of Big Sur.

THE PACIFIC GROVE ART CENTER, 568 Lighthouse Avenue (831/375-2208). The Art Center has two of the largest galleries in Northern California. This is an excellent place to find the works of local artists.

MUNICIPAL GOLF COURSE, 77 Asilomar Avenue (831/648-3177). The municipal course offers eighteen holes, a clubhouse, golf equipment rental, electric carts, and a driving range. This course, which backs on the ocean, is a rare golfing bargain, with relatively low nine- and eighteen-hole greens fees.

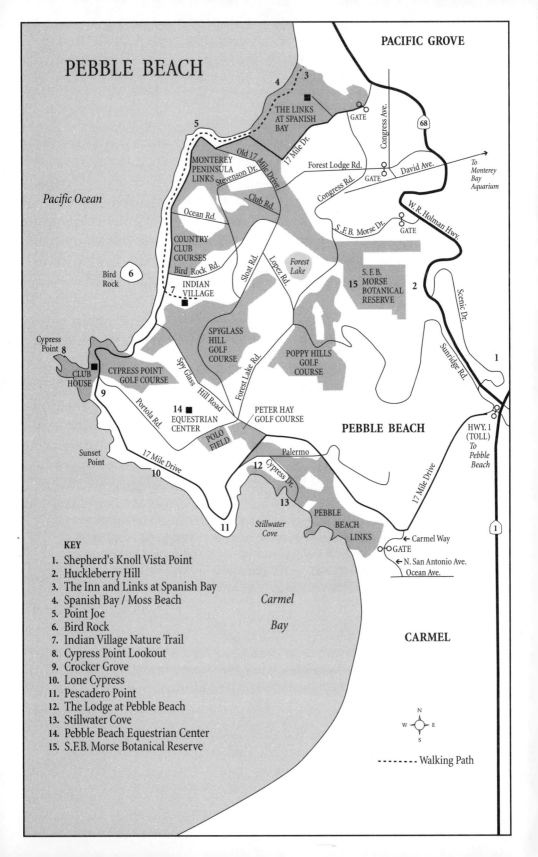

PEBBLE BEACH

PACIFIC GROVE

Pacific Ocean

THE LINKS
AT SPANISH
BAY

GATE

Congress Ave.

68

Old 17 Mile Dr.

17 Mile Dr.

Forest Lodge Rd.

David Ave.

To Monterey Bay Aquarium

MONTEREY
PENINSULA
LINKS

Stevenson Dr.

Congress Rd.

GATE

Club Rd.

S.F.B. Morse Dr.

GATE

W. R. Holman Hwy.

Ocean Rd.

COUNTRY
CLUB
COURSES

Bird Rock Rd.

Forest Lake

S. F. B.
MORSE
BOTANICAL
RESERVE

15

2

Bird
Rock

6

7   INDIAN
VILLAGE

Sloat Rd.

Lopez Rd.

Scenic Dr.

Cypress
Point   8

SPYGLASS
HILL
GOLF
COURSE

POPPY HILLS
GOLF
COURSE

Sunridge Rd.

1

CLUB
HOUSE

CYPRESS POINT
GOLF COURSE

Spy Glass Hill Road

Forest Lake Rd.

9

Portola Rd.

14   ■
EQUESTRIAN
CENTER

PETER HAY
GOLF COURSE

PEBBLE BEACH

HWY. 1
(TOLL)
*To
Pebble
Beach*

Sunset
Point

17 Mile Drive

POLO
FIELD

Palermo

17 Mile Drive

10

12   Cypress Dr.

1

11

13

*Stillwater
Cove*

PEBBLE
BEACH
LINKS

← Carmel Way

GATE

← N. San Antonio Ave.

Ocean Ave.

*Carmel
Bay*

CARMEL

KEY
1. Shepherd's Knoll Vista Point
2. Huckleberry Hill
3. The Inn and Links at Spanish Bay
4. Spanish Bay / Moss Beach
5. Point Joe
6. Bird Rock
7. Indian Village Nature Trail
8. Cypress Point Lookout
9. Crocker Grove
10. Lone Cypress
11. Pescadero Point
12. The Lodge at Pebble Beach
13. Stillwater Cove
14. Pebble Beach Equestrian Center
15. S.F.B. Morse Botanical Reserve

N
W   E
S

-------- Walking Path

CHAPTER 4

PEBBLE BEACH

THE BEACH, THE FOREST, THE GREENS

P ebble Beach is a gated enclave of residences—some of which are true mansions—and forests and golf courses. Seventeen Mile Drive winds through the area and leads to several points of interest, the most popular of which is the Lone Cypress.

GETTING READY

BEST TIMES TO VISIT AND SPECIAL EVENTS

On a morning tour you might catch a glimpse of a wobbly fawn nuzzling its mother in the forest on one side of Seventeen Mile Drive as surfers and playful otters catch a wave together on the other. If it's the golf you have come for, according to Pebble Beach Links golf pro Soney Bae the best time to play golf is "early, early morning, about seven o'clock." At any time of the day you can enjoy a trail ride, relax with a book on the sands of a sheltered cove, tour a posh residential area, or walk among more than one hundred varieties of wild flowers, some fragile dune dwellers found nowhere else in the world. Every evening, as the sun dips through wind-whipped skies, a bagpiper plays a farewell tune. You will find him walking the headlands between the Inn at Spanish Bay and the ocean.

Crowds vary more with events than seasons in Pebble Beach. Seventeen Mile Drive is closed to tour traffic during the AT&T Golf Tournament in early February. A favorite time to be in Pebble Beach is during the Concours d'Elegance in early August. Equestrian shows are featured in August, March, and April. In May the top-rated Del Monte Kennel Club Dog Show stars on the greens around the Lodge at Pebble Beach. Regattas in Stillwater Cove start in May and continue through September. Golf tournaments tee off almost every month.

Wildlife-viewing times are another consideration for trip planning. Pods of whales blasting geysers and breaching offshore can be seen best in late December and January. Dappled fawns are born in spring and summer and can often be observed at close range. Wildflowers bloom year-round and most profusely in spring.

Golf is the daily event at Pebble Beach. Seventeen Mile Drive meanders through some of the most famous golf courses in the world. Unless you are a guest at the resort, tee times may be difficult to arrange at the public course of your choice.

CLIMATE AND CLOTHING

The best time to play golf is September to November. In the usually mild winter months it's not unusual to see golfers dressed in short sleeves running through rain with golf clubs bouncing on their backs. Wind and fog are common but below-freezing temperatures are extremely rare.

What you wear at Pebble Beach will mirror how you choose to spend your time. Since the area combines fine resorts, forests, beaches, casual horseback trail riding, and fashionable golf, your wardrobe may vary from dinner jackets and evening wear to tennis shoes and hiking clothes. Bring binoculars for wildlife viewing and for golf viewing, which also may be wild if Bill Murray is on the course.

TOUR LENGTHS

Seventeen Mile Drive from Pacific Grove to Carmel through Pebble Beach takes twenty minutes. With light sightseeing at major attractions, set aside at least two hours. Pebble Beach offers a full day, weekend, week, and lifetime of possibilities for relaxing and learning. If you do not choose an extended stay you can still experience the many moods of Pebble Beach by traveling through it early, on the way to Carmel, and again later, on the return drive.

HIGHLIGHTS FOR KIDS

The spotting telescopes at Bird Rock are kid-friendly, and the walk along the nature trail across the road is level and inviting. Beach inlets along Seventeen Mile Drive are favorite play areas for families. Unfortunately, the waves and currents are treacherous along this stretch of exposed coast. The Pebble Beach Equestrian Center offers trail rides through the forest.

Golf professionals here offer free golf instruction to Monterey Peninsula youth. Reasonably priced Peter Hay Golf Course is a great par-three course for beginners of all ages. Visitors who try a bucket of balls at the driving range will gain new respect for Tiger Woods.

WILDLIFE WISDOM

The number of visitors to this area increases each year. The treasured environment of this area appears rugged but is actually quite fragile, dependent in its natural balance on responsible tourism. No plant or animal life should be disturbed or removed. The deer in this area have very little fear of people.

Drivers need to pay special attention to speed limits and keep watch for deer darting onto roadways, especially at dusk.

The temptation to feed animals such as cute ground squirrels and calling gulls is easier to resist if you are aware that overpopulation of one species endangers others, and that food from people spreads disease. Animals catching their own food provide great moments for human spectators.

VISITOR INFORMATION

You can enter Pebble Beach through any of the five fee gates. The Highway 1 Gate and the Pacific Grove Gate lead to the most scenic drives. The cost for tourists is $7.25 per car at this writing. Gatekeepers clear those who are guests of residents, and resorts refund the entrance fee to diners and lodgers. To help drivers locate and remain on Seventeen Mile Drive, the center lines of the entire route have been painted red. A walking path leads into Pebble Beach by way of a slat-board walkway at the south end of Asilomar Beach, and another walking path begins at the Pacific Grove Gate. Bicyclists can enter free at any gate. On holidays and weekends bicyclists may enter only through the Pacific Grove Gate. Bicycle rentals are available in Pacific Grove, Monterey, and Carmel (see the Resource Guide, pages 356–7).

A visitor-use pamphlet will be handed to you at the gate. No overnight camping or fires are permitted. Fire danger is usually extreme. Swimming in the rough water anywhere along Seventeen Mile Drive is hazardous; the undertows and sneaker waves are powerful, even at the wading level. Keep your eye on the ocean while wading or playing near the surf.

Courtesy for golfers is expected. Maintain quiet on the backswings. Hiking isn't allowed on golf cart paths or on courses. For information about events or gates or to ask questions, call the Pebble Beach information line (800/654-9300).

PARKING

Parking is provided in pullout areas along Seventeen Mile Drive. Parking at Stillwater Cove is behind The Lodge. Parking for events is in designated areas, with shuttle bus service.

ALTERNATE TRANSPORTATION

County transit buses do not serve Pebble Beach. Private tour buses include Pebble Beach in coastal tours. If you have all day and love exercise, use my favorite way to see Pebble Beach, with a combination of walking or biking and horseback riding. You can rent bikes (pages 356–7), and reserve trail rides (831/624-2756). A leisurely walk from Asilomar Beach to a point parallel to Bird and Seal Rocks (two and a half miles) and then, crossing the street, along the Indian Village nature walk takes about three hours (at an athletic pace, one and a half hours). Trails from here connect with the equestrian center. A one- or two-hour trail ride reveals miles of incredible vistas. If you're walking you can hike back or call a cab. Pack drinks, snacks, and a backpack picnic. You can also stop at a restaurant at Spanish Bay along the way and choose from such selections as a giant panfried chocolate chip cookie or Roy's potstickers with a lobster miso sauce.

REST ROOMS

Since this is primarily a forest, golf, resort, and residential area, finding a rest room is not always easy. Public rest rooms are located a couple of miles south of the Pacific Grove Gate at the Bird Rock turnoff and, closer to the Carmel Gate, at Stillwater Cove.

WHERE TO STAY

A tradition of elegance and the highest standards prevail in the only two lodgings available in Pebble Beach. For golf and room reservations at the resorts call 800/654-9300. AX, MC, V, and other cards are accepted at all resort facilities.

THE INN AT SPANISH BAY. In an architectural blending of Spanish and Old Monterey styles, four stories of rooms feature elegant custom-made oversized furniture, six hundred square feet of floor space, fireplaces, Italian marble baths, and either an outdoor deck or a patio. Approximately half of the rooms offer sweeping ocean views of the wild coast and the Spanish Bay golf course. Amenities include tennis, pools, award-winning fitness center, and restaurants. 831/647-7500. For two from $275 to $350; suites from $575.

THE LODGE AT PEBBLE BEACH. Located in the heart of Pebble Beach, surrounded by the famous Pebble Beach Links, and opening to beautiful ocean vistas, this grand resort has kept pace with the times. Most of the rooms are set in cottage clusters. Warm interior pastels complement architecture of Spanish and Italian influence. The service is impeccable. Wood-burning fireplaces. Four fine restaurants. Priority golf tee times, complimentary airport transportation, tennis, swimming, and fitness facilities. 831/647-7500. For two from $330 to $450; suites from $825.

RESTAURANTS

FORMAL

CLUB XIX (at the Lodge at Pebble Beach). The meals are exquisitely prepared with every detail attended to. Dine by a wall of windows with a view
of the eighteenth hole and the ocean. The Symphony of Club XIX appetizer
offers tastings of six selections including truffle-laced vichyssoise. Continue
with elegant French cuisine. Lunch is served at a French bistro with patio dining. Jackets are requested at dinner. 831/624-3811. AX, MC, V; others also
accepted. Entrees mostly under $30.

SEMI-FORMAL

THE BAY CLUB (at the Inn at Spanish Bay). Fresh orchids, elegant seating,
and marble counters inside set off spectacular ocean views. Truly gracious
service. Contemporary and classical Northern Italian cuisine. Dinner.
831/647-7500. AX, MC, V; others also accepted. Entrees mostly under $25.

CASUAL

CLUBHOUSE BAR & GRILL (at the Inn at Spanish Bay). In a pro-shop
atmosphere, dine outside or in. Choose the patio on a sunny day and the
view of golf and beach will detain you past any prior appointment, except
perhaps tee time. Breakfast, lunch, and dessert. Skillet-baked chocolate chip
cookie smothered with a hot fudge sundae. You can indulge yourself and get
a gate-fee refund. Open 6 a.m. to 3 p.m. 831/647-7500. AX, MC, V; others
also accepted. Entrees mostly under $15.

ROY'S (at the Inn at Spanish Bay). Serves fine "Euro-Asian" cuisine.
Families, couples, and singles all feel comfortable here. Diners are treated to
sweeping ocean vistas or views of the exhibition kitchen. Counter seating is
available for walk-ins. The mood is vibrant. Menu items range from the esoteric escargot cassoulet with garlic and cabernet sauce to teriyaki short rib
pizza. Breakfast, lunch, dinner. 831/647-7500. AX, MC, V; others also
accepted. Entrees mostly under $15.

STILLWATER BAR AND GRILL (at the Lodge at Pebble Beach). View the
eighteenth fairway, Carmel Bay, and the coastal mountains from grand windows. Lively dining in an upbeat setting. Dining is on two levels; a long
curved bar room is splendid for drinks or dining. Fresh seafood specialties
include coriander-seared ahi tuna. Weekly specialties highlight the exquisite

Sunday brunch. Breakfast, lunch, dinner. 831/624-3811. AX, MC, V; others also accepted. Entrees mostly under $25.

THE TAP ROOM (at the Lodge at Pebble Beach). An English pub with an eclectic collection of golf memorabilia, this is where golfers relax and share great stories. Prime rib, vegetarian platter, and lighter fare. Voted "Best Late Night Restaurant." Lunch, dinner, late-night service; full bar with thirty-six varieties of beer. 831/624-3811. AX, MC, V; others also accepted. Entrees mostly under $15.

DIRECTIONS

Pebble Beach is accessible from fee gates near Ocean Avenue in Carmel, Highway 1 at the Highway 68 intersection, on Highway 68 into Pacific Grove (the S. F. B. Morse Gate), and in Pacific Grove (the Country Club Gate and the Seventeen Mile Drive Gate).

For more spectacular views include Pacific Grove's section of the drive in your Pebble Beach–entry route. Drive around Ocean View Boulevard in Pacific Grove, pass Asilomar State Beach, then connect with Seventeen Mile Drive at Sunset Drive (call 831/624-3811 for gate information); or continue on Sunset to Highway 68, driving to the top of Highway 68 to enter Seventeen Mile Drive at the Highway 1 Gate for spectacular summit views.

Direct Route from the Monterey Bay Aquarium. *Drive up David Avenue to Forest Avenue (on the Pacific Grove map). Turn right at Forest Avenue and immediately move into the left-turn lane; turn at the first street, which is Sunset Drive/Highway 68. Drive west on Sunset until you come to the second stop sign. This is the intersection of Sunset and Seventeen Mile Drive. Turn left on Seventeen Mile Drive; you will soon see the gated entrance.*

From Highway 1. *Take the exit for Highway 68, Pacific Grove/Pebble Beach. This leads directly to the Highway 1 Gate; enter Pebble Beach and follow the scenic route around the summit.*

INTRODUCTION TO PEBBLE BEACH WITH HISTORICAL HIGHLIGHTS

Serene one moment, wild the next, the route of panoramic Seventeen Mile Drive through exclusive Pebble Beach is world renowned. Five gated entrances invite the traveler to nine miles of spectacular coast, towering pine forests, rare wildflowers, cypress groves, and seven world-class golf courses. Exquisite residences and luxury resorts are interspersed in this Edenlike atmosphere, cradled between Pacific Grove and Carmel.

The area known as Pebble Beach lies within the Del Monte Forest, thick with tall, closed-coned Monterey pine and a rare grove of indigenous Monterey cypress. A century ago thick, impenetrable forests grew from inland to the dunes and highlands above the ocean's edge, on lands now shared with world-famous golf courses and estates. Archaeological studies of the area, including an important discovery in Pebble Beach in 1991, reveal that Del Monte Forest was inhabited by people for five thousand years before the first Spanish explorers landed. These earlier inhabitants, often described as the Ohlone people, may have been the distinct dialect and family group called the Rumsien people. They were probably predated here by the Esselen, who later moved down the Big Sur Coast. Tools such as bone awls and arrowheads, still found at Pebble Beach, show the importance of the area as a food-gathering territory. Such archaeological sites today include Spanish Bay, Cypress Point, Fanshell Beach, Pescadero Point, Stillwater Cove, and the oceanside stretch of Pebble Beach Golf Links, including the famous seventh hole at Arrowhead Point.

Pounding in winter, lapping gently on calm days, the relentless ocean waves meet the rocky promontories and scenic beaches along the six-mile ocean frontage of Pebble Beach. The forest and dunes provided shelter from strong ocean winds for Juan Gaspar de Portola, who camped at Spanish Bay, just south of Asilomar Beach, during his 1769 expedition for Spain. During this first expedition he explored the areas around the Monterey Bay but missed his landmarks and lost his bearings. He returned to his post as governor of Baja California with the misunderstanding that he had not found Monterey Bay. The following year cannons roared when a land expedition led by Portola and Father Crespi met the companion ship the *San Antonio*, with Father Serra aboard. Ground was broken the next day for the presidio and mission.

After Rumsien inhabitants were driven away from Spanish, Mexican, and early California settlements, Pebble Beach remained a primitive forest, sharing some lands with grazing cattle and sheep. Two Mexican land grants, El Pescader (the Fishing Place) and Punta de Pinos (Point of Pines) Rancho, encompassed a major part of present-day Pebble Beach, from 1835 to 1860.

In 1840 El Pescader was owned by Dona Maria del Carmen Barreto, who sold it for an adobe in Monterey. The Lodge at Pebble Beach stands at about the center of the old ranch, and the Dona's ghost is said to roam the cypress trees (probably losing sleep over her selling price of five hundred dollars for the whole four thousand acres).

Eventually the land was acquired at a sheriff's trustee sale by the famous land wheeler and dealer David Jacks of Monterey, who in turn sold it in 1879 to the Pacific Improvement Company, the holding company for Southern Pacific Railroad. Jacks leased back some of the land to graze cattle and sheep. Charles Crocker of the "Big Four" railroad empire proposed the old Del Monte Hotel in Monterey, which was built as a magnet to draw the very rich to the Monterey Peninsula. Pebble Beach became the recreation destination for visitors to the hotel. The original Seventeen Mile Drive, several miles longer than today, circled the peninsula from the old hotel and back.

The road was described by J. R. Fitch, a travel writer of the late 1800s, as being at first "a waste of sand through which horses plodded laboriously." By 1887 a "fine graveled highway permitted rapid trotting" as hotel guests traversed in grand tally-hos pulled by three matched pairs of lively horses. The brisk ride took several hours and then some. An elaborate picnic near where the Lodge stands today was the highlight of a stay at the Del Monte. Fifty wagon coaches completed the Seventeen Mile loop trip each day. President Theodore Roosevelt rode the loop on horseback, roughrider style.

The name Pebble Beach was garnered, according to Fitch and later others, from a section of especially "pebbly" beach by the then-soon-to-be-built first lodge. "One bit of this bay is worth passing notice. It is known as Pebble Beach, because of the myriads of pebbles that take the place of ordinary sand. The waves come in with a peculiar swish on these loose pebbles, and their constant action results in beautifully rounded specimens of all kinds and of every shade of color. The Beach is a favorite resort for collectors of pebbles, but the search usually proves disastrous to clothes and shoes, since the waves come up with great rapidity, and yet so noiselessly that the incautious seeker after pebbles, finding too late that he cannot escape in this yielding mass, is overcome by the water and receives a thorough drenching." The beach by Stillwater Cove still swishes with pebbles, though many fewer in number than in the 1880s as reported by Fitch.

The mansions of Pebble Beach were mere dreams in those days. The only settlement was a Chinese fishing village at Stillwater Cove, which, along with Jacks's dairy barn, occupied the seventeenth green of the present-day Pebble Beach Golf Course. The Chinese, prohibited by law from owning land, originally leased the land from Jacks for six dollars and two dozen abalones each month. In 1888 the village had more than thirty inhabitants. After the drive opened for tourists the villagers offered what may have been Monterey County's first commercial souvenirs—polished abalone shells, sold at a stand. Jung San Choy, the last Chinese villager, left in 1912 following the demise of the village from age, changes in the fishing industry, immigration laws, and development of surrounding land.

The "Duke of Del Monte," Samuel F. B. Morse, nephew of the inventor of the telegraph, served as a successful manager of the Del Monte Properties. In 1919 Morse and partner Herbert Fleishhacker, president of Anglo Bank in San Francisco, bought the Del Monte holdings for $1.3 million. It was through the vision of Morse that Pebble Beach developed as a golf resort with exclusive residences.

The original lodge burned the day after Christmas, 1917. A reconstructed lodge and a golf course designed by amateur golfer and real estate salesman Jack Neville, now famous as the "Links at Pebble Beach," opened the same year Morse began his new company. Golf had a new mecca.

The oldest and most grandiose estates stretch over the land south of the Lodge to the border of Carmel. Most of these opulent mansions were built before the Depression of the 1930s. The style imposed on all construction was Spanish or Mediterranean. Between the mansions and Highway 1 and in a few other parts of Pebble Beach Monterey pine forests grow thick with lush undergrowth. Highway 1 to the east climbs Carmel Hill.

From numerous horseback surveys Morse divided Pebble Beach into four areas: the Lodge area; Cypress Point, which was to welcome one of the most privately exclusive golf clubs in the United States, still owned primarily by the one hundred founding families; the Country Club area, which extended into present-day Pacific Grove; and the highlands sports area, which now includes the S. F. B. Morse Botanical Reserve. Through the leadership of Morse, lots were plotted away from major vistas, to protect the open ocean views.

From the opening of the links, Morse's intention was to attract the rich and famous both as residents and visitors. Some of the memorable visits have been Douglas Fairbanks in the 1920s, Prince George in 1928, Bing Crosby in 1947 at his first pro-am tournament, John F. Kennedy, a senator when he posed on the lawn in front of the Lodge, Ringo Starr of the Beatles, riding incognito at the height of their popularity in 1966, and Luciano Pavarotti, singing at a fund raiser in 1991.

Nothing has brought more fame and celebrities to Pebble Beach than the Crosby Golf Tournament, which first opened in 1947. Pros, amateurs, and celebrities come together for a week of golf and the famous clambake dinner that accompanies the tournament. Bob Hope described the Crosby as "a place for the elite, where ocean and golf ball meet."

Today the Crosby lives on in the AT&T Pebble Beach National Pro-Am.

The initial purse was $10,000; in 1998 it was $2,000,000. The original venues were Pebble Beach Links, Cypress Point, and the Monterey Peninsula Country Club. Spyglass Hill replaced Monterey in 1967 and Poppy Hills replaced Cypress Point in 1991. In 1993 Bill Murray took golf into theater on the links with comic skits at each tee. In his final high jinks he carried a woman into the sand pit on the eighteenth and then sunk a twenty-foot birdie for the best finishing shot. The bleachers of normally sedate golf fans went wild. In 1997, the tournament set record attendance figures when Kevin Costner teamed with Tiger Woods. In 1998 Tiger Woods returned to play with his father, but El Niño caused play to be suspended until August.

The present owner of the Pebble Beach Company is the Lone Cypress Corporation. Its holdings include 2,300 of the 5,300 acres in Pebble Beach. Included in these acres are the two resorts and three golf courses: Spyglass Hill Golf Course, The Links at Spanish Bay, and the Pebble Beach Course. The corporation also owns the equestrian center, other acreage, a realty company, artistic rights, and the famous Lone Cypress logo. Controversial plans are underway to add more housing and another golf course and to move the equestrian center. This new ownership polished Pebble Beach, to gain a return invitation for the U.S. Open in the year 2000. Morse, who died in 1969, referred to Pebble Beach as "a garden for generations to enjoy."

TOUR: SEVENTEEN MILE DRIVE

If your pleasure is golf, you probably intend to take an intimate tour of a very special set of eighteen holes. To take full advantage of the variety of activities that Pebble Beach offers you might also include a visit to the beach, Point Joe, a resort, the cypress grove and the Lone Cypress, Bird and Seal Rock lookout, and a slow drive by an enormous mansion or two. Also explore other areas of Pebble Beach that are less known but included in this guide; consider this tour of Seventeen Mile Drive an invitation to all the offerings highlighted along it.

Wildlife is especially abundant here. Enthralled drivers have been known to leave their Mercedes in the middle of the road with doors wide open as they rush to take a picture. More than a hundred varieties of plants and two hundred birds, a forest of trees, and a constant parade of sea, tidal, and land animals will bring you so close to nature you may wish you could grow roots.

If you enter Pebble Beach at the Highway 1 Gate you then wind back under Highway 68 to the turnouts for the Shepherd's Knoll and Huckleberry Hill vista points. In 1989 a fire burned the forest and several residences at Huckleberry Hill. The thousands of small pines you see are the natural seedlings of the burned pines—a forest renewing itself. Winding down the wooded hills you intersect Seventeen Mile Drive where it enters Pebble Beach from Pacific Grove.

Gardens grace the turn from Seventeen Mile Drive to Spanish Bay. If it is close to sunset roll your windows down as you turn and you may hear a bagpiper welcoming you to the Inn at Spanish Bay, the newest and largest resort of the area. You can park in the main parking lot and wander through shops, enjoy a meal, or walk to Spanish Bay.

A gated driveway leads to the Residences at Spanish Bay. The Inn and Residences are operated by the Pebble Beach Company, which describes their style as "new traditionalist." They are the largest structures on the coast: a 270-room luxury hotel and several fine shops and restaurants. Rolling sand dunes covered with native grasses and wildflowers are more than twenty feet tall and encapsulate the look of the eighteen-hole golf course here. Visit the Ansel Adams Gallery (831/375-7215) to view fine photography.

Back on Seventeen Mile Drive take the next right and the beautiful breakers off Moss Beach, which fronts Spanish Bay, roll into view. Due to its variety of undersea habitats this area has the greatest diversity of marine algae on the Monterey Peninsula. It was already famous in *Picturesque California* in 1887: "This is Moss Beach, famous for the delicate specimens of sea moss washed up every day at high tide. These are as infinite and as graceful in design as the coral, and one of the favorite pastimes of the dwellers at Pacific Grove is the floating out and preserving of these mosses." One of our family's favorite pastimes is to get pizza and calzones from Allegro Gourmet Pizzeria in Pacific Grove and picnic at tables here, then stroll the boardwalk through the dunes. (Allegro's will deliver to the beach for large groups.)

Point Joe is an easy walk to the southwest of Moss Beach and is the next natural stop if you're driving or biking. The offshore area here has been dubbed "The Restless Sea" for the wave action caused by its underwater topography and meeting of ocean swells. Turbulent waves smash from different directions, then clash and crisscross for some of the most unusual and wildest surf in California.

Waves crash over rocky Point Joe, conjuring ghosts of shipwrecks, but by the 1890s a small Chinese wooden fishing village had been built along the rocky point. During the abalone rush of the 1850s hundreds of Chinese had arrived in the Monterey area to harvest the shellfish, which had multiplied in numbers since the overkilling of its natural enemy, the sea otter. The abalone harvesting took place at two places along the Pebble Beach shore, Point Joe and Stillwater Cove. The rocks claimed many ships, including the coastal steamer the *Saint Paul* which wrecked off the rocks in 1896. The Chinese salvaged the lumber for future buildings. Today experienced surfers ride the waves with abandon.

After the turn of the century only a solitary Chinese man named Joe fished, tended a herd of goats, and sold trinkets at this point. He was a familiar sight as he walked from the point to Monterey with a cat on his shoulder. It is not known whether the point was named for Joe or whether Joe was named for the place he lived, but the two are linked and no other reason for the name Point Joe remains.

As you leave Point Joe to meander down Seventeen Mile Drive, exclusive residences dot the forest side. Farther south huge mansions hug the cliffs above the ocean and guard their own private beaches. Movie and TV stars, old and new rich, and corporations have estates here. Architectural styles vary from the early Spanish Colonial preferred by Morse to old southern mansion to Cape Cod to modern. Some of the names on gated entrances disclose or hint at the identity of occupants. Past the Lodge on Seventeen Mile Drive, "Wit's End" still identifies the home of late cartoonist Jimmy Hatlo.

Who needs a mansion when you can carry a roomy, comfortable house on your back as you enjoy beachfront property with a solar-heated pool? You might not be caused to ogle by his domicile, but you can enjoy the little hermit crab's antics as you investigate the many tidepools along the walking path connecting Point Joe with Bird and Seal Rock.

In late December and January, then lessening through March, this path and the picnic tables at the bottom of Ocean Road are perfect vantage points to watch the migration of gray whales. Pods of geysers line the horizon. Occasionally they get close enough for you to see the massive hulks breach and flukes slap the water.

One Christmas as I was making breakfast a puff of white caught my eye in our ocean-view window. I blinked my eyes, not sure if late-night wrapping had made me weary. Three more white steamy fountains and . . . Whale ahoy! We actually packed our Christmas dinner, tablecloths, and fine china and celebrated the day at the beach. It's a widespread enthusiasm here; if you need a conversation piece to break the ice with locals just mention whales.

The greens of the Monterey Peninsula Country Club's Shore Course extend to the other side of Seventeen Mile Drive below Point Joe. Membership in this private club was used to entice the home buyers of this area. Some deeds still come with membership.

As two offshore islands come into your view just south of Ocean Road, you hear barking sea lions challenging each other for offshore lounging rocks. At first you think there are just a few. Then as your eyes focus you see hundreds of pinnipeds, the majority of which are California sea lions, resting on Bird and Seal Rock (which actually is several rocks). Their barks can be heard for miles through the calm air of evening and morning. For close-up viewing, telescopes line the shore.

One day as friends of mine were walking at the beach, a young sea lion dodged up and down in the water and became so caught up in its game of pitch and roll that a wave washed it onto the shore. It paused for a moment, looked them in the eyes as if asking, "What are you doing here?," then waddled back into the frothy surf.

The birds used to share the larger island until Morse came up with the industrious plan to scrape the bird guano off of it to use as fertilizer for the golf courses and appease the surrounding residents, who didn't like the rocks' appearance or odor. The pinnipeds apparently liked the rocks guano-less and moved there, displacing the birds. However, the larger rock is still marked on maps as Bird Rock and the smaller one as Seal Rock.

You might think a sea gull is a sea gull, period. Check out the beaks, feet, wings, feathers, and colorings to distinguish the many varieties that share the smaller rock roost with cormorants, sandpipers, kingfishers, and the rare blackfooted albatross. Brown pelicans glide by on their way to better fishing at Stillwater Cove.

Each year from late January through spring, wintering Canadian geese give free manicures to surrounding golf courses. Throughout the year jack rabbits race golf carts and raccoons' eyes shine bright from the brush at night.

Herds of deer graze freely on the greens. In early summer the air is heavy with expectation as fawns are born in surrounding brush. Around September bucks sprout majestic antlers. One of the unusual deer you might see, an albino buck, is known as the Ghost of Pebble Beach.

Across the road from Bird and Seal Rock a nature trail winds through the dunes, past a pond, and into a forest oasis. A picturesque private residence called the Gingerbread House borders the trail.

The trail is an easy loop hike. Sand verbena, Menzies wallflower, and lupine hold the fragile dunes. Up the hill beneath the pines, globe lilies, California iris, and ceanothus are guarded by poison oak and milk thistle. If you stay on the wide path you and the plants will be happier. The trail loops at a large grassy clearing known as Indian Village.

Although historians are not clear on the authenticity of an actual Indian village located here, Morse related, "The legend of the place is that the Indians had used it as a sort of a cure; that when they were sick they came there to camp and that after they had stayed here a few days and taken of the waters of the spring they frequently felt better. . . . It is an interesting thing that they should have a spa comparable with Saratoga and Baden-Baden."

Back on Seventeen Mile Drive you soon see a sign on the left for the Spyglass Hill Golf Course. Robert Louis Stevenson reportedly found the places for his book *Treasure Island* along the Monterey Coast. Each hole at this course is named after a place or character in the book. Hole one, an island in the sand, is aptly named Treasure Island. Long John Silver, Bad Dog, and friends are all represented. The demanding course combines dunes and forest. A cafe here offers burgers and refreshments.

About a half-mile south of Spyglass Hill Road, Fan Shell Beach lies along the turn of the road. This white-sand beach is perfectly crescent-shaped. Is that why the sands sing? Truly, they do. If you walk along the sand and drag your feet, high-pitched tones will follow your movements. A midden of piled abalone shells was found nearby from early tribal days. Apparently, this has been a favorite picnic spot for centuries. Pink sand verbena and Menzies wallflower grow here on the dunes, which also provide a home for the black legless lizard.

The drive now passes through the very private Cypress Point Club. Morse engaged the well-known Santa Barbara architect George Washington Smith to design the Cypress Point Clubhouse. The exclusive club was started in 1928. More recently its exclusivity caused it to be dropped from AT&T tournament play. The course was designed by Scottish architect Alister Mackenzie. The famous par-three sixteenth hole is separated from the back tee by an ocean gorge.

As you drive by the Cypress Point Course take the turnoff for the Cypress Point Lookout. On a clear day, from this spectacular lookout you can see twenty miles south. Black oystercatchers, western gulls, and cormorants nest on rocks offshore. In the spring, a dark canvas covering with holes cut for peeping naturalists covers the fence that separates the lookout area from the beach, which is the birthing place for Pacific harbor seals. The Pebble Beach Company participates in the Harbor Seal Protection Program along parts of the coastline in Del Monte Forest. The Pacific harbor seal is a true, or earless, seal, which spends equal amounts of time on land and in the ocean. The female seal is a devoted parent, but noise from tourists can cause the adults to stampede, crushing the young ones. Docents lead very quiet tours to educational groups. Viewing by the public, with the exception of organized groups, is not allowed every year. Call the Pebble Beach Office for information (831/647-7500).

Across the drive, in Crocker Grove, thirteen acres of cypress grow in a protected reserve. The Monterey cypress grows wild in indigenous groves only in this stretch of roadway and at Point Lobos. The oldest and largest single Monterey cypress grows in this protected grove. The distinctive greenery of these trees masses at the top, forming a dark canopy. The lower branches die but remain as twisted, gnarly arms.

At the midway point on your tour, a turnout and slat-board walkway provide the opportunity to view and photograph the Lone Cypress. Access beyond the lookout has been restricted because of extreme soil compacting

The Lone Cypress

and danger to the tree. The gnarled tree, hugging its rugged precipice above the waves, is portrayed on the Pebble Beach logo. Twisted and alone, it is the sentinel of its precarious perch. It's definitely camera time.

At Pescadero Point the white sand beaches of Carmel and Point Lobos are glimpsed from the best benches on the drive. This is where major developer Frank Devendorf first envisioned the future Carmel. Legend has it that this outlook is where the ghost of Dona Maria del Carmen Barreto, owner of this land in the days of Ranch El Pescadero, roams at night.

The large marble estate you will pass near here is known as the Crocker Castle. Built as a marble Byzantine castle for Mrs. Templeton Crocker of the banking and railroad fortune, this mansion contains many rooms and has indoor and outdoor arches made of thirty-two kinds of marble. The private beachfront was heated by underground pipes.

Continuing south, the drive curves inland to the Lodge, the village, and the famous Pebble Beach. The stately lodge blends Old World elegance with comfort. The public is invited; dine and shop, play golf, and of course stay as long as you like. You'll enjoy the walk through the outer lobby, down the steps, and into the Terrace lounge. Through tall French windows you'll see the green of Pebble Beach's eighteenth fairway. This was the finishing hole for the 1972, 1982, and 1992 U. S. Open Golf Tournaments. Pebble Beach will host the U.S. Open in 2000.

In August, the need for homes that have garages with a three-car minimum becomes apparent. Garage doors that have remained closed all year open and large car-carrier semis twist through Pebble Beach: destination, the eighteenth green. You'll rub your eyes and wonder if you're dreaming about another era as classic cars traverse the roads, heading for the Pebble Beach Concours d'Elegance. This epitome of classic car shows is the anchor event of a summer automotive weekend in Monterey County.

You won't need a classic car to enjoy the vicinity of the Lodge. A post office, bank, service station, and deli-market serve residents and visitors. Relax and enjoy people watching, as well as a deli sandwich on picnic tables near the post office.

The village offers an array of shops. You might really need the bank after viewing the mesmerizing art at the Coast Gallery, especially the marine and wildlife sculptures.

Behind the Lodge, you can walk between the links to beautiful Stillwater Cove. Public parking is also available at the cove. On any day you'll likely see pelicans speed-diving for food and golfers power-swinging to hit wayward balls back to the greens from the beach. The water here is relatively calm. Public boat launching is permitted, with certain restrictions. You'll get a unique view of the coast and resort if you kayak over the glassy surface of the cove.

Continuing on Seventeen Mile Drive after your sojourn in the Lodge area, you can enter Carmel by staying to the right. If you bypass Carmel and continue on the original drive you'll climb through a canyon and be treated to sweeping views at Shepherd's Knoll and Huckleberry Hill. Seventeen Mile Drive ends at Highway 1.

WHAT ELSE TO SEE AND DO

THE GOLF COURSES. The private Cypress Point and the public Pebble Beach golf links rank number three and number five in *Golf Digest*'s ratings of the top one hundred courses in America. The public Spyglass Hill and the Links at Spanish Bay also receive high ratings. Three other courses in Pebble Beach, the public Poppy Hills and the private the Shore and the Dunes of the Monterey Peninsula Country Club, share the wondrous surroundings. The Peter Hay, a reasonably priced public nine-hole par-three practice course, lies inland from Seventeen Mile Drive. Reservation lines are open from 7:30 a.m. to 6:00 p.m. on weekdays and from 8:00 a.m. to 5:00 p.m. on weekends.

PUBLIC GOLF COURSES

PEBBLE BEACH GOLF LINKS, adjacent to the Lodge at Pebble Beach. 831/624-3811, 800/654-9300. Site of the annual AT&T National Pro-Am Golf Tournament. Eighteen holes, 6,806 yards, par 72.

PETER HAY PAR 3 GOLF COURSE, near the Lodge at Pebble Beach. 831/624-3811. Nine holes; very reasonable greens fees; gate-pass refunded.

SPYGLASS HILL GOLF COURSE, Stevenson Drive and Spyglass Hill Road, Pebble Beach. 831/624-6611. Eighteen holes, 6,810 yards, par 72.

THE LINKS AT SPANISH BAY, at the Inn at Spanish Bay, Pebble Beach. 831/624-3811, 800/654-9300. Eighteen holes, 6,357 yards, par 72.

OTHER RECREATIONAL FACILITIES

PEBBLE BEACH EQUESTRIAN CENTER, Portola Road, Pebble Beach. 831/624-2756. This Currier & Ives–lookalike facility with green lawns, rail fences, and white-painted board-and-batten buildings offers trail rides and private lessons. Thirty miles of riding trails weave through Pebble Beach. The finest horse trainers and showriders of the West Coast gather here each summer for annual horse and dressage shows. If Pebble Beach development plans are approved, the equestrian center will move to an abandoned quarry.

S. F. B. MORSE BOTANICAL RESERVE, in the northeast area of Pebble Beach. Turn left at Bird Rock Road from Seventeen Mile Drive. Hiking trails begin in the Bird Rock–Congress Road area. In the spring, wildflowers bedeck the thirty miles of trails that loop through Pebble Beach. Naturalists associated with the Pacific Grove Natural History Museum sometimes lead nature walks of the S. F. B. Morse Botanical Reserve. This eighty-six-acre reserve is the only place in the world where Monterey and Bishop pines grow together. Huckleberry Hill is the highest point of the area. After the area was submerged by ocean, millions of years ago, the wave-cut marine terraces of Huckleberry Hill were left with Pleistocene deposits of poor-draining claypan soil and acidic podzol, having only enough nutrients and support for the usually towering Bishop pines and the endangered endemic Gowen cypress to grow as a stunted "pygmy forest." The Gowen cypress is known to occur only at this location and at Point Lobos State Reserve. Many other rare and endangered varieties of plants also are found here. Harvest mice, jack rabbits, deer, and an occasional mountain lion (yes, in Pebble Beach) find homes in or pass through this area.

CHAPTER 5

CARMEL

THE VILLAGE AND ENVIRONS

Snowy white beaches, shady lanes, and meadow trails grace the one-mile-square village of Carmel-by-the-Sea. As a historic haven for professors, artists, and writers, Carmel-by-the-Sea retains a commitment to the arts, a strong community identity, and respect for individualism, while busloads of visitors are charmed by its storybook architecture, unique shops, and galleries. Woodland and meadow trails lead from the downtown area and the surround, known as Carmel, to the historic Mission San Carlos Borromeo De Rio Carmelo, which was the headquarters for Spanish colonial growth in California.

GETTING READY

BEST TIMES TO VISIT AND SPECIAL EVENTS

On weekdays in October and November you might be one of a handful of visitors wandering through the sunny village. During Christmas season, the absence of neon lights here and the presence of carolers heralds a scene similar to a Norman Rockwell painting. If it does chance to rain, this is one of the best getaways-turned-stormy imaginable. Carmel has a plethora of warming fireplaces. One of the largest and most popular is in the library. Spring wildflowers along the coastal and woodlands trails are an added plus March through June.

If you are visiting just for the day plan to arrive before 9 a.m. during the summer—especially on weekends—and also on holiday weekends throughout the year. Have breakfast or enjoy one of the coastal or woodland walks. This way you'll be able to find a parking place and see the village before the crowds. Later in the day traffic can be bumper to bumper for one mile up Ocean Avenue and onto Highway 1. The best entrance route in high seasons is from the Carpenter Street or Rio Road exit from Highway 1.

Most shops open at 10 a.m., although more and more are opening at 9 a.m. on weekends. The shops begin to close around 5 p.m. The Plaza (downtown shopping center) stores stay open later seasonally, and some shops stay open later on particular nights. On Friday evenings during the summer artists open their studios for art walks.

CARMEL

KEY

1. City Hall
2. Church of the Wayfarer
3. Tuck Box
4. Piccadilly Park
5. Carmel Plaza (Mall)
6. Dovendorf Park
7. Park Branch Library
8. Youth Services & Local History
9. Eastwood Bldg.-Hog's Breath Inn
10. Carmel Business Assn. Visitor's Center
11. Post Office
12. Village Corner
13. Carmel Art Assn. Gallery
14. First Murphy House and Park
15. Harrison Memorial Library
16. Pine Inn
17. Frank Lloyd Wright House
18. Tor House
19. Carmel Mission
20. Mission Ranch
21. Lester Rowntree Arboretum

20. Sunset Center
21. Cherry Foundation
22. Forest Theatre

City ordinances prohibit music in eating establishments. Nightlife is conversation in pubs (some are open until 1 a.m.) and walks on the beach. Some of the restaurants serve later than 10 p.m. and have wonderful outdoor firepits. The Mission Ranch, just outside the city limits, and the Rancho Carmel restaurants across Highway 1 offer livelier nightlife.

Special events to plan for include: the Rio Resolution Run (call the Treadmill, 831/624-4112) on January 1; this is a cross-country run on trails, beaches, and roads. The Tor House Garden Party is held in late spring. In April the internationally renowned Big Sur Marathon (831/625-6226) sponsors a marathon and fun 5K walk-run. In May the Carmel Gallery Alliance (831/642-2503, www.carmelga.com) plays host to the Carmel Art Festival, which includes a sculpture-in-the-park exhibit, youth art show, and artists' demonstrations. The Bach Festival (831/624-1521), three weeks of concerts, is usually scheduled during July and August. The autumn Arts and Crafts show takes place in September.

CLIMATE AND CLOTHING

Bring a sweater or jacket for the cooling fog. Locals and visitors dress stylishly casual. Bring a comfortable pair of walking shoes and pack binoculars for bird watching at the lagoon.

TOUR LENGTHS

If you asked most regular visitors how to see Carmel in an hour you'd get disbelieving looks. However, one afternoon I asked various Australian tourists how they had spent the one hour in Carmel that had been allotted to them by their bus guide. The sweatiest had chosen to jog down the Mission Trail. Those with packages had shopped. Some had wandered the galleries. All were glowing.

Can you spare a week or long weekend for just Carmel? Check into a historic inn and, if you have to, misplace your car keys. If your visit must be shorter, try for at least a half-day. Schedule a minimum of two hours for the village walking tour, one hour for the mission, and two hours for the coastal and woodland trails.

HIGHLIGHTS FOR KIDS

The dunes at Carmel Beach invite kids to roll their way to the beach.

Carmel celebrates its birthday with a great hometown Halloween costume parade. Several theater groups including Dance Kids Inc. (831/624-3729) and Pacific Repertory Theater (831/622-0100) offer plays to watch. Some youngsters who vacation here on an extended stay end up joining the actors. The Forest Theater (831/626-1681) offers a selection of live theater, classes, and summer outdoor movies under the stars with occasional fog. For kids this is the best theater in the world. They can bring bags of snacks and laugh at old comedies.

Artists can often be found in tucked-away studios throughout the village. Just observing the changing canvas is magical. At Carmel Bates Cafe, artist Bill Bates provides instructions for "How to Draw a Carmel Cottage." Highlands Sculpture Gallery (831/624-0535) on the west side of Dolores between Fifth and Sixth is an especially friendly gallery where visitors are encouraged to touch the sculpture.

Dedication to quality education is a strong community value. The Harrison Memorial Library Park Branch (831/624-4664) in this community has a complete library for youths. As with all libraries in the county, kids enjoy a great summer reading program here.

Carmel Valley Racquet and Health Club (831/624-2737) offers an excellent camp and membership opportunities for families.

Glazes (831/624-0204) ceramics workshop offers opportunities for artists of any age to paint on a fine selection of ceramics.

WILDLIFE WISDOM

The presence of kelp beds at the north end of Ocean Beach toward Pescadero Point almost guarantees otter sightings. Tidepools dot the shoreline there and south of Carmel Point. Gaze over the horizon from December through February for the spouting of gray whales. Bring binoculars for the abundance and variety of birds at the River Beach lagoon.

VISITOR INFORMATION

Since there are no street numbers in the village, if you ask about a certain location you'll receive instructions such as "the third house up from the northwest corner" of a given street. Residents and businesspeople have a warmth and patience uncommon in a fast-paced world.

Pick up a copy of the free *Carmel Pine Cone*, the *Sun*, *Coast Weekly*, the *Review*, or the *Monterey County Herald*'s "Go!" section at newsstands for the latest village news and information about events and gallery showings. The Carmel Business Association Visitor's Center, open 9 a.m. to 5 p.m. Mondays through Fridays with extended summer hours, is located on the second floor of the Eastwood Building, San Carlos Street between Fifth and Sixth Avenues, 831/624-2522. Special gallery events including receptions and art exhibitions are included in the twenty-four-hour *GuestLife* magazine Gallery Events Line at 831/645-7700.

Mediterranean Market in Carmel

PARKING

At the western beach end of Carmel Village free all-day parking is available in the Ocean Beach lot and on lower Ocean Avenue. Around the village you might get lucky and find a free all-day parking spot on Junipero Avenue, south of Ocean Avenue. Free parking is also available in the city lot located about three blocks from the center of the village at the corner of Junipero Avenue and Third Avenue. The maximum parking available on most streets near the center of the village is ninety minutes. Overtime parking is ticketed every day of the week.

You can pay to park at Carmel Plaza's underground garage (from Junipero Avenue, turn right at Seventh Avenue and right on Mission Street) or at the lot next to Sunset School on Eighth Avenue and Mission Street. Rates for the Sunset lot are $1 per half hour with a $14 maximum.

ALTERNATE TRANSPORTATION

Monterey Transit (831/899-2555) serves Carmel with hourly service. Buses leave and return to the Monterey transit center. Carmel is rather hilly for bike touring, but some areas by the Carmel River Beach make for a great residential and sea-view ride. Many enjoy the ride to Point Lobos. Call Bay Bikes (831/625-BIKE/2453) for free bike delivery.

REST ROOMS

Public rest rooms are located at the base of Ocean Avenue at Carmel Beach and also five blocks up from the beach just north of Ocean Avenue on Lincoln, at First Murphy Park (behind the Pine Inn). At the top of the business district rest rooms are located in the Carmel Plaza and across the street at Devendorf Park.

PLACES TO STAY

Carmel has truly wonderful lodging opportunities. These are some of the places that offer the flavor of Carmel. Many more await you.

IN CARMEL, WITHIN WALKING DISTANCE OF THE VILLAGE AND BEACHES

COBBLESTONE INN (on Junipero Avenue between Seventh and Eighth Streets). Cobblestones from the Salinas River cover the exterior of this inn. Teddy bears, country pine furniture, floral wallpaper, and fireplaces in every room create the warm feeling of a country home. Full breakfasts, afternoon wine and hors d'oeuvres, and late-night cookies are served in a cheery lobby and parlor filled with early American antiques, an original carousel horse, and handmade crafts. Each room has a refrigerator stocked with complimentary soft drinks. All private baths. Special suites available. Special-occasion packages. Friendly, thoughtful service. 831/625-5222. MC, V; others also accepted. For two, mostly from $95 to $180.

CYPRESS INN (Lincoln Street and Seventh Avenue). A grand hotel, the Cypress Inn has a Moorish Mediterranean facade. Warm-toned interiors with floral fabrics. Many ocean-view rooms. The unique tower suite offers views to Point Lobos. A decanter of sherry and continental breakfast are complimentary with each room. Movie posters in the cozy cocktail lounge feature Doris Day, one of the owners, whose love of animals is extended to guests; this hotel is pet-friendly. Locals out for a walk with their dogs often stop by the lounge. 831/624-3871, 800/443-7443. AX, MC, V. For two, $110 to $285. Off-season rates available.

GREEN LANTERN INN (Seventh Avenue and Casanova Street). Carmel-stone walkways lead through gardens to a variety of rooms, ranging from very cozy to spacious with lofts. Both European feeling and Old Carmel ambiance. Some individual cottages. Many rooms have special features. The Teak Room was designed especially for writers. Hobbit ceilings lead to a private attic retreat with an antique desk lighted by an ocean-view dormer window. The inn is just a few blocks to town or the beach. All rooms have private baths; some, fireplaces. Homemade bread, muffins, cereals, fresh fruit, and beverages are served for breakfast in a French-country dining area or outside in the courtyard. Afternoon tea and wine. 831/624-4392. AX, MC, V; others also accepted. For two from $120 to $175.

HAPPY LANDING INN (Monte Verde between Fifth and Sixth Avenues). Built in 1925 as a family retreat, this early Comstock-designed inn offers quintessential bed and breakfast lodging at moderate rates. Carmel-stone paths lead through a country garden with gazebo and pond to pink cottages with wood cathedral ceilings and antiques. Set back from a quiet wooded street, the inn is an easy walk to beaches and the village. All rooms have private baths; some, fireplaces. Breakfast served in your room. Early room reservations suggested. 831/624-7917. MC, V. For two from $90 to $110. Suites, $145.

LA PLAYA HOTEL (Eighth Avenue and Camino Real). This Mediterranean-style historic hotel, which began as a large private estate, has grounds that were voted by locals as the loveliest garden walk in Monterey County. Oriental rugs cover terra-cotta floors in the stylish lobby. Warm yourself by the white-marble fireplace. Spanish-style room decor. Seventy-five units on three levels, many with ocean views. Private patio rooms available. Cottages have sleeping accommodations for up to eight adults, full kitchens, wet bars, patios, wood-burning fireplaces. Full-service hotel. Pool, spa. Terrace Grill Restaurant with courtyard dining overlooking the gardens, and a convivial pub. While near the pub, walk through Carmel's history in extensive displays of photographs. 831/624-6476, 800/582-8900. AX, MC, V; others also accepted. Rooms for two from $120 to $220; suites $215 to $395, cottages $215 to $495.

MISSION RANCH (26270 Dolores Street, just outside the city limits, by the mission). Clint Eastwood saved this former ranch and resort from razing. The restoration's award-winning attention to detail has preserved the charming exteriors of the former century-old farmhouse, creamery, and barn, and the 1930s cottages. Handmade quilts, trademark oversized furniture, and Carmel stone fireplaces add special touches to renovated and newly built rooms. Rooms are clustered in different sections. Barn rooms are standard units; meadow-view units are more deluxe with views to the ocean beyond. The six units in the Martin Farmhouse are arranged around a central parlor. Tennis courts. Twenty-one acres to enjoy, complete with grazing lambs. Lively full piano bar and Mission Ranch Restaurant. Pastoral views opening to panoramic ocean vistas. It's an easy walk to Carmel River Beach, a twenty-minute walk to the village. 831/624-6436, 800/538-8221. Fax: 831/626-4163. AX, MC, V. For two from $95 to $225.

OUTSIDE OF CARMEL: CARMEL HIGHLANDS

See the next chapter (page 167), on points south, for information about the Highlands area, a two-mile stretch of coastline that begins four miles south of Carmel. I mention it here because the Highlands Inn (831/624-3801), with the California Market casual restaurant and ultradeluxe Pacific's Edge Restaurant (831/622-5445), caters to Carmel visitors. I have often been stopped on Ocean Avenue by disoriented people trying to find the Highlands. Go south, my friends.

OUTSIDE OF CARMEL: CARMEL VALLEY

A popular lodging place for visitors to Carmel-by-the-Sea, Carmel Valley has tennis, golf, and sunny summer weather. Various lodges attract many to this area. For a tour of it see the Carmel Valley section (page 232).

RESTAURANTS

If you move to Carmel don't bother to pack your kitchen. One couple I know dines out five days a week. These are some favorites. There are more than sixty restaurants in Carmel. More are noted under The Village Tour (page 149).

The first three restaurants are ones we enjoy more if our young children are not with us.

IN CARMEL-BY-THE-SEA

CASANOVA (Fifth Avenue and Mission Street). Nooks, fireplaces, and open-air dining create a romantic setting in this Spanish-style historic home. Italian and French country-style three-course dinners melt any palate and heart. The grilled rack of lamb is a house specialty. The owner or maitre d' will lead you on a personal tour of the more than 20,000-bottle hand-excavated wine cellar under the restaurant. Hollywood stargazing for those who are looking. American-style breakfasts, Sunday brunch and Italian and French lunches are also served (831/625-0501). MC, V. Three-course dinners from $24 to $37.

FRENCH POODLE (Fifth Avenue and Junipero Avenue). In this elegant third-generation French restaurant the chef-owner prepares delicate, complex sauces. Specialties include abalone, duck, lamb, and fresh-daily fish. 831/624-8643. AX, MC, V. Entrees from $16 to $26.

LA BOHEME (Dolores Street and Seventh Avenue). Walls designed to look like a village surround exquisitely set tables and bench seating. One choice of entree is served each evening, with an alternative vegetarian selection available. Diners savor the freshest ingredients and meticulous French preparation. A monthly menu is available at the restaurant. All dinners are prix fixe and include soup and salad garnie. 831/624-7500. www.laboheme.com. MC, V. Prix fixe $21.75.

BULLY III (in the Adobe Inn, Dolores Street and Eighth Avenue). In your choice of a lively pub or casual English lodge dining room, a variety of American dishes featuring prime rib is served. Pub fare featuring tasty prime rib reuben is available in the lodge dining room on weekdays. Lunch and dinner. 831/625-1750. AX, MC, V; others also accepted. Pub selections, mostly under $10. Dining room entrees mostly under $20.

CAFE BERLIN (on the west side of Junipero Avenue between Fifth Avenue and Sixth Avenue). A Bavarian eatery, the cafe is popular with diners who enjoy authentic German food. Sauerbraten and goulash are favorites. 831/626-8181. Lunch and dinner. AX, MC, V. Entrees from $9.95 to $18.95.

CAFE NAPOLI (Ocean Avenue between Dolores and Lincoln) and LITTLE NAPOLI (Dolores near Seventh). Italian flags and garlic braids adorn these two sister restaurants where lively conviviality gives diners the feeling of being in Italy and Carmel simultaneously. Attentive waitstaff will converse with you in Italian at your pleasure. The portions are delicious and beyond ample. If the Ocean Avenue line is too long, the host will escort you to Little Napoli, where beam ceilings and a warming fireplace add a romantic touch. Menus are identical. Begin with bruchetta topped with pomodoro, pesto, or cambonzola cheese. A dozen pizzas and seven salad selections complement a variety of southern Italian pastas. My personal favorite, the cannelloni tricolor, looks like an Italian flag, with alternating red marinara, white alfredo, and green pesto sauces—and tastes like the best of two worlds. Open daily. Lunch and dinner. 831/625-4033. MC, V. Entrees from $8 to $16.

CARMEL BATES CAFE (on Mission Street between Ocean Avenue and Sixth Avenue). Lei Lei Bates prepares fresh homemade scones and homemade jams. You'll also find a dose of local humor on the walls covered with Bates's insightful cartoons—as well as the opportunity to talk with the artist who will share memories of Carmel. Request a scone in place of toast to accompany your perfectly cooked omelette and herbed cottage fried potatoes. Breakfast and lunch. 831/624-1922. MC, V. Selections from $4.

CHEZ CHRISTIAN (in the Court of the Golden Bough on Ocean Avenue at Monte Verde Street). This bistro with a cozy home feeling serves fine French cuisine, featuring pastas, seafood, and duck. Great burgers highlight indoor and outdoor lunches. Lunch 11:30 a.m. to 2:30 p.m. Fridays and Saturdays. Dinner 5 to 9:30 p.m. Tuesday through Sunday. 831/625-4331. MC, V. Dinner entrees from $15 to $19.75.

CHINA GOURMET (Fifth Avenue between Dolores Street and San Carlos Street). Casual surroundings and friendly, gracious service highlight Mandarin Chinese fare. Tasty kung pao chicken. Lunch, dinner, or take-out service. 831/624-3941. AX, MC, V; others also accepted. Entrees from $7 to $10.

FLYING FISH GRILL (Mission Street between Ocean Avenue and Seventh Avenue, Carmel Plaza). At this local favorite, colorful wooden fish fly over fifteen slatted redwood booths constructed by chef and owner Kenny Fukumoto. Fresh fish entrees rooted in Asian cuisine are prepared with artistic and meticulous care. California roll, a sushi roll with crabcake and avocado, is one of eight first courses. Almond seabass and seafood (*yosenabe*) clay pots are top choices. 831/625-1962. AX, MC, V; others also accepted. Entrees from $16 to $19.

FORGE IN THE FOREST AND THE GENERAL STORE (Fifth Avenue and Junipero Avenue). Years ago this really was the general store, with a telegraph office in front. Metal sculptures were welded in the forge. Today, cheery gardens make a delightful spot for an outdoor casual lunch. Original board-and-batten walls frame the wine cellar–style dining room. A fire pit and hand-carved bar warm the inviting pub for foggy days and late nights. Great hamburgers, quesadillas, and Chinese chicken salad for lunch. Grilled prawns are a favorite for dinner. A special wine cellar room is perfect for private parties (eight to twelve). Murder Mystery Dinners are organized on selected evenings and upon request. Lunch, dinner, Saturday and Sunday brunch. 831/624-2233. MC, V. Dinner entrees from $9.95 to $17.

GRASINGS (on the corner of Sixth and Mission). With sterling culinary résumés, chefs Kurt Grasing and Narsai David bring delectable coastal cuisine to this bright, comfortable restaurant. Grasing prepares the entrees and David contributes international travel experience and research. Grilled duck breast with bitter chocolate and raspberries and a polenta tower with grilled vegetables and a spicy tomato sauce are just a few of the tempting entrees. Grasing also excels with fish and shrimp. In addition to the sensational à la carte entrees, the special Grasing Menu features a prix-fixe three-course meal. Dinner and lunch. 831/624-6562. AX, MC, V. Dinner entrees from $13.50 to $18.75.

HOG'S BREATH INN (San Carlos Street between Fifth Avenue and Sixth Avenue). Visitors often want to know where to find Clint Eastwood's first restaurant. Go to the gas station at the corner of Fifth and San Carlos. Cross to the opposite side of San Carlos. Walk toward town for about fifty yards along San Carlos. You will see two ten-foot poles, one with an old-fashioned gas lamp on it and one with a tusked hog's head. Walk between the poles, down the walkway, and you'll find the Hog's Breath Inn. The outdoor patio with fireplaces is lively and refreshing. Mounted boars' heads are focal points of the interior restaurant. The pub/lounge is a popular late-night spot. Complimentary hors d'oeuvres are served Sunday through Thursday between 4 and 6 p.m. The menu items refer to Eastwood film names and characters—examples include the Dirty Harry Burger and the Mysterious Misty tuna sandwich for lunch. Lunch and dinner daily. Sunday brunch. Full bar open until 2 a.m. 831/625-1044. AX, MC, V. Dinner entrees from $10 to $24.

THE COTTAGE (Lincoln Street between Ocean and Seventh). Handpainted arches lead to fireplace-warmed rooms with wonderful food. Quintessential cottage atmosphere. Beveled lead glass enhances the Snug Room and Stone Room, which can be reserved for groups. Heavenly hollandaise sauce on seven selections of eggs Benedict, panettone French toast, great omelettes, and more. Locals vote the soups—especially the artichoke soup—the best on the Peninsula. Continental dinner selections include pizzas and ravioli. Breakfast and lunch daily. Dinner Thursday through Saturday. 831/625-6260. MC, V. Dinner entrees from $7.50 to $14.95.

PÂTISSERIE BOISSIERE (Mission Street between Ocean Avenue and Seventh Avenue, Carmel Plaza). Candlelight, a warming fire, and comfortable tables offer a relaxing venue for lunch or dinner. Pasta selections, quiche, and dinner pies are among the selections. Delectable European desserts and an extensive list of coffees are served all day. If you are looking for a delicious picnic at the beach or on the woodland trails, call in advance for the picnic menu featuring an assortment of sandwiches on baguettes, a veggie burger, and a snow crab and rock shrimp salad sandwich. Lunch daily. Picnic menu, Monday through Friday. Dinner, Wednesday though Sunday. 831/624-5008. AX, MC, V. Dinner entrees from $8.95 to $13.95.

OUTSIDE CARMEL-BY-THE-SEA

The next three restaurants are samples of the many eating places located across Highway 1 from Carmel Village, in the Crossroads Center and Barnyard shopping areas. Take the Rio Road exit east. Turn at the first right for the Crossroads. For the Barnyard turn left at the next street, Carmel Rancho Boulevard. Look left for the large groupings of Western wood buildings, lit with garlands of white lights at night.

RIO GRILL (in the Crossroads Center, 101 Crossroads Boulevard). A local favorite, the Rio Grill has a lively atmosphere. Paper table coverings for the artists or kids with you. Nouveau Southwestern-Californian decor. Baby-back ribs and smoked salmon tostadas are samples on a menu that features regional ingredients and innovative California cuisine with a Southwestern flair. Lunch, dinner, lounge with full bar. 831/625-5436. AX, MC, V. Dinner entrees from $13 to $23.

ROBATA (3658 The Barnyard). A traditional setting with a Japanese garden, Robata has been voted the best Japanese restaurant in Monterey County. Sushi; tempura and fried oysters; mesquite grill cooking to perfection. Dinner only. 831/624-2643. AX, MC, V. Entrees from $11 to $21.

ROBERT KINCAID'S BISTRO (217 Crossroads Boulevard, at the Crossroads). Thick beams, burnt-sienna washed enclaves, and arched doorways provide a romantic ambiance. Eighteenth-century Tuscan and French Provincial furnishings add to the feel of a French country inn. Acclaimed as a favorite local chef, Robert Kincaid offers menus that showcase his style of classic French cuisine. The crisp roast duckling half, sliced, with cherry sauce was voted best duck on the Peninsula by the *San Francisco Chronicle*. The one-page menu changes often. Dinner only, Monday through Saturday. 831/624-9626. AX, MC, V, and others. Entrees from $17.95 to $26.95.

INTRODUCTION TO CARMEL WITH HISTORICAL HIGHLIGHTS

"I wandered out to the point and looked across to the deserted beach and sloping forests, and thought it was one of the most beautiful resort sites ever conceived." A hundred-some years after developer Charles Devendorf thus envisioned Carmel, hundreds of thousands of visitors each year agree. The wonder is that this one-mile-square "storybook hamlet in the forest" also maintains a strong residential community with ecologically important coastal, forest, and wetlands habitats. Carmel's future depends on the delicate balance struck by developers, artists, preservationists, families, and merchants who live side by side but are often worlds apart in their ideas of what Carmel is to be.

Many businesses, including the neighborhood drugstore and bakery, serve residents' needs as they have for decades. Home delivery of prescriptions and the tradition of a free cookie for the neighborhood youngster continue on the same streets with what is probably the greatest number of galleries and specialty shops per capita of any city in the United States. Through the years, numerous forest, ocean bluff, and village walking trails—some centuries old—have served as quiet passageways for the first inhabitants, the missionaries, a throng of famous writers and artists, and locals. In summer the sidewalks running the length of the Ocean Avenue business district stay packed with visitors.

The pure white sands that first caught Devendorf's eye in the 1890s still rise in sixty-foot dunes from the foaming waves at Ocean Beach to sculpt

DIRECTIONS

From the Pebble Beach Tour. *If you are continuing from the Pebble Beach tour (page 120) follow the signs on Seventeen Mile Drive that direct you to the right to Carmel. You will exit Pebble Beach through the Carmel Gate. After the first stop sign follow the curve of the road. The eucalyptus trees on your right were a wind-break for an original rancho. The oldest house in Carmel, built in 1864, is hidden from street view behind shrub fences. You will now be traveling south on San Antonio Avenue, which at the next stop sign intersects Ocean Avenue. Turn right and you will enter the beach parking lot. This is one of the lots where you can park all day. From here it is a delightful tree-shaded five-minute uphill walk to the first shops and galleries.*

If you are in a hurry to shop or dine, and you want to skip the uphill walk and save the beach until later, then turn left at Ocean Avenue instead. Drive up the hill nine blocks. Turn right at Junipero Avenue. You will drive by the Carmel Plaza (and pass tour bus parking); the village tour connects at the Plaza, on the north side of Ocean Avenue. You can also begin the tours at any point in the descriptions, as they are loop tours.

Ocean Avenue can be very congested. It is better to drive on a parallel street such as Seventh Avenue on busy days.

From the Monterey Bay Aquarium. *Follow David Avenue up the hill to its intersection with Route 68/Forest Avenue, and turn left. Travel east to Highway 1, staying in the right lane to enter Highway 1 south. Continue below.*

To Carmel, for Highway 1 travelers. *Carmel is one and a half miles south of Pacific Grove and four miles north of Point Lobos. From Highway 1 take the Ocean Avenue exit. Travel west, down-hill, past one stop sign. For Carmel Plaza turn left at the next stop sign, onto Junipero Avenue. Or continue on Ocean Avenue down the hill to park at the beach or start a tour there.*

From Highway 1 southbound. *An alternate entrance to Carmel is via Carpenter Street. Travel south on Highway 1 past the Highway 68/Pacific Grove exit for one-half mile. Turn right at the first light, which is the Carpenter Street exit. Follow truck route signs. Turn right on Third Avenue (city parking is available at the corner of Third Avenue and Junipero Avenue), then left at Junipero Avenue, and continue four more blocks to the village.*

To Mission Carmel and Mission Trail Park. *From Highway 1 take the Rio Road exit (one mile south of the Ocean Avenue exit). Travel one-half mile west. Look for Mission Carmel on the left. Parking is available at and around the mission, and Mission Trail Park is across the street. For the Carmel River Beach follow Rio Road to Santa Lucia Street and turn left. After about five blocks turn left on Carmelo Street, which leads to the large parking lot near the lagoon at the beach.*

Carmel's western boundary. The expansive beach is hemmed by emerald Pescadero Point to the north and the rugged Abalone Point to the south. These two headlands block the intrusion of river and ocean sediment, which darken so many California beaches. The powerful winter waves of El Niño in 1998 devoured much of the sands from Carmel Beach; the gentler waves of summer may take a number of years to replenish the shore.

The dazzling sands of Ocean Beach are the result of sixty million years of earthquake and volcanic action. Colliding plates of the earth's crusts caused molten magma to form deep under the earth's surface. Earthquakes and collisions thrust the magma, which had cooled to form granite, upward. Ground smaller and smaller by relentless waves, the pure quartz crystals and feldspar of the exposed granite whitewash the shores at Ocean Beach.

A cypress-canopied walking path winds above the dunes and melds with the narrow and windy Scenic Drive, which curves with the city limits along the ocean's shoreline south to the Carmel River. In January 1603 the Spanish explorer Sebastian Vizcaino explored "a copious river descending from high-snow covered mountains." During rainy season, this river is like a liquid chainsaw artist, carving new patterns in its banks daily as it flows under Highway 1 to its outlet at Carmel River Beach on the southern outskirts of the city limits.

In honor of the Carmelite fathers who were his chaplains Vizcaino named this river "El Rio Carmelo." The name "Carmel" refers to the order of monks who founded their monastery at Mount Carmel in the Holy Land in the thirteenth century. From 1603, "El Rio Carmelo" is one of the oldest

Eurocentric place names in the United States—it beat Plymouth Rock by several years.

When the Spanish landed they were met by the first inhabitants of this land, a peaceful tribe of people who were later identified in mission records as the Rumsien. The Rumsien settled in at least two places in Carmel, one close to this river and the other one by San Jose Creek, to the south. In 1993 rushing storm-swollen waters of the Carmel River washed away sand dunes from an ancestral site at Carmel River Beach that may date back four thousand years. More than twenty mortars for acorn grinding were uncovered. Most archaeologists believe the Esselen tribal group was here prior to the Rumsien.

The beautifully restored Mission San Carlos Borromeo Del Rio Carmelo, known as Mission Carmel, lies near the southeastern border of Carmel. Father Junipero Serra, founding father of the California missions, was dissatisfied with the first, 1770 mission location in Monterey. In 1771 he moved the mission to Carmel, which he described as "a locality indeed most delightful and suitable because of the excellent quality of the land and the water supply necessary for abundant harvests." It also exemplified Serra's desire for a division between church and military, especially to keep the Rumsien and Esselen, as well as women of other groups, separated from the often raucous soldiers. The military remained at the Presidio in Monterey. Father Serra went on to found nine more missions. He envisioned a great stone church, but a wooden chapel and adobe outbuildings were his headquarters until his death in 1784. He was buried in the sanctuary of his beloved mission at Carmel. The stone church was not completed until 1797; later yet, when the mission was restored, he was buried under its altar. Two centuries after Serra's death Pope John Paul II attended beatification ceremonies in Carmel as part of the steps to sainthood for Serra.

The missions were funded by an endowment fund set up by the Jesuits, transferred to the Franciscans, and then held in trust by first the Spanish and subsequently the Mexican government. They served a dual purpose, to expand the teaching of Christianity to aboriginal peoples and to serve the Spanish government as the means to subjugate the tribal populations of California lands.

During the Carmel mission period the Rumsien and neighboring Esselen people were both enticed from and forced to leave their native villages and to relocate onto mission land. The natives who were Christianized were called *neophytes*. They were put to work, often against their will, building the mission, planting and tending the surrounding orchards, and caring for the mission cattle.

The mission system had been abandoned by 1836. The Mexican government had divided the mission land among settlers, with some neophytes

Mission San Carlos Borromeo Del Rio Carmelo

receiving land shares. The dwindled numbers of Rumsien and Esselen who had survived disease and relocation were scattered. Although both the Rumsien and Esselen tribes have been declared extinct by the U.S. government, a number of direct Esselen and Rumsien descendants continue their ceremonial traditions and those of other tribes. The Ventana Wilderness Camp near Carmel Valley is one center for tribal information.

At the mission site by the 1860s, "Cattle had free access, broken columns were strewn around, thousands of birds lived in nooks," according to the written captions under historic drawings that hang on interior mission walls. Once a year a mass was held among the ruins to commemorate the feast day of its patron saint, San Carlos Borromeo, a leading Catholic reformer of the Counter-Reformation. Robert Louis Stevenson attended the event in 1879 and suggested that the Monterey newspaper start a fund drive for restoration of the buildings. Private donations were then collected from visitors, who were brought by horse-drawn tally-hos to the abandoned mission as part of the Seventeen Mile Drive tours offered by Hotel Del Monte. A roof was raised, but authentic restoration did not begin until a half-century later under the direction of Harry Downie.

In the late 1800s the presence of the mission and the Methodist community of Pacific Grove were the inspiration for a "Catholic resort" to be known as Carmel-by-the-Sea. Abbie Jane Hunter from San Francisco, founder of the Women's Real Estate Investment Company in San Francisco, joined investor Santiago Duckworth in the venture. Her cottage at the corner of Guadalupe Street and Fourth Avenue is beautifully preserved and includes Carmel's only woman mayor, Jean Grace, in its long succession of owners. The majority of early lots were bought by San Francisco school teachers and administrators.

The railroad was not extended to Carmel, Duckworth developed other interests, and the dream of a Catholic resort folded. By 1901, three-quarters of what is now Carmel-by-the-Sea was owned by San Francisco attorney Frank Powers and his wife, artist Jane Gallatin Powers, whose father was president of one of the largest hardware, steel, and iron companies on the Pacific Coast. Eschewing a fancy mansion, the couple chose to live in a rustic log cabin with a dirt floor. The cabin can still be seen on the dunes at the northern border of the town. In 1902, financier Frank Powers teamed up with Charles Devendorf to form the Carmel Land Development Company. Devendorf's first marketing brochure was addressed to "School Teachers of California and other Brain Workers of Indoor Employment." Prospective buyers and resort guests were met at the Monterey train station, then transported for the half-day trip by buckboard stage. Some of the male passengers would walk partway when the straining horses couldn't make it up the steep hill to Carmel.

Stanford University professors had homes built along Camino Real, soon to be known as Professor's Row. Word of Carmel spread and was caught by George Sterling, a San Francisco poet and fellow member of the San Francisco Bohemian Club with Frank Powers. Devendorf and Frank and Jane Powers encouraged artists and writers, and they came—some to visit, some to stay. One of the first, writer Mary Austin, wrote in a "wik-i-up" tree house. Obscured from view, her first home is maintained as a private residence. The Mary Austin minipark honors her contributions to the literary and Carmel world.

Xavier Martinez, like many other San Francisco artists, had his studio and much of his work destroyed in the earthquake of 1906. San Franciscans fleeing their devastated city swelled the population of Carmel. The arty group, known as the Seacoast Bohemians, grew in numbers and local recognition. Names associated with this group and Carmel either as visitors or residents included Jack London, Sinclair Lewis, Upton Sinclair, William Rose Benet, and Xavier Martinez. Their community was headlined in a 1910 *Los Angeles Times* as a "Hotbed of Soulful Culture, Vortex of Erotic Erudition."

The unbohemian side of Carmel in those days boasted a dozen stores, two stables, a school, and a library. The community was close to what Devendorf actually described, an "all round healthy little town."

The natural beauty and freedom of the area attracted photographers. Edward Weston moved to Carmel in 1929 and set up a small portrait studio. Through his close-ups of rocks and details of trees and other natural objects Weston brought nature's own designs into the area of the abstract in art. His four sons joined him in Carmel. Brett Weston and Cole Weston shared exclusive printing of their father's work after he was stricken with Parkinson's disease in his later life. Cole Weston managed the Carmel Sunset Cultural Center in the late 1960s and, together with Ansel Adams and others, formed the Friends of Photography. Although relocated from Carmel to San Francisco in 1987, the nonprofit organization continues to play a leading role in fostering creative photography.

When I talked with the energetic Cole Weston, now famous in his own right as a color photographer and director of local plays, about his childhood memories of Carmel, he told of being able to run from the top of Ocean Avenue to the beach through a natural pathway of vacant lots. Nowadays one still hears more rustling of leaves than rumbling of car engines on pine-scented residential streets. The winding roads that lead to residential areas have neither sidewalks, streetlights, nor numbers. One story goes that early bohemian artists and writers kept the numbers off to make it almost impossible for Internal Revenue agents to find their houses. In 1953 a bill was introduced in the California State Legislature that would withhold state gas tax funds from cities without house numbers. Rather than change the numbering system Carmel's city attorney called for a movement to secede from the state. The state bill failed, and Carmel remained in California.

Distinctive architecture helps with directions and highlights Carmel's respect for individualism. Poet Robinson Jeffers commissioned a house of stones carted up from the beach and added rooms and a three-story adaptation of an Irish tower with his own hands. With this Tor House as a base and inspiration, Jeffers wrote and published several volumes of poetry seemingly endemic to this area. His long narrative poems welded his own individual spirit with that of soaring hawks and granite and tapped the raw sensuous beauty of the coast southward through the Big Sur area.

Throughout the village, hand-carved and hand-forged gates lead to log cabins, redwood board-and-battens, thick-walled colonial revival homes, Spanish villas, subterranean modern structures, and the only Frank Lloyd Wright home on the Monterey Peninsula. Cottages in the storybook style developed by Hugh Comstock and emulated by others dot the residential and business sections. Several of the residences and homes in Carmel have entrances or exteriors that are covered with a soft, irregularly shaped stone with creamy golden coloring. Known as Carmel stone, these sedimentary rocks are quarried at the base of the Santa Lucias in Carmel Valley. Some of them might be from the quarry presently owned by Clint Eastwood.

Ocean Avenue descends from Highway 1 through the upper residential section to the village core. At the east end of the business section Junipero Avenue intersects Ocean Avenue. To your left a sign points uphill to the Mountain Theater, where patrons are warmed by firepits on cool nights as a tradition begun in 1910 of enjoying plays under the stars continues. Dame Judith Anderson starred here in Jeffers's first successful play, *The Tower Beyond Tragedy*.

The relatively steep Ocean Avenue, known as the Devil's Staircase in its dirt road days, remained unpaved for years with consent of the majority of citizens as a deterrent to the village's development for tourism. A Bill Bates cartoon (he's a well-known Carmel artist) lampooning the present road shows the driver of a car turning into a skeleton as he waits for a chance to cross Ocean Avenue, packed with cars and tourists, on a typical summer weekend. This main artery is lined with an array of historic businesses, intriguing shops, and the usual sweatshirt and cup collectibles stores.

Inns were built as buffers between business and the surrounding residential section. Businesses are also zoned as resident-serving and tourist-serving. Attempts by the city council to enlarge the tourist-serving section of the city are met with referendums and full-page newspaper ads to "Save Carmel."

The post office is the heart of the village for residents. Since their houses have no numbers, residents collect their mail here every day. Outside the front door and around their boxes they share personal tidbits and discuss the latest hot political topic—whether it be the rerouting of the freeway or the permit denial for a tree's removal.

Some of the best-kept secrets in Carmel are found on side streets and along narrow walkways. Tucked in Spanish-style courtyards and English garden alcoves, specialty shops and museum-quality galleries offer anything from Gucci fashionware to keepsake hand-quilted vests, from Remington sculptures to canvases being created in the moment by artists outside their front doors, from Guatemalan rainmakers to antique violins, from hand-carved carousel horses to Eastwood-signature oversized leather chairs.

Romantic cottages and luxury inns with ocean views share wooded nooks with bistros, patisseries, and elegant restaurants. From the historic Pine Inn you can view the forest of Pebble Beach, which grows into the northern border of Carmel. From bay-view rooms you can see Carmel Beach. The snowy sands extend north to rocky outcroppings and the emerald links of Pebble Beach.

Along with your favorite shop and place to view a sunset, Carmel offers plenty of benches for people-watching. Many tourists are watching for

Carmel's most famous citizen, actor and Academy Award–winning director Clint Eastwood, who served one term as mayor beginning in 1986. Eastwood fans flooded the town during the duration of his term, seeking him and settling for Eastwood posters, cups, and a meal or drink at his co-owned restaurant, Hog's Breath Inn. The most asked questions from tourists are still about his where-abouts.

Since its beginning Carmel has been a community with an independent spirit. On each Halloween, children and dignitaries still parade down Ocean Avenue to mark the day and commemorate the town's founding. Through years of community action the beaches remain bare of commercial development. Issues are passionately discussed in town meetings.

Knowing where to find the best of Carmel while avoiding the throngs of tourists that swarm the village on high-season weekends is an insider's art. When tree-lined Ocean Avenue, the main thoroughfare, is packed you can feel like a sequestered guest as you explore hidden passageways to one-of-a-kind shops and wander peaceful forest trails described in this chapter. Then relax on beaches shared only with gentle breezes, perhaps an artist with easel perched on a rocky outcrop, and the glances of a bobbing sea otter.

TOURS

How should you see Carmel? Slowly. One suggestion would be to complete the village tour first. It features the shops, galleries, and history of the village core—one of the most charming and popular shopping areas in America. To complete the day or to fill another one choose portions or all of the coastal and woodland walks, especially at Carmel Mission, to experience the beautiful natural environment. As you plan your day first consider phoning the cultural and historic destinations of interest to you for special programs and schedule changes.

THE VILLAGE TOUR

This tour can be completed in one hour but it would be better to allot at least three, and it could last three weeks. In Carmel you are either "north of Ocean" or "south of Ocean." Let's begin with the south side of Ocean Avenue. This would be on your right as you walk uphill from the Carmel Beach. (If you are starting at the Plaza at the top of Ocean, skip ahead in this text to Devendorf Park, page 156. All tour buses park at the Plaza.)

From its beginning Carmel has been known as a village in a forest. Native Monterey pines fill the upper slopes while gray-foliaged oaks hug the lower lands. Trees help decipher the history of the location. Before you cross Ocean Avenue, at the northwest corner is the largest tree in the village, a blue-gum eucalyptus that measures twenty-two feet and eight inches around at the trunk. The most popular theory about this tree, a native of Australia, is that its seed was probably brought here by early Spanish explorers or mission padres. The tree possibly marked old rancho boundaries. A walking-tour map to sixty-one of the city's heritage trees is available at the visitor's center.

As you walk uphill on Ocean, as throughout Carmel, twisted cypress, spreading oaks, tall eucalyptus, and native Monterey pine shade your walk. Devendorf sold many lots with the condition that the buyers agree to plant trees. One of Carmel's first laws prohibited the cutting of trees without city approval.

A drawing by local artist Bill Bates shows a house on fire as the owner yells to the firemen: "To hell with the house; save the trees." The community is currently evaluating its stringent tree ordinances because of the numerous trees that have fallen as a result of El Niño storms and pitch pine canker.

The first business on your right as you walk up Ocean Avenue is the Lamplighters Inn—located at Ocean Avenue and Camino Real. These story-book cottages with picturesque lanterns are one of Carmel's oldest (1916) and quaintest tourist courts. If you have children with you they will enjoy visiting the elves in the front courtyard.

While many of their garrets have disappeared in Carmel, there are many local artists who still display their work in Carmel's galleries and shops. In the local tradition some artists still create by gallery windows, or doors, as well as in back rooms. More than sixty galleries crowd Carmel. They often offer special shows and feature particular artists along with museum-quality collections. Some galleries are mass-production print and art dealers. There is no more pressure to buy art in stores of reputable dealers than in a museum. You will walk by some of the especially memorable galleries on this tour. On Dolores Street, between Fifth and Sixth Avenues, about a dozen are grouped in what is sometimes called Gallery Row. A Carmel gallery guide is available at the visitor's center and at many galleries.

From the corner of Monte Verde and Ocean, city hall is located half a block south on Monte Verde Street. (On another outing you might choose to hike directly up the parking lot and steps behind city hall to see the gardens of Wayfarer Church, with their outlet to Lincoln Street, described on page 152.) City hall is memorable mainly for some of the mayors that Carmel has voted in. Perry Newberry posted ads that admonished, "If you truly want Carmel to become a boosting, hustling, wide-awake, lively metropolis, DON'T VOTE FOR PERRY NEWBERRY." More than twenty years ago, Mayor Barney Laiolo took the law into his own hands and dressed in a disguise to help police stop drug deals in a local park. Clint Eastwood, by being Clint Eastwood, increased world recognition of the hamlet, but many cite his support of the Carmel Youth Center as an endearing accomplishment in his mayoral term.

For this tour, continue on Ocean Avenue. A few doors up, the aromas of chocolate and candies will sweeten your walk if you stop in at the Cottage of Sweets (831/624-5170), outlet for the Carmel Candy and Confections Company. California Wine Truffles and old-fashioned favorites await you. Imported English candies are also popular. We buy English Allsorts here for the outdoor Forest Theater movies. The Cottage of Sweets is cited as the original ticket booth area of the Golden Bough Theater, which opened in 1924 to accolades as the "crown jewel of small American theaters," but burned twice during separate productions of *By Candlelight*. Four entrances invite visitors through what remains, the rebuilt Court of the Golden Bough. The founder, Edward "Ted" Kuster, had been a successful lawyer in Los Angeles with a yen for theater and a continuing relationship with his former wife Una and her later husband, the poet laureate of the Central Coast, Robinson "Robin" Jeffers.

The present court retains the original architecture, which has influenced many of Carmel's buildings. Fouratt-Simmons Real Estate is located in what was the lobby of the Golden Bough. A delightful miniatures shop named the Impulse Shoppes (831/624-3200), a coffee and tea specialty shop and more are tucked inside.

Continue on the south side of Ocean. The Seven Arts building at the corner of Lincoln and Ocean has launched many Carmel artists. You can view the lighting of the old studio at the Carmel Bay Company (831/624-3868), which follows the tradition of an old mercantile. It carries a fine selection of furnishings including one-of-a-kind salvaged wood furniture created by a local father-and-son team. Walk upstairs to bathe in the light of Edward Weston's former studio, now part of the store. With the exception of the stairway entry, the building and studio room remain the same as they were sixty years ago. Weston made a number of portraits here, including his famous one of Steinbeck and those of his second wife, Charis.

Halfway up the block on Lincoln is the Spanish Colonial–style La Rambla, which was built in 1929. Typical of this style are its thick whitewashed walls with irregularly placed windows, tile roofs, and decorative ironwork. An arcade leads through the center of this building to the Shop in the Garden (831/624-6047), where you'll find the metal artist Milton Williams Jr. continuing the work of his late father. At a garden corner you may observe him soldering artistic sculptures and whimsical fountains while his mother cuts artistic details such as delicate leaves. More than thirty-five years ago the senior Miltons bought this little backyard garden, then basically dirt with one fruit tree. Now their creations of countless waterfalls, copper and brass garden creatures, and lanterns share the courtyard with trees and lush greenery.

Find benches to rest on in the peaceful, Biblical gardens of the Church of the Wayfarer (831/624-3550) at the corner of Lincoln Street at Seventh Avenue. Planted in 1941, all the plants in this mature garden, such as aloe, tamarisk, rosemary, and olive, are labeled with their Biblical reference in either the New or Old Testament. Established in 1904, this Methodist Church is the oldest continuously operated church in Carmel. Its picturesque setting is a favorite for weddings. Eighteenth-century hand-carved Italian paneling graces the inside. Services as well as seasonal concerts are offered, with a new, thirty-two rank Soenstein pipe organ. Since each rank is a stop and provides for an additional instrument, you can imagine the quality and richness of tones.

Back on Ocean Avenue enjoy the aromas and tastes of the Carmel Bakery—Carmel's oldest, established in 1923 (831/626-8885). A full sandwich selection is available here also. You'll soon be walking by a hidden-away park that has benches for relaxing and for enjoying bakery treats. Another bakery, Wishart's (408/624-3870), at the top of Ocean on the north side, will entice you again midway through your walk. There, if a local child walks in with mom or dad, the kid will probably get a pat on the head, the daily joke, and a free cookie from the person behind the counter.

Farther up Ocean Avenue; the home store of Villeroy & Boch, the largest ceramic manufacturer in the world, offers first-quality merchandise at 30 percent below retail. People line up on those special days when Carmel resident Isabelle Von Boch, great-granddaughter of the founder, signs pieces, often to benefit Carmel schools.

Three doors up, the Robert Talbott Shop (831/624-1747) is a success story born in Carmel. In 1950 banker Robert Talbott and his wife Audrey left New York with young son Robb for Carmel. Audrey began making ties as gifts for friends and hand-sewed the first ties she sold. What began as a cottage industry with attention to detail and selection of the finest silks, cottons, wools, and linens has grown to a staff of two hundred. Production studios and offices are located on the Monterey Peninsula. The first shop was opened in Carmel in 1958. Another store is at the Lodge at Pebble Beach, and a third is in New York. Their outlet store is located in Carmel Valley; see page 236.

Follow Der Ling Lane for a short detour to the topiary gardens of the Dovecote and the light-radiating Thomas Kinkade Garden Gallery (831/626-1927). A showcase luminescent painting portrays the gallery itself.

Dolores Street, the next right turn from Ocean, is a study in Spanish colonial revival architecture. Note the outside staircases and upper porches. Halfway down the first block, a semicircle of benches, a stone drinking fountain, and a wooden gate frame the entrance of peaceful little Piccadilly Park.

Before 1981 the hanging plants and overflowing flower pots of the Piccadilly Nursery occupied this space. Threatened with development of the space into more shops after the nursery closed, the city purchased the lot. A moss-lined lane winds back from the gate to a fish pond, a tiny waterfall, and shaded English armchair–style benches. Volunteers from the city's Garden Society are completing a historic garden restoration.

Next to Piccadilly Park locals and visitors enjoy the friendly service and specialty ribs at Fabulous Toots Lagoon (831/625-1915). Just beyond, the New Masters Gallery (831/625-1511) displays original paintings and sculpture by more than sixty artists from four continents. Amid this selection of contemporary and historic art, you might view an "Audience with the Cardinal"—not in a church but among the illustrated one-liners on the animal kingdom found in the fine pun art of local Will Bullas. "A strong reality on this planet is a smile," is the Bullas perspective. "It disarms better than the threat of guns . . . I enjoy making people laugh . . . it's good medicine." Farther along Dolores, two blocks northeast of Eighth, the Digital Giraffe (831/624-1833, www.giraffe.com) presents the award-winning digital painting of Corinne Whitaker.

Across the street from the New Masters Gallery the gingerbread-style Tuck Box (831/624-6365) is a local favorite for afternoon tea. Lunch and dinner are also served. Built by Hugh Comstock in 1926 the Tuck Box followed in style his Hansel and Gretel Cottages, which you can see on the east side of Torres Street between Third and Fourth Streets. He built the original fairy-tale house for his wife's doll collection and business, and each cottage cost $100 to build. In 1993 the Hansel and Gretel Cottages were listed together for sale at $450,000. Comstock constructed at least eighteen Carmel buildings.

Walk a few doors south to the El Paseo Building. In this courtyard with its brick flagstones you'll see two Spanish figures that were sculpted by Joe Mora in 1928. The real estate office here has early Carmel photos and maps and warm fireplaces for cool days. If you are interested in real estate many long-time residents who now sell real estate will share their stories of the town— for example, about Charles Devendorf. In the early 1900s he was the genial real estate sales and land management end of the Carmel Land Development Company; until the city was incorporated he also was the leading town official, and did everything from helping deliver babies to settling builders' disputes. Perry Newberry, a writer, actor, and later preservationist mayor of Carmel, bought his Carmel lot for five dollars down and five dollars a month in 1910. In 1924 Devendorf reported he had traded some Stockton land he owned for Carmel acreage. Today, if you could trade your five-acre Stockton ranch with pool for a tiny-plotted Carmel board-and-batten fixer-upper you'd be getting a good deal.

As you walk back toward Ocean Avenue you can experience the artist's love affair at three special galleries. I drive the Laureles Grade summit over Carmel Valley (page 240) almost daily during the winter and spring to catch the play of fog and shadow. You can have the same experience and save the gas at Gallery Twenty One (831/626-2700), the hometown headquarters of Carmel resident artist Eyvind Earle. Ask for the invitation to view Earle's original oils in the viewing room. His eighty-one years of experience with layers of dark pigments and the creation of mist on canvas catch the essence of the Central Coast region.

Continue to the Bleich Gallery (831/624-9447) where Pebble Beach impressionist master George Bleich greets visitors on most Saturdays throughout the year. Bleich and his two sons painted their way around the world in the summer of 1997. You and your family can commission a painting that you create together with the artist in his Pebble Beach Studio (831/372-2717). Along with the painting, you'll receive a video of the entire process.

Light captured through the eye and lens is displayed at Photography West Gallery (831/625-1587). Monterey photographers such as Morley Baer and John Wimberley in addition to Ansel Adams and Edward and Brett Weston are displayed and sold.

Back on Ocean, head north again and look for the first archway called Las Tienda. At the archway the Sierra Club Shop (831/624-8032) is open Monday through Saturday 12:30 to 4:30 p.m. Hidden farther back in the courtyard, Caffe Cardinale Coffee Roasting Company offers indoor and patio seating.

The Doud Arcade is the next walkway that leads from Ocean to a courtyard of shops. Remodeled in the 1980s, the arcade now houses a variety of shops including Sun Country (831/625-5907), which specializes in kaleidoscopes and the glass creations of owner Ray Anderson, and Paolina's (831/624-5599), an indoor bistro. Exit on San Carlos.

At Thinker Toys (831/624-0441) on the corner of Seventh and San Carlos Avenue, the world of children's play is a world of imagination, warmth and creativity. No toys for violent play are sold at this store.

Between Seventh and Eighth at Reiners Stone House Terrace you can watch the Carmel street scene from a rooftop aerie while enjoying freshly made pasta at La Dolce Vita (831/624-3667). Try the crab ravioli with champagne cream sauce. Carmel is a dog lovers' town and the best behaved of local pooches join their "dads and moms" on the patio.

The Pasta Palate (831/625-6508) in the inner Terrace makes up to twenty-eight thousand tortellini a day. Visitors watch dough rollers and presses move the pasta to cutting blades. Choose from a variety of ingredients and colors. The goat cheese with sundried tomato is one of the owner's favorites. Fresh made-today pasta and sauces are available for takeout.

Across the street from Thinker Toys, Nielsen Brothers Market (831/624-6441) offers picnic fare, fresh fruit, and quality champagne. The wine shop stocks a selection of fine and vintage wines, including a Yquem, the famous wine from the Sauternes region of France, priced at more than eight hundred dollars. A mural of sights in Carmel painted by Bill Bates covers a wall outside the market.

For a few minutes' rest or a meal stop, take the insider passageway that begins on the other side of the building by Nielsen Market; pass through the Carmel Square Shops (the Owl's Nest has more than five hundred teddy bears and you will see more Bullas creations at Bullas Fun Art) to find a narrow walkway at the back left. Walk around and downstairs to emerge at the Court of Fountains. The glassed-in gazebo shops reflect the sparkles of the shooting fountains, and garden benches invite you to stay awhile. Anton & Michel Restaurant (831/624-2406) serves moderately priced lunches and dinners with deluxe food and service. Write a letter on handmade paper with an antique pen from Bittner's Fine Stationery & Writing Accessories (831/626-3510). Enjoy watching an artist at her easel: Lisa Bryan paints watercolor maps of the region, chronicles of her world journeys, and creates pictures of horses ready to gallop from the paper. Her son, Ashley Day, joined her in the production of the beautiful sketches of Carmel-by-the-Sea and the Monterey area collection (831/626-5435, www.modernweb.net/sketches).

Outside the courtyard, On the Beach Surf Shop, Inc. (831/624-7282) sells boogie boards, wet suits, and anything else you need to join the beach fun.

On Ocean Avenue at the corner of San Carlos Street a World War I arched monument designed by Carmel architect Charles Green fills the center divider. The monument replaced a horse trough; though it was made obsolete by the automobile the road was still unpaved when the monument was completed, since locals thought paving the roads might bring progress.

The Carmel Plaza, a three-level shopping center, fills the block at Ocean Avenue and Junipero Avenue. Gardens, fountains, and an outdoor fire pit are flanked by fifty stores and restaurants. Construction of this block-sized shopping center was stalled for two decades in the 1950s and 1960s as townspeople debated its size and needs in proportion to the town's.

As you enter the Plaza from Ocean Avenue you pass the Plaza Restaurant, on your right, which has a varied menu to fit the preferences of almost everyone in your party. Desserts here are scrumptious, even just to look at.

The Carmel Plaza Dollhouse is a short walk in. The custom-made revolving doll house was built to one-inch scale in 1984 at a cost of $25,395. Its draperies and soft goods are handmade, and many furnishings are signed by their artists.

Books Inc, on the entry level, offers an excellent collection of books on Monterey, Carmel, and the Central Coast. The Cheese Shop (831/625-2272) offers tastes of cheeses from around the world—more than 350 varieties of cheese. If you'd like both wine and cheese, the shop offers a selection of California and imported wines. They will ship your choice for you.

Tour bus parking is at the Plaza exit to Junipero Avenue. This is the midway point of the tour, where the loop back to the beach parking lot begins.

Cross Ocean Avenue at Mission Street. At the Mediterranean Market (831/624-2022), hanging dry sausages and gourmet cheeses indicate that this is a great place to get sandwiches, fine wines, gourmet food items, and deli fare for a picnic at the beach or just across the street at Devendorf Park. Other places to get picnic and food-to-go items on this side of Ocean Avenue include 5th Avenue Deli and Catering Co. (831/625-2688) between San Carlos and Dolores, Bruno's Market and Deli (831/624-3821) on Junipero Street, and Friar Tuck's (831/624-4274), which provides incredible service, at the corner of Fifth and Dolores.

After enjoying the Mediterranean Market walk down Ocean Avenue to the Nature Company (831/624-1334) to enjoy art, books, and fine gifts that celebrate the earth's beauty. Also on Ocean Avenue is the Dansk II shop, an outlet store. In the next block, between San Carlos and Dolores Streets, the Carmel Drug Store stands as a town landmark: it's been in business since 1910.

Back at Devendorf Park near Mission Street, artists, children at play, old timers, and picnickers share green lawns and manicured gardens and sometimes a concert. "The Patriarch," a Coast live oak recognized as the largest in the village, shades the southwest corner. This tract too was once within developer Charles Devendorf's holdings. He lowered the price on ocean frontage and threw in the park as an incentive to get citizens to vote for a resident-launched city deal to save ocean dunelands. It worked. Voters approved the deal in 1922.

Walk along Mission Street. A left turn at Sixth Avenue leads to the Firehouse, First Aid Center, and Harrison Memorial Park Branch Library (831/624-1366), the children's library and local history room annex, acquired when Clint Eastwood was mayor. In addition to children's library services the building also houses the Carmel History Library.

Back on Mission you can cross Sixth and find Carmel Fly Fishing & Outdoor (831/626-4537), featuring Orvis products and guides for summer fishing trips—depending on the conditions of local steelhead populations. Across the street, the catch is still fresh at Katy's Place (831/624-0199), a popular place for breakfast and lunch, home of twelve types of eggs Benedict.

Continue until you reach the Mission Patio Shops on Mission Street between Fifth and Sixth. Ambrose Pollock Furniture Maker (831/624-8145), located in the Mission Patio, displays Ambrose Pollock's expertly crafted wood furniture. Pollock explores the sensuous lines of Ranch- and Mission-style furniture. He worked as a cabinet maker in Hawaii in the seventies. "I breathed enough sawdust that it got in my blood system. Now we're insepa-rable." Pollock's furniture begins with the search for the perfect wood. The wood is crafted to become functional art. In addition to fine furniture his cre-ations range from the papal altar and podium created for Pope John Paul II's mass at Laguna Seca in 1987 to the handcrafted bookstore at the aquarium. If you are in town for any duration, take advantage of his wood-shop classes.

Double back to the entrance to the mall walkway. In this Carmel-style "mall," really a pleasant courtyard of galleries and the Club Jalapeño Restaurant (831/626-1997), you will have a great chance of viewing the artist at work and feeling the connection to the creative spirit that has always defined Carmel. In the Siner Gallery (831/625-9628) you'll find quality etch-ings of California landscapes, particularly of the Central Coast. Two of Jeff Siner's fine etchings hang in the White House. The bright high-beamed gallery space also has a number of his oils. You can find Siner at the back of the gallery, often completing three-dimensional drawings of fine collectible ceramic buildings.

At the Andrew Jackson Gallery (831/626-8354, www.baylife.com/web/ajackson/home.htm), the colors glow with surreal intensity and the "dreamscapes" reflect the artist's dreams. Jackson, an observant student of John Mason, was voted best local artist in the *Coast Weekly* Readers Poll in 1997. At the Zimmerman Gallery (831/626-9500), Marc Zimmerman enjoys the dialogue and access people enjoy at his studio. He studies nature in its outdoor realm and back in the studio, "I interpret, make it personal."

In the Eastwood Building, next door on San Carlos Street, take the eleva-tor or walk upstairs to the visitor's center operated by the Carmel Business Association (831/624-2522). Helpful staff will answer your questions and provide maps, art walk guides, and event information.

Next, walk to the Richard MacDonald Galleries (831/624-8200) on San Carlos between Fifth and Sixth. Here the power of MacDonald's figurative art creates a dramatic and sensuous experience for the viewer. When I visit I feel almost as if I've bought a ticket to a passionate concert or theater perfor-mance. MacDonald created the nationally acclaimed twenty-four-foot bronze monument *The Flair,* now permanently installed in Georgia International Plaza, to celebrate the 1996 Olympics.

After wandering along San Carlos Street, take the Secret Garden pathway to Dolores Street. This whimsical garden lane is the backyard of a home that used to front Ocean Avenue. At the center of the lane the Garden Gate shop is open 10 a.m. to 5 p.m.

Near the garden pathway, Em Le's Restaurant (831/625-6780), owned by sports newscaster John Madden and partners, offers an old-fashioned soda shop and memorable French toast. In the Pantilles Court adjacent to Em Le's, you can find Pat and city council member Paula Hazdovac working and creating at Two Sisters Designs (831/625-1203). They offer handmade and beaded jewelry, hand-dyed silk scarves, dresses, and more. The post office, the gathering place for the community, is around the corner on Fifth Street.

Turn right at Dolores Street, doubling back to enjoy the side streets. Several galleries dot this area. At the corner of Sixth Avenue and Dolores Street you'll spot the Village Corner. This Spanish-style one-story building with outdoor dining is a cherished gathering spot and nostalgic heart-place for locals. In the late 1970s plans for a two-story building at the site surfaced and a citizens group called "Old Carmel" led a Save-the-Village-Corner campaign.

Around the corner from Dolores on Sixth Avenue, the Weston Gallery (831/624-4453) features prints by the finest nineteenth- and twentieth-century photographers. Prints by Ansel Adams, Edward Weston, and the Weston sons Brett and Cole are focal points of the gallery, which is also the exclusive representative for work directly from photographer Yousuf Karsh. Gallery shows change frequently. One of the most popular is of eighteenth- and early-nineteenth-century prints. The gallery includes a prime selection of photography art books, as well as boxed notecards of the artists' prints of local sights.

Across the street, the Lynn Lupetti Gallery (831/624-0622) features her enchanting figurative paintings where people are painted on the same canvas with "Magic People" of literature and dreams. The entire collection of J. A. Pippett's whimsical sculptures is also presented here along with a selection of bronze sculpture and Tiffany-style lamps.

The sculpture garden back on Dolores Avenue between Fifth and Sixth Avenues leads to the Carmel Art Association Galleries (831/624-6176), which display the works of seventy-five local painters and sculptors. Originally situated in the Seven Arts Building, the Carmel Art Association was formed in 1927 by local artists to organize to display their talents and protect their place in Carmel. Membership in this cooperative included locals Salvador Dali, Armin Hansen, and seascape painter William Ritschell.

Only originals are offered for sale in the gallery. For nine months, special one-person shows fill one of the five display floors. At the show's opening reception the public is invited to mingle with local artists and association patrons. Special retrospective shows offered in autumn trace important influences on California art by such early association members as Mary De Neale Morgan, Donald Teague, and Armin Hansen. Some of these shows are so popular that lines form in the sculpture garden.

Near the Art Association Galleries, the courtyard, El Prado de Su Vecino, which means "the passageway of your neighbor," leads from Dolores Street through a variety of shops to Lincoln Street. Animals are beloved in Carmel so the S.P.C.A. benefit shop is the recipient of top-of-the-line clothing donations. Hours are daily 10 a.m. to 4 p.m. You'll emerge through the Cortille San Remo onto Lincoln.

Across the street is the M. J. Murphy house, home of the Carmel Heritage Welcome Center, open Wednesday through Sunday 1 to 4 p.m. (831/624-2781). The family home of one of the major builders and designers in Carmel, this house was lifted by crane over the tops of businesses and homes from its original location up Ocean Avenue. During the week it serves as a community center. Shows of historical and artistic significance rotate throughout the year. A small park with rest rooms is adjacent to the Murphy House.

The Harrison Memorial Library, at the corner of Lincoln Street and Ocean Avenue, was one of the most famous buildings that M. J. Murphy designed, this one in consultation with architect Bernard Maybeck, who designed the Palace of Fine Arts in San Francisco. The library was a gift to the city from Ella Reed Harrison in memory of her husband, Ralph Chandler Harrison, who had served as a California Supreme Court justice from 1890 to 1903. Light and airy, and with more than eighty-two thousand volumes to be enjoyed by a huge fireplace, this adult library could be your perfect gift to yourself on a foggy afternoon. Ninety-five percent of the town's residents hold library cards. A walking-tour guide to the library's paintings and sculptures is available at the reference desk.

The courtyard of the Pine Inn (831/624-3851) connects across Lincoln Street and also to Murphy Park. Before you leave Ocean Avenue look up the street and imagine it as the bumpy dirt road of 1904 and a two-story hotel on thundering logs is rolling toward you.

Recycling isn't new. Original sections of the Pine Inn were formerly the Hotel Carmelo, which was built from the old Tivoli Opera House in San Francisco. Charles Devendorf had the hotel moved down the hill on pine logs to greet guests at its present closer-to-the-beach location. M. J. Murphy refitted and enlarged the hotel in 1905, which has since seen many additions.

Brick walkways edged with hedges and gardens weave through sections of the Pine Inn here. Walk through an original beveled-glass door to the lobby. The same antique clock that timed Devendorf's early sales and kept time at gala dances keeps the pulse of the present lobby, which is textured with deep red silks, velours, and leathers, and furnished with antiques from his development days.

Il Fornaio (831/622-5100) at the Pine Inn offers pasta, pizza, and meat and poultry specialties in a choice of dining areas: inside the hotel, in the garden room, or on the rooftop. Coffees and baked goods are savored in a round fresh-air-filled bakery section. Locals gather at the circular plank table. The selection of fresh baked breads available here was voted best in the county in 1997.

Just south of the Pine Inn, the Lobos Lodge (831/624-3874) at Monte Verde and Ocean Avenue was built as a buffer between residences and the business district and as such is the last commercial location at the foot of Ocean Avenue. Traditional and antique quilts, reasonably priced quilted apparel, and quilting supplies warm your last glance at Carmel shops in California Quiltmakers (831/625-2815), which is tucked into the hotel's first courtyard.

THE COASTAL AND WOODLAND WALKS TOUR

Scenic walking trails traverse the areas west of Highway 1. They connect to almost anywhere you want to go in the village.

THE BEACHES AND TOR HOUSE. Ocean Beach is the wide expanse of snowy white sands that grow into the dunes hugging the parking lot at the bottom of Ocean Avenue. Parking also can sometimes be found along Scenic Drive. Stairways lead down to the beach from several points along Scenic. The only public rest rooms for this beach are located near the parking lot.

The waves here are beautiful but dangerous. No swimming or wading is advised on any Carmel-area beach. News clippings back to the city's founding tell of heroic saves and tragedies. The people you see surfing or skim boarding have been taught to swim here; they understand the currents and undertows.

You will get a feel for Carmel's international reputation as you watch people from all over the world descend the dune from the Ocean Avenue parking area to the beach flats. Some people begin elegant arm-in-arm strolls and end up laughing as they wade through the soft dunes. Some race their dogs in downhill dashes. How do the dunes stay white? Once a month community member Clayton Anderson organizes the Neighborhood Association to scour the sand with metal scoops and waste bags. If you see beach walkers in orange jackets give them a wave of thanks. Responsible visitors keep the sands clean for the next wave.

Once at the ocean's edge, walk toward the northern end of the beach, scrambling over granite rocks as you go. If the tide is low peek into tidepools. Sea otters especially enjoy the feeding grounds of these northern beach waters. In early spring this is an excellent spot to see mother otters with babies riding on their upturned chests. A path climbs to a rocky outcropping and an expansive view.

After enjoying the rocky area head back down the beach. Probing the wet sands for tasty crustaceans, shorebirds such as willets and sanderlings might scurry along the tide line with you.

To discourage mobs of people the exact date for the annual Sand Castle Contest is not announced until one week before the contest. A general theme embraces entries ranging from whimsical to political. Three-foot-tall sand mice guard a detailed Cinderella's castle for one entry while a lifelike whale collapses an oil platform as another. Each year a local architects' group replicates a notable Carmel building in the sand. In the afternoon the judges, usually a group of local architects and civic notables, award seashells and the coveted golden shovel for the "Grand Sand Award."

Return to the bluffs by way of one of the staircases or back through the dunes—especially, if it's sunset. You may be joined by many local shopkeepers and artists who walk here for the evening event. The sky bursts with colors reflected on the shimmering beach. Dark headlands and silhouettes of cypress trees frame a sun dipping through an erubescent sky that may be on fire one night and softly blushing through the fog on the next.

Scenic Drive and a walking path parallel the beach and offer spectacular views for one and a half miles. The shady walking path along Scenic resounds with the crashing of waves and meanders into sunlit patches of beautifully planted scenic bluffs. Benches along the way invite you to view breakers, gliding pelicans skimming the waves in summer and, in the winter, the geysers of migrating whales. Close by, a hummingbird may be feasting on native plants.

To extol the twelfth-night winter celebration a group of residents continues a Carmel tradition along this route. Old Christmas trees are dragged to the beach, usually at the bottom of Thirteenth Avenue. Toasts to the New Year are raised as a bonfire of the branches lights the evening sky.

The pathway ends at the Frank Lloyd Wright–designed house at the point just past Martin Way. Completed in 1954, the house was declared by the architect to be "durable as rocks, transparent as a wave." The exterior is thin-layered stone with a porcelain enamel roof.

The road becomes a narrow cliff-hanger after it passes the Frank Lloyd Wright house. As you walk or slowly drive past Ocean View Avenue, look up to your left. For a moment you will feel transported to Ireland as the stone Tor House and Keats-inspired tower fill the grassy knoll above you. Writer Robinson Jeffers (1887–1962) arrived in Carmel in 1914. Jeffers commissioned M. J. Murphy to build a house of ocean stone on the cliff. With his own hands and later those of his twin sons, Jeffers added to the home, which he named Tor House. Charlie Chaplin, Carl Sandburg, Charles Lindburg, and Edna St. Vincent Millay were among those who visited. For his wife, Una, he built a three-story adaptation of an Irish tower with thousands of granite rocks that he wheelbarrowed up from the beach below his house. Una loved the works of Keats, who had witten poetry in a similar tower in Ireland. Each day Jeffers built, a hawk would circle around him and sometimes light on the structure, which Jeffers later named Hawk Tower. Unicorn statues and wall moldings beloved by Una, artifacts and rocks from throughout the world, personal mementos, and the Jeffers' furnishings are on view during hourly tours of the unique home and tower, Fridays and Saturdays. Call (831/624-1813) for reservations; the location is Stewart Way, off Scenic Avenue.

To reach Carmel River Beach follow the panoramic but hair-raising Scenic Drive to the end at Carmel River Beach, or travel back to Junipero Avenue and loop around to Rio Road. The Carmel River meanders through wetlands and a bird sanctuary before it flows to the sea during rainy seasons. When the lagoon is filled and threatens to flood, bulldozers arrive to push the summer buildup of sands aside and let the river rush free. Crowds gather on the shore to toast and cheer the annual event.

The lagoon is a birder's paradise. On the hillside hovering marsh hawks, sparrow hawks, and red-tailed hawks glide and dive. Great blue herons and egrets stand and elegantly turn at the marsh's edge. Mallards and coots paddle by, and dip and dive.

After the river is dammed, usually sometime in spring, you can walk over and up an easy slope to a smooth service-road trail. In spring and early summer lupines and paintbrush flowers highlight mixed bouquets of surrounding wildflowers. Along this trail you'll see various paths leading down to picturesque coves. Artists often set up easels here and on the rocky crags.

Numerous benches dot the hillsides and pathways along your walk. One of the inland paths leads to a large wooden hillside cross, which marks the site of the Portola-Crespi Spanish explorers party of 1769. The party, searching for Monterey Bay, left a message at the foot of a cross they erected here. "[We have] made every effort to find the Port of Monte-Rey; penetrating well into the mountains, skirting it along the shore, in spite of its ruggedness, but all in vain." (This is the party that retreated to San Diego and returned to recognize Monterey Bay the next year.) At the cross there is a panoramic view of the bay and Point Lobos and the river's route from the mountains.

Follow the road again to a gnarled, rocky promontory. Climb the wooden steps up to the outlook. Breathe deep: this view is a sweep. You'll see the pristine bay at beautiful Monastery Beach, which extends in a sandy crescent north to San Jose Creek. When rushing river water prevents your crossing from Carmel River Beach, or if you want to begin at Monastery Beach, you will need to drive on Highway 1. Turn west off 1 onto Ribera Road just south of Rio Road or turn right after you pass the little red Bay School. You can also park at Monastery Beach.

Many people mean Monastery Beach, also known as San Jose Creek Beach, when they talk about the Carmel Beach. Busy with locals and scuba divers on weekends, the postcard-perfect beach offers many private stretches of sand.

THE MISSION. Mission San Carlos Borromeo Del Rio Carmelo (831/624-3600), located one-half mile west off Highway 1 on Rio Road, is open for visitors every day. From Carmel River Beach drive or walk along Carmelo Street, then turn right at Fifteenth Avenue, which becomes Lasuen and leads to the mission. The walk takes fifteen to twenty minutes.

In the summer and on weekends busloads of visitors view the authentically restored Mexican baroque church, its two museums, and the flowering gardens. Off season, it is so deserted you can almost hear footsteps from the past as you walk in the old mission cemetery and view relics. Masses are offered year-round, and special concerts fill the basilica one of only two in the western United States.

The exterior of the outbuildings that now surround the "cells" of Father Serra and Father Lasuen has been left unplastered in sections to reveal the original adobe brickwork. A landmark Moorish star tower and vaulted ceiling cover the basilica, which displays historic oil paintings and religious statues. Father Serra's private room is in the interior hallway between the gift shop and the first restored room.

Inside the first restored room, the *Serra Cenotaph* by sculptor Joe Mora was originally built as a sarcophagus for Serra. The sculpture grew too large in scope and is now a freestanding monument composed of kneeling figures and a small grizzly bear.

Two museums on the grounds depict early California life and the story of the loving restoration of the mission that was directed by cabinetmaker Harry Downie, who scoured records to restore the mission in exacting detail. Flanking the mission are gardens and a cemetery dating back to its origins. An estimated three thousand Esselen and Ohlone tribespeople are buried on the mission grounds. A self-guided tour leads through the church, museums, and grounds.

WOODLAND AND MEADOW TRAILS. Before there was pavement, before there were wide, dusty roads, Father Serra and mission workers journeyed from the Carmel Mission to Monterey and back along a web of narrow walking trails. Today you can follow the footsteps of Father Serra, beat the traffic and parking of modern times, and enjoy wooded glens and carpets of wildflowers along these same trails, which are preserved in Mission Trail Park. There is a loop trail within the park that leads though the Lester Rowntree Memorial Arboretum. The loop trail is a leisurely hour-and-a-half walk.

You can pick up the trails at any of several locations. On Mountain View Avenue walk to the top of the avenue, where it ends. (Only limited parking is available.) From the bridge there, walk to your right to enter the park. The main entrance is located at Rio Road, just across from the Carmel Mission. A gateway entrance at Junipero and Eleventh Avenue is about a half-hour walk from the mission and three easy blocks to shops. Few cars can be accommodated at the entrance marked by a small sign near the Flanders estate section of the park, located off a narrow residential stretch of Hatton Road.

If you travel up to the Mountain View Avenue bridge, a few steps up from the Serra trail leads to the Flanders trail stairway. The Doolittle nature trail connects to this trail and winds back to the Rio Road starting point. Picnickers will not find tables in the glens along the way, but the Rowntree Arboretum has many benches.

From the Rio Road entrance across from the mission, the Serra trail and Willow trail lead to Eleventh Avenue. Highlights of the Serra trail include a redwood glen and serene canyon. Clusters of benches invite you to sit and listen to bird symphonies and the rainy-season murmur of a nearby stream. Surrounding houses are obscured behind forest groves. A generation ago the trail up to Mountain View Avenue would sparkle some nights with a parade of candles in coffee cans as neighborhood groups made their way up the hillside, past the Eleventh Avenue bridge, to the Mountain Theater.

WHAT ELSE TO SEE AND DO

SUNSET CENTER. At the corner of San Carlos and Eighth Avenue (831/624-3996), the center is the location of several special events in Carmel. Sunset Center is a former school that now houses a theater plus meeting rooms and studios where instruction is offered. Granted Historic Preservation status, the building will be remodeled rather than torn down if any changes are made to improve or expand the building. Through the efforts of citizens the annual Bach festival brings artists of renown for two summer weeks. Concerts are at the Sunset Center and the Mission. The city also sponsors a playwriters' contest, with the winning play presented at the center in summer.

CHERRY FOUNDATION. At Guadalupe Street and Fourth Avenue (831/624-7491) the Cherry Foundation combines an art gallery, instructional center, and performing arts center. Peaceful gardens surround the former home of inventor Carl Cherry and his artist wife, Jeanne D'Orge.

LESTER ROWNTREE MEMORIAL ARBORETUM. There is very limited parking at this easy-to-miss location off Hatton Road. It's best to use the Rio Road entrance from Mission Trail Park. Walk up Doolittle nature trail, which is the main entrance to the park. It is located to your right as you stand with your back to Rio Road. California native plants, many of which the garden's founder collected on her trips through California's wilderness, are labeled and grouped in discrete environments, such as desert, woodland, and chaparral. Redwood benches offer good views throughout the garden.

THE BARNYARD AND CROSSROADS. East of Highway 1, off Rio Road. A large windmill marks the redwood buildings of the Barnyard, where the gardens are a palette of flowers during every season. Local watercolor artists set up their easels or paint flat on the walkways. The Thunderbird Bookshop and Restaurant (831/624-1803) offers a wide selection of books, an informative lecture series, and weekend concerts for children. You can browse through books, then enjoy garden and mountain views while savoring menu items from the restaurant. At the northern end of the Barnyard, Succulent Gardens & Gifts (831/624-0426) displays the largest selection of waterfalls in the country. Succulents are usually in best supply beginning in March. Across the street, steel, iron, and bronze are pounded and shaped over a pit of hot coals in the working forge of award-winning metalsmith Chris Axelsson (831/624-3909). Hundreds of tools used to handle and form the metal and control the fire hang on the barnlike walls. Hand-forged sculptures, lighting bases, gates, and furniture are displayed and sold in a room adjacent to the forge.

The Crossroads provides live jazz, along with a selection of shops and top-rated restaurants. Through a large viewing window you can watch DJs in action during live broadcast hours at KRML 1410 AM studio. Walk next door to the Jazz Store, the world's first all-jazz store, for a selection of compact disks, posters, and original jazz photographs, a selection of percussion instruments, and Jazz Festival apparel. Part of the store is designed for the Jazz Series concerts scheduled throughout the year. Call for a schedule of concerts (831/624-6432).

Creativity continues at Glazes (831/624-0204) ceramics workshop where anyone, trust me, can paint their design on a ceramic gift, be it candleholders or a giant pasta bowl. Twenty-four crafters can play at one time as individuals or in arranged parties. This site is very popular for birthdays and bridal showers. For out-of-town crafters who want to paint their ceramics and have them shipped home, Glazes is conveniently located two doors from Mailboxes Etc. (831/625-2800).

The Treadmill (831/624-4112) shoe store and more is the local information center for runners' events. If you've been on the run, the Power Juice Company (831/626-6577) will squeeze you fresh organic juices of any combination you desire.

CHAPTER 6

HIGHWAY 1 SOUTH COAST ROUTE

POINT LOBOS, BIG SUR, HEARST CASTLE, AND ON TO CAMBRIA

Ninety miles of spectacular coast stretches south from Carmel to the southern border of the Monterey Bay National Marine Sanctuary. San Simeon, home to Hearst Castle, and Cambria are included as natural extensions of the route.

GETTING READY

BEST TIMES TO VISIT AND SPECIAL EVENTS

The scenery and curves of Highway 1, the coast route, are best suited for daylight traveling. Traffic is heaviest in summer, the traditional vacation season: sun warms the inland valleys, rivers and creeks offer refreshing dips, and rangers lead hikes and campfire programs. In autumn and spring the route is less crowded and the fog lifts sooner for clear views. As the number of visitors drops, so do the rates for lodging. Ask about winter rates and room specials. The California Transportation Department describes Highway 1 as a safe road in winter. However, travelers need to be advised that minor slides and some major ones do occur. Drought years have seen the fewest. Most of these slides are cleared within an hour by maintenance crews that live along the highway. Motorists are urged to use common sense. As on any mountainous road, hazardous conditions are going to occur along Highway 1 in stormy weather.

When I asked for information about special events at Point Lobos, Chuck Bancroft, the ranger answered, "We open every day." Agreed, every day along this route is special. Check Wildlife Wisdom, below, for nature's parade of events. Gatherings include: In February, as Masters of Food and Wine gather at the Highlands Inn (831/624-3801), international star chefs and vintners present cooking classes, tours, wine tastings, and gourmet meals. Call to get on the mailing list. Tickets sell out as soon as offered. In April, the

BIG SUR
SOUTH COAST
AND
INLAND
VALLEYS

MARINA

PACIFIC
GROVE

SAND CITY

PEBBLE
BEACH

MONTEREY

SEASIDE

SALINAS

CARMEL

LAGUNA SECA
REC. AREA

San Juan Grade Rd.

Abbott Rd.

Spreckels Blvd.

River Rd.

68

TORO
REGIONAL
PARK

SPRECKELS

CHUALAR

POINT LOBOS
STATE RESERVE

1

G16

Laureles Grade

CARMEL
HIGHLANDS

Soberanes
Point

GARRAPATA
STATE PARK

Ford Rd.

4

CARMEL
VALLEY
VILLAGE

Chualar
River Rd.

Alta St.

Gonzales
River Rd.

GONZALES

To Pinnacles
National
Monument

2

Center St.

3

Bixby
Point

Palo Colorado Rd.

Carmel Valley Rd.

Cachagua

5

Tassajara

101

146

Point
Sur

6

JAMESBURG

CHEWS
RIDGE

Foothill

Ft. Romie Rd.

SOLEDAD

ANDREW
MOLERA
STATE PARK

G16

PARAISO
SPRINGS

Metz Rd.

PFEIFFER
BIG SUR
STATE PARK

Tassajara

Paraiso
Springs Rd.

Partington Cove

TASSAJARA
HOT SPRINGS

Arroyo Seco
Road

Elm Ave.

GREENFIELD

JULIA PFEIFFER
BURNS STATE
PARK

LOS

VENTANA
WILDERNESS

Central
Ave.

Esalen Institute

PADRES

NATIONAL

KING
CITY

1

FOREST

Limekiln Cr.

Gamboa Point

San Lucas Rd.

LUCIA

LIMEKILN CREEK STATE PARK

Kirk Cr.

Nacimiento-Fergusson Rd.

Jolon Rd.

PACIFIC VALLEY

Mission Rd.

MISSION
SAN
ANTONIO

Jolon Rd

Jade Cove

Lockwood Jolon Rd

101

WILLOW
CREEK

Willow Cr.

Mission
Rd.

JOLON

Cape San Martin

MAIN
GATE

*Pacific
Ocean*

HUNTER
LIGGETT
MILITARY
RESERVATION

GORDA

Lake
San Antonio

New Pleyto Rd.

WINERIES

1. Chateau Julien
2. Georis Winery
3. Bernardus
4. Heller Estate Durney Vineyards
5. Galante Vineyards
6. Joullian Vineyards

Pleyto Cemetery Rd.

San Antonio Rd.

MONTEREY COUNTY
SAN LUIS OBISPO COUNTY

Ragged Point

N
W   E
S

Lake
Nacimiento

San Antonio Rd.

Big Sur International Marathon (831/625-6226) also offers a 5K walk/run, when Highway 1 is closed to morning traffic. In late October runners fill Julia Pfeiffer Burns State Park during the beautiful Big Sur River Run (831/667-2315). Also in October, artists display the largest collection of Big Sur and Monterey jade (nephrite) ever assembled in one spot, at Pacific Valley's Jade Festival (805/927-5574).

CLIMATE AND CLOTHING

There are fifty or so microclimates between Highway 1 and the eastern reaches of the Santa Lucia Mountains. It is said that every thousand feet you climb vertically represents an inland climate span of one hundred fifty miles. People grow macadamia nuts and small bananas on sheltered headlands and inland valleys, as though this were the tropics. In summer you can hike from thick fog to a heat wave in a few hours. The average high temperature for January is sixty degrees; average low, forty-one degrees. In July the average high temperature is sixty-eight degrees; average low, fifty-two degrees. Pfeiffer State Beach is beautiful, but the wind-blown sands can sting your face any day of the year. The rainy season lasts from November through early April and the rain produced ranges widely, from twenty inches annually along the coast to more than sixty inches at higher elevations.

You can dress fancy for the Highlands, and you don't have to dress at all for some of the beaches. Casual, layered clothing is the norm for travel along Highway 1. Good hiking shoes, sunscreen, a canteen, a camera, and binoculars are advised. Once you've started hiking some of these trails you won't want to quit. Bring a swimming suit for dips in the rivers and at protected China Beach at Point Lobos. The water is, however, freezing at the beaches, and the surf is dangerous at most. The surfers you see along the coast are experienced ocean swimmers.

TOUR LENGTHS

Highway 1 can certainly offer a week's worth of views and pleasures. For Mickey Muenning, the architect of Post Ranch and the Hawthorne Gallery, a two-week vacation has lasted twenty years. If your schedule will allow only one day to drive Highway 1 you can have an enjoyable day, with time for a few walks and a few stops at galleries or restaurants. It would be best to explore Point Lobos on a separate day, but don't miss it if this is your only chance; allow at least three hours. Point Lobos is one of the best places to bike in the area. For the one-day drive, the easily accessed half-hour hike to the McWay Waterfall at Julia Pfeiffer Burns State Park and the hour creek-trail hike in Pfeiffer Big Sur State Park are suggested walks. The gallery at Ventana Resort displays works by local artists and is well worth a part of your day. For the day drive, plan an hour driving time for thirty miles. There are numerous signs, yellow with black lettering, at the beginnings of curves. Their speed limits are the suggested safe speeds for the curves only, and drivers should resume a normal safe speed after leaving them. Two types of drivers cause difficulties on Highway 1: the driver who speeds and the driver who drives too slow rather than pull over at any of the numerous turnouts, to view the magnificent vistas.

HIGHLIGHTS FOR KIDS

Camping in Big Sur is perfect for kids. The State Parks have interpretive programs and some form of Junior Ranger program each summer. At Andrew Molera State Beach, the horseback rides are along easy terrain. The River Inn is a perfect place to dangle toes in the water and relax on, as one child I know well says, those "giant's wood chairs." Kids also like to brag about the giant hike up to the Big Sur Lighthouse Station.

WILDLIFE WISDOM

Marine and inland wildlife abound year-round. In the summer the birds are the first to catch my eye. Legions of pelicans fly along the coast. At some cliffs along Highway 1 golden eagles soar alongside your car windows. Sometimes it feels as if you are flying with them. Migratory marine birds, most notably Brandt's cormorants, nest at the bird-rock island at Point Lobos from spring through summer.

Of the marine mammals, sea otters and harbor seals are the ones seen year-round. Otters are best observed in the kelp beds at Point Lobos, Soberanes Point, Julia Pfeiffer Burns State Park, Big Creek, Limekiln Beach, Kirk Creek, and Alder Creek. Seals give birth on the beaches of Point Lobos, especially Whalers Cove, in the spring. Sea lions are most often seen from August to March.

Deer, raccoons, squirrels, and an occasional bobcat are among the animals that inhabit the mountains. Mountain lions, wild boar, and rattlesnakes rarely cross your path but do inhabit this region. When we first camped at Pfeiffer Big Sur some twenty years ago we didn't take the wild boar reports seriously. During the night the pounding of many hooves in our campsite awakened us and our tent was jiggled by rooting boars. Stay calm if you come upon a herd of these fellers. Noise can provoke them. Backing away easy is advised; if charged, rangers say, climb the nearest tree. Damage to possessions, let alone people, is quite rare. Herds of boar can be seen in the daytime from the high ridges. Mountain lions usually avoid human trails. None of the hundreds of hikers I have talked to has ever seen one but rangers do report sightings. If you are in the back country, it is advisable to carry a stick just in case. Rattlesnakes may show up in Big Sur; be careful before putting hands on rocky ledges or sitting on rocks or logs.

When the crowds leave at the end of summer Big Sur seems almost reborn. In the warm sunny autumn weather the leaves of maples, sycamores, and cottonwoods wave in yellow and orange. Poison oak, which is prolific off the trails, turns fiery red. In October the first monarch butterflies begin arriving for the winter months. The eucalyptus grove by the historic Cooper cabin in Andrew Molera State Park is a good viewing location.

From mid-December through February gray whales begin to be spotted with regularity offshore as they migrate to and from the warm lagoons in Baja California. Some of them come within fifty feet of the shore. If you pull off the road at any turnout with a good ocean view and watch the water closely, you will probably be rewarded with a white geyser and perhaps a full body breach. Light conditions of late afternoon make the whales easier to see. Prime whalewatching spots are found at Point Lobos, Garrapata State Park, Point Sur Lighthouse (access is by guided tour only), and Julia Pfeiffer Burns State Park. During the peak five weeks of the season you can join a ranger-led whale watch. The rangers will provide binoculars and share displays of whale bones and baleen, and informational handouts. Call Pfeiffer Big Sur State Park (831/667-2315) for specifics.

Wildflowers bloom on hillsides and meadows in March and April, tapering off in May. The Garrapata hike offers some beautiful varieties, but don't pluck any; picked wildflowers wilt quickly and their seeds are lost for the coming years. Fire danger is extreme during dry summer and autumn months. Campfires need to be legal and tended.

VISITOR INFORMATION

Most of the land adjacent to Highway 1 is private property. Check at Forest Service Offices for registration requirements for hiking the back country. You may need to purchase an Adventure Pass. Hike and enjoy posted trails and parkland. These numbers serve public lands: Point Lobos State Reserve information, 831/624-4909; USDA-Forest Service Big Sur Station, 831/667-2423; USDA-Forest Service Main Station in King City, 831/385-5434; Pacific Valley Station, 805/927-4211; California Department of Parks and Recreation, Monterey District, 831/649-2836; Big Sur District, 831/667-2315; California State Parks Information Line, 916/653-6995. For more visitor's information call the Big Sur Chamber of Commerce, 831/667-2100. For San Simeon State Park, call 805/927-2035. For road conditions call the CALTRANS state-wide road information line, 800/427-7623.

Point Lobos, An Illustrated Walker's Handbook, by Florence Thompson, from Inkstone Books, is a good reference for the natural history of Point

Lobos. *Hiking the Big Sur Country,* the 1998 edition by Jeffrey Schaffer, from Wilderness Press, is an excellent guide for the coast and Santa Lucia Mountains from Carmel River Beach to Lucia. Pick this book if you want a good source for extended backpacking trips.

Pick up a tide table before you begin your journey. They are usually available free at chain drugstores and sporting goods stores. Along Highway 1 almost every market has them. Plan your visits to tidepool locations to coincide with low tide.

ALTERNATE TRANSPORTATION

From April to October, Monterey-Salinas Transit line 22 serves Carmel, Point Lobos, Carmel Highlands, Yankee Point, Garrapata Beach, Bixby Creek Bridge, Point Sur Light Station, the River Inn, Pfeiffer Big Sur Park, Pfeiffer Beach, Ventana Inn, and Nepenthe. Buses depart from the Monterey transit center and offer a relaxing ride. Call 831/899-2555 for complete information. Otter-Mobile Tours (831/649-4523) offers an excellent and relaxing tour.

PARKING

There are more than three hundred turnouts on the west side of the highway. Take advantage of the great views. If you find yourself with a line of five vehicles behind you, pull over. If you are leaving your car by the roadside and embarking on a hike, lock your vehicle before leaving it. Take valuables with you.

PLACES TO STAY

CARMEL HIGHLANDS

HIGHLANDS INN (four miles south of Carmel at signs, above Highway 1). This is a romantic destination for newlyweds. One hundred forty-two units, set on cliffs above crashing surf and twisted cypress. All suites with whirlpool baths and fireplaces. 831/624-3801. AX, MC, V; others also accepted. For two from $240 to $300.

NORTHERN BIG SUR COAST

BIG SUR LODGE (within Pfeiffer Big Sur State Park). Sixty-one garden court cottages with redwood decks, in the midst of Big Sur Park. Close to hiking trails. Some rooms include fireplaces and full kitchens. Restaurant and grocery store on premises. Conference facilities. Swimming pool. 831/667-2171. MC, V. Three different rate seasons. In summer, for two, from $100 to $120.

BIG SUR RIVER INN (just off Highway 1, one mile from the entrance to Pfeiffer Big Sur State Park). One of the most relaxing experiences on the Central Coast is an afternoon here planted in a wooden chair in the middle of the Big Sur River. Renew your spirits with excellent food and drink in the rustic dining room. In the evening you will find music by local bands and conversation by the warming fireplace in the thick timbered redwood lounge. If you stay all night the rippling water will serenade you. The inn is divided in two sections; one group of buildings is located across the highway. Reserve a room in the section on the river-facing side. All rooms are furnished differently and many feature strong accents of redwood in the craftsman style. Winter specials include a candlelight dinner and hearty breakfast. Pool for summer swims. Small craft and clothing stores are in the near surround. 800/548-3610. AX, MC, V. For two from $99.

DEETJEN'S BIG SUR INN (just off Highway 1, approximately four miles south of the entrance to Pfeiffer Big Sur State Park). This inn is registered as a national historic site. Rustic cabins under the redwoods, near the babbling Castro Creek, have dark woods, antiques, Oriental and country throw rugs, and hand-hewn doors in rooms, each with its own name and history. Some rooms feature Deetjen's handcrafted furniture. Cabins range from tiny to two-family size. Walls are planks of locally milled or scavenged redwood. As walls are thin, guests with children must rent two adjacent rooms. TV? Never. Favorite pastimes here are renewing relationships, cozy honeymoons, walking in the forest, and writing and reading journals that are passed on from guest to guest. Most rooms have private baths; some have fireplaces, some full kitchens. Reserve at least two months in advance. 831/667-2377. MC, V. For two from $70 to $140.

GLEN OAKS MOTEL (on the east side of Highway 1, a few miles north of Pfeiffer Big Sur State Park). This clean post adobe has fifteen rooms. Only in Big Sur would this standard-style motel seem a little unusual. Pleasant room decor and flower gardens by the walkways. The motel is slightly set back from the highway. An added bonus is the Glen Oaks Restaurant, just across the street. Textured ceilings. No credit cards. 831/667-2105. For two from $115.

POST RANCH INN (west of Highway 1, approximately thirty miles south of Monterey, across the highway from the Ventana Inn entrance). The newest inn on the Big Sur Coast has spectacular ocean views and also redwood, oak, and madrone forests, fern grottos, and meadows. Located on ninety-eight acres of coastal ridge, set well back on the ocean side from Highway 1, the thirty deluxe rooms meld with their surroundings. Wildflowers grow on the sod roofs of five ocean houses that are recessed into the ridge. Seven tree houses are built on stilts to protect the roots of surrounding redwoods. Rooms offer the ultimate in privacy while preserving ocean and starlit views through expansive use of glass. Intricate wood interiors, slate floors, and marble baths. Sierra Mar restaurant offers regional cuisine for guests and reserved seating for visitors. When Highway 1 was closed for months during the 1998 visit of El Niño, the Post Ranch delivered guests in helicopters. Complimentary morning yoga. Two pools, fireplaces, state-of-the-art music systems, and minibars. A spa offers exercise equipment and massages. Drivers escort guests from parking areas to the secluded ridge. 831/667-2200, 800/527-2200. AX, MC, V; others also accepted. For two from $290 to $450.

VENTANA INN (inland from Highway 1, a little more than two miles south of Pfeiffer Big Sur State Park). Everytime I visit here deer are grazing nearby. The secluded mountaintop adult resort of sixty-three accommodations is set within meadows framed by forests and spectacular ocean views. Rooms have light-cedar walls and high ceilings; many rooms have fireplaces. Some have private Japanese hot baths; some townhomes have whirlpools; two pools and Japanese hot baths are shared. Walk along nature trails or through meadows to Ventana's quintessential California-cuisine restaurant. TV, pay movies. Complimentary evening beverages. 831/667-2331, 800/628-6500. AX, MC, V; others also accepted. For two from $190 to $480, summer season.

SOUTHERN BIG SUR COAST

ESALEN INSTITUTE (on the ocean side of Highway 1, fifteen miles south of Pfeiffer Big Sur State Park). Most people stay here while attending workshops in a variety of disciplines over a weekend or during the week. Spaces do open up for people who just want lodging, board, and baths. Rooms have two single beds, dressers, and desks. Some have spectacular ocean views. No TVs, radios, or telephones. Clothing is optional around pool and bath areas. Rooms include three meals with primarily vegetarian cuisine. "Animal is served about three times a week." Reservations are taken as early as seven days in advance for nonworkshop participants. Drop-in vacancies do occur; call prior to arriving. The heavy rains of El Niño caused a landslide that destroyed the historic mineral baths, but Esalen is constructing a new grouping of cliffside mineral baths. These are open to anyone from 1 to 3:30 a.m., with reservations and fee. All lodging includes three meals. 831/667-3000, 831/667-3023. AX, MC, V. For two, $230.

LUCIA LODGE (twenty miles south of Pfeiffer Big Sur State Park). Nestled in cabins, a group of ten very rustic rooms sits on the edge of an oceanside ridge. Dark slat-wood walls and beamed ceilings. Fine-quality beds and showers. Units seven through ten offer incredible views of Lucia Bay and the southern Big Sur coastline. Outside your room, ocean watching and a reading bench offer the only recreation on this isolated headland. The Lucia store and restaurant are a short walk around the bend. 831/667-2391. MC, V. For two from $82 to $165. The more expensive rooms offer the better views.

RAGGED POINT INN (off Highway 1, fifteen miles north of San Simeon). Panoramic southern Big Sur views from rooms set on a cliff above the ocean. A pathway for an invigorating walk is cut across a rugged cliff to the beach below. Nineteen large, modern rooms with high sloping, textured ceilings. The environs include a restaurant, an ice cream and smoothie snack area, espresso bar, outdoor areas with serene decks and incredible views, an art gallery, a small store, and horseback riding opportunities. All buildings are housed in earth-pleasing woods and glass. TV, coffee, and full baths. 805/927-4502. MC, V. For two, mostly under $100.

CAMBRIA AND SAN SIMEON

In Town

OLALLIEBERRY INN, 2476 Main Street, Cambria. The town's first "chemist" lived in this fully restored historic bed and breakfast inn with six guest rooms. A century-old redwood tree, cottage gardens, and caring proprietors welcome guests. Each room has special touches. The Olallieberry Room features blue, lavender, and white wall coverings, a ceiling canopy, and an antique chaise lounge. All rooms feature Victorian-era or similar furnishings, linens, and wall coverings. Sunken tubs or antique claw-foot tubs and showers. A comfortable creekside cottage area has been added to the original house. Outside, enjoy the creekside setting, with town just a half-block away. Full breakfast and afternoon hors d'oeuvres with wine and sparkling water included. 805/927-3222. MC, V. For two, most rooms from $85 to $115.

THE SQUIBB HOUSE, 4063 Burton Drive. The Squibb house bed and breakfast is a newly restored Victorian in the heart of Cambria. The house was built in 1877 by Fred Drake, a Civil War veteran and young schoolteacher. Paul and Louise Squibb, the last inhabitants before the house became an inn, were especially beloved by the town. Bruce Black has kept the house as true to itself as possible, keeping the original fir floors and old distorted glass.

Historic photographs of the home hang on the walls, and many of the original furnishings remain. In addition, Black handcrafted a set of furniture specifically for the house. Five rooms with private baths. Continental breakfast of scones, brioche, fruit, and cheeses. Complimentary afternoon wine tasting. 805/927-9600. MC, V. $95 to $140, single or double occupancy.

Along Moonstone Beach Road

FOG CATCHER INN, 6400 Moonstone Beach Drive, Cambria. This new inn is across the road from Moonstone Beach. The thatched roof and gardens are complemented by floral linens in the rooms, for an English-botanical ambiance. Pine walls, vaulted ceilings, rattan chairs, and special touches such as carved ivy lamps add to this inn's charm. Fireplaces in each room. Some rooms have sweeping shore views. Locally crafted garden benches invite you to relax in ocean-view gardens. Full breakfast included with room. Mini-microwaves, VCRs, and honor bars. 800/425-4121, 805/927-1400. AX, MC, V; others also accepted; for two from $80 to $135.

SAN SIMEON PINES (five miles south of San Simeon, near Cambria, at Moonstone Beach). Set in the pines and cypress, with an easy stroll to Moonstone Beach, this is a casual resort for families or adults. Large rooms with high sloping ceilings, some with fireplaces. Mementos of the area's past accent the lobby and tree-shaded lawns—brands from Hearst Ranch, whale bones set along a pathway, an old quicksilver-mining cart, and a climb-aboard tractor. Clubs are loaned for the practice par-three golf course. Solar-heated pool, complimentary coffee. Although some rooms are by the freeway, they are virtually soundproof and are landscaped for privacy. 805/927-4648. AX, MC, V. For two, most rooms from $70 to $90.

In the Pines

CAMBRIA PINES LODGE, 2905 Burton Drive, Cambria. The grand redwood Warren Leopold–designed and hand-carved doors offer a fitting welcome to the main lobby of the rebuilt historic Cambria Pines Lodge. The previous lodge burned in 1991. Reconstruction in light-pine wood has stayed faithful to the historic architecture and ambiance. There is a lively lounge, and indoor or deck dining. One hundred twenty rooms range from rustic cabins to comfortable suites with pinewoods views. The grounds reflect a place in the pines rather than well-manicured or cared-for gardens. Many tour bus groups lodge here. The rate for suites will be appreciated by families. Conference facilities. Indoor pool, spa, volleyball. Duraflame log-burning fireplaces, refrigerators, and microwaves in some rooms. 805/927-4200, 800/445-6868. MC, V; others also accepted. Suites available. For two from $60 to $100.

J. PATRICK HOUSE, 2990 Burton Drive, Cambria. Set in the Monterey pine forest above the town of Cambria, the main house in this bed and breakfast is an authentic log cabin that houses the living and dining areas as well as one upstairs guest room, "Clare." This large room is suitable for families and offers a brass-and-white-iron headboard above a king-sized bed; a private bath; and a real redbrick log-burning fireplace. (Due to town regulation J. Patrick House is one of very few accommodations that can offer real log fireplaces.) Seven additional rooms are in the carriage house, each with its own unique and tasteful country decor. Beds are dressed in hand-stitched quilts. Breakfast. Evening hors d'oeuvres complemented by fine wines. 805/927-3812, 800/341-5258. MC, V. For two from $115 to $180.

CAMPING

To really feel the beat of Big Sur's heart, you might choose to camp in the fresh air in wooded canyons or on oceanside cliffs. Advance reservations are advised at the very popular Pfeiffer Big Sur State Park and Limekiln State Park. All national forest campgrounds and Andrew Molera State Park are available on a first-come-first-served basis. Summer weekends are popular camping times; try to get to your destination early in the day on Friday to get a campsite. Tent camping is advised, as weather is unpredictable and many animals visit during the night.

CAMPING ON THE NORTHERN BIG SUR COAST

ANDREW MOLERA STATE PARK (twenty miles south of Carmel). Twenty walk-in camp sites on an open field; often windy. An easy hike to the ocean. First come, first served. PARK NET 800-444-7275. $5 each night.

BOTTCHERS GAP NATIONAL FOREST CAMPGROUND (at the top of Palo Colorado Road). Oak and madrone campground with views of Pico Blanco and Ventana Double Cone Mountains. 831/385-5435, 800/280-2267. Ask for drinking water from park host but bring your own in case the supply is low. $5 day use. $10 each night.

PFEIFFER BIG SUR STATE PARK (near the Big Sur River, twenty-five miles south of Carmel). Two hundred eighteen sites, many under the redwoods, some along the banks of the Big Sur River. Campgrounds are spaced for some privacy. Trailheads for many hiking trails begin here. Warm showers, convenience market. PARK NET 800/444-7275. AX, MC, V. $22 each night.

VENTANA CAMPGROUND (the turnoff from Highway 1 is near Ventana Resort). Sixty-two secluded privately owned campsites under the redwoods next to Post Creek, which trickles slowly in the summer. Warm showers. Trails lead to Ventana Restaurant for the wilderness gourmand and to some of the best views in Big Sur. RVs are not recommended. 831/667-2688. $20 each night.

Four other Big Sur Valley private resorts offer cabins and/or campgrounds located between the River Inn and Pfeiffer State Park:

BIG SUR CAMPGROUND AND CABINS. The campgrounds and cabins are clustered under redwood trees; many front their own beach along the Big Sur River. Cabin styles include tent cabins, older trailer cabins, A-frames, and newer, bright, spacious units. All cabins have free-standing fireplaces. This resort includes hot showers, laundry, store, playground, and jumbo river tubes to rent. Tent, trailer, and RV sites. Thirteen cabins and eighty-two campsites. 831/667-2322. Cabins from $45 to $150. Camping $24 each night for two people with added costs for additional cars and people.

RIVERSIDE CAMPGROUNDS AND CABINS. Two wood-paneled rustic cabins with beam ceilings and a larger lodge with five cabin-style rooms share a knoll above the river. The thirty-plus campsites are in an open clearing surrounded by trees; many are next to the Big Sur River. Hot showers and RV sites. 831/667-2414. Cabins and lodge rooms from $45 to $90. Camping $24 each night for two people with added costs for additional cars and people.

RIPPLEWOOD RESORT. This resort includes a store with a community bulletin board and photographic display area, a comfortable home-style breakfast and lunch cafe, and seventeen rustic, lived-in cabins. Cabins one through nine sit along the Big Sur River. Cabins ten and eleven are situated along Highway 1 under coastal redwoods. Cabins twelve through seventeen are located at the edge of the woods behind the store. 831/667-2242. Cabins from $70 to $90.

FERNWOOD RESORT. This resort was built in 1938, above the former site of Highway 1, which now passes close by the front of the restaurant and lodging units. Sixty-six campsites flank the Big Sur River below the resort. In 1998, owner Bob "Tassi" Robinson kept the resort open for lunch and dinner throughout the four-month closure of Highway 1. Money was scarce and tabs were many. Together with his friends, he used a tractor and iron chains to grab an eighty-seven-foot old-growth redwood tree that was floating down the rain swollen river here. Robinson milled the tree into two twenty-six-foot-long bars for the inside and outside service areas. Other hand-milled oversized redwood tables of Robinson's creation are set throughout the restaurant. Reasonable meals and the bargain all-you-can-eat Saturday and Sunday night barbecue are some of the best priced meals in Big Sur. You can barbecue your own select cut of prime meat on the back deck. For desperate sports fans in the wilderness, a satellite dish beams the "hottest games" into the bar and casual redwood-beamed dining area. A gift and women's clothing shop and the Fernwood market share the premises with the basic roadside accommodations. 831/667-2422. Camping $24. Rooms $90.

CAMPING ON THE SOUTHERN BIG SUR COAST

KIRK CREEK NATIONAL FOREST CAMPGROUND (twenty-eight miles south of Pfeiffer Big Sur State Park, just north of Nacimiento-Fergusson Road). Thirty-three sites in an incredible ocean-ridge setting. Painters are here with their easels, writers have their journals on their knees, naturalists scan the waters with binoculars. Campers here are radiant; they probably have the best camping views on the West Coast. 831/385-5435. $16 each night.

PLASKETT CREEK NATIONAL FOREST CAMPGROUND (thirty-six miles south of Pfeiffer Big Sur). Forty-five campsites, close together in an open field and among trees. Sand Dollar Beach and picnic area is a half-mile away. 831/385-5435. $16 each night.

LIMEKILN STATE PARK (twenty-six miles south of Big Sur). Forty-three tent and RV campsites. Some of the campsites have privacy; most are set close together. The surrounding area—beach, stream, and redwood forest—is truly a find. Showers and store. For information about the park call 831/667-2403 and for reservations call PARK NET 800-444-7275. Rates are adjusted seasonally and range from $14 to $22.

CAMPING AT SAN SIMEON

SAN SIMEON PARK (just beyond the north end of Cambria off Highway 1). This park includes two campgrounds. Both sections offer picnic tables and fire rings. San Simeon Creek Campground has 143 campsites set in an open field and along San Simeon Creek. This developed park has rest rooms, showers, and picnic tables. Washburn Campground is set on an open flat knoll. This primitive site does not include showers or flush toilets. For information about the park call 805/927-2035 and for reservations call

PARK NET 800-444-7275. Rates for San Simeon Creek are adjusted seasonally and range from $14 to $17. Washburn sites are one-half the San Simeon
Creek fee.

RESTAURANTS

CARMEL HIGHLANDS

HIGHLANDS INN, THE CALIFORNIA MARKET (five miles south of Carmel).
Of the inn's dining choices this is the more casual. Sweeping ocean views,
from indoor or deck seating. Salads, sandwiches, fresh fish, and California
cuisine. Breakfast, lunch, and dinner. 831/624-3801. AX, D, MC, V. Entrees
mostly under $15.

HIGHLANDS INN, THE PACIFIC'S EDGE RESTAURANT. This is the home
of the Masters of Food and Wine culinary event that features menus and
demonstrations by master international chefs. Stunning architecture
and walls of glass enclose the restaurant. The waves crash seemingly beneath
your window table. California and other versions of American cuisine are
featured. Locals vote this the best restaurant to entertain someone you'd like
to impress. Grande Spectator Wine Award for outstanding wine selection.
Jackets suggested for men. 831/624-3801. AX, D, MC, V. Entrees mostly
under $30. Prix fixe menu $40.

NORTHERN BIG SUR COAST

BIG SUR RIVER INN (two miles north of Pfeiffer Big Sur State Park). This
casual roadside lodge with redwood beams and a stone fireplace has a creekside deck; after lunch you can relax on outdoor rockers or cool your toes in
the creek while sitting on rustic wooden chairs. The local Abalone Stompers
liven up the deck with music on weekends. Delightful lunches feature the
River Inn Burger, salads, sandwiches, pasta, and fresh fish. Dinners offer grill,
seafood, and pasta selections. Friendly service. 831/625-5255. AX, D, MC,
V. Dinner entrees mostly under $15.

DEETJEN'S BIG SUR INN RESTAURANT at Deetjens Big Sur Inn (just off
Highway 1 approximately four miles south of the entrance to Pfeiffer Big Sur
State Park). There is a warm homestead feeling here, with redwood walls,
fireplaces, candlelight, and classical music. Rack of lamb with herbal crust,
roasted duck, and fresh pasta and coastal fish are specials nightly. Beer and
wine are served; the wine list features wines from Monterey County. Hearty
breakfast menu. Try blueberry pancakes for your day on the road. Dinner
reservations advised; sittings every fifteen minutes. Breakfast, lunch, dinner.
831/667-2378. MC, V. Dinner entrees mostly under $20.

GLEN OAKS RESTAURANT (just off Highway 1 a few miles north of Pfeiffer Big Sur State Park). When dining on the Peninsula you will hear people raving about the pasta and service at Glen Oaks. The intimate size of the restaurant, copper-chimneyed fireplace, redwood tables, and works of local artists create a cozy feeling here. Glen Oaks also has a good reputation for fresh seafood. 831/667-2264. MC, V. Dinner entrees, $8 to $14.

NEPENTHE (three miles south of Pfeiffer Big Sur State Park on Highway 1). Open redwood beams blend with the cliffside environs of trees and ocean. Nepenthe is derived from a Greek word meaning "no sorrow." Also at Nepenthe, the Café Kevah for breakfast, lunch, or espresso offers wonderful views. Below the cafe, the Phoenix Shop features jewelry, clothing, and crafts from throughout the world. Lunch, dinner, full bar. 831/667-2345. AX, MC, V. Dinner entrees from $17 to $25.

ROCKY POINT (eleven miles south of Rio Road, Carmel). Expansive glass windows and outdoor deck seating capture incredible oceanfront views. Powerful floodlights illuminate the cliffs and water after dark. Located on a rocky promontory, this restaurant offers fine steaks, fish, and vegetarian specialties. Breakfast, lunch, and dinner. 831/624-2933. D, MC, V. Dinner entrees from $17 to $32.

SIERRA MAR (at the Post Ranch Inn, west of Highway 1, approximately thirty miles south of Monterey, across the highway from the Ventana Inn entrance). This restaurant is located high on a magnificent ridge with miles of ocean views, constructed with expansive use of glass, slate, and exotic woods. Four-course prix fixe menus offer the freshest vegetables and seafood and the highest-quality meats. Each course is served on its own style of plate, ranging from handblown glass to hand-thrown terra-cotta. Menu items are available à la carte. Lunches include salads, sandwiches, and main courses that are consistent with Big Sur–area prices. Reservations are required for lunch and dinner. Fine French and California wines. 831/667-2800. AX, MC, V. Prix fixe menu $58. You may select a course from the set menu, entrees $29.50.

VENTANA INN RESTAURANT (at Ventana Inn, inland from Highway 1, a little more than two miles south of Pfeiffer Big Sur State Park). Rough cedar beams, eye-level ocean views, wood tiles, bistro chairs, and a large outdoor hearth fireplace combine for a relaxing atmosphere. Grilled salmon with artichokes and pasta with rock shrimp and basil may be on the menu, which varies to feature fresh ingredients. Lunch and dinner. Reservations advised. 831/667-2331. AX, MC, V. Entrees mostly under $25. Prix fixe menu $45.

SOUTHERN BIG SUR COAST

LUCIA LODGE (twenty-four miles south of Pfeiffer Big Sur State Park). Here enjoy spectacular outdoor seating. Your cliffside seat overhangs the ocean and, in a suggestion of a tropical Big Sur, a small grove of banana trees. Views span a series of jade coves south to Cape San Martin. Fresh fish selections, and a heaping fish-and-chips basket. Meat and pasta also served. Lunch only. 831/667-2391. MC, V. Entrees mostly under $15.

CAMBRIA AND SAN SIMEON

BRAMBLES DINNER HOUSE, 4005 Burton Drive, Cambria. Built in 1874 as a family home, this quaint cottage offers gracious American dining. Dark wood accents, candlelight, red-cloth-draped tables, and deep-hued carpeting create ample ambiance. Menu includes blackstrap molasses bread, baby-back pork ribs, seafood brochette, and oakwood-broiled steaks. Victorian ornaments decorate trees in the restaurant during the Christmas season. Dinner. 805/927-4716. AX, D, MC, V. Entrees mostly under $15.

IAN'S, 2150 Center Street, Cambria. Soft lighting and romantic booth and alcove seating underscore a relaxed elegance. The owner and chef, Ian McPhee, is a master at combining seemingly discordant tastes and decor into sensational environs. The menu changes often, as McPhee likes creating new choices. The California cuisine—fresh local vegetables daily—comes in ample portions. Try the chocolate cake with lime and caramel sauce for dessert. When Ian is on break he mingles with guests on the steps of the renovated and enlarged Victorian restaurant. Sunday brunch, weekend lunches, nightly dinners. 805/927-8649. AX, D, MC, V. Entrees mostly under $15.

ROBIN'S, 4095 Burton Drive, Cambria. Batiks, oak furnishings, and a stonehearth fireplace enliven this wood-beamed home. A columbine and bougainvillea trellis surrounds the outdoor patio. Eclectic international selections include prawns, hot Sri Lanka chicken curry, pasta, and quesadillas. Take-out orders for incredible picnics. Lunch and dinner. 805/927-5007. MC, V. Entrees mostly under $10.

DIRECTIONS

Travel to Highway 1. From the Monterey Bay area drive south on 1 passing the exits for Pacific Grove and Carmel. Big Sur country begins just south of Carmel.

INTRODUCTION TO THE HIGHWAY 1 SOUTH COAST ROUTE, WITH HISTORICAL HIGHLIGHTS

Highway 1 snakes along ninety miles of legendary raw and rugged coast from Carmel to the Carpoforo Creek, just north of San Simeon. The road cuts across the young Santa Lucia Mountains, which rise from relentless waves to heights of five thousand feet and are still growing. Miles of mountain and sea vistas remain virtually wild and free. Early Spanish explorers called parts of these lands "Ventana," meaning window. Anthropologists and geologists are not sure whether this name refers to an eroded natural ocean bridge or the canyons that open with windowlike views. Many people feel the window is of a deeper sort, an opening of the spirit, emotions, and creativity.

The spirit frees itself quickly at Point Lobos, just three miles south of Carmel. Countless artists, photographers, and writers have walked its paths. Landscape artist Francis McComas called Point Lobos "the greatest meeting of land and water in the world." Its ragged, isolated coves and churning waters are said to have inspired Robert Louis Stevenson to write *Treasure Island*. Edward Weston and Ansel Adams photographed the area and Robinson Jeffers drew from its power for his epic poems.

Point Lobos is now protected for its rare and indigenous gnarled cypress trees and populations of marine and land animals. The reserve features a museum building used formerly for shore whaling and abalone fisheries, otherworldly rock formations, and both meadow and forest walks, as well as wave-sculpted coves where the ocean seems to boil and sea otters raft while *los lobos* (the sea lions, called sea wolves by Spanish explorers) roar into the wind. In the early 1900s Point Lobos was a favorite picnic spot for many locals. In 1933 it was saved from being divided into hundreds of parcels to become a state reserve. In 1960, 750 underwater acres were added to create the first marine reserve in the country. Point Lobos lovers rejoiced in 1993 when the Big Sur Land Trust announced it had secured an extra 1,700 acres, formerly slated for a resort, to be added to the reserve. More than 400 acres are now open to the public.

Rock mortars of previous civilizations can be found at the end of the Point Lobos Moss Cove trail. Rumsien tribes and earlier the Esselen gathered and hunted food in this area. The Esselen inhabited the lands between the Big Sur Point and the upper portions of the Arroyo Seco and Carmel Rivers. South of the Esselen, the Salinans lived in the coastal areas around what is now Lucia. The largest group of the first tribes, the Chumashan, lived from south of the Salinan to what is now San Luis Obispo. Descendants of the Monterey and northern Big Sur coastal tribes often refer to themselves as Ohlone. According to Ohlone legends, Pico Blanco, a high marble peak often visible from the road and on inland hikes, is the embryo of all civilization. It was here, according to the stories, that Coyote brought civilization to people.

Most locals refer to the lands five miles south of Point Lobos as the northern tip of Big Sur. Carmel Highlands lies between the two meccas of wilderness. Originally developed by Charles Devendorf and Frank Powers of the Carmel Land Development Company, the Highlands features a collage of homes that blend with land and sea.

When Cabrillo sailed up the coast in 1542 he noted, "There are mountains which seem to reach the heavens and the sea beats on them." As they stood on mountain vantage points in Monterey the early Spanish settlers in the area described the mountainous region to the south as El Pais Grande del Sur, the great land to the south, now translated as Big Sur.

For some Monterey County stalwarts, Big Sur ends at the Monterey and San Louis Obispo county line. The contours of the Santa Lucia Mountains suggest that the natural boundary of Big Sur lies farther south, where sheer mountain cliffs meet the valley owned by the Hearst Corporation at the Carpoforo Creek. Hairpin curves, jagged cliffs dropping off to boiling surf and the brilliant blue water beyond, redwood forests, lush creekside settings, and thirty bridges punctuate the eighty-some miles from the northern to southern boundaries. Capes, streams, and beaches bear the names of early settlers: Mount Manuel, Pfeiffer Ridge, Post Summit, Cooper Point, Dani Ridge, Partington Cove, and others. Some of their descendants still live in Big Sur. The main community along the route also bears the name Big Sur. For this history and the tours that follow, Big Sur refers to the eighty-mile stretch of land along the coast.

About twelve hundred people live along this stretch. More than five hundred live in the six-mile stretch known as the Big Sur Valley, where numerous resorts and businesses and Pfeiffer Big Sur State Park line the highway. People here are bound by a respect for their environment. Many are here to lead a remote and private life. Long dirt driveways lead to unique homes, many hand-built by the owners. For early settlers, the Big Sur experience was surely fearful. They were visited by grizzly bears, forest fires, and nature's storms, and the nearest stores were at least a two-day pack trip away. The oldest surviving structure along the Big Sur coast was built in 1861 on the 8,949-acre Rancho El Sur, owned and cattle-ranched by Captain John Roger Cooper. You can still peek into his cabin at Andrew Molera State Park. After the secularization of the missions the Mexican government formed two land grants in "El Sur Grande." Cooper had acquired Rancho El Sur from his nephew, Juan Bautista Alvarado, the then provisional governor of California. When Cooper died the land grant was divided among his five children. His granddaughter Frances Molera sold the land at a reduced price to the Nature Conservancy in 1968 with the condition that it remain undeveloped and be named for her brother Andrew, who had died in 1931.

More than any other settler's name, Pfeiffer (pronounced by the family as "pie-fur") is most synonymous with Big Sur. In 1869, during the years when the government offered one hundred sixty acres of government land free to families who would homestead parcels for five years, Michael and Barbara Pfeiffer along with four children and a small stock of horses and cattle set sail from San Francisco on the old sidewheeler *Sierra Nevada* for a two-day journey to Monterey. The trek overland to the unknown southern lands was even longer. They built their first cabin on the beach south of the Big Sur River. Later John Pfeiffer, one of their sons, homesteaded what is now Pfeiffer Big Sur State Park.

From the 1880s until the early 1900s Big Sur was an industrial center of the county, and boom settlements brought greater populations to the area than in present days. Throughout the area tanbark oak trees were lumbered for tannic acid, used in tanning, inks, and astringents; mules pulled tons of bark along narrow mountain paths on wheeled carts named "go devils" to boat landings along the coast. Limestone was smelted in giant redwood-fed lime kilns in Bixby Canyon and Limekiln Canyon; an aerial tram transported the lime from the settlement at Bixby Canyon to the company boat waiting at Bixby Landing. Thousands of redwood trees were lumbered or cut to fire the kilns. On the Big Sur River, the Ventana Power Company generated electricity.

As the redwoods were cut to bare numbers the lumber and lime industries faltered. The population dropped, and the tourist industry took on new importance for those who stayed on. The John Pfeiffer home was opened to lodgers at $3 a night.

Dr. John Roberts, founder of Seaside, a physician who rode the twisted coastal trails for days at a time to care for patients, proposed that Highway 1 be built as a scenic highway. Funds became available for highways that were necessary for the nation's defense, and the word "scenic" was dropped; in

1919 the state legislature appropriated $15 million for the construction of this road for the defense. Chinese laborers and convict labor provided much of the labor to build it. Highway 1 was finally opened in 1937, though traffic was limited—during World War II it was restricted by gas rationing and periodic closing of the road by the military.

After the war, artists, photographers, and writers settled the area. Headlines such as "Sex and Anarchy in Big Sur," a *Harper's* expose about Partington Ridge resident Henry Miller, author of *Tropic of Cancer,* brought the area new attention. Later the Esalen Institute opened, a center for personal growth. Crowds began to seek out Big Sur for its beauty.

That the beauty has remained, mostly undeveloped and preserved for future generations, is to the credit of people like John Pfeiffer, who donated a large portion of his land for Pfeiffer Big Sur State Park, and the Lathrop Browns, who donated landed for Julia Pfeiffer Burns State Park. Great credit is due Margaret Owings, who founded the Friends of the Sea Otter and, together with her late husband, Nathaniel, and Nick Roosevelt, led communities to write master plans that preserve the coast from lines of houses, hotels, and golf courses. "It was natural, I never looked for anything, it just fell into my lap. Thirty years ago on late evenings a mountain lion howled in the canyon behind our house and we could follow its tracks in the morning. Then one day a neighbor shot it for a bounty. I just couldn't let that animal die in vain." Owings was instrumental in obtaining legislation to end the bounty payments. If you are a Californian who voted for Proposition 70 in 1988 and 117 in 1990, you can thank yourself for preserving much of this land for wildlife habitat and viewshed protection. With additional funds, the nonprofit Big Sur Land Trust continues to add acreage to the fifteen thousand acres it has already shielded from development.

TOURS

Addresses are not very useful on this route. However, the State of California has instituted two systems for setting mileage and locating destination points. White markers along the highway marked with black writing mark the distance north from the San Luis Obispo/Monterey County line. During the floods and slides of 1998 many of the markers were lost or covered with deposits of earth. The state also has a system of sixteen white markers for scenic overlooks and I will use them as guidelines for some turnouts. Both of those marker systems are dependent on road and maintenance conditions and do not mark all locations covered in this tour. For the purposes of this tour I have included markers along Highway 1 marked with distances. "S" marks the numbers of miles south from Rio Road near Carmel and "N" marks the number of miles north from Hearst Castle, a distance of 89.7 miles.

For some people the "Big Sur state of mind" begins farther down the coast near Malpaso Creek; for others it begins as soon as they cross the Carmel River Bridge. Years ago the State of California purchased the oceanside fields of artichokes you see here for a flood plain for the Carmel River. In 1997 Clint Eastwood donated most of his inland acres of artichokes to the Big Sur Land Trust. Many people hope that after two consecutive years of flooding, the artichoke fields will be allowed to be replaced by natural flood plain habitats.

At a mile past the bridge you will see the entrance and the high towers of Carmelite Monastery. Eleven cloistered Carmelite sisters reside here. The massive beam ceiling of the church is supported by grand pillars of marble. The serene grounds are open to the public for meditation and quiet enjoyment until 4:30 p.m. daily. Sunday mass is said at 9 a.m. and is open to the public.

THE POINT LOBOS TOUR

The Point Lobos State Reserve entrance is 2.2 miles south of the Highway 1 and Rio Road intersection and 1.2 miles north of the Highlands Inn entrance. The park opens at 9 a.m. and closes at 5 p.m. daily. As the duration of daylight lengthens in late spring and summer, the closing time is later and is posted at the entrance. In summer it is usually 7 p.m. All walking and picnicking must be done in designated areas. For each vehicle, there is a $7 entrance fee which includes one map; walkers and bikers are admitted free. Entry is limited to 450 visitors at any one time. The park fills to its limit of visitors early on summer weekends. On busy days, visitors may wait in line to enter on a one-vehicle-out, one-vehicle-in basis. Drivers may park along Highway 1 at their own risk and walk for five or ten minutes to the park entrance. All bikers must stay on paved roads. Monterey transit bus 22 is a good alternative to cars.

Guided walks and Whalers Cabin Museum access are offered as staffing permits. A schedule for the day is posted at the entrance station. The museum is usually open daily from 11 a.m. to 3 p.m. An information station at the Sea Lion Point parking area is staffed by docents from 9 a.m. to 4 p.m. Docent-led tours are very informative, presenting introductions to the history, geology, flora, and fauna of the park, though they are not operated on a given schedule. (Call before you arrive in the park for the days, times, and focus of tours; 831/624-4909.)

All fishing and collecting of marine life or natural objects is prohibited. Scuba diving at Whalers Cove is often spectacular. You must reserve in advance, as only a limited number of dive teams are allowed each day. To make reservations: ptlobos@mbay.net or 831/624-8413.

The west side of Highway 1 covers 525 acres above ground and 712 underwater acres. The newest addition to Point Lobos, encompassing 1,700 acres, is on the east side of Highway 1. (At the time of this writing it had not yet been opened to the public.)

The twisted formations, giant boulders, eroded hollows, and strange conglomerates here have been the thrill of many a photographer and the awakening of many a latent geologist. Some treasures are hidden except to the most trained eyes. On the tour that Todd Bliss of Bio-Tours (831/375-5089) gives of the area he points out one of the rare phenomena of Point Lobos known as the K-T line. This line contains traces of iridium brought by the theorized impact of a giant meteor, which is to have collided with the earth sixty-five thousand years ago and is credited with changing conditions on land that caused the abrupt disappearance of the dinosaurs.

For your own discoveries, get a map of the reserve at the entrance or the Information Station at the Sea Lion Point parking lot. Plan to spend two to three hours if you are going to just walk the trails. Also at the Sea Lion Point Information Station docents are available to answer questions and sell you a book or poster.

Point Lobos State Reserve has about ten different trails that are short and relatively flat. (Still, it is a good idea to wear sturdy shoes.) This tour covers three of the main trails.

WHALERS CABIN AND THE CARMELO MEADOW TRAIL. The Carmelo Meadow trail provides a short connection between the entrance station and the Whalers Cove area. Access this trail about ten yards past the entrance station. All trails in the park are clearly marked. Around you invasive rattlesnake grass shakes in the wind. The grass entered the park about twenty years ago on the blades of a grass mower. Follow the trail through a forest of Monterey pine and coast live oak. Monterey pine cones need the heat from an unusually hot day or a fire to open. A controlled burn of this area in 1993 provided the heat for Monterey pine cones to open; most of the young trees you see date to that time. The trail then winds through open Carmelo Meadow. A number of sedges and grasses native to California grow here as well as non-native plants introduced by early settlers and cattle ranchers. In 1890 Carmelo Meadow was the site of a proposed 1,000 lot housing subdivision known as Point Lobos City. The 0.1-mile easy trail meets Granite Point Trail on the bluff above Whalers Cove. Here you will find a bench where you can lose yourself in the offshore antics of otters, or in late spring, watch a baby harbor seal waddle up by mom.

Whalers Cove can also be reached by turning right on a service road, just past the entrance station. Picnic tables, rest rooms, and parking are located here. Divers usually fill the available parking slots early.

Built as one of several cabins by Chinese fishermen in the 1850s, Whalers Cabin now houses several exhibits that document the cultural history of Point Lobos. Next to the cabin, the Whaling Station Museum displays the ropes, harpoons, and tools of Portuguese whalers who arrived at Point Lobos in 1862. Panels describe the whaling operation and family life. Large pots called try pots were used to melt large chunks of whale blubber. Two of these pots and an almost one-hundred-year-old finback whale skeleton can be seen outside the museum.

In the mid-1890s, marine biologist Gennosuke Kodani began an abalone fishery with workers from his native village of Chiba, Japan. From 1899 to 1927, together with property owner Alexander Allan, the Kodani family operated an abalone cannery on what is now the Whalers Cove parking area. Whalers Cabin was used as a processing plant.

Granite Point Trail begins at the museum. A mass of scrub flowers frame each side of you as you walk along bluffs. The trail enters a forest area, then leads to the now abandoned site of the Kodani home. A segment of the trails unveils a now peaceful lookout of a hidden pit scoured by granite miners. Farther on, the trail connects with Moss Cove trail, which leads to evidence of the earliest inhabitants—the grinding rocks found at Ichxenta Point.

BIRD ISLAND TRAIL. This trail leads to China and Gibson beaches, the only two beaches in the reserve where swimming is allowed. The water is very cold, but you may enjoy a refreshing dip. This .7-mile trail offers a variety of animal life and scenery with good views of Bird Island. The trail takes about twenty minutes to walk.

Walking from the entrance, just past the ranger station, follow the South Plateau trail left 1 kilometer to the Bird Island trail. If you drive in, follow the main road around the information station at Sea Lion Rock and turn south past Weston Beach and then Hidden Beach to dead-end at the Bird Island trail. You will find parking spaces, a picnic area, and rest rooms.

The Bird Island trail first leads up a set of stairs to a knoll, a favorite from which to spot migrating whales. You can also spot large, rounded Bird Island from this point. The trail enters the edge of a Monterey pine forest. These pine trees are host to several species of birds, such as the pigmy nuthatch (a small bird with a blue-gray and white throat). It chips out nesting cavities thirty or more feet high in the trees. Here you may also encounter the ground squirrels that eat the seeds, plants, and insects abundant in this forest. Next the trail crosses the hillside facing the sheltered emerald green baylet of China Cove. A long, steep set of stairs descends to the white sands of China Beach. If the tide is out you can look into the small cave at the base of the cliff. In the water you can see floating brown kelp. Both giant kelp and bull kelp are found here. Egrets can often be seen in this sheltered cove, walking on the kelp blades.

Back up the steps, continue on the path to a second spur. Here a second set of stairs leads down to Gibson Beach. Large boulders strewn about on the beach look like giants' marbles.

From above Gibson Beach the trail heads west to an ending loop. The larger of the two rocks you see is Bird Island, a refuge for Brandt's cormorants, western gulls, and pigeon guillemots. Although brown pelicans no longer nest here, they can still be found roosting in the summer and fall.

CYPRESS GROVE TRAIL. This .8-mile trail is one of the most popular in the park. It passes through the Allan Memorial Grove of Monterey cypresses and comes out along the clifftop to provide views of the ocean. The trail begins at the Cypress Cove parking area. This is a loop trail that takes about forty-five minutes to walk.

The path splits a short distance from the information station. During spring the native wild lilac, ceanothus, blossoms pink and blue along the first stretch to ocean vistas. You will probably hear the barking of sea lions before you see them. The Spaniards called his area Punto de los Lobos Marinos: Point of the Sea Lions (literally, of the sea "wolves"). One short side trail leads to North Point and a good view of Cypress Cove. Another features spectacular vistas of the ocean and the waves crashing on the ragged outcroppings. From here you can look across Carmel Bay and see the brilliant white sands of Carmel Beach.

After leaving the vista point the trail heads through a Monterey Cypress Grove named in honor of A. M. Allan, who in the early 1900s bought the land to keep it from being subdivided by developers into Point Lobos City. Allan set up a toll gate in later years when autos and picnickers flocked to the area. Allan's family donated the cypress grove to the state when Point Lobos became a reserve in 1933. This is one of two last remaining indigenous Monterey cypress groves anywhere. The oldest trees here are probably two hundred years old. As you look coastward to the Pinnacle, the northernmost point in the reserve, you will see the gnarled, twisted trunks of trees sculpted by battering winds. To survive the winds, the trees adapt with a response called "buttressing": a thin part of the trunk faces the wind while the trunk grows thicker on the opposite side to brace the tree.

Scientists theorize that the cypress formerly grew in huge forests along the coast. The conifer is easily grown from seed and since discovering the native groves here and across Carmel Bay in Pebble Beach, people have planted cypress trees extensively. The tree is so adaptable and easily reproduced that it is a puzzle why this tree's natural range is limited to the two tiny groves.

The trail turns past South Point, with a descent back to the trailhead. Close by you can join the Sea Lion trail for good wildlife viewing.

THE BIG SUR TOUR

It is best to allow a full day for the Big Sur drive if you are planning to complete the entire route. Highway 1 through Big Sur is slow, twisting, and scenic. Allow time to stretch your legs. I strongly suggest this as a one-way trip for the day with an overnight along the way or at a southern destination. The largest community along this section of the coast is in Big Sur. A six-mile-long stretch along the Big Sur River is the home for approximately five hundred people. The community is a collection of rustic homes as well as restaurants, resorts, general stores, and specialty shops. It is well known as a rural retreat and artists' colony.

There are no other towns between Carmel and Cambria, so you should plan to take most of your supplies with you. There are small rural communities with a gas station, deli, artist galleries, and small shops, so you can pick up small items if needed. It is always a good idea to take water and wear good walking shoes.

After leaving Point Lobos you drive through Carmel Highlands, a collection of architecturally stunning homes perched on rocky cliffs. Homes here complement the rugged coast and sometimes appear much smaller than their actual size. In Carmel Highlands, a Carmel stone gas station and espresso bar shares a corner at Fern Canyon Road with the Sculpture House and Gardens Fine Arts Gallery (831/624-2476). Across Fern Canyon Road, at Gravity Gardens, you can picnic by the balanced rock sculptures that line Highway 1. Here, Jim Needham shares his wisdom for creating precariously balanced rock figures. "Center yourself. Come in contact with the earth and the rocks will balance." He shares some lighthearted philosophy as he surveys the eighty tons of rocks he has personally transported here. "In life, make sure the things you hold on to are heavy and of no value—then you can really test your attachment." The balanced rocks may collapse if touched; this is not an appropriate place for small or energetic children or pets. As you continue south on Highway 1, for the turnoff to Highlands Inn (831/624-3801), watch the left side of the road.

Just past Carmel Highlands, the steep canyon walls of Malpaso Creek mark the beginning of Big Sur country. At Malpaso, meaning "bad crossing" in Spanish, let your mind wander back to the times when no bridges crossed the steep ravines, and imagine the hardships of early travelers. Clint Eastwood liked the sound of this crossing and used it as the name of his production company, Malpaso Productions.

5.4 S, 84.3 N. Garrapata State Park's northern boundary is two miles south of Carmel Highlands Drive. Rugged coastline and sweeping ocean views especially from Rocky Ridge trail make this a representational slice of the Big Sur coast. As the park has been open to the public only since 1983, it is still relatively untraveled. Within it along Highway 1 are sixteen numbered (unless signs are vandalized or dislodged by roadwork) state highway turnouts that lead to a variety of scenic overlooks. The only safe waterfront access is at the highly visible Garrapata Beach at the southern border of the 3,067-acre park. For day-use only, the park has as facilities only outhouses,

Rocky Creek Bridge

between turnouts 13 and 14 and between 15 and 16. Turnout 10's trail leads to a good example of the war of land and sea; waves are wresting a large shoulder of granite from the shore.

5.7 S, 84 N. From this turnout you can view Soberanes Point, a major headland that resembles a giant clippership jutting into the ocean.

6.8 S, 82.9 N. Seventy-yard-long turnout 13 marks the beginning of the oceanside Whale Peak trail system, Rocky Ridge trail, and the Soberanes Canyon trail. Clusters of cypresses that were probably planted as windbreaks by the Soberanes family, early settlers of the area, now hide an outhouse. These cypress also mark the rocky promontory of Soberanes Point. Around the back of a small headlands, a bench offers a great spot to sit and watch the ocean, especially for whales.

To hike to a creek setting and memorable views, hike the inland Soberanes Canyon trail and the Rocky Ridge trail. "Garrapata" means wood tick in Spanish, so tuck in your pant legs and stay on trails in this area. A main trail begins behind an old barn. After crossing Soberanes Creek you will come to the sign for the beginning of Soberanes Creek trail. Rocky Ridge trail and Soberanes Creek trail form a loop back to your starting point. I recommend ascending the first trail that veers right, Soberanes Creek trail, which is a little steep for a while as it winds through a bushy ridge, then enters a small red-wood forest. You will need to cross the creek a few times before you climb to a grassy path. Sometimes in the very early spring multitudes of ladybugs hatch here. You will be treated to panoramic ocean views as you descend a path dotted with golden yarrow, bush lupine, and sage.

9.3 S, 80.4 N. As the road widens and some oceanside houses come into view, several dirt parking areas mark the Doud Creek entrance to the accessible and inviting sandy stretches of Garrapata State Beach. Here you can walk the coastal bluffs for about five minutes, then descend a rather steep hill and traverse stepping stone bridges across Doud Creek. This is the more rugged entrance to the beach; a staircase entrance is accessed from pathways located across the bridge, .3 mile south of this turnout. Some isolated sections of Garrapata Beach are preferred spots for clothing-optional preferences.

9.6 S, 80.1 N. Highway 1 widens. Several hundred feet of dirt roadside parking area mark the staircase approach to Garrapata Beach. Families enjoy sand play here, but the waves are treacherous. The uplifted shelves of rock and eroded surfaces create a dramatic backdrop for the crashing waves.

10 S, 79.7 N. The official vista point allows a close look at abalone cove, a deep bay covered with swirling kelp. This is usually a good spot to view a sea otter or observe the black Brandt's cormorants.

10.8 S, 78.9 N. Rocky Point Restaurant (408/624-2933), "excellent food on the edge of forever," serves lunch and dinner on a point rumored to have been used by pirates and later bootleggers. Sweeping views of the unfolding coastline, including the gigantic hill of Point Sur and Rocky Creek Bridge, are some of the best on the coast. The picturesque bridge span is often mistaken for the famous Bixby Bridge. Downhill from the restaurant, waves have carved a natural arch out of a cliff on the shoreline.

11.1 S, 88.6 N. Palo Colorado Canyon Road, carved along the Palo Colorado ("tall red wood" in Spanish) fault, winds four miles as a very narrow one-and-a-half-lane twisty road before widening and eventually ending at Bottcher's Gap National Forest Campground. Drive slow for the curves and extra slow to watch for children and animals along the way. Lower Palo Colorado Canyon Road is darkly shaded by tall, closely set redwoods, and dotted with a surprising number of homes and cabins.

At Bottcher's Canyon a number of trails lead to the Ventana Wilderness. There are stories but no evidence or pictures that a land bridge once spanned Bottcher's gap, forming a natural window, the "ventana" of the wilderness. At 3,709 feet Pico Blanco, meaning "white peak," towers over the southern section of the gap. The tons of white-gray marble that form the peak are the largest chunk of the oldest metamorphic rock in the parks. Geologists theorize the peak was formed millions of years ago when river sediments in Mexico or even farther south were pressed, heated, and folded by an underriding of the earth's crust. Pico Blanco rode north by movement of the San Andreas fault.

13.1 S, 76.6 N. Along your drive and various sojourns you have probably been catching great views of the stunning 260-foot-span Bixby Bridge. You can travel the Old Coast Road by turning left just before you cross the bridge from the north; from the south take an immediate right after crossing the bridge. Before the bridge was opened in 1932, Old Coast Road was the only route available for traversing the coast. For veteran Big Sur travelers who want a change of pace or photographers in search of sweeping coastal views this ten-mile-long, graded dirt road is a pleasant, but very curvy, backroad route. It requires up to an hour to travel. If you want to hike here look for the trailhead along the way. You can walk by the Little Sur River, bounded by redwoods, ferns, and in spring shade-loving flowers. Stay on the trail. The "no trespassing" signs here are strictly enforced. Backpackers and long-day hikers, note this trail connects with the Pico Blanco camp trail. The Old Coast Road winds along hillsides, into dark stands of redwoods, along the river, and up through more redwood groves to top-of-the-world views. Hawks and eagles may be soaring in the skies around you. The road ends at the Highway 1 entrance to Andrew Molera State Park.

Bixby Bridge, one of the world's highest single-span concrete bridges, stretches 700 feet, rises over 260 feet high, and features a 320-foot arch over the V-shaped Bixby Creek Canyon. The bridge took more than a year to build. Its continued existence symbolizes the successful fight by Big Sur residents to stop the widening of Highway 1 into a four-lane freeway. Before you leave try to imagine the tram here in the early part of the century, carrying limestone from the lime kilns down to ships waiting at Bixby Landing in the cove below.

14.3 S, 75.4 N. Just be happy you aren't running the Big Sur Marathon as you climb this steep grade to Hurricane Point, probably the most wind-blown point on the highway. A massive slide in January 1998 destroyed the road here and closed it for four months.

16.5 S, 73.2 N. The Little Sur River flows through a horseshoe valley carving new channels at whim as, during wet winters and springs, it flows to the ocean. In the dry season the river collects in a lagoon behind a sandbar built by wind. Pico Blanco is easily spotted from the turnoff here. The beach is on private land. Even from your lookout you can see that the waves are too treacherous for swimming or even wading here, as along most of the coast.

18.5 S, 71.2 N. Atop the 370-foot-tall block of lava that resembles a large pillow, facing cold mists and sweeping winds, is the Big Sur Lightstation, the only lightstation on the West Coast with all its nineteenth-century buildings intact. A hundred feet below the cluster of keepers' buildings a working lighthouse hugs the side of the mound. The lightstation as a whole is connected to the shore by a tombolo (sand bar). Early Big Sur residents sometimes benefitted from the cargos of wrecked ships, such as the linens and wagons on the *Ventura*, which wrecked in 1875.

The first light was a large multiwick kerosene lamp surrounded by an approximately six-thousand-pound Fresnel lens that projected a beam visible for fourteen nautical miles. The lighthouse was controlled automatically after 1972. Today the light and radio beacon are computer-directed and project a beam for twenty-four nautical miles. The original lens can be seen at the Monterey Maritime Museum.

The collection of intact buildings and architectural features and workmanship of the unique rough-cut sandstone, including rock keystones and arched doorways, prompted the reclassification of the lighthouse as Point Sur State Historic Park. Volunteer-led guided tours include the lighthouse, the keepers' houses, the blacksmith shop, and the barn, where livestock was kept for food and transportation. Cormorants and seagulls fly eye-to-eye with tour groups alongside a cliffside walk to the lighthouse. On sunny days the view is spectacular. On foggy days rocks offshore are swallowed from view. The Central Coast Lighthouse Keepers, a group of California State Park volunteers, is presently working to preserve the lightstation for future generations. The buildings sustained considerable damage in 1997 and 1998 and viewing may be restricted in some areas.

Tours are currently offered every Saturday at 10 a.m. and 2 p.m. and Sunday at 10 a.m., weather permitting. Moonlight tours are also scheduled to coincide with the full moon. Visitors who wish to go on tours should arrive one-half hour before the scheduled times. Meet along the west side of Highway 1 at the locked gate, a quarter mile north of the Point Sur naval facility. Depending on the number of volunteer guides available, tour size may be limited. Tours last two-and-a-half to three hours and include a walk of approximately one-half mile up an access road with a 360-foot rise in elevation. There are two flights of stairs; the longest has sixty-five steps. Admission is $5 per adult, $3 for ages thirteen to seventeen, and $2 for ages five to twelve. Wear comfortable walking shoes, bring coats, and dress in layers, even if Highway 1 is sunny; the weather is unpredictable. Since the tour includes steep cliffs without barriers it is not recommended for small children, and strollers are not permitted. No pets, food, or drink are allowed. Call prior to your trip; contact the Big Sur State Park Office: 831/667-2315.

The lands beyond Point Sur are part of the El Sur Ranch, the largest remaining cattle ranch along the coast. The 7,100 acres included in the ranch were part of an original Spanish land grant, a common history for many of the ranches in Big Sur.

21.4 S, 68.3 N. Andrew Molera State Park, Big Sur Ornithology Lab, and Molera Trail Rides (831/625-5486 or 800/942-5486) share the same entrance on the west side of the highway. We like to cook a pancake and Corralitos sausage breakfast at the riverside barbecue area in the park, then spend the rest of the day riding, hiking, or biking the numerous trails within these 7.4 square miles. The Camp trail, which merges with the Headlands trail, is the only year-round coastal access route, because it doesn't cross the river. However, it does not access the main beach, which is cut off by the river. The trail begins as a river-bordering road to an open-field walk-in-only campground, which has a few special wooded spots. Beyond the campground you'll pass through a eucalyptus grove favored by migrating monarchs from November through March. When it is cold or foggy the orange and black butterflies fold their wings, to resembling dry leaves hanging from the trees. The historic Cooper cabin is nestled in this grove—where the road narrows to a trail. If you want beach access continue ahead. If you take the Headlands trail spur you'll climb to where some thoughtful person has set some of the best-located benches along the coast. Look up and you may see a red-tailed hawk soaring or an American kestrel hovering. Nature planted a hedge of ceanothus around the bench, and in spring the sweet blossoms frame the expansive ocean view.

Take someone you love along if you climb higher, to the tip of Molera Point to view the little cliff-shrouded beach to the north. This overlook is my pick for the most romantic place on the coast. The Big Sur River flows free to the ocean below. The golden sands, the rocky headlands, and the aquamarine waters intertwine, as the wind whispers secrets in your ear. . . . Another love affair unfolds offshore as surfers glide in the waves. Sometimes when my feet are feeling a little weary from the mile-long walk to the beach, I'm humbled by a surfer running the distance with board tucked underarm. Remember, the waves here are dangerous for those of us who aren't experienced surfers.

The Big Sur Ornithology Lab serves as a research center at Andrew Molera. As you hike through the park you may come upon green nets spread between trees. The nets need to remain undisturbed. Occasionally you will see a bird wrapped in one. Rest assured, a scientist will be along soon to free it. The ornithology lab allows scientists to study environmental concerns. For instance, the increased presence of a previously rare bird may indicate environmental changes in its usual habitat.

Bicycles are allowed only on the Camp trail, Creamery Meadow trail, and Ridge trail. To walk along Molera Beach you'll first need to cross the Big Sur River. During summer months there is a footbridge a short distance from the entrance parking lot that leads to the beach and Creamery Meadow trails. More trails are mapped in a brochure you can pick up from the ranger. Molera Trail Rides offers a selection of two- and three-hour rides, which lead through redwood groves, along ocean bluffs, and over beaches in the park. Luncheon and sunset rides are available.

25.2 S, 64.5 N. The ice cream bus, adjacent to the River Inn, welcomes travelers to the community of Big Sur. Ice cream, shakes, and floats are signals that this sunny inland valley can get pleasantly warm. Parking is located in front of the River Inn and behind the village shops. If you are here on a weekend afternoon, check whether the local Abalone Stompers are jazzing it up on the River Inn deck. The inn offers a grassy expanse to a river beach where patrons pull their chairs into the water and dangle toes or soak hike-weary feet. This is a fun place to stretch and wander galleries and shops. The Heartbeat Gift Shop (831/667-2557) offers a selection of wood drums, other musical instruments, and jewelry. You might want to check out the resorts with private campgrounds and cabins along the next couple of highway miles: Big Sur Campgrounds and Cabins, Riverside Campground and Cabins, Ripplewood Resort, and Fernwood. Four gas stations, several delis, and a small grocery line this route. Across the street from the clean and comfortable Glen Oaks Motel, the Glen Oaks Restaurant (831/667-2264), owned by long-time residents, serves an elegant meal and special Sunday brunch. Just a half-mile south of Glen Oaks, Saint Francis of the Redwoods Catholic Church (831/624-1271) holds mass in the open air.

26 S, 63.7 N. When most people say they're going to Big Sur they are headed for Pfeiffer ("pie-fur") Big Sur State Park, which offers day use and more than two hundred campsites with facilities. It is located thirty minutes north of Julia Pfeiffer Burns State Park, which offers day hikes and four walk-in campsites. Favorite activities at Pfeiffer Big Sur include wading in the river which meanders through the park's 810 acres and participating in the park's many interpretive programs. You can spot deer during the day. You might lose anything that is not locked and secured to the bandits of the night, those wide-eyed raccoons.

Redwoods, ferns, a babbling creek, and a small waterfall await day visitors on the half-mile mostly level Pfeiffer Falls trail. This is a gentle leg-stretcher for the whole family. The best swimming holes I've heard about in the area are some boulder hops away, up the River Gorge trail. This trail is not an official, maintained trail but is one of the two most popular in the park. The gorge should never be entered alone, during rainy weather, or when a strong current exists in the river. It is ideal for hot summer days and can get quite crowded then. The trail begins at the north tip of the campground as the East-Bank trail. By early summer, campers have usually built a stepping stone crossing on the river about three hundred yards up the trail. Once across you need to scoot over some large boulders to the edge of a large rock-lined pool. The water temperature is warmer than the ocean, but still brisk. On the Oak Grove trail you will pass a homesteader's cabin. A ring of rocks surround the graves of the children of the Innocentis, the first family to settle in Big Sur.

26.4 S, 63.3 N. About one-half mile south of the entrance to the Pfeiffer Big Sur State Park you will see the entrance to the Big Sur Station. This is a multi-agency facility served by California State Parks, the U.S. Forest Service, and CALTRANS. Information about Big Sur in general, plus road conditions and hiking trails, is available here. Maps are provided and also sold along with books and postcards. This is a good place to ask for information regarding Adventure Passes, which are required to hike and backpack on some public lands that are not served by private concessions. If you are taking a stove into the back country you will need a permit.

Big Sur Station is also the trailhead for hikes to Ventana Wilderness Camp and Sykes Hot Springs. The hike to the hot springs is more than nine miles one way so you will need to plan for at least two days. The trail to Sykes Hot Springs is one of the most popular back-country hikes in the park, but many people who hike it feel it is overrated. Parking here costs $4 a day. Day hikes from this point traverse some steep terrain, but the beauty of the back country is worth it.

Just beyond Big Sur Station, on the west side of Highway 1, Pfeiffer Beach is located at the end of Sycamore Canyon Road—from the north, the second right turn you can make south of Big Sur State Park. After the movie *The Sandpipers*, with Elizabeth Taylor and Richard Burton, was filmed in 1965, the area attracted many tourists in search of idyllic life-with-beach. Pfeiffer Beach is one of the most beautiful beaches I have ever seen. Immense wind and wave sculpted rocks, ocean-powered blowholes, and eroding rock arches beckon. However, the winds here can be outrageous and the sand stings even the most ardent seeker. Traffic and parking problems led to limiting to the number of cars permitted entry each day. There is a $5 day use fee.

27.1 S, 62.6 N. Big Sur Center with its deli and United States Post Office and Big Sur Bazaar (831/667-2197) featuring quality organic personal care items and creations by local artisans are located next to Loma Vista Gardens on the west side of Highway 1. Sixty-year-old cacti mark the entrance to Loma Vista which was built in 1937 by Alice and Steve Jaeger as the first filling station and diner on the newly constructed highway. The Jaegers knew the perfect location for a cactus garden; when fog shrouds the valley, this spot is usually sunny. The Jaegers were also known for their prize-winning begonias. The Big Sur Garden Company (831/667-2818) continues their tradition of selling begonias, cacti, and pottery. In one of the original greenhouses here, A Shop in the Garden sells vintage clothing, herbal products, and jewelry. A great view of Mount Manuel is garnered on the steps of the Loma Vista Cafe (831/667-2450).

28 S, 61.7 N. On the inland side of the highway you will spot the red farmhouse which belonged to the Posts, one of the early homesteading families in Big Sur. Today the farmhouse marks the entrance to the Ventana Inn. Although they are both on original Post Ranch land, the entrances to the Ventana Inn and Post Ranch Inn are found here, on opposite sides of Highway 1. Even if you eat and lodge elsewhere on this trip, consider taking the daily 2 p.m. tour of the ecologically and architecturally stunning Post Ranch Inn. Call first to confirm the tour (831/667-2200). The Gallery at Ventana (831/667-2331) is a showcase for artists who live or have a long history of residence on the Big Sur coast. Marble sculptures of sea life and whales by Warren Arnold swim about you. His dream is to bring a series of whale sculptures to outlooks along the sanctuary. The layered wood sculptures by the door, so alive I could almost feel them breathe, are the works of Edmund Kara, the carver of the large phoenix at Nepenthe.

28.7 S, 61 N. Nepenthe's corner of the world used to be owned by Orson Welles, purportedly as a planned but never materialized hideaway for Rita Hayworth, his wife for a short time. Lolly Fassett, granddaughter of Frank Powers (developer of Carmel), and her husband, William, bought the property from Welles and developed Nepenthe, a Big Sur landmark. Stairs and paths lead huffing visitors to the main restaurant, to the Phoenix Shop, with crafts, jewelry, and clothing from around the world, and to the Café Kevah, where guests are treated to exceptional views. Designed by Rowan Maiden, a former apprentice to Frank Lloyd Wright, the building was probably the first commercial destination on the coast to assimilate the lines of sky and coast. The *Dark Angel*, a stunning redwood and mosaic sculpture by Big Sur artist and forty-year resident Cyril (Bus) Brown, stands tall to transport souls above the Phoenix Shop. Although Nepenthe has expanded and mellowed through the years, it still offers visitors an artsy, in-step-with-Big-Sur aura, heightened by treetop coastal views and occasional glimpses of famous visitors.

Immediately beyond Nepenthe, on the inland side of the highway, the stunning Hawthorne Gallery (831/667-3200) displays contemporary art. The gallery represents the artwork of the multi-talented Hawthorne family as well as work of selected internationally known artists. From his studio overlooking the gallery and coast, Gregory Hawthorne creates provocative imagery that meshes painting and sculpture in full color human figures, steel wall puzzles, and free-standing abstract forms. A large metallic cowboy rides on a sunlit wall, water cascades through huge granite fountains, and sunlight plays in massive blown-glass shells. For gallery director Bebe, the connection and display of the gallery holdings within the stunning architecture is itself an art. The panoramic ocean-view from upstairs is unsurpassed.

29 S, 60.7 N. The Henry Miller Memorial Library (831/667-2574) is just south of Nepenthe, one of the writer's favorite haunts. For seventeen years, *Tropic of Cancer* author Miller lived and wrote south of here atop Partington Ridge. His friend Emil White started a collection of Henry Miller materials and entertained the many visitors who flocked to the coast hoping to catch a glimpse of the author with a satyr's reputation. Today visitors enter through large wooden gates and a sometimes serene, sometimes lively sculpture garden. The library is really a light and airy gallery, which features first and out-of-print editions of Miller's books, some of the artist's paintings, and memorabilia. Some of the treasures are under glass, some are available to purchase, but none are available for library loan. Drumming classes on the lawn, life-drawing classes, art retrospectives, and ongoing presentations by local artists and writers sometimes share the space.

29.2 S, 60.5 N. Slow down or you will miss the inland dirt road to Deetjen's Big Sur Inn. This collection of rustic cabins and a memorable lodge, built by Norwegian carpenter Helmut Deetjen from old wharf timbers and driftwood, nestles under redwoods by Castro Creek. A nonprofit foundation operates Deetjen's, now a national historic monument. Summer rooms are often booked months in advance. Breakfasts and lunches are casual. Candlelit dinners are served on Staffordshire china to a background of classical music. Helmut used to tell guests that music, nature, and art were the only important things in life.

32 S, 57.7 N. After traversing some sheer cliffs visible from the Castro Canyon Bridge and Grimes Point turnoff you'll see the Coast Gallery (831/667-2301), tucked into the inland side of Lafler Canyon. The gardens and driveway of this gallery were washed away in a slide, but the gallery remains stalwart at the edge. The canyon is named for a former editor and friend of Jack London's. Legend has it that Lafler slept in the hollowed-out trunk of a redwood tree before moving to a ridge-hugging stone house. The legend makes the Coast Gallery, housed in two round antique redwood water tanks, all the more fitting. Handmade candles have been dipped at a studio here since 1958. A summer artists-in-action program sometimes provides an

opportunity to talk with the local artists and craftspeople who display their work at the gallery. The Coast Cafe (831/667-2301) serves lunch, baked goods, coffee, and estate bottled wines, and offers great views from the rooftop seating.

34.1 S, 55.6 N. To hear ocean waves crack like no other place on the coast, walk through a hundred-foot tunnel, view a grove of stunted redwoods that defy scientific knowledge, and enjoy reflective waters by sparkling deep blue surf, take a hike through Partington Canyon and Cove, which mark the northernmost boundaries of Julia Pfeiffer Burns State Park. The trail begins at an iron gate on the west end of Partington Creek Bridge, then descends rather steeply for a quarter of a mile to Partington Creek. Upstream, the trail leads to an outhouse. Downstream the route continues a short way to a junction. Straight ahead the trail leads though redwoods to a tiny beach. Supposedly, redwoods can't live this close to the ocean because of intolerance to salt air. Well, you're here and so are they! Retrace your steps to the junction and turn right, cross a footbridge, then picture sleds of tanbark oak as they were pulled through the tunnel. John Partington built the tunnel for his tan oak cutting and shipping operation at Partington Landing. As you walk through the six-foot-wide, eight-foot-high tunnel to the beach, the waves crash against cliffs pitted with caverns. You can still see the rusted remains of the landing. Experienced scuba divers explore the kelp beds here; clearance is given through Pfeiffer Big Sur State Park.

37 S, 52.7 N. A short, level walk to McWay Falls punctuates the beauty at this main entrance to Julia Pfeiffer Burns State Park. The quarter-mile trail takes about twenty minutes. From the parking lot descend the first set of stairs to your left to see the tiny McWay Creek ripple over rocks shaded by redwoods. Then, accompanied by waters rushing ever faster, turn right and walk along a path decorated by orange sticky monkey flower, spring-blossoming pink ceanothus, and in autumn, the beautiful scarlet of poison oak (far from your reach if you stay on the path). The path leads through a tunnel under the coast highway to an overlook where you can watch the creek plummet fifty feet to foamy ocean waters, at high tide, or to a sandy beach, at low. Across from the falls, isolated cypress trees pull nutrients from a rock that is being torn from the main headland by constant surf pounding. To the best of my knowledge, this is the only place on the California coast where a creek forms a waterfall directly into the ocean.

In addition to the waterfall Julia Pfeiffer Burns State Park offers trails through the redwoods and along the creek. Usually, it's sunny here which makes this a favorite picnic location.

39.8 S, 49.9 N. A wooden sign on the west side of the road marks an entrance to the reservations-only Esalen Institute (831/647-3005), which has offered seminars emphasizing human potential and values for more than thirty years. Seminars range from weekend-participant to three-month-resident and internship programs.

Esalen was frequented by Esselen and perhaps Salinans for the soothing hotsprings in the cliffs above the ocean here. Shell mounds and in some places mortars are found. September 1993 marked the first time a workshop given by local Esselen descendants teaching the ways of indigenous peoples has been offered at Esalen. In 1860 Thomas Slate, reportedly crippled with arthritis, lost all symptoms after soaking in the springs repeatedly for several weeks. Slate bought the springs, and in the Esselen way, opened them to any and all who needed or wanted soaks. Slate's Hot Springs were bought by Dr. and Mrs. H. C. Murphy from Salinas. Their son Michael cofounded the Esalen Institute here in the 1960s. Today, with millions of cars traveling Highway 1 annually, the public soaking hours are limited to 1 to 3:30 a.m. and only by reservation (831/667-3047). Overnight accommodations are sometimes available, depending on attendance at seminars.

45 S, 44.7 N. Even though it has double arches, Big Creek Bridge is often mistaken for Bixby Bridge. The four-thousand-acre Big Creek Ranch lands around the bridge were purchased in 1977 by the Nature Conservancy. The University of California operates a large portion of the former ranch as the Landels Hill–Big Creek Reserve.

49.8 S, 39.9 N. In 1895, Wilbur Harlan hiked down the coast from Santa Cruz to land around the present community of Lucia. The Lucia Restaurant, convenience market, and rustic cabins are set on land the Harlan family homesteaded.

Just south of Lucia on the right hand side a white cross marks the entrance to the Immaculate Heart Hermitage, New Camaldoli. Camaldolese Monks, whose order was established in the Apennine Mountains of Italy in the year 1012, bought part of the Harland land for hermitage. Visitors are welcome to attend daily masses and are reminded by a mildly worded sign to observe the quiet contemplation of the order. Retreat facilities are open to men and women for a usual stay of three days. For reservation information you can write Immaculate Heart Hermitage, New Camaldoli, Big Sur, 93920, or call 831/667-2456.

52.1 S, 37.6 N. Limekiln Creek flows to a sandy cove beach shared by campers and day users of Limekiln State Park. Forty-three campsites are spread through three environs a stretch of one of the southernmost coastal redwood forests, ocean bluff, and beach sand. Ranger Beth Atwood wears two hats here as site ranger and land-based ranger for the southern section of the Monterey National Marine Sanctuary. She answers every question you have or could dream up about your natural surroundings. When the creek is rushing in the spring she will help you spot the spawning steelhead trout. A nature trail that borders Limekiln Creek leads to large rusted metal cylinders and massive brick ovens, where limestone from the surrounding canyon was smelted into lime. Hundreds of thousands of barrels of lime were shipped off at the cove here, much of it bound for San Francisco to rebuild sidewalks lost in the 1906 earthquake. Along the trail millions of carbonated skeletons of marine organisms compacted in white limestone lie at the base of redwoods, a waterfall churns over a fallen redwood to fill a tranquil pool, thimbleberries bear sweet fruit, and lush carpets of sorrel bloom pink and white from April through September. Back at the beach kayaks skim the cove; check with the helpful staff for surf information.

54 S, 35.7 N. The trailhead for the Kirk Creek trail, also known as the Vicente Flat trail, begins across from the Kirk Creek Campground. Here you can climb steep switchbacks as Highway 1 shrinks to a hairline S below. All along the trail, mountains and seashore form expansive views. The trail takes about one hour to walk to the crest. It then continues to Vicente Flat Camp.

54.2 S, 35.5 N. Many tour books and some motel personnel recommend scenic Nacimiento-Fergusson Road to the Salinas Valley and Highway 101 for the ultimate ocean views. The road is a narrow, twisty cliffhanger. In some places where rocks have slid from sheer cliffs the road isn't wide enough for one car, much less two. For a complete description, see the Inland Excursions chapter (page 213). The only time I would recommend this road is when Highway 1 to Big Sur is closed. The views are great but I'll choose hiking Kirk Creek any day.

54.5 S, 35.2 N. Mill Creek flows to the Pacific Ocean just south of Nacimiento-Furgusson Road. Picnic tables with a small accessible beach nearby make this a good place for snacks or lunch.

57 S, 32.7 N. A driveway leads up a small inland slope to the foundation of the burned and closed Pacific Valley Center. Your attention may be diverted from the ocean as hang gliders and parasailers take to the skies on the coast side. This area has become a very popular launching and landing area for these sports; reserve a permit in advance by calling the Pacific Valley Station of Los Padres National Forest (805/927-4211).

58.4 S, 31.3 N. The Pacific Valley Station of Los Padres National Forest operates primarily as a fire station.

58.7 S, 31 N. At Sand Dollar Beach you'll find a clean, pleasant picnic area with fire pits and a rest room. To reach the crescent-shaped beach, where you can sometimes find sand dollars among the rocks, cross a meadow and walk down the stairs. The sand here was washed out in monster storms of the late 1990s. Sand usually washes from this beach every winter and deposits in a type of sand reservoir offshore. In summer the sand returns, but these storms were so massive people are wondering if the sand is still offshore and if the sandy Sand Dollar Beach will return.

59.2 S, 30.5 N. Plaskett Creek Campground is set in an open clearing alongside a creek. Plaskett Cove marks the northernmost boundary of jade coves.

59.8 S, 29.9 N. A Los Padres National Forest sign that marks Jade Cove designates the series of coves that stretch from Plaskett Creek on the north to Willow Creek on the south. With the exception of Willow Creek the coves are only accessible by descending steep cliffs subject to crashing waves and this is not recommended.

Local jade or nephrite is most readily found at low tides following winter storms. The jade along the cliffs has been picked over for years, and most pieces found now have been freed from immersed reefs of serpentine and washed onto shore by high waves, which leave them lodged between rocks along the cliffs. Most local jade is a darkish blue-green color. The jade you find may have a dull appearance until you rub it against your cheek or dip it in water. Jade has a soapy feel and is stronger than steel, so a nail or knife won't scratch it.

61.5 S, 28.2 N. A road on the ocean side leads down to Willow Creek Beach, where you'll find a picnic area and rest rooms. Plan to be here at low tide if possible, particularly for the tidepooling, which is sometimes more rewarding than the jade hunting. Kids love to do both. Watch for sneaker waves along the shore.

62 S, 27.7 N. Willow Creek Road, on the east side, is a very precarious road with little to recommend—no ghost town remains of the historic Los Burros mining district. The Gold Rush boom town in these hills burned to the ground. A few diehard prospectors work private claims, which are not open to the public. If you are going this way, stay on the road. Four-wheel drive is required.

64 S, 25.7 N. Gorda, renamed by its most recent owners as Gorda Springs, is a relaxing spot near a landslide-prone section of the road. The road washed out on February 2, 1997, and for months the road was closed then opened to one lane as CALTRANS workers reinforced it to become what locals refer to as "The Great Wall of Gorda." One year, one month, and one day later a 1998 storm sent a waterfall of mud down the hillside between the restaurant and the gas station but the Great Wall held, some say the best of any stretch of road along Highway 1.

Founded in 1878 as an important stagecoach stop, Gorda made national news in 1979 when Kidco Limited Ventures, a corporation of four children, bought the settlement using money allegedly earned by killing gophers, selling horse manure, and raising earthworms. The corporation failed to make mortgage payments. Gorda now offers the Whale Watcher Cafe, gas station, general store, and a set of newly remodeled cabins, some of which house the people who work in Gorda. Many old-time travelers will miss the jade gallery and studio that were once here. Two pet llamas and pygmy goats have taken up residence on a protected hillside. The Gorda Cultural Center, a room with books to trade and check out, the restaurant's delicious homemade desserts, and tasty impromptu outdoor barbecues keep a sense of the simpler past in Gorda Springs. For travelers, the accommodations are greatly improved. Of the six cabins, referred to as houses, five have wonderful ocean views (805/927-4600). One cabin is primarily rock, the others are panelled in warm woods. The Gorda's only palm tree shades the palm house; the redwood house is redwood panelled and furnished with redwood furniture. Four newly remodeled rooms with Jacuzzi tubs and ocean views are located above the general store. Access to hiking trails is nearby. Several sculpted waterfalls and fountains highlight the natural spring water which flows here. Although the restaurant patio is close to Highway 1, the planted gardens and incredible whale watching views take your mind off the cars. There is a prime location for viewing marine mammals on a bluff across the highway from the center. The beach below Gorda is a designated sanctuary for a growing colony of elephant seals.

70.8 S, 18.9 N. Keep your eyes on the road but, once into the turnoff, view the Salmon Creek waterfall. Many trails, including one that leads behind the waterfall, begin here at an abandoned ranger station.

74.6 S, 15.1 N. Ragged Point is the last southern destination point in Big Sur and, northbound, the first turnoff for this stretch of coast. Walk behind the Ragged Point Restaurant (805/927-5708) to view the dark green Santa Lucia Mountains plunging to the sea.

77.9 S, 11.8 N. The San Carpojo Creek flows at the dramatic base of the southerly Santa Lucias. Rangelands belonging to the Hearst Corporation extend from the banks of this river.

SAN SIMEON AND CAMBRIA

Points of interest along this stretch include Hearst Castle, San Simeon State Beach and Sebastian's General Store, a seasonal elephant seal colony, and the town of Cambria. Fifteen miles of coastal plains and rolling foothills stretch south to the little business center of San Simeon and farther south to Cambria. The open lands you drive through are the private property of the Hearst Corporation. At one time the Hearst family owned forty-five thousand acres of Central Coast property. If you glance from time to time to the south you will see the outline of Hearst Castle. Thirteen miles south of the Carpojo Creek you will come to the turnoff for San Simeon Landing and, a

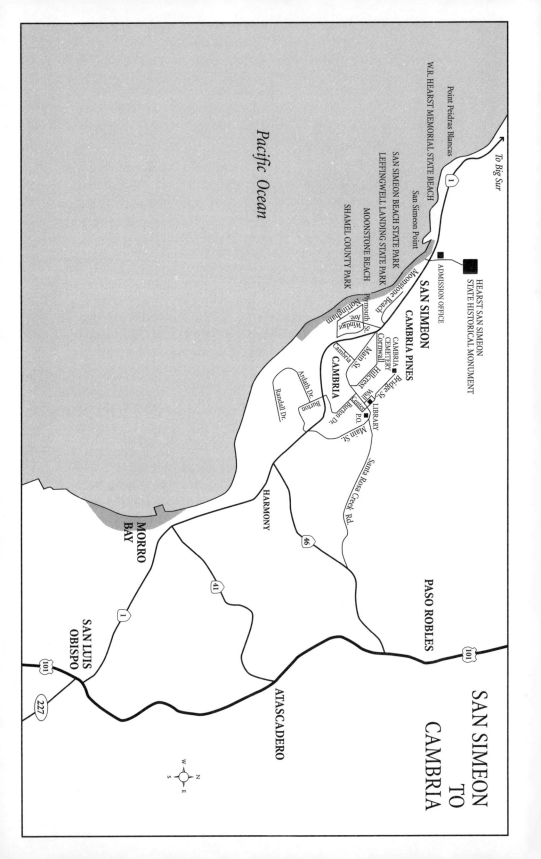

SAN SIMEON TO CAMBRIA

Pacific Ocean

To Big Sur

Point Peidras Blancas

W.R. HEARST MEMORIAL STATE BEACH

San Simeon Point

SAN SIMEON BEACH STATE PARK

LEFFINGWELL LANDING STATE PARK

MOONSTONE BEACH

SHAMEL COUNTY PARK

Moonstone Beach

ADMISSION OFFICE

HEARST SAN SIMEON
STATE HISTORICAL MONUMENT

SAN SIMEON

CAMBRIA PINES

Nottingham

Windsor Ave.

Plymouth St.

Main St.

Cambria

CAMBRIA CEMETERY

Cornwall

CAMBRIA

Ardath Dr.

Randall Dr.

Burton

Bridge St.

Hillcrest

Main St.

Burton Dr.

Center

P.O.

LIBRARY

HARMONY

Santa Rosa Creek Rd.

MORRO BAY

46

41

1

SAN LUIS OBISPO

227

101

101

ATASCADERO

PASO ROBLES

N
W   E
S

little farther south, the entrance road to the tour-staging area for Hearst Castle. If you are interested in taking a tour of the castle, make advance reservations, especially in the summer. If you have not made reservations or want to look around before doing so you should go directly to the center for tour information.

ELEPHANT SEALS

Two road turnoffs provide excellent places to spot elephant seals. The turnoffs are located eight miles south of the Monterey County line and four miles north of San Simeon. Five elephant seals were reported here in 1988. The colony now numbers in the 5,000 range and they breed and pup here. BAY NET docents, recognizable in their blue jackets, answer questions and provide binoculars everyday in summer, on weekends during high population times, and on occasional weekdays. See Chapter 1, page 43–44, for more information about elephant seals. As of this writing, the land enclosed by fences belongs to the Hearst Corporation, and trespassing for a closer look is not allowed.

HEARST CASTLE

Although it is often referred to as a castle, William Randolph Hearst never used that description for the large estate on the hill; to him it was always "La Cuesta Encantada," the enchanted hill, or La Casa Grande. His guests were invited to come to "the ranch." Many visitors are surprised when they come looking for a European castle. Hearst employed Julia Morgan to design not a castle but a Spanish plaza of the 1500s. Julia Morgan's adaptation of Hearst's wishes and the surrounding landscape does in fact combine a Spanish church and a plaza on the hill.

William Randolph Hearst was the only child of millionaire miner, senator, and rancher George Hearst and of Phoebe Apperson Hearst, who was herself known for her philanthropic contributions that included the founding of the P.T.A. While a senator, George Hearst acquired his major coastal land holdings. William enjoyed summers at the San Simeon site, which was originally used by the family for lavish camping expeditions. In 1887, when he was twenty-three, William convinced his father to give him ownership of the financially failing *San Francisco Examiner*. William Hearst turned the fortunes of the paper around and began building a publishing empire. Between 1890 and 1920 he acquired thirty newspapers, more than a dozen magazines, eight radio stations, and several film studios. He married Millicent Murray in 1903, and they had five sons, but the couple had separated by the 1920s. After the death of his mother, Phoebe Hearst, in 1919, William Hearst began a building fantasy with her good friend Julia Morgan, California's first woman architect, who had designed buildings in Berkeley and Pacific Grove for the family. In later years actress Marion Davies was his companion and hostess at the "Ranch on the Hill."

To furnish the lavish estate, Hearst, with Morgan advising, began an antique-collecting spree. The rooms were created as museums, and the state of California, which now has ownership of the ranch, presents them as such. Hearst Corporation–owned warehouses still stocked full of unused antiques line the shore at San Simeon Landing. In addition to accumulating antiques Hearst collected, in effect, the largest zoo in the West at the time.

The Hearst Castle visitor center is free to the public but the castle can be visited only by guided tour. Four distinct daytime tours of the estate are offered. Four to six tours, each with a duration of about two hours leave each hour, beginning at 8:20 a.m. until the last scheduled daytime tour at 3 p.m. If you opt to take more than one tour a day plan to space tours at least two hours apart. Evening tours are also available on most Friday and Saturday evenings during spring and fall. Advance reservations can be made by calling the Park Net ticket reservation agency (800/444-4445). At this writing, tours are $14 for adults and $8 for children. The evening tour is $25 for adults and $13 for children ages 6 to 12. All vehicles park at a visitor staging area, and buses take visitors up the hill. As you ride up you may catch glimpses of zebras on the hillside.

Tour I is suggested for first-time visitors. The guide greets you like you are a guest of the "Ranch." Several landings of steps lead to the hundred-foot-wide outdoor Neptune Pool, with a panoramic view of the San Simeon coast through a Greco-Roman temple facade. Marble figures, including Venus rising from the foam of the sea, surround the pool. Although you might love to bask by that pool all day, Tour I continues with one of three guest rooms, a ground-floor tour of the castle, which Hearst called "La Casa Grande," and a look at the tiled indoor pool. The Casa Grande features rooms layered with silk Persian rugs and Flemish tapestries. Everywhere you look, furnishings are of fine craftsmanship: Etruscan vases, cabinets with gold inlay, and precision-cut crystal.

As you enter the dining room on the tour you are made to feel like an invited guest. Hearst's only requirement for his guests was that they attend dinner. It was served on a three-hundred-year-old refectory table surrounded by a decorative display of silver. Diners joined a privileged list, including world leaders such as Winston Churchill, President Coolidge, and the king and queen of Greece. Hollywood celebrities included Charlie Chaplin, Greta Garbo, and Cary Grant.

You leave the dining room in the same fashion as Hearst's guests. You are invited to view a 1930s newsreel in the private theater where Hearst invited his guests to watch "home movies." In the lobby you'll see the wondrous—for that time—light bulbs in full view.

On the last stretch of Tour I, see the tiled indoor pool that took eight men three and a half years to finish. Not just any tiles, these have thin sheets of gold fused in Venetian pressed glass. Hearst wanted the tiles to resemble the lapis lazuli tiles of a fifth-century mausoleum.

Although five tours are available, you may find that one or two make a comfortable experience. Tour II features the upper floors of the Casa Grande, including the Gothic Suite, which was used as Hearst's private quarters; the library, with its collection of ancient Greek vases; and the kitchen and pantry areas, which were similar to those of a grand hotel. Tour III visits the smallest of the three guest rooms and the last, uncompleted guest room. Tour IV is especially recommended for photographers, as it focuses on garden areas, rooms of the large guest house, and the wine cellars. Tour V, the evening tour, leads you through Casa Grande, the pools and gardens, the largest guest cottage, and a 1930s newsreel shown in the theater. Docents are dressed in fashions of the 1930s and wander the rooms and gardens as though at a garden party.

The newest grandeur at the visitor's center is the five-story National Geographic Theater featuring surround-sound. One film tells the story of the Hearst family; another stars the giant whales of the ocean. More films about marine life in the Monterey Bay National Marine Sanctuary will be developed expressly for this theater. Adult admission is $7.

When you descend from the hill, the cove at San Simeon waits for you with natural treasures. Although regarded by locals as the sunniest and most gentle of nearby beaches, the cove is still posted for rip currents.

SAN SIMEON LANDING

The building-construction foreman at Hearst Ranch and the present-day cattle workers got the beachfront property at San Simeon Landing. People on first visits to the landing often ask if their Spanish-style residences and the adjoining warehouses are California missions.

San Simeon Landing prospered in the 1850s as a whaling station and later as the center of a ranching and mining district. Sebastian's General Store was one of forty-five buildings that formed the community. A long pier and visiting ships were the community's link with the outside world, as no roads served the area. By the late 1870s the population had declined but grew again when William Randolph Hearst began building his estate.

Sebastian's General Store (805/927-4217) is now the only separately owned piece of property surrounded by Hearst land. An outdoor takeout window serves fish, burgers, sandwiches, and fries for patio dining. Inside the store you can find a multitude of items including Italian fishermen's hats, hand-painted Victorian birdhouses, chocolate dolphins, and picnic supplies.

The Hearst Corporation is planning to develop land around San Simeon landing and the visitor's center. The development is a widely discussed project up and down the coast.

A small San Simeon commercial development begins about two miles south of the landing, at the edge of Hearst-owned land. Several restaurants, motels, residential apartments, and galleries are located here. The California Carvers Guild (805/927-4718) showcases sculptures.

CAMBRIA

Two miles down the road, the little but growing town of Cambria is the gentle grand finale of this tour. Moonstone Beach hugs the northern border of the town, which was a boom whaling and mining settlement and now draws many artists. You can hunt for opalescent moonstones at the beach. The whales slip in very close to the shore during late winter and early spring. Cambria invites you to stroll its downtowns—both of them. Take the first downtown Cambria entrance. Newer West Main Street offers pickle tasting, book browsing, a toy soldier factory, an old-fashioned bowling green, and a one-room schoolhouse now converted to a community art studio. The "Pinedorado Grounds" are a mix of fair buildings and some historical structures that include the old town jail and a historic lighthouse.

Old downtown features a mix of galleries, shops, and restaurants in hundred-year-old Victorians and well-designed replicas of such. The people strolling along with you are scattered about rather than packed. The athletic looking couple may be heading for Cambria Bicycles (805/927-5510), known throughout the world as one of the best assemblers of bikes made up of parts from the best manufacturers; each bike costs $2,500 or more. Galleries attract a variety of tastes; customers range from those looking for museum-quality glass at the Seekers Collection & Gallery (805/927-4352) to those questioning the very essence of life and art at the What Iz Art gallery, where walls are painted with faces and slogans. Cue balls click at Old Camozzi's Saloon, and local musicians pick tunes at Molly's, a coffeehouse. You can pick up some fresh fruit at Soto's family-run market, savor some sweet low-sugar pie or jam at Linn's (800/676-1670), and find a serene bench behind the picket fence at Heart's Ease Garden and Herb Shop (805/927-5224).

Santa Rosa Road winds inland from downtown, through bucolic countryside and wooded vales. Linn Fruit Stand and a variety of other roadside produce stands dot the landscape. If you drive a little farther down the coast from Cambria turn off Highway 1 to visit the tiny stop of Harmony. Here, good food, music in the courtyard, tasting of San Luis Obispo County wines, and an extensive crafters' gallery and potters' barn are worth the amble.

WHAT ELSE TO SEE AND DO

"Tell them to get out of their cars and walk around, touch the ground, smell the mix of pine and sea, redwood and river glen—just don't walk on private property or land that is not marked with paths": so say Big Sur residents.

CHAPTER 7

INLAND EXCURSIONS

CARMEL VALLEY, SALINAS VALLEY,
THE PINNACLES,
SAN JUAN BAUTISTA

Carmel Valley and Salinas Valley are the interior heart of the Central Coast region. Carmel Valley Road and River Road are connecting links to farms, wineries, ranches, and resorts. Lake San Antonio and Lake Nacimiento are southern valley destinations.

GETTING READY

BEST TIMES TO VISIT AND SPECIAL EVENTS

Carmel Valley Road and Highway 68 to Salinas are busy during weekday mornings 7 to 9 a.m. and afternoons 5 to 6 p.m. Highway 1 south from Monterey to Carmel Valley Road can be thick with cars on three-day weekends and summer weekends.

The California Rodeo rides into Salinas in mid-July; advance ticket sales are suggested (831/757-2951). Motels throughout the area fill up early. The more intimate Carmel Valley Fiesta enlivens Carmel Valley in midsummer (831/659-4000). Also in summer, usually in July, the Steinbeck Festival features tours, movies, and speakers highlighting the life and writings of native son and Pulitzer and Nobel Prize–winner John Steinbeck. The festival is offered by the National Steinbeck Center (831/796-3833). The Soledad Mission Grape Stampede in September offers a showplace for vintners, great barbecue, and the unusual bare-footed grape-stomper's competition. In October, the Salinas Valley International Mariachi Festival whirls into the Salinas Sports Complex and Sherwood Hall (831/758-7477).

Nature offers special events too. Plan for eagle-watch tours at Lake San Antonio from December to March. Wildflowers burst into bloom along back roads and on hillsides from April through June. In May, Lake San Antonio sponsors a wildflower show and biathlon.

The southern lakes, San Antonio and Nacimiento, are crowded during summer when the air is hot and the water is warm. Camping is usually available at Lake San Antonio. You'll stay cooler if you sightsee in the morning.

WINE TASTING

The experience of wine tasting in these valleys is rather intimate. Small groups gather and converse with wine experts. Tastings and tours get crowded during the height of crush when the pace is exciting. Only nature knows the exact dates of crush. Varying with the weather, crush normally lasts from the middle of August to late September or early October.

Seven distinct appellations in Monterey's coastal valleys and benchlands account for an impressive diversity of wines. Monterey County has more than forty thousand acres planted in premium varietal wine grapes. The wines vary from world renowned to starter wineries, from mass produced to the private reserves enjoyed by a few in the know. Maps and event information are available through Monterey Wine Country Associates, a nonprofit organization comprised of forty growers and vintners (831/375-9400, www.wines.com/monterey). A Taste of Monterey, 700 Cannery Row, Monterey, serves as the ultimate visitor's center for the county's wineries. See page 75.

Many tasting rooms, some off backcountry roads are elegant, others are cozy. Some offer breathtaking views. Tasters are welcomed as honored guests who have braved a journey. Choosing a designated driver or using a driver service is highly recommended if more than one winery is on your list. AgVenture Tours is a local tour company specializing in agriculture and wine-tasting tours (831/643-WINE).

Special events begin in April with the Salinas Valley Wineries Open House, a weekend of tasting, tours, music, and culinary treats (831/678-0300). In August, tents fill the Custom House Plaza in Monterey for the Winemakers' Celebration weekend. Enjoy wine tasting, gourmet food, and music. At one of the many educational displays, you watch as a cooper forms a round barrel from flat wood. On Sunday many wineries host open houses with hors d'oeuvres and entertainment (831/375-9400). November brings the Great Wine Escape Weekend. More than fifteen wineries host open houses. Enjoy winemaker dinners where the winemakers pair food and wines and are available to converse with throughout the meal. Also, receive special discounts at local restaurants, hotels, and inns. Transportation provided or drive yourself (831/375-9400). The listings here include the wineries with tastings at scheduled hours.

CARMEL VALLEY

In order of approach for those driving inland from Highway 1:

Chateau Julien Wine Estate, 8940 Carmel Valley Road. At this boutique winery situated on sixteen acres in mid–Carmel Valley, wine tasting and tours offer the feeling of joining old friends. The use of French-Swiss chateau architecture with high interior ceilings and stained glass parallels Chateau

Julien's use of the French traditional methods for aging wines in new French oak. The winery produces more than eighty thousand cases including private reserve wines. Grapes are hand-picked from growers throughout Monterey County. Chateau Julien was the first local grower to feature the California Italian wines Sangiovese and Trebiano. These specialty wines and private reserve wines are available for purchase only at the tasting room. Winemaker Bill Anderson and assistant winemaker Marta Krastzeck host winemaker dinners with festive dancing. The tasting room is open from 8:30 a.m. to 5 p.m. weekdays and on weekends from 11 a.m. to 5 p.m. Tours are scheduled, with reservations suggested, at 10:30 a.m. and 2:30 p.m. weekdays. The winery offers several events during the year, including a summer jazz, wine, and food extravaganza (831/624-2600).

BERNARDUS, 5 West Carmel Valley Road, Carmel Valley Village. Bougainvillea drapes the trellised entrance of this tasting location, a former Bank of America. The wine is presently stored in the vault. Many people come to the village specifically to visit the Bernardus tasting room, and the hosts make the visit memorable. The focus wine is the Marinus, an estate-vineyard Bordeaux blend.

Bernardus's estate vineyards, Jamesburg and Featherbow Ranch, are fifteen miles farther up the valley; take Cachagua and Tassajara Roads through the scenic hills. The Jamesburg Vineyard lies on the rolling hills of a 1,500-foot plateau. More than three hundred coastal live oaks have been preserved to live among carefully planted vines. The warm Carmel Valley conditions with daily variations caused by the ocean breezes are perfect for the hot-weather cabernet and merlot grapes. The tasting room in Carmel Valley Village is open daily 11 a.m. to 5 p.m. (800/223-2533).

GEORIS, 4 Pilot Road, Carmel Valley Village. Lush flower gardens and koi ponds surround outdoor tables at this relaxing wine tasting retreat. Bread and cheese are offered with tastings of merlot and cabernet. In the winter, tasters move inside to enjoy sips by a wood-burning fireplace in an early California adobe home. Visitors can wander throughout the grounds and the adobe home which houses a gift shop, rooms for private parties, and the company offices. Distinctive furnishings, collected by owner Walter Georis while on trips to Mexico, are also available for purchase. Walter Georis, proprietor of the renowned Casanova restaurant in Carmel, brings impeccable standards to his traditional European-style full-bodied merlot. The wine is in high demand and is completely allocated at the time of its annual release. Reserves are held for the tasting room, area restaurants, and specialty shops.

The tasting garden is open Thursday through Sunday from noon to 4 p.m. (831/659-1050).

HELLER ESTATE DURNEY VINEYARDS, 69 West Carmel Valley Road, Carmel Valley Village. Two large metallic figures dance outside the tasting home of this acclaimed vineyard. More artwork by well-known artist Toby Heller graces the tasting room and gift shop. According to owner Gilbert Heller, "Durney wines are produced entirely from our estate vineyards and our grapes are organically grown without pesticides or herbicides." The Autumn 1997 *Quarterly Review of Wines* described the 1992 Durney cabernet sauvignon Private Reserve as "A perfect example of what a Carmel Valley cabernet sauvignon is capable of doing . . . beware, Napa!" The tasting room in Carmel Valley Village is open Monday through Thursday 10 a.m. to 5 p.m., and on weekends from 11 a.m. to 5 p.m. (831/659-6233).

RIVER RANCH, WHITE OAK GRILL, 19 East Carmel Valley Road, Carmel Valley Village. River Ranch vineyards can be spotted near Laureles Grade Road, three miles west of Carmel Valley Village. This two-and-one-half-acre vineyard yielded five hundred cases of chardonnay and pinot noir in 1996. Tasting is enjoyed in the wine room at the entrance to the White Oak Grill. Chef and owner Terry Terflinger manages the winery. One hundred years ago a different liquid prevailed here when the White Oak Grill building was the creamery of the local dairy. Terflinger, with partner Marilyn Beach, removed years of layered paint to expose the original redwood walls. From the vented cupola, natural light fills the dining area. The White Oak Grill offers an excellent selection of wines at very reasonable prices (831/659-1525). Open Thursday through Monday 11 a.m. to 2:30 p.m. and 6 p.m. to 8:30 p.m.

GALANTE VINEYARDS AND GALANTE GARDEN ROSES, 18181 Cachagua Road, Carmel Valley. If you are looking for the "Days of Wine and Roses," you have arrived. Twelve thousand rose bushes with gorgeous blooms and fragrance grace this seven-hundred-acre ranch. Plan your trip for between May and October to see the blooms and ripening grapes. The road is windy and remote, but the views are breathtaking in every season. The estate cabernet sauvignon draws lines of tasters at local wine festivals and events. The atmosphere is friendly, relaxed, and welcoming. Several concerts are offered each summer, which benefit local charitable organizations. Seatings for concerts are on lawns strewn with rose petals. At Galante, the vineyard manager, winemaker, or owner hosts your private tasting and tour. Tasting and tours are by appointment only. (800/425-2683/GALANTE).

SALINAS VALLEY TASTING ROOMS

As many different routes lead to these tasting rooms, the listings are arranged in alphabetical order. Winery locations are noted throughout the tours in this chapter. The varied soils and temperatures in Salinas Valley provide for six appellations, yielding an ever-impressive variety of harvest.

CHALONE VINEYARD, Stonewall Canyon Road and Highway 146, Soledad, adjacent to the west side of the Pinnacles. In 1922 Bill Silvear and his family planted chardonnay and chenin blanc wine grapes on this remote hillside. The original vines are still growing and producing fruit for Chalone's fine wines. The old vines and added vineyards grow in decomposed granite and limestone soil, and during drought years, with sparse rainfall. The adverse growing conditions produce strong vines and distinctive fruit. From the balcony and tasting room window you can enjoy incredible vistas from the Gabilan to the Santa Lucia Mountain ranges. The tasting room is open on weekends from 11:30 a.m. to 5 p.m. or call to visit during the week. All tasting times and appointments should be confirmed before you visit because of the remoteness of the location (831/678-1717).

CLONINGER CELLARS, 1645 River Road, Salinas (near Gonzales). Cloninger Cellars is located on the sloping benchlands of the Santa Lucia Mountains. Cooler nights, cool ocean breezes, and rocky soil are ideal for chardonnay and pinot noir. Cloninger's chardonnays have scored among the very best in the county. Grapes for cabernet sauvignon are grown in the Carmel Valley, just past the village. The ocean breezes are less influential there and the hotter climate is perfect. Cloninger is a young winery located in the buildings of an old dairy farm; the tasting room is in a renovated farmhouse. When I visited, one of the owners was tending the rock-lined koi and water turtle pond he designed for visitors' enjoyment. Picnic tables add to the country feeling. The barrel room is often open for visitors along with the tasting room. Tasting hours are Monday through Thursday 11 a.m. to 4 p.m., Friday though Sunday 11 a.m. to 5 p.m. (831/675-WINE/9463).

HAHN ESTATES AND SMITH & HOOK WINERY, 37700 Foothill Road, Soledad. To reach the tasting room you will drive for 1.5 miles along a dirt road within arm's reach of cabernet sauvignon grapevines interspersed with chaparral. Even in December, roses bloom at the head of each row. Fog may cover the trellised vines at the base of the road, while sun warms those on the higher alluvial slopes. Variances in sun exposure affect the flavor of the harvest and also the choice of bottling. The sweeter, sun-drenched grapes strengthen the heavier Smith & Hook wines, which are made for longer aging; the lighter-flavored grapes blend well into the softer Hahn Estate wines that are bottled at the same winery. The winery is set on an alluvial fan overlooking the site where the first vineyards were planted for the Soledad Mission in the 1770s. The gravel-laden soil of the sedimentary slopes makes this prime grape-growing country. A 428,000-gallon redwood barrel, which was used by the Almaden winery as an aging barrel, now serves as a reserved tasting room. A larger, more elegant tasting room is located in a house set among oaks. The views from the expansive deck stretch across the broad Salinas Valley to the peaks of the Pinnacles perched on the Gabilans. A warming fireplace is ready for winter tasting days. Views from a nearby lookout are worth the hike. Estate-bottled Smith & Hook cabernet sauvignon, merlot, *viogner,* and Hahn estate tastings are offered. Wine can be tasted daily from 11 a.m. until 4 p.m.; tours are available upon request. (831/678-2132).

JEKEL VINEYARDS, 40155 Walnut Avenue, Greenfield. Visitors walk under a spreading arbor before entering the farmhouse-style tasting room. A mounted deer head fashioned from grape vines greets tasters. Jekel Vineyards produces johannisberg riesling, chardonnay, cabernet sauvignon, pinot blanc, and pinot noir. Cabernet franc—long the favored blending grape of Bordeaux-style cabernet sauvignons—is bottled as a singular varietal with berry- and pepper-laden results. In years of the noble rot, *Botrytis cinerea,* which sweetens grapes, a late-harvest dessert wine is offered. Grounds are extensive for wanderings and picnics under the wisteria are pleasant. Tasting hours are 10 a.m. to 5 p.m. daily (831/674-5522).

PARAISO SPRINGS VINEYARDS, 38060 Paraiso Springs Road, Soledad. Family-owned and operated, Paraiso Springs Vineyards perches on an escarpment of the Santa Lucia Mountains. The spacious tasting room, gift shop, and entertainment facilities open to a deck with sweeping views of the valley, across to the Gabilans and rugged outlines of the Pinnacles. Grapes grown at this vineyard location are part of the Santa Lucia Highlands appellation, the coolest appellation in Monterey County. The soil conditions and varied canyon and bench locations are perfect for quality chardonnay, pinot blanc, pinot noir, johannisberg riesling, and gewurztraminer. The assets of talented winemaker Philip Zorn bring gold ribbons and *Wine Spectator* ratings of 90-plus to Paraiso Springs. Claudia Smith, one of the family owners, credits "fastidious attention to wine making, care of the grapes, and skill with chemistry."

Twenty thousand cases of Paraiso Springs wines are released yearly.

Limited releases of port, the newest wine; syrah; late-harvest pinot noir; and late-harvest reisling are available only at the tasting room. When I visit Paraiso Springs, a member of the family is always there. The feeling of family commitment is strong, and somehow that makes a great wine taste even better. The tasting room is open from 12 to 4 p.m. on weekdays and on weekends from 11 a.m. to 5 p.m. (831/678-0300).

SCHEID VINEYARDS, 1972 Hobson Avenue, Greenfield. Look for the big American flag! The entrance to Scheid Vineyards is a direct exit from Highway 101. Northbound travelers will need to cross southbound lanes. Inside the tasting room, you forget you just exited a freeway. You also forget you are in a remodeled one-hundred-year-old barn. The subdued yellow plaster walls, bleached floors, and natural lighting create a pleasant tasting room. I enjoyed the opportunity to compare the tropical fruity flavors of the Scheid Monterey chardonnay and the crisp, green-apple, lighter flavor of the Scheid San Lucas Valley chardonnay. Scheid is publicly traded and plans to offer its premium wines at a discount to holders of its common stock. Call in advance for trellis vineyard tours. The tasting room is open daily from 10 a.m. to 5 p.m. (831/386-0316).

VENTANA VINEYARD, 2999 Monterey/Salinas Highway 68. A wall covered with gold and blue ribbons greets visitors at the tasting room of Ventana Vineyards, which deserves special recognition as the most award-winning single vineyard property in the United States. The Gold Stripe estate bottled chardonnay has a record of eighteen years of consecutive awards, including gold medals in the San Diego National Competition. Grapes for this vineyard flourish in the Arroyo Seco appellation, located along the banks of the Arroyo Seco River in the heat of southern Monterey County. The fruity sauvignon blanc and peppery cabernet sauvignon are especially notable. The tasting room is open daily from 11 a.m. to 5 p.m. (831/372-7415).

CLIMATE AND CLOTHING

Spring is my favorite season here, an average seventy degrees with occasional rains. In summer, coastal locals trade the fog for bathing suits by heading up the closer Carmel Valley, for resort pools or river swimming; Carmel Valley is a very pleasant average eighty degrees, Salinas Valley about ten degrees hotter. The southern lakes regions are much hotter, with one hundred-degree temperatures common. The wilderness areas and Carmel River areas do flood occasionally in winter. Call ahead about Los Padres National Forest road conditions. Snow blankets the hills once or a few times a year.

Shorts and short sleeves greet the heat in summer and autumn. Bring sweaters for afternoon and evening breezes. Some winter days in the valleys can be in the eighties, so bring some light clothes in any season. Bring umbrellas and coats in the winter just in case a cold front moves in. Some fine restaurants, especially in Carmel Valley, request that men wear dinner jackets.

Scenic roads and incredible photo opportunities await you on this tour. Cameras and binoculars are advised.

HIGHLIGHTS FOR KIDS

Hartnell Junior College (831/755-6700) offers a summer university for ages seven and older.

Garland Park, Toro Regional Park, and Fort Ord Public Lands offer easy and rewarding hikes for kids.

Barlocker's Rustling Oaks Ranch (831/675-9121) in the Salinas Valley and the Holman Ranch (831/659-2640) in Carmel Valley offer horse camps and glimpses of farm life.

TOUR LENGTHS

Carmel Valley Village and Salinas are both about thirty minutes from Monterey and the aquarium and twenty minutes from Highway 1 exits. Laureles Grade, located a few miles from Carmel Valley Village, connects the two valleys. Carmel Valley offers many choices of places to stay on an extended visit to the Central Coast area or for the week or weekend.

Lake San Antonio or San Antonio Mission can be reached in two hours from Monterey by River Road or Highway 101. A leisurely drive to an afternoon eagle-watch tour or back from a morning tour makes a pleasant full day trip. Lake San Antonio campgrounds, the Hacienda at Lake San Antonio or the resort condos at Lake Nacimiento are good overnight destinations after a day tour of valley roads. Some pleasant creekside, first-come, first-served campgrounds are located at the Salinas Valley side of the Nacimiento-Fergusson Road. King City and Soledad offer lodging possibilities midway—especially well positioned if you are considering a following day-trip to the Pinnacles. The drive from Monterey to San Juan Bautista takes forty minutes.

WILDLIFE WISDOM

Deer, squirrels, jack rabbits, and coveys of quail are plentiful. Rattlesnakes inhabit the rolling hills and mountain areas; be careful before putting hands on rocky ledges or sitting on rocks or logs. Some of this tour borders land preserved by the taxpayers of California with Mountain Lion Habitat Preservation Funds. No attacks on humans by mountain lions in this tour area have been reported but during drought years the big cats come to lower elevations and attacks on family pets are reported. As a precaution, if you go hiking in Garland Park and the Los Padres National Forest lands with children, keep them close and carry a stick.

In 1919 Russian wild boars were brought to a hunting preserve in South Carolina from the Ukranian Mountains. Five years later, thirteen boars were shipped to the Los Padres forest region; they mated with wild domestic swine, and hundreds of bristled, tusked wild boar now roam the Santa Lucia Mountains. If you encounter a wild boar stay calm and back away quietly; noise can provoke a charge. If one does charge, rangers advise, climb the nearest tree. Damage to possessions, let alone people, is quite rare.

Bald eagles and golden eagles winter at Lake San Antonio. In the Pinnacles, raptors such as falcons, kestrels, and golden eagles can be spotted at the peaks from January to July. A dozen varieties of lizards, deer, and gray foxes can be viewed there year-round. Thousands of slow-moving tarantulas search for mates on the east-side roads and dirt paths in the fall.

VISITOR INFORMATION

Fort Ord Public Lands (831/394-8314) provides information about hiking, mountain biking, and horseback riding mentioned in these tours.

Call Fort Hunter Liggett Range Control for information about Nacimiento-Fergusson Road, which is sometimes closed. The number to call

Bald Eagle

is the same number as that for the Painted Salinan Cave, which is listed in the National Historic Registry and offers examples of cave painting by the area's earliest inhabitants (831/386-2503).

Monterey County Parks (831/755-4899) offers information about popular eagle-watch boat tours and reservations for camping in area county parks. The three county park campgrounds in this tour area are at Laguna Seca, San Lorenzo Park in King City, and Lake San Antonio.

Fremont Peak State Park (831/623-4255) is located close to San Juan Bautista. For more information about Pinnacles National Monument, call 831/389-4462.

The Monterey County Tourism Center has extensive information about the area and the entire Monterey County (San Lorenzo Park, 1160 Broadway, King City 93930; 831/385-1484). The National Forest Service district headquarters for the Los Padres National Forest is in King City (406 South Mildred Avenue, 831/385-5434). The National Forest Service Station is located on Cachagua Road off Carmel Valley Road (831/659-2612).

The *Californian,* the daily Salinas paper, lists events in its Thursday "What's Fun" section, and the *Monterey County Herald* has event information in the Thursday "Event" and "Go" sections. "Go" is also available free at newsstands. The *Carmel Valley Sun* offers local and event news for Carmel Valley, Carmel, and the south coast. Locals keep informed at information boards that are posted outside many of the small community shopping areas or post offices.

ALTERNATE TRANSPORTATION

Monterey-Salinas Transit serves Carmel Valley with hourly buses from the Monterey transit center (831/899-2555). Several buses travel to Salinas. Bus service does not extend to southern Monterey County.

PARKING

Parking is available and free at most locations. If you park your car along the road or in parks, lock it and take your valuables with you.

PLACES TO STAY

CARMEL VALLEY

LOS LAURELES COUNTRY INN (10.5 miles east of Highway 1, just past the Laureles Grade turnoff). This historic country inn was once owned by the Hotel Del Monte and the Vanderbilts. White picket fences, a large library, knotty-pine patio rooms, country rooms, and premier suites; beamed ceilings in a comfortable lodge-type lobby with a crackling fire. Conference area in the former equestrian center. Du Val's Restaurant is in the restored front porch of the original lodge, built in 1890. A mahogany-paneled bar has entertainment by local musicians. 831/659-2233; in California, 800/533-4404. MC, V. For two from $100 to $450; $100 to $130 average.

QUAIL LODGE, 8205 Valley Greens Drive (off Carmel Valley Road, a little more than three miles from Highway 1). A Mobil Travel Guide five-star-rated resort. Guest rooms overlook 245 acres of pastoral golf course dotted with ten lakes and mountain vistas. The more deluxe accommodations feature patio rooms and suites and terrace rooms; the Executive Villa has private hot tubs and luxurious appointments. Guests of the lodge receive full privileges at the private Quail Lodge Golf and Tennis Resort. Conference, entertainment, and banquet facilities available. Country elegance prevails at the Covey Restaurant. 831/624-1581. AX, MC, V; others also accepted. For two from $175 to $345.

ROBLES DEL RIO LODGE, 200 Punta Del Monte (above Carmel Village). This oldest of the operating inland resorts is fully restored to last another century. French country decor, peaceful setting, panoramic views of the valley and mountains. Lodge rooms and cabins. Breakfast included. Complete meeting and banquet facilities. Outdoor tiled pool, spa, and full-service restaurant. 831/659-3705, 800/833-0843. MC, V. For two from $90 to $190.

STONEPINE, 150 East Carmel Valley Road (in upper Carmel Valley just past Carmel Village; on the right opposite Las Tulares Road). A Relais Chateau Gold Star–rated resort. Eight lavish suites, some with secret rooms, in the Chateau Noel, which was the private estate owned by Helen Crocker Russell. Helen and Henry Russell were famous in the 1930s, 1940s, and 1950s as the most prestigious thoroughbred breeders west of the Mississippi. The equestrian center offers a quality riding program. Fantasy, elegance, and gracious service. The butler will pick you up at the airport in a Rolls Royce. 831/659-2245. AX, MC, V. For two from $225 to $750.

SALINAS VALLEY

BARLOCKER'S RUSTLING OAKS RANCH BED AND BREAKFAST, 25252 Limekiln Road, Salinas. Bring the family for a weekend of ranch fun or escape on wine tasting tours while the kids camp here. Also great for the adult in search of serenity or the weekend cowhand experience. One cottage under the oaks and five rooms in the ranch house. All rooms have private baths. This is a horse boarding and working ranch. The breakfast is one of the freshest you will find anywhere. 831/675-9121. MC, V. Rooms from $90 to $150.

KEEFER'S INN, Canal Street, King City (from U.S. 101, exit at Canal Street). Built like a Dutch village, this inn has forty-eight units, a putting green, and a family restaurant. 831/385-4843. AX, MC, V; others also accepted. For two, from $50.

LAUREL INN, 801 West Laurel Drive, Salinas (from U.S. 101, exit at Laurel Drive). Air-conditioned rooms, pool, hot tubs, sauna, some fireplaces. 831/449-2474. In California, 800/354-9831. AX, MC, V; others also accepted. For two, from $60.

SOUTHERN EXTENSION

THE HACIENDA GUEST LODGE (on Fort Hunter Liggett, in Jolon, near Mission San Antonio). Designed by Julia Morgan as William Randolph Hearst's Milpitas ranch house, this Spanish revival hideaway may be Monterey County's best-kept secret. Reserve a high tower room, then walk the curved staircase to enjoy a private enclave with beam ceilings, arches, and carved-wood treatments. Pedestal sinks in the baths keep the aura of the 1930s. Four rooms have queen beds. Six of the rooms have private baths. Five smaller "Cowboy Rooms," named for the cowboys who stayed here to tend Hearst's herds, are appropriately priced for "no in-room plumbing." The drawback to the ultimate quiet retreat is the juxtaposition of lodge and sometimes noise-creating military facilities. Beautiful hiking and biking trails are nearby for the quiet retreat. Bowling, a movie theater, and summer-only swimming add to the recreation possibilities here. Fishing and hunting packages are also available. "This place attracts people who want to get away from the city—there's nothing here," offers hostess Schillene Torres. Dine in the lounge beginning at 1700 hours (that's 5 p.m.) Monday through Saturday. Lunch Monday through Friday and Sunday. Guest lodge reservations 831/386-2900; restaurant 831/386-2446. Two-bedroom apartment from $125; tower rooms from $50; other rooms from $28.

NACIMIENTO LAKESHORE LODGES (at the resort, on the shores of Lake Nacimiento; for directions, see page 254). Lakeview townhomes on a quiet rise, all with lake views. High ceilings, fireplaces, and modern kitchens. Romantic for just two. Large units accommodate eight to ten people per lodge; with adjoining units, up to sixteen. 800/323-3839. $130 to $210.

PARKFIELD INN AND V6 RANCH, 70403 Parkfield Road, Parkfield. This log-style inn features six western-style rooms bordering on thousands of acres of open oak-graced land at the Varian Ranch. It is not actually on the ranch but it's close enough. Four rooms offer spacious lofts. Massive rock, wagon parts, and a wildlife scene highlight the Rock Room. The Gathering Room is available for reunions or retreats of up to fifty people. Continental breakfast. Coffee makers, toaster ovens, and refrigerators in all rooms. Ranch is open to all guests for hiking or riding. Horseback riding packages available. 805/463-2421. $68 to $89.

Lodging is also available in Paso Robles, farther south along Highway 101.

RESTAURANTS

CARMEL VALLEY ROAD VICINITY

THE COVEY, at Quail Lodge, 8205 Valley Greens Drive, Carmel Valley (on Carmel Valley Road, 3.4 miles beyond Highway 1). Here find country elegance, with polished pewter, fresh flowers, Audubon prints, and a warming fireplace. Views of fountains and lakes. Nooks for quiet conversation. The European cuisine includes beef, lamb, poultry, seafood, and locally grown produce. Extensive wine selection. Piano bar. Men are requested to wear jackets. Dinner. 831/624-1581. AX, MC, V. Entrees from $20 to $30.

THE RUNNING IRON RESTAURANT AND SALOON, East Carmel Valley Road and Via Contenta, Carmel Valley Village. A stuffed mountain lion and a boar's head watch over the passage from the lively bar to the restaurant. Hundreds of pairs of boots hang from the ceilings. Barn-burning chile and barbecued baby back pork ribs. 831/659-4633. AX, MC, V. Entrees mostly under $10.

THAI BISTRO, 55 West Carmel Valley Road, Carmel Valley Village (Thai Bistro II is at 159 Central Avenue in Pacific Grove). At this local favorite, patrons enjoy valley views and outdoor dining. *Laub-gai* (chicken simmered in lime juice, with shallots, mint, and chiles) is especially recommended. Vegetarian fare is available. Lunch and dinner. 831/659-5900. MC, V. Entrees mostly under $10.

WAGON WHEEL COFFEE SHOP (on Carmel Valley Road in the Valley Hills Shopping Center just past the Quail Lodge turnoff). A breakfast and lunch favorite with locals, this coffee shop has old Western saddles and bridles hung outside the front door. Inside, branding irons, saddles, spurs, and chaps decorate wood-paneled walls. Hearty and tasty Western breakfasts, including butter-pecan waffles; later, calamari burgers. Open 7 a.m. until 2 p.m. every day. 831/624-8878. No credit cards. Selections mostly under $8.

WILL's FARGO, Carmel Valley Road, Carmel Valley Village (in the center of the village). In a turn-of-the-century Victorian setting you can select your own steak, cut to your specifications, from the attractive display case. Fresh seafood, lamb, and chicken are also offered. Tuesday through Sunday. 831/659-2774. AX, MC, V. Entrees mostly under $20.

HIGHWAY 68 VICINITY

The following restaurants are located off Highway 68 between Highway l and River Road.

TARPY's ROADHOUSE, Highway 68 and Canyon Del Rey. Dine alfresco in a sunny, European-style courtyard surrounded by trellised gardens or indoors in the dining rooms of this old stone roadhouse. The stonework varies from room to room and includes fossils as well as a shell-lined fireplace. American country favorites with innovative touches include Indiana duck served on sweet-corn succotash with an apricot mint glaze and molasses bourbon pork-chops. Full-service bar. Lunch, dinner. 831/647-1444. AX, MC, V; others also accepted. Entrees mostly under $20.

SALINAS VALLEY

CASA TERESA, 185 Kidder Street, Soledad. The super burritos and chile verde at this family-owned restaurant with the atmosphere of a town reunion are often prepared by Teresa, who teaches the art of better Mexican cooking to chefs on the Monterey Peninsula. Lunch, dinner. 831/678-2480. MC, V. Entrees mostly from $3 to $10.

GUTIERREZ AND RICO DRIVE IN, 61 Sherwood Drive (corner of East Ross), Salinas. At this beach-look restaurant the Mexican seafood items are area favorites. Other menu items are also authentic and tasty. 831/424-8382. No credit cards. Entrees mostly under $10.

KEEFER's, Canal and Highway 101, King City. Melt into the comfortable booths here after a day's drive. A lighthearted Swedish mural gives counter seating a warm feeling. Hearty American and continental selections. Friendly service for the whole family. Breakfast (open 6:30 a.m.), lunch, dinner. 831/385-4843. MC, V. Entrees mostly under $10.

THE PUB, 227 Monterey Street, Salinas. With oversized, comfortable booths and wood paneling, this is a classic steak and rib house. Open-flame-grilled barbecued chicken, huge slabs of prime rib. Lunch, dinner. 831/424-4261. AX, MC, V. Entrees mostly under $15.

SPADO'S, 66 West Alisal Street, Salinas. Mention Spado's in Salinas and eyes sparkle. Two generations before him, chef/proprietor John Spadaro's family traveled from Sicily to the Monterey Peninsula. Blending heritage cuisine with California pizzazz, fresh Salinas Valley produce, and a number of Monterey County wines, Spado's pleases business diners, residents, and visitors. Bright murals and lively dining set a "city-style" mood. Local fans favor the Parmesan-crusted lamb shanks served over soft polenta and the pork chops stuffed with smoked mozzarella. The hot-burning white oak oven flavors herbed chicken and pizzas. A landscaped courtyard opens for alfresco dining. Lunch Monday through Friday, dinner every night. 831/424-4139. AX, MC, V. Entrees mostly under $12.

STEINBECK HOUSE, 132 Central Avenue, Salinas. In a Victorian family home containing memorabilia, photos, and original furnishings of John Steinbeck's family, weekday lunch only is served, in two sittings. Gourmet fare features seasonal vegetables of the area. Set daily entree; menu changes monthly. Call ahead for reservations and entree selection. Local wines available by the glass. 831/424-2735. Lunch entrees under $10.

DIRECTIONS

For the Carmel Valley loop which travels to Carmel Valley with an alternate route over Laureles Grade.
From the Monterey Bay Aquarium follow Lighthouse Avenue to Pacific Avenue. Continue on Pacific Avenue to Sherman Street. Follow entrance signs to Highway 1 and head south. Take the Carmel Valley Road turnoff, at the signal light, which is one mile south of the Ocean Avenue exit for Carmel and seven miles north of Point Lobos.

For the Northern Salinas Valley tour of River Road and its cut-offs, and the southern extension from the Highway 68 beginning points; *from the Monterey Bay Aquarium,* follow Lighthouse Avenue to the city of Monterey. Move to the right-hand lane after you go through the tunnel. Turn right at Camino Aguajito. Follow Camino Agualito to the end, and follow the signs to Highway 1 north. From 1, take the Highway 68 east exit.
From Highway 1 heading either direction, take the Highway 68 east exit, which is on the northern border of Monterey at Del Rey Oaks.

INTRODUCTION TO THE INLAND AREA WITH HISTORICAL HIGHLIGHTS

When local artist Marie-Louise Rouff compares the Carmel Valley to other Central Coast landscapes, her words reflect her pictures. "The colors are less diffuse, the shadows cast are darker. Mountains lie there like breathing human forms."

John Steinbeck was a native son of Salinas, and many of his novels drew on the surrounding landscape. In *East of Eden* he called the Salinas Valley "a long narrow swale." The Gabilan range on the east he described as "light gay mountains full of sun and loveliness and a kind of invitation, so that you wanted to climb into their warm foothills almost as you want to climb into the lap of a beloved mother." In contrast he described the Santa Lucias, on the west, as "dark and brooding."

The Carmel Valley and the Salinas Valley share agricultural and historical roots as they stretch inland and southward from the Monterey Bay Area. Each has a rhythm that complements the other, each its own chamber of California's heartland. The tours in this chapter of each valley begin with turns east off Highway 1 near Monterey, but the two tours take different routes inland. They intersect, forming an inland excursion loop, near Greenfield.

Cutting through the Santa Lucias, the Carmel Valley is the narrower, more intimate, more westerly of the two—the valley of sun to the people fogbound along the coast in the summer. The dark backdrop is the verdant redwood and pine forests of the Los Padres National Forest. Carved by the Carmel River, which can run swift in winter and only trickle through shaded pools in summer or drought years, the Carmel Valley begins at Highway 1 almost as a sister to Carmel. Not to be claimed by it, this valley has its own form and beauty. The Santa Lucias' high peaks on the Carmel Valley Road's southern side melt to gentle hills on the northern side. The road passes the Crossroads, Rancho Carmel, and Barnyard shopping centers at its Highway 1 entrance. Rolling hills separate the road from Monterey and, farther inland, Salinas and the Salinas Valley area. Due to its prime location, availability of land, and balmy weather, the Carmel Valley has faced intense and increasing pressures to develop. Resorts, many of which serve golf or equestrian enthusiasts, and residences share the valley with agricultural and wilderness land.

Miles broader than the Carmel Valley and anchored by the largest submerged river in California, the Salinas Valley is the agricultural heartland of the Central Coast region, the "Salad Bowl of the Nation." The Salinas River, one of the longest rivers in the state, is unusual both in running north and in being one of the largest submerged rivers in the United States. Just as the river flows peacefully (it surfaces at shallow levels), the Salinas Valley has a restful quality, in its spreading farmlands and open vistas. As the current building boom moves south from the Santa Clara Valley the fresh air and open views are cherished with the knowledge that they may be ephemeral, the makings of tomorrow's postcard collections. For the many Californians who grew up in now-urbanized areas, such as the orchards of San Jose, groves of Orange County, or once-discrete, now suburbia-absorbed small agricultural towns, stretches of the Salinas Valley remain like the places they remember. For readers of Steinbeck, the fields and open grasslands are yet the "Pastures of Heaven."

Highway 101 cuts through the center of the Salinas Valley. River Road, on the western side, offers a more intimate view of it. During celery-harvesting season on the western side of the valley the spicy fragrances are heady along River Road, clearing the mind and rousing the imagination.

Footsteps of the early inhabitants can be traced in both valleys. On the north side of Carmel Valley Road, about three miles from Highway 1, the gnarled El Encino del Descanso (the "Oak of Repose") holds a small religious shrine. The Rumsien and Esselen peoples who had been converted to Christianity used to stop here on the way to the Carmel Mission for burials. The Esselen territory extended east to what is now Soledad. Today, farther up the Carmel Valley in a section known as the Ventana Wilderness, the descendants of the Esselen tribe are rebuilding Esselen ceremonial grounds as they petition the government for official tribal recognition. South of the Esselen the Salinas Valley was first inhabited by the "Salinan," the name the Spanish gave to the people who lived along what the Spanish called the Salinas or, translated, "salty" river. The Salinans' name for themselves has not survived, although some descendants live throughout the Salinas Valley.

Two missions were founded in the Monterey County stretch of the Salinas Valley. Some parts of Mission Soledad have been restored near its fragrant rose garden and small chapel. A nearby ranch was the setting Steinbeck used for *Of Mice and Men.*

Farther south the western boundary of the Salinas Valley rolls into the Fort Hunter Liggett Military Reservation, now divided by a number of military and government uses. The reservation surrounds the painted cave of the Salinan people and the restored Mission San Antonio de Padua, which stands on the edge of pine and oak wilderness. A little more than two hundred years ago the missions were all outposts in wilderness, but they were not isolated from people. When Mission San Antonio was established in 1771, about twenty Salinan villages lay in a twenty-some-mile radius around the mission.

Nearest to Mission San Antonio, the typical Salinan village of Chacomex hosted several quadrangular houses averaging ten square feet in size. The roof consisted of a lattice of poles thatched with tules, which were lashed with strips of bark.

The missionaries recognized the temperate climate and gravel-laden soils of the alluvial fans at the base of the mountain ranges to be highly compatible with their European viticulture. A mission-period winery can be viewed at Mission San Antonio. Today, the Salinas and Carmel valleys are prime wine-grape areas. Several wineries and tasting rooms welcome visitors; tons more grapes are shipped throughout the state for processing.

By the 1830s Mexican and Spanish land grants had divided the valleys of the Rumsien, Esselen, and Salinan into enormous ranchos: Don Jose Manuel Boronda and his wife Maria Juana Boronda were among the first grantees to live on the land.

Many of the large ranchos that divided the Salinas and Carmel valleys after the mission period passed from the original Mexican owners after the Mexican-American War, because of the bureaucratic difficulties to keeping the land that were built into the treaty ending the war, in 1848. Starving cattle and the parched grasslands of the drought of the 1860s sent many ranchos into foreclosure. A hundred thousand cattle grazed Monterey County in 1860, but by 1864, after the dry years, the number had dropped to thirteen thousand. David Jacks, land baron of Monterey County, became a prime landowner.

Dona Boronda sold the golden *queso del pais* (cheese of the country) made on her rancho to Santa Lucia goldminers and Monterey markets. In the 1880s more dairies came to the valleys, among them those of David Jacks. Several local stories, including the Boronda version, lay claim to the origins of Monterey jack cheese. It is not clear whether this name came from David Jacks's marketing of it or from the heavy wooden "jacks" that pressed down on the cheese while it aged.

After the livestock tragedies of the drought years, landowners turned miles of rangeland into wheat fields. Labor contractors spread groups of dispirited tribal peoples through the valley each summer to harvest grain, but according to writings by historian Sandy Lydon their numbers dropped sharply because of disease. Chinese laborers were brought in by labor contractors from San Francisco. Many of the Chinese had worked the gold fields or had been released from railroad work when lines were completed.

Claus Spreckels brought the sugar beet to the Salinas Valley in the late 1880s and built a seven-story sugar factory near Salinas. Yearly "campaigns," as the harvests were called, saw wagons, train cars, and later trucks haul out the yields of thousands of acres of sugar beets. Parts of Steinbeck's novel *Tortilla Flat* and both movie versions of *East of Eden* were filmed in the "Sugar King's" company town of Spreckels.

The Southern Pacific Railway whistled through the valley, shipping first the grain and then the beets and cheese, and made or broke the towns along the central Salinas Valley. Towns such as Chualar, Soledad, and Gonzales were built on the freight train routes; Highway 101 connects many of these shipping towns today. Salinas, at the northern end of the valley, is the governmental, agricultural, and business center for Monterey County. People of Hispanic descent are the majority of the population and contribute leadership and their traditional celebrations to the city. In the surrounding valleys Hispanic workers are today's prime tenders of the agricultural fields.

Now it is "King Lettuce" that surrounds Salinas and stretches eastward toward the Gabilan Mountains. New shopping malls are also spreading northeast of Salinas, along the 101 corridor. Directly across from the Northridge Shopping Center travelers can pick up the San Juan Grade Road and travel northeast through the Gabilans to the old mission town of San Juan Bautista. From vantage spots along the narrow rutted road the grand vista of the Salinas Valley stretches to the sea.

The interior of narrow Carmel Valley is void of major shopping centers. Sugar beets were planted to entice the railroad to extend to Carmel but didn't succeed as a crop. Some of the original creamery buildings for Monterey jack cheese house businesses in Carmel Valley Village, the diminutive population center of this valley. The pickup trucks and cowpunchers are for real in this village: this is a ranching area. Also in the eclectic Carmel Valley Village, the Hidden Valley Music Center presents baroque, opera, and chamber music as well as theater and dance performances year-round. Local artisans exhibit at local festivals and shops.

When asked what changes he'd seen in the last twenty years the assistant fire chief of Cachagua, a relatively isolated community along Carmel Valley Road, smiled. "Everyone says the newcomers are going to change the valley. I've noticed more how it changes them."

Undaunted by change, within the southern Gabilan Mountains in the Pinnacles National Monument golden eagles soar above the wild rugged peaks of a remnant ancient volcano, gliding and circling. The trees that shade the rolling grasslands around Lake San Antonio and the pines by Lake Nacimiento, farther to the south, are winter homes to migrating bald and golden eagles. From their vantage point especially there is wilderness here still, wilderness prowled by the mountain lion and respected by the Rumsien, the Salinan, the Esselen, cut through with dusty mission trails—now cut much more by the fields of farmers from many lands, the resorts that cater to seekers of sunlit quietude, and the residences of present generations.

TOURS

The Carmel Valley tour follows the Carmel River, then turns inland to Carmel Valley Village. Beyond the village the winding road leads as the gateway to many locations in the Los Padres National Forest. Once you have completed the Carmel Valley Road tour you can cross to the Salinas Valley tour by driving Laureles Grade Road north to Highway 68. The tour follows Highway 68 to Salinas with turnoff for Spreckels and then continues along pastoral G-17, which is alternately named River Road, Fort Romie Road, and Arroyo Seco Road. From Greenfield, the terminus for the Northern Salinas Valley tour, you can also connect to the southern lakes tour. Visitors bound for San Juan Bautista and/or Gilroy can reach them via Highway 101 from Salinas. The Pinnacles National Monument can be reached from San Juan Bautista or Soledad.

THE CARMEL VALLEY TOUR

The tour begins at the intersection of Highway 1 with Carmel Valley Road. Heading inland from the intersection, the first right turn is Carmel Rancho

Boulevard, which leads to three shopping centers: the Crossroads, Carmel Rancho, and the Barnyard. The restaurants and some shops here are featured in the Carmel chapter (page 129). The first left from Carmel Rancho Boulevard leads to a small center and the Cornucopia Community Market which offers fresh organic produce as well as a number of prepared picnic foods. On the west side of Carmel Rancho Boulevard, the Bagel Bakery serves a palate-pleasing assortment of bagel sandwiches.

Just past the boulevard turnoff, a wooden sign on Carmel Valley Road welcomes you to Carmel Valley. Behind the sign a fence straddles the Carmel Rancho parking lot and fields of furrows dug in the rich Carmel River basin-land. The fence is the first of many to separate disparate uses of the landscape in this valley. Golf ball drivers and cattle drivers share a common scenery. Christmas tree farms, fresh-egg ranches, winery tasting rooms, cattle ranches, golf courses, and hybrid begonia nurseries occupy this bucolic valley once known for pear orchards and creameries.

The valley is wide at this point, and the Carmel River flows far from your sight, near the base of the mountains. Along the route the river will weave closer and entice you to leave your car and listen to its swift wet-season rumbling and gentle summer babbles, very much the same as Steinbeck described in the book *Cannery Row.*

> "The Carmel is a lovely little river. It isn't very long but in its course it has everything a river should have. It rises in the mountains, and tumbles down a while, runs through shallows, is dammed to make a lake, spills over the dam, crackles among round boulders, wanders lazily under sycamores, spills into pools where trout live, drops in against banks where crayfish live. In the winter it becomes a torrent, a mean little fierce river, and in the summer it is a place for children to wade in and for fisherman to wander in. Frogs blink from its banks and the deep ferns grow beside it. Deer and foxes come to drink from it, secretly in the morning and evening and now and then a mountain lion crouched flat laps its water. The farms of the rich little valley back up to the river and take its water for the orchards and the vegetables. The quail call beside it and the wild doves come whistling in at dusk. Raccoons pace its edges looking for frogs. It's everything a river should be."

Traffic often moves too quickly and turns are easy to miss on this scenic road. It is imperative that drivers slow at the several school zones along the route. From Highway 1 to Carmel Valley Village nonstop takes about thirty minutes.

The first greens you see are on the two eighteen-hole championship courses

234 Monterey Bay: The Ultimate Guide

of the Rancho Cañada Golf Course. The public courses crisscross the Carmel River. Reservations are recommended (831/624-0111). In addition to great golf the Rancho Cañada Golf Club serves an excellent Friday night fish buffet.

After the road narrows to one lane, greens again carpet the valley floor, around the rooms of the Mobil-rated five-star Quail Lodge Golf Resort. Eleven lakes that dot the landscape provide refuge to migratory birds. The resort land previously housed the Carmel Valley Dairy, which was owned by the Dwight Morrow and Charles Lindbergh families. The famous aviator used it as a getaway. A new luxury home development is being built on the adjoining six hundred acres of Quail Meadows, where the understanding is, "If you can see it from the road you can't build it." Maseratis, Lamborghinis, Ferraris, and other automotive jewels take over the practice greens at the Concours Italiana, which is held at the resort in late August of each year.

At the next sharp right on Carmel Valley Road past Quail Lodge, the Valley Hills Shopping Center welcomes you to country living. Check the bulletin board for the latest livestock and community concerns. Egg-laying guinea hens cackle on top of antique stores within close proximity to Quail Lodge.

Roosters strut and rabbits scurry around pickup trucks being filled with hay at the next driveway. The Hacienda Hay and Feed store is a must stop if you have children or want a western barnyard experience. In October the hay bales are piled high and filled with Halloween surprises at the store's haunted hay house, for kids and brave adults.

October is also pumpkin-picking time at the farms along Carmel Valley Road. Some fruit and vegetable stands are open year-round, some just for the summer-autumn harvest. Just past Hacienda Hay and Feed, the farm stand at Earthbound Farms offers an excellent selection of organic produce and also hosts summer events.

A right turn on Schulte Road leads to Saddle Mountain Recreation Park. This hundred-acre park is open year-round for camping. Tepee tents are an option but are not the style of dwellings used by the Rumsien/Ohlone, who slept under the open skies during warm months and also lived in round willow- and tule-covered ruks. A three-and-one-half-mile hiking trail leads to an elevation of a thousand feet for a panoramic view. On clear days you can see across the bay to the Santa Cruz Mountains.

At Chateau Julien (831/624-2600), 8940 Carmel Valley Road, wine tasting and tours offer the feeling of joining old friends at the boutique winery situated on seven country acres. Many other wineries are located along the Salinas tour and in the Santa Cruz Mountains.

The Holly Farm (831/625-1926), which provides gardens for private parties, and the Carmel Valley Water Gardens (831/622-POND) share the next right turn. At the Water Gardens, nursery stock pools and artistic ponds hold numerous imported and domestic koi and forty varieties of water plants. Blooming water lilies and pond poppies are favorites. The gardens are open to the public Wednesday through Saturday, 9 a.m. to 6 p.m.

Your next stop may be Mid Valley Shopping Center, which has restaurants, a grocery store, a deli, and a movie theater. You might want to get foodstuffs here and take them to Garland Ranch Regional Park, an excellent hiking and picnic spot, three miles up the road. The five-thousand-acre Garland Park, located eight and one-half miles from Highway 1, includes picnic areas by the Carmel River, a field of old farm equipment, and miles of hiking trails.

Two bridges lead across the river to the visitor's center in the dry months. The wider year-round green bridge is located on a trail that begins about a hundred yards west of the parking lot by the mailbox at 700 West Carmel Road. If you pause at the bridge and look north you will see a dense cottonwood grove, one of the best examples of riparian woodland that remains along the Carmel River. Beyond the bridge veer left for the visitor's center, which is open 10 a.m. to 2 p.m. on weekends. In the field of old farm equipment from ranch days the picnic tables alongside old hay wagons are inviting places to have snacks or lunch. So are small coves at the river near the other entrance from the parking lot.

Three of the scenic trails include the lupine loop, the buckeye nature trail, and the waterfall trail to the mesa. The lupine loop is a sea of blue flowers from April through June. A Rumsien grinding rock site and large midden lie at the terminus of the buckeye trail. Every season here has its highlights, but the spring wildflowers bedazzle more than the bees.

Garland Park is one part of the Monterey Peninsula Regional Park District (831/659-4488), all parks of which feature free admission. The new Cooper Ranch addition to Garland Park, one-half mile west of the green bridge on Cooper trail, is the only area of Garland Park open to mountain bikes. Equestrians have open access to the park trails, with the exception of the terrace trail, buckeye trail, Siesta Point trail, and portions of the waterfall trail.

Back on Carmel Valley Road you intersect Laureles Grade, which connects to Highway 68 about midway between Monterey and Salinas. The views over the mountaintops and the descent from the Santa Lucia Mountains make this road a good return route or side trip.

Los Laureles Lodge is to the left on Carmel Valley Road, just past Boronda Road. The Los Laureles Rancho was sold in the 1880s to the Pacific Improvement Company for the Central Pacific Railroad, which needed a source of water for the newly opened Hotel Del Monte. Some seven hundred Chinese laborers built the original San Clemente Dam on the Carmel River and laid twenty-three miles of pipe to the Hotel Del Monte. The Los Laureles ranch house was enlarged and a number of cabins added to create an inland destination for guests of the Del Monte, who rode up Carmel Valley Road on horse-pulled tallyhos to take the air or to stay and hunt or fish. During Prohibition this was the place where Hotel Del Monte guests imbibed in bootleg liquor.

After the property changed hands again, Muriel Vanderbilt Phelps Adams acquired it to raise racehorses. The present Los Laureles Lodge is restored as a historic country inn. Upon his retirement, Monterey County's "Singing Sheriff," Pat Duval, opened his popular DuVal's restaurant here (831/659-3426).

After driving through pastoral hills you come to Carmel Valley Village, the first shops of which were designed to resemble a Mexican village. Spread along Carmel Valley Road, the village has businesses that are set back from the road. A community park with picnic areas, public pool, barbecue pits, and children's play area complete with one of the first fire engines in the valley is located in the eastern end of the village.

The village is an eclectic arrangement of shops, galleries, bakeries, and markets. The Talbott Tie Factory Outlet offers neckware, fabric, shirts, and accessories at reduced, outlet prices (831/659-4540). Across the street studios offer fine handcarved furniture and wood sculptures. The Carmel Valley Market offers groceries, choice meats, and collector bottles of fine wines (831/659-2472).

The White Oak Properties complex on Carmel Valley Road between Paso Hondo and Esqualine Road is the historic heart of the village. The white clapboard building with the cupola was built in 1890 to process milk from the Los Laureles Dairy Ranch, for the old Hotel Del Monte in Monterey. A rod-controlled lever opened the sides of the tower to take advantage of afternoon breezes, cooling the milk. The round trip to Monterey for a four-horse wagon loaded with milk or cheese took at least eight hours in the dry season, and longer when the roads were muddy from seasonal rains. William Hatton managed this dairy and others so successfully that he was able to purchase the Rancho Cañada de la Segunda at the entrance to the valley. The Hatton Canyon, which parallels Highway 1, was part of his landholdings. The White Oak Grill, now located in the former dairy building, encourages visitors to relax under the oaks and feel the serenity of the valley.

When you are ready to continue past Carmel Valley Village travel north on Carmel Valley Road, which becomes Tularcitos Road and is best identified as G-16. It leads through hills and meadows with some sharp curves for thirty miles to Greenfield and the Highway 101 connection. Cabernet grapevines spread on both sides of the road as you leave the village and continue on.

About 4.5 miles past the village you'll come to the turnoff for the very narrow Cachagua Road, which winds through very sharp turns to Los Padres Dam, Los Padres National Forest, and then connects with Tassajara Road to loop back to G-16. The entire loop from the village is about twenty-nine miles. If you want a more relaxing and less winding drive to the same locations wait for Tassajara Road, which branches off Carmel Valley Road 7.5 miles farther (11.5 miles from Carmel Valley Village).

Between Cachagua Road and Tassajara Road on G-16 keep a look out for the 21.8 milepost and a dirt road on the north side. This is the right of way to the Blomquist Open Space. Before you visit the area you need to pick up a permit in Garland Park (at its visitor's center or the district office in the Cooper Ranch addition; see page 235). It's a four-mile hike down the dirt road to the open space, which features open woodlands, an old cabin site, and serenity—a lovely place to enjoy Central Coast wildflowers in the spring.

G-16 cuts through a hill just before a road marker identifies your next right turn as Tassajara Road. About 1.5 miles past the Carmel Valley Road intersection, Tassajara Road forms a Y with Cachagua Road. John James founded the small unincorporated settlement in the area in 1867. From 1904 to the end of the stagecoach era James Ranch was a stagecoach stop for visitors bound for the hot springs resort at Tassajara. Miss-it-if-you-blink Jamesburg is another 1.5 miles down Tassajara Road. In former days, some settlers here trapped live grizzly bears, supplementing incomes by ox-carting them to Monterey for bull and bear fights. Ladybugs were gathered in the springtime and sold to Salinas farmers, to protect their crops from pests.

To view the Jamesburg Earth Station turn right, on Cachagua Road, at this Y junction. If you want to visit Tassajara Zen Center or Ventana Wilderness Station keep to your left, on Tassajara Road.

The turnoff for the Jamesburg Earth Station is plainly marked on the right-hand side of Cachagua Road, 3.5 miles past the Y junction. A large-dish antenna at the AT&T facility stretches a hundred feet across and stands more than ten stories high. This is the major U.S. station for international satellite telecommunications in the Pacific Ocean region. The station operates twenty-four hours a day, seven days a week.

For more hiking, drive past the Jamesburg Earth Station and a small store and turn left at Nason Road. A narrow, rutted road will lead to the San Clemente Dam and backcountry trails.

On Tassajara Road from the Y junction the route is rugged and cut with sharp curves. About 1.5 miles beyond the Y an older home is the site of the Jamesburg refreshment stand and the staging area for Tassajara. For those staying overnight at Tassajara, a four-wheel-drive stage, which costs $30, leaves here at 11 a.m. daily during the summer season. The staging area and the Tassajara Zen Center are closed to visitors from September to May. Just past this staging area the paving ends. The final portion of Tassajara Road will climb to the high Chews Ridge, pass the turnoff for the MIRA astronomy station, and then drop to the Tassajara Zen Center (see below). Note that it is best suited for standard transmission and preferably four-wheel-drive vehicles.

Ventana Wilderness Expeditions (831/625-8664), which offers daily two- and three-hour trail rides as well as overnight trail rides into the Ventana Wilderness, is located on Tassajara Road, 6.5 miles from Carmel Valley Road (including three and a half miles of dirt road). It is owned and operated by the Nason family, which has pioneer and Esselen roots. A re-created Esselen village is opened to visitors and school groups. Trail rides meander by small streams and through oaks and pines to Chews Ridge, the highest peaks of the Santa Lucia mountain range. Incredible views of the Ventana Wilderness, the Monterey Bay, and the valleys greet ridge-top visitors. Reservations are strongly recommended for all rides.

Continue on Tassajara Road to Chews Ridge, which offers an eagle's view of the Carmel and Salinas valleys and, west, over the Los Padres National Forest to the Pacific Ocean. Snow sometimes blankets the ridge in winter, inviting youngsters to try out their sleds. The sign to the left for MIRA marks the ten-mile rutted dirt road to the Monterey Institute for Research in Astronomy. It is an observation, education, and research facility, the center-piece of which is a thirty-six-inch reflecting telescope that weighs six tons. "Using gravitational lenses to determine the scale of the universe is one of our primary research efforts," explains director and researcher Dr. Bruce Weaver. Open houses are held throughout summer and fall (831/883-1000).

No water is available at the U.S. Forest Service campgrounds of White Oaks Camp and China Camp located along Tassajara Road. It is beyond China Camp that a standard transmission is suggested. The fourteen-mile trip from Jamesburg to Tassajara Zen Center takes about an hour and fifteen minutes. Full tanks of gas and adequate car cooling systems also are advised.

Seventeen hot mineral springs flow out of the Tassajara mountainside. Tassajara is a monastic community established by the San Francisco Zen Center at the Tassajara hot springs. During the winter it is closed to visitors for intensive Zen training sessions. April is a transition month, with visitors invited to work at the resort in preparation for the summer months. In the summer visitors have the opportunity to stay in rustic cabins and share in Zen instruction and meditation. Families and individuals may also share day use of the hot springs, scenic hiking trails, smooth rock water slides, and swimming pool without joining the instruction. In 1993 the famous bath-house and baths were relocated upstream due to danger of rock slides from the surrounding hillside, which was weakened by the earthquake of 1989.

The vegetarian meals are offered for overnight guests only, so pack in picnics for day use. Some areas are clothing optional. All visitors should make reservations (415/431-3771).

Back on G-16 (which is also signed Carmel Valley Road and Tularcitos Road) your day is complete or Laureles Grade Road will connect you with Highway 68.

You may notice that a few of the surrounding hills have dark green patches that persist while neighboring hillsides are dried brown and yellow. With the reintroduction of native grasses that covered the hills here two hundred years ago, the hills stay greener longer, and the grasslands don't crowd out sprouting oak trees. Only 2 percent of the grasses you see on the hillsides of California are native. During the rancho days the cowhide was the "Monterey Dollar." Cattle preferred the native perennial grass and overgrazing led to its demise. Annual grass and weed seed, brought with livestock or bags of barley from Europe, took over. As reported to the *Monterey County Herald* by a lead researcher, "plots of native grasses seem to attract more native insects, more bees, butterflies, beetles, maybe mice, owls, and hawks—all kinds of things cascade from putting the base of this ecological pyramid back in order."

THE SALINAS VALLEY TOUR

From Monterey, Highway 68 east, also known as the Monterey Salinas Highway, leads to Salinas and delightful backroads connections that parallel Highway 101 south to Greenfield. The tour begins on Highway 68 at its intersection with Olmsted Road (which leads north to the Monterey Peninsula Airport and south to Jacks Peak; for particulars about the park at Jacks Peak and directions see the Monterey chapter, page 65). Leaving Olmsted Road behind, as you drive east along Highway 68 cattle graze on the grassy meadows to your right as you weave through oak woodland and chaparral. Just one mile north of Olmsted Road on 68, turn left to visit the three establishments at Tarpy's Stonehouse. Here Ventana Vineyards Tasting Room offers wine tasting, Tarpy's Roadhouse serves acclaimed American cuisine, and Langdon Williams & Castleberry (831/372-2418) invites you to wander among an eclectic collection of antiques.

The Ventana is the first of several tasting rooms and wineries you can visit along this tour. Monterey County has the largest number of acres planted in premium-varietal wine-producing grapes of any county in California. Growers match wine grape varieties to the climate regions and soil types. In Europe, for example, the German Riesling region is relatively cool and the French Bordeaux regions are warmer. Salinas Valley's cool weather is especially suited for cooler grape varieties such as riesling, gewurztraminer, pinot noir, and chardonnay. Cabernet sauvignon, cabernet franc, and merlot thrive in the warmer areas south of Soledad and on alluvial fans west of Soledad.

Laguna Seca is most famous for its many auto racing and motorcycle racing events, and recently famous also for in-line skating and mountain bike racing. The Grand Prix of classic car races comes to Laguna Seca in mid-August. These prestigious races feature two hundred varieties of classic cars, including Maseratis and Ferraris. A good spot from which to view the races is the top of the hill looking down at the racecourse. The famous corkscrew section is also an exciting view from the other side of the hill. (For information and tickets to auto and motorcycle races call 800/327-SECA.)

In March quieter but highly competitive groups of racers whizz down the hill and around the curves. In-line skaters, road racers, and mountain bikers compete in separate events at Laguna Seca at the Sea Otter Classics. (For information, call 650/367-7797.)

Just beyond Laguna Seca, Highway 68 intersects Laureles Grade, which is a scenic fifteen- to twenty-minute drive over the rolling Santa Lucias to mid–Carmel Valley Road. At the summit of Laureles Grade Road, views extend over Carmel Valley to the ocean. If the time and weather are opportune, the fog rolling in from the ocean can be caught as sunlit shimmers in the valley.

About two miles past the Laureles Grade intersection a gas station and minimart mark the Corral de Tierra intersection on Highway 68. George Vancouver, the English naval captain who explored the Pacific Coast in the period 1792 to 1794, viewed a fascinating sandstone formation in the area of what is now known as Corral de Tierra Road. "I was . . . there gratified with the sight of the most extraordinary mountain I had ever beheld. . . . The whole summit of the mountain appeared to be wholly supported by these columns rising perpendicularly with the most minute mathematical exactness." This sandstone formation, known as the Castle, is located on the private lands of the Markham Ranch and looks like a sand sculpture more reminiscent of Utah or Arizona. You can view it, at a distance, from Corral de Tierra Road by looking to your left when you are 1.3 miles past the intersection. For viewing, a pull-out to accommodate two or three cars is located just before the road enters the oak groves. People who have hiked to the Castle claim it is more memorable from the road than from close range. The Castle, or "Castle Rock," as Steinbeck called it, is featured in the beginning of his short story "The Murder." Beyond the view of the Castle, Corral de Tierra Road enters the canopy of a towering oak grove. Although the buildings were located elsewhere, the setting of Steinbeck's *The Red Pony* depicts the Corral de Tierra area. Roads throughout the area are laden with curves and dotted with small ranches.

Blanchard's Wood Sculptures is located .8 mile up Highway 68 from the

Corral de Tierra Road intersection. Mammoth bears, redwood seals, and an old prospector with a hopeful face are among the forty wood sculptures that surround Steve Blanchard as he carves the chainsaw masterpieces. His art is deafening but he'll take off the earmuffs and talk awhile. "When you're writing a story you have a general idea of what you're going to say but you don't know the exact words you'll be using. It's the same with carving. I can see the statue in the wood, then as I get going I cut here and cut there. It evolves." Most of his huge statues won't fit in your trunk, but he'll ship them to you. Toro Place Restaurant is located next door. This local favorite serves ample and tasty country breakfasts and lunches (831/484-1333).

On the left, just a short way past San Benancio Road, the Fort Ord Lands provide a parking lot and staging area for access to the Toro Creek trail. Head for the hills on a walking trail that hugs this seasonal creek. In winter the creek rages after storms. Notice its northerly direction; it is flowing away from the direction of the ocean to meet the Salinas River. If the creek is flowing you will not be able to cross to the hills. If you walk north to the section just beyond a view of a landslide-scarred hill, let your sense of hearing and a small path lead you to a clearing and view of six or more small fifteen-foot waterfalls. These are known locally as "Wolf's Falls." No, there aren't any wolves here. The falls are named after a third-grader who discovered them. If the streambed is dry, cross it at an area across from the grade school's baseball diamond; a hike up the hillside will earn you sweeping views of the Fort Ord Lands and Salinas.

The entrance to Toro Regional Park is on Highway 68, about four miles north of Laureles Grade, which places it thirteen miles from Monterey and six miles from Salinas. This 4,700-acre park includes a nature center, picnic grounds, playgrounds, and miles of walking and horseback riding trails that wind through the wooded hillsides.

After Highway 68 becomes a divided road the first exit leads to River Road, which is the bucolic alternative to Highway 101. To take it south, skip to page 246. To visit Spreckels and Salinas continue on Highway 68.

SPRECKELS AND SALINAS. Spreckels Boulevard, which intersects Highway 68 just beyond River Road, leads south into the town. Just as you enter Spreckels a canopy of white-rimmed black walnut trees extends over the road. After Claus Spreckels was expelled from the sugar fields in Hawaii by its king and his supporters, in 1886, he started a sugar beet factory in Watsonville. When the focus of sugar beet planting moved to the Salinas Valley, "King Sugar" Spreckels chose it as the location for the largest sugar factory in the United States. This factory town grew nearby. After shutting down in 1982 the factory was laid waste by the wrecking ball, but the sugar storage bins, a warehouse, and the company town remain as if frozen in the past. Parking is easy on the block-long downtown section of Spreckels Boulevard. The successful new figure around the area is Billy Broccoflower, a muscular green superhero with a head of broccoflower, the combination of broccoli and cauliflower that offers more vitamins than either. He entertains at local festivals and around schools, inspiring people to eat five vegetable servings a day. His namesake seed was developed at Tanimura and Antle (T&A), one of California's largest growers and shippers of vegetables. The corporate headquarters are set in a palm-tree-shaded oasis just outside of town.

Back on Highway 68 your ride to Salinas may be punctuated by motorists in a hurry. This is a major commute route. The hurrying along this route isn't new. Back in the mid-1800s stagecoaches rushed to a tavern on land that would become Salinas. Elias Howe owned the tavern, which was at the intersection of the routes for stages from Monterey to San Juan Bautista and from San Francisco to Los Angeles, and he placed bets on which would arrive there first. Business prospered so much that the neighboring stop, at Natividad, had to shut down.

Today Salinas is the population center, the industrial hub, and the governmental center of Monterey County. As is the case in many growing cities Salinas faces crime problems. These tour areas are in parts of the city commonly visited.

As you drive into Salinas, Highway 68 becomes south Main Street. A walking tour of the 100 block of Main Street shows many refurbished old town buildings, dating from the 1890s through the 1930s.

Ten antique stores cluster around the entrance to "Old Main." At Country Peddler Antiques (831/424-2292) you can find a 1930s kitchen gadget or expertly finished one-hundred-year-old Victorian furniture. Olde Town Antiques (831/754-3627) houses twenty-one dealers in a twelve thousand square foot historic bank building. Oldtown Salinas Antique Faire offers free appraisals and a festive atmosphere on the third Sunday of each month from 9 a.m. to 4 p.m.

At the top of Main Street the new National Steinbeck Center brings John Steinbeck's books to life in a vivid juxtaposition of stage sets, films, and discovery centers. The thirty-seven thousand square foot structure is the city's elegant reconciliation and honor with its native son. The Steinbeck Center provides research access to a collection of more than thirty thousand letters, manuscripts, artifacts, oral histories and film archives related to Steinbeck's works.

In a series of changing exhibits, visitors actually join the characters and settings of Steinbeck's books. In the Cannery Row exhibit, adults and kids

examine some of Doc's specimens, look through microscopes at slides of marine plankton, and enjoy scientific study with trained docents. Woody Guthrie's music fills the air at Hooverville, where visitors walk into a migrant worker's cabin and tent, share chores, and view film clips about the real workers who lived these lives. In the Mexican Plaza, visitors enter the world of *The Pearl, The Forgotten Village,* and *Viva Zapata.* Films give way to real storytellers, musicians, and dramatic readings. The Rocinante, the camper driven by Steinbeck in *Travels with Charley,* is one of many major Steinbeck artifacts that authenticate the center. Around every corner, in every drawer and through every doorway, visitors find a multisensory approaching the center's twenty-three different sections. The archival vault holds thirty thousand Steinbeck items: manuscripts, letters, autographed first editions, gallery proofs, posters, photographs of Steinbeck, and more. Research facilities are available for scholars and others who want to learn more about this native son. Just as the Monterey Bay Aquarium exhibits *Fishing for Solutions* to promote thought and action about the dwindling oceanic reserves, so, too, this center will hopefully push for solutions to homelessness and farmworker conditions in the new millenium.

Several Steinbeck events are coordinated throughout the year from the Steinbeck Center Foundation office. During the first two weeks of August the town honors Nobel– and Pulitzer prize–winning author John Steinbeck during the annual Steinbeck Festival. Each year one of Steinbeck's books is the focus for events, which include plays, films, barbecues, walking tours, and special lectures. For information about Steinbeck and events call the National Steinbeck Center (831/796-3833).

Turning left from Main on West Alisal leads to the courthouse, the oldest section of which dates to the mid-1930s. Joe Mora's sculpted heads of the pioneers of Monterey County history watch modern events from the outer walls and inside the courtyard.

From the courthouse turn right on Church Street to Central Avenue. The stately Victorian at 132 Central was John Steinbeck's family home and contains family photos, memorabilia, and Victorian furnishings. The restored home was rescued by the nonprofit Valley Guild, which bought it when the diocese of Monterey put it up for sale in 1972. The home is open weekdays, when the volunteers staff a luncheon tea room and book and memorabilia store. Gourmet weekday lunches that feature produce fresh from the local fields and local wines are served in the original living room, parlor, and dining room. The room Steinbeck was born in, his bedroom until his sister was born, is the reception area of the house. Reservations are necessary for lunch or for group tours of the house (831/424-2735).

Follow Church Street south to 110 West San Luis Street. A nearly lifesize statue of the author stands in front of the John Steinbeck Library. The archival collection which began at this library is now housed in the new vault at the Steinbeck Center.

To view the Boronda Adobe, a new cultural museum under construction, and the beginnings of a "Street of History Museum," drive west on Central with a right turn on Davis, following well-marked signs. The Boronda Adobe was built by Eusebio Boronda, son of the Borondas who were the first permanent rancheros in Carmel Valley, and it is the oldest structure at the site. Partially furnished as it was in the mid-1800s, the adobe also includes the genealogy of the Boronda family and early photographs.

Nearby is the original red one-room Lagunitas Schoolhouse, moved here from San Juan Grade Road. Rows of old wooden desks and old maps greet twentieth-century visitors inside this 1896 schoolhouse, which was made famous in Steinbeck's *The Red Pony*. An old Victorian home designed by William Weeks is being restored on the property and will feature furnishings of 1898. A new twelve-thousand-square-foot cultural museum will feature a panorama of the various cultures that have contributed to Monterey County. For information on when the buildings are open call the Monterey County Historical Society (831/757-8085).

Steinbeck used to be a controversial figure in Salinas, as his descriptions of the agricultural fields often were raw and they exposed wretched conditions. Now another major event in Salinas—the California Rodeo, usually held the third week in July—provokes a different kind of showdown in the new West. The event brings to town opposing forces in the best of the rodeo stars from throughout the Western United States and the most concerned of the animal rights activists. The cowboys and cowgirls and adoring fans are definitely in the majority, with tickets for seating at the rodeo necessary in advance of events. The rodeo is now presented in the new Sports Complex. Night time action is drawing even more crowds.

Everyone seems to love the preparation and camaraderie. For two weeks prior to the event in the shopping centers throughout Salinas, windows are painted with Western scenes, store clerks wear Western clothes, and even the models in a local fashion show ride horseback. Parades and barbecues add to the festivities. The rodeo grounds are located at Sherwood Park, a ninety-nine acre recreational facility on North Main Street. Not to be missed at Sherwood Park are three gigantic hat sculptures by Klaes Oldenburg.

Hats, trucks, and anything else you need can probably be found in the major shopping centers along Highway 101 at Northridge and Harden Ranch. Major department stores as well as local shops populate the malls here. For specialty shopping you might want to take the John Street exit off Highway 101 (north or south) and turn left at Work Street to visit the

Dinnerware Outlet (831/422-4962) of Franmara, Inc. It claims to be the only factory in the United States that designs porcelain with "in-glaze" techniques practiced in Europe. The company imports hard-paste (high-fired) Pillivuyt French culinary and Czech Spirito porcelains, and artisans decorate them according to individual or business requests, then fire them in a Limoges-type kiln. Tours are given depending on the production schedule.

RIVER ROAD. If you turned south from Highway 68 onto River Road before reaching Highway 101 and Salinas, continue south. For the next twenty-three miles River Road winds through acres and acres of rows and rows of lettuce, stumpy broccoli bushes, carrots, celery, asparagus fronds—just about anything you need for a soup or salad. Roll down your windows to smell a mixture of vegetable fragrances forgotten by city dwellers. Weathered redwood barns, horse ranches, and turning wooden windmills dot the landscape. Depending on the season, a wide slow-moving track of water or the swirled dry weeds of the Salinas River bed drift in and out of view. Farther south, rows of vineyards stretch along the road and many wineries open their doors for wine tastings and tours. You may also have miles of views of slow-moving farm equipment, if you get behind a tractor or truck loaded with harvest. They usually don't pull over; this is their road. Approach curves with the understanding that tons of tomatoes may weigh down a truck just around the bend, since you don't want to be smashed into sauce. Cars and trucks also pull out of blind driveways.

In your south-facing view the Santa Lucia and Gabilan mountains seem to merge at the point of a V. In reality the ranges never meet. I love to follow this changing illusion while driving River Road.

About four miles south of Highway 68, Vision Quest (831/455-1914) opens its exotic animal kennels to public tours. Joseph the MGM lion, famous for his role in *George of the Jungle*, lives here, along with an elephant, tigers, monkeys and other animals that perform in movies and television. Tours at the exotic animal attraction are given at 1 p.m. each day and cost $5 per person.

About nine miles south of the Highway 68 intersection River Road merges with Chualar River Road to cross the Salinas River over the Chualar River Bridge and eventually connect with Highway 101. Before merging and crossing the bridge, veer right to continue on River Road. Limekiln Road intersects River Road three miles south of Chualar River Road. You will turn off River Road for Barlocker's Rustling Oaks Ranch (831/675-9121) at 25252 Limekiln Road. One last limekiln can be sighted from the ranch, kids can pet animals at farm pens, and picnics can be enjoyed on the grass under spreading oaks. Weekend horse camps for kids here offer options for parents who want to enjoy adult wine-tasting excursions. For even the adult weekend cowhand, the owners will teach cattle cutting and other ranch skills.

A few miles farther on River Road the first acres of grapevines spread their arms along the roadside. At 1645 River Road a sign on the left-hand side of the road will direct you to the Cloninger Cellar Winery (831/675-WINE).

Back on River Road, seven miles south of the Gonzales River Road intersection, you will come to a fork in the road. At this point River Road becomes Fort Romie Road, the left fork. If you are on a wine-tasting excursion, take the right fork Foothill Road, to Smith & Hook Winery, which is known for its cabernet sauvignon. Picnics under the oaks or on the decks of the meeting room treat visitors to grand vistas of the Salinas Valley. Views from a nearby lookout are worth the hike. See page 217.

You won't find an actual fort on Fort Romie Road. In the depression of the 1890s the Salvation Army in collaboration with other groups set up a moderately successful colony or, utilizing the military terms of the Salvation Army, "a fort"of unemployed workers and their families here. Several of the farmers in the area are their descendants. At a little more than a mile up Fort Romie Road you can take a right turn for a side trip to Mission Soledad. The mission was built as the thirteenth member of the chain in 1791 and has not received the facelifts and complete restorations of others in the area. Crumbling ruins of the old mission lie beside a restored chapel and museum of mission and ranch artifacts. In July and September lively barbecues and fiestas fill the mission grounds. For the rest of the year the mission is quiet; a stroll through the patio rose garden and a picnic on benches invite quiet reflection on the past.

Fort Romie Road next intersects with Arroyo Seco Road. You can turn left at this intersection for a two-mile side trip to Soledad, one gateway to the Pinnacles National Monument. Soledad has roots as an Italian-Swiss dairy community and currently, with an approximately 85 percent Hispanic population, is the first community in Monterey County to have an all-Hispanic City Council. Several taquerias here sell piñatas and household items along with handmade tortillas. You will feel comfortable speaking either English or Spanish.

If you turn right at the Arroyo Seco intersection you can travel six miles to Paraiso Hot Springs Resort. You will first intersect with Foothill Road. Across from the fork, a road leads up the alluvial fan to the family-owned Paraiso Springs Vineyard (831/678-0300). See page 218.

Paraiso Springs Road cuts through open fields to the foothills of the Santa Lucia Mountains. Palm trees sway over the green lawns surrounding two pools and the Victorian cottages that once served turn-of-the-century guests at Paraiso Springs Resort (831/678-2882). The Victorians are now long-term rentals, and short-term overnight guests stay at a campground or at small, rustic cabins on the hillside. The day-use fee for the heated mineral pools and enclosed hot pool room is $25 per person. Guests can camp and use pools for $30 per person with a $5 added charge for the hot pool. Cabins with full use of facilities rent for $125. Guests I spoke with chose this retreat for the mineral pools and to get away from urban life. Overnight guests and drivers who just drop in for a sandwich and refreshing drink can enjoy the panoramic view from the dining area, and also the early-times news articles and pictures posted in the lodge.

Beyond the intersection with Paraiso Springs Road, Fort Romie Road continues as Arroyo Seco Road. The Highway 101 connection at Soledad offers a more direct route to Greenfield. If you continue on Arroyo Seco Road south, turn left at Elm Avenue (G-16), which leads to Greenfield and Highway 101. To connect with River Road or with Highway 101 continue east on G-16, which is now the eastern stretch of Arroyo Seco Road. After six miles Arroyo Seco Road intersects Elm Avenue, leading to Greenfield and Highway 101. (You can take 101 south for the southern lakes and mission tour, page 249.) Alternately, you can follow Arroyo Seco/G-17 as it turns left and loops north to Highway 68, which leads west to the Monterey Peninsula and northeast to Salinas and Spreckels. To follow the loop north keep your eyes open for the G-17 markers, as road names change; Arroyo Seco Road veers right to connect with Highway 101 at Soledad. To join River Road, leave Arroyo Seco Road and jog left at Fort Romie Road, which, farther north, becomes River Road. This backroads route parallels Highway 101 and takes nearly the same time as 101 to approach the Monterey Peninsula, but it is much longer on scenery (reverse the Northern Salinas Valley tour, below).

Greenfield is one of the most productive agricultural areas of the Salinas Valley and one of the fastest-growing communities in the state. As the Highway 101 population corridor reaches farther and farther south, the pressure faced by farmers to sell their land for development increases. Miles and miles of open land in the Salinas Valley has been protected by the California Williamson Act, an agricultural preservation program, which has given farmland owners incentives for keeping their property in agricultural use. Owners have been eligible for substantial tax breaks in exchange for agreeing not to develop their property. The act has kept farming and ranching in Monterey County feasible.

Known as the "Broccoli Capital," Greenfield gained national fame when locals sent a truckload of broccoli to Washington, D.C., after then-President Bush announced he hated broccoli. The summer broccoli festival features parades and tasty and unusual broccoli dishes such as deep-fried broccoli and broccoli ice cream. Music, entertainment, and arts and crafts booths anchor the festival, which is surrounded by agricultural fields. The Jekel Vineyards (831/674-5522) winery is located at 40155 Walnut Avenue. A proposed aircraft museum may change the face of Greenfield. Charles Nichols, who owns the world's largest private collection of World War II–era aircraft, has chosen land near Greenfield as the site of a museum, theater, and conference center.

THE SOUTHERN LAKES AND SAN ANTONIO MISSION TOUR

The area south of Greenfield is vintage California. Eagles soar above their nests at Lake San Antonio, over the remnants of an old stage stop at Jolon and near the remote San Antonio Mission. Reach Greenfield by traveling south either on Highway 101 or on the Highway 68 and River Road route, or take the longer Carmel Valley Road route. Before King City exit the freeway at Jolon Road to travel directly to Jolon, the lakes, or Mission San Antonio. Sometimes sections of the military reservation in this area are closed due to training maneuvers (though Jolon Road, G-14, is not affected by the closures). Remember to call Fort Hunter Liggett Military Range Control (831/386-2503) if you plan to travel the Nacimiento-Fergusson Road (which connects to Big Sur) or to fish in the reservation reservoirs. Also call if you plan to visit the Salinan Painted Cave; in 1993, due to vandalism problems, it became necessary to arrange for a guide to accompany visits. Advance phone notice is imperative, and access is not always permitted, unless you arrange for an archaeologist who has been approved by the military.

King City is about ten miles south of Greenfield. To visit the Monterey County Agricultural and Rural Life Museum in the southern Salinas Valley marketing hub of King City, before picking up Jolon Road take the Broadway/King City exit from Highway 101, turn right, and follow the signs to San Lorenzo Regional Park.

KING CITY. Central King City is forty-five miles south of Salinas and about one mile south of the G-14 or Jolon Road exit from Highway 101. In San Lorenzo Regional Park, several buildings at the Monterey County Agricultural and Rural Life Museum bring the old Salinas Valley to present-day visitors. A barn structure displays the parade of inhabitants in the valley from Salinan times, through the early mission settlers, the pioneer farmers, and those of recent times. Mortars and pestles, horse-drawn plows and reapers, hand-operated drills, hand-cranked household appliances, and wine-making tools are displayed against backdrops of their eras. In the main barn a tourism center provides comprehensive information about all areas of Monterey County. The latest museum under construction explores what may be the number one issue in Monterey County today, water supply and irrigation. Through past overuse, water tables have dropped, allowing saltwater intrusion into the most northern Salinas Valley. This intrusion has resulted in strict water monitoring of farmers and strong disagreements at county supervisors' meetings.

The museum barn is open year-round seven days a week, from 10 a.m. to 5 p.m. The other buildings are open from April to November, Saturdays and Sundays, 1 p.m. to 4 p.m. As they are staffed by volunteers not all buildings are open every weekend; call for museum information (831/385-1484). RV and tent camping is available through the Monterey County Parks (831/755-4899).

WEST TO JOLON FOR SOUTHBOUND 101 TRAVELERS. To proceed with the southern extension tour, once you have exited Highway 101 at Jolon Road (G-14), follow it to the intersection of Mission Road. Here you have three choices: (1.) Continue via Mission Road, which leads north to the Fort Hunter Liggett entrance gate, Mission San Antonio, Fort Hunter Liggett's Hacienda Restaurant and Lounge, the Salinan Cave, Santa Lucia Memorial Park, and the Nacimiento-Fergusson Road cut-over to Big Sur. (2.) Continue on Jolon Road, south, which leads to Lockwood, and the North Shore of Lake San Antonio. (3.) Continue on Interlake Road, which leads to the resort side of south shore Lake San Antonio and proceeds farther south to Lake Nacimiento.

NORTHWEST TO LAKES AND MISSION ROAD FOR NORTHBOUND 101 TRAVELERS. Exit on Jolon Road, 1.3 miles north of Bradley on Highway 101. Either turn left on Lake Drive for Lake Nacimiento and the southern route to the south shore of Lake San Antonio or drive north eight miles to the New Peyto Road entrance to north shore Lake San Antonio; seven miles farther will bring you to Lockwood and the intersection of Interlake Road and Mission Road. Turn left on Interlake Road for an alternate route to the south shore of Lake San Antonio or continue via Mission Road which leads north to the Fort Hunter Liggett entrance gate, Mission San Antonio, Fort Hunter Ligget's Hacienda Restaurant and Lounge, the Salinan Cave, Memorial Park, and the Nacimiento-Fergusson Road cut-over to Big Sur.

On the beginning of Jolon Road as it eases west from King City, you will see acres of flat farmland that extend to gentle hills covered with rows of grapes, isolated collections of farm buildings, and old corrals. Oil wells and modern metallic windmills dot the midsection before it winds along rugged slopes of oak forests interspersed with chaparral. Then the road heads straight through a thick forest of ancient California oaks. Majestic valley oaks and blue oaks, many more than two hundred years old, tower and weep. The blue oak is the most familiar variety in this area. Viewed from a distance it has a bluish cast, thus the name.

At close range the acorns of the blue oak can be recognized as shorter and fatter than those of the valley oak. Of all the deciduous oaks, the tribal inhabitants of California picked the valley oak as their first choice for acorns, the one main food source that the Salinans, Yokuts, Esselen, and other tribes could depend upon. Acorns were also a highly traded item among tribes, as different acorns were utilized for their different tastes. A single family might gather as many as five hundred pounds for a year's supply. The acorns needed to be dried, then peeled and pounded. Since they contain bitter tannic acid they were also leached until the brown juice from them ran clear. Bedrock mortars in the Lake San Antonio area and around the Salinan Cave remain as the remnants of this laborious process.

The miles of oaks resemble panoramas of oaks in the American South that are covered with Spanish moss. The long grayish green tassels hanging from the trees are actually lichens called granny's nets. Salinan mothers used lichens for a type of baby diaper, as they are soft and absorbent.

About seventeen miles inland from Highway 101 three old structures form the map destination of Jolon. Bare cement slabs are all that remain of the bulldozed Jolon General Store, restaurant, and trailer park. Originally called Holamma or "Valley of the Dead Oaks" by Salinans who settled the area, Jolon was first visited by the Spanish when Gaspar de Portola trudged through the area in 1769 on an expedition to find Monterey Bay.

Prospectors traveling the Santa Fe Trail in search of gold following its 1848 discovery in California passed through the present town of Jolon on their way to Pacheco Pass. To provide a place for them to eat and rest Antonio Ramirez built a small adobe inn, the ruins of which are located on the right side of Jolon Road just before you enter the town. Later the inn became an important stage stop on the Camino Real, the main route between San Francisco and Los Angeles.

In 1871 the inn property was purchased by Lieutenant George Dutton and Captain Thomas Tidball of the U.S. Cavalry. They ran the inn as a post office, saloon, and stage stop. Tidball later moved down the road to establish his own hotel and store. Placer mining brought settlers to the area in the 1870s. The ranch lands around the town were eventually acquired by William Randolph Hearst. Today ruins of the hotel are sheltered from devastation by a wooden roof, and the Hearst property is part of Hunter Liggett Fort.

A little farther up the road the quaint 1884 Saint Luke's Episcopal Church, built in Prairie Gothic style, holds regular services. Early Jolon settlers are buried in the old cemetery behind the church. Across the road the Tidball store remains in well-preserved condition.

Jolon Road turns south to Lockwood and other destinations. Travelers who exit Highway 101 by Bradley and drive north to this stretch of Jolon

Road are first greeted by miles of vineyards. In autumn, acres of gold-leafed vines give new meaning to the "golden hills" of California. Jolon Road climbs through vineyards to chaparral to pine forests. Just around the bend from a nopales cactus farm, Jolon Road dips to traverse a level valley known by locals for years as "Hungry Man's Flats." Lockwood Post Office and General Store share a spot on the road in an area now sustained by dry farming of wheat and barley. Judy Grindstaff, postmistress of the Lockwood Post Office, explains that the area was named in 1888 for Belva Ann Lockwood, the first woman nominated for president of the United States.

To continue to the San Antonio Mission, Salinan Painted Cave, and Nacimiento-Fergusson Road, turn right on Mission Road. Shortly after, stop at the access gate staffed by the Fort Hunter Liggett military police. Mission San Antonio de Padua is 4.5 miles farther on Mission Road. The officers at the gate will give you directions to the Salinan Painted Cave only if you have made prior reservations for an escort.

THE SALINAN PAINTED CAVE AND MEMORIAL PARK. The cave is located at the top of the eastern foothills of the San Antonio River Valley. The painted cave is about twenty feet long and thirty feet wide. Some of the pictographs on the walls resemble humans and others are geometric: circles, lines, and crosses. The crosses are a focal point, as they are arranged at angles and have circles at different points. It is not known whether the inhabitants of various Salinan villages in the area used the caves for hunting maneuvers, for shelter, or for religious or spiritual ceremonies. The pictographs may also have been recreated by the Salinan people from drawings left by a more prehistoric people. The red in the pictographs is from the iron oxide rock hematite. The white could be from limonite or gypsum. The black is from charcoal or manganese ore. The roofs of the caves are blackened with the soot of many fires.

Although descendants of the tribe remain, the tribe itself is considered ethnologically extinct. The Spanish explorers and missionaries noted this to be a peaceful tribe that had no history of war but would partake in long discussions to end differences. The simplicity of their lifestyle served the tribespeople for more than a hundred generations, but it could not compete with the strange diseases and the treatment they received from Spanish, Mexican, and American settlers on the land.

Santa Lucia Memorial Park is about twelve miles north of Mission San Antonio. This area is known as the Indians Ranch and was settled by the Salinan Encinales family, postmistress Judy Grindstaff's maternal ancestors. At the park you can find the adobe home of Perfecta Encinales, now in the restoration process, and acres of eighty varieties of mission grapes.

MISSION SAN ANTONIO DE PADUA. Local tradition has it that the original site of the 1771 San Antonio Mission, the third in the string of missions founded by Father Serra, is at or near the old military cemetery by the Nacimiento-Fergusson Road and Jolon Road intersection. By 1773 the mission complex had been moved to the confluence of the San Miguel and San Antonio rivers. The mission was named for the Franciscan Saint Anthony. After the secularization period the mission deteriorated; it was near ruins by 1949, when the Hearst Foundation funded a restoration directed by Harry Downie, who had restored the Carmel Mission. The inside walls and the front facade of the church are part of the original building. The museum is the old *convento* with many artifacts of mission life. The mission's original eighteenth-century wine press sits under walls decorated with Spanish paintings from the eighteenth and nineteenth centuries. A painted guidonian hand, a mnemonic device for the musical instruction of the Salinan choirs, covers one wall. Artifacts of the Chumas nation, those of the first inhabitants of areas to the south, and of the Salinan are displayed in an entrance room, as is an extensive collection and description of native plants and their uses. Frescos of the old mission and ecclesiastical items decorate the inside of the church, where a statue of Saint Anthony that dates back to the mission's beginning stands behind the altar. A mural on one of the outside walls honors the site of the first marriage in California.

Mission San Antonio is isolated from population centers and is off the usual tourist routes. The walk to the old grist mill is so quiet grasshoppers can be heard flittering in the wild oats along the dirt path. The Franciscan friars who live at the mission are friendly. The grounds, church, and museum (831/385-4478) are open daily from 9 a.m. to 4:30 p.m.

The buildings of the U.S. military across the road are located between the mission, quiet isolated grasslands, and the grand Spanish colonial revival–style Milpitas Ranch House. Designed by Julia Morgan, the architect of the Hearst Castle at San Simeon, this hacienda is now open to the public for strolling, dining, or guest lodging. Here, William Randolph Hearst entertained Clark Gable, Spencer Tracy, Herbert Hoover, and other notable guests in the 1930s.

Retrace your way back three-quarters of a mile from the mission to the intersection of Mission Road and the Nacimiento-Fergusson Road. Along the way you'll pass the the road to Santa Lucia Memorial Park.

Nacimiento-Fergusson Road is an extremely curvy road that connects the Salinas Valley with Big Sur. Los Padres National Forest Campgrounds at Ponderosa and Nacimiento Creekside, situated next to a pleasant creek on the inland lower elevations of the road, are worth a side trip, but I do not recommend the entire trip along the narrow road.

If you do continue, the Los Padres National Forest ranger facility, near the summit on Nacimiento-Fergusson Road, offers information, maps, camping permits, registration for wilderness backpacking, rest rooms, and water. Just past the summit, Cone Peak Road, an ungraded mountainous road, leads north and upward from Nacimiento-Fergusson Road seven miles to the Cone Peak Lookout, which offers a commanding view of the ocean and the Santa Lucia Mountains. Cone Peak Road is often closed to vehicular traffic due to fire danger. Nacimiento-Fergusson Road intersects Highway 1 at Kirk Creek, three miles south of the Limekiln Creek Campgrounds on the Big Sur tour (page 191).

LAKE SAN ANTONIO AND LAKE NACIMIENTO. Both lakes are set back from dams and serve as reservoirs for county water. The blue waters of Lake Nacimiento contrast with its surrounding verdant pine-covered mountains. Lake San Antonio is situated in a vale of rolling hills, studded with oaks and some pine.

Back at Jolon, arriving from Highway 101 or backtracking from Mission San Antonio, turn south on Jolon Road (G-14) to continue to both lakes. First, to reach the south shore of Lake San Antonio, turn south (right) at the intersection of Jolon road with Lockwood Jolon Road. This road becomes Interlake Road (G-14). Pass the turnoff to the old Pleyto Cemetery Road and continue to the south shore for the nature center, ranger office, a self-guided nature walk, eagle tours, camping, mobile home (cabin) rentals, the Spring Wildflower Festival, and a large marina with store and playground.

The northern end of Lake San Antonio, which offers scenic camping, ranger information, and a second marina, is not always open. To reach the northern section of the lake from the intersection of Jolon Road and Lockwood Jolon Road, continue east on Jolon Road (now G-18). Turn right at New Pleyto Road.

In spring the hills are awash in delicate and vibrant wildflowers. Bountiful lupines, wild lilac, and chemise set the hills ablaze with color from March to mid-May. When the fleeting wildflowers have gone, spring has turned to summer.

A nature center at the lake offers a look at wildlife of the area and written guides and maps, local artwork, and historical displays. One display includes information about Pleyto, an abandoned homesteader's town now covered by the reservoir. By some accounts the name "Pleyto" was derived from the Spanish word for "lawsuit." The Spanish who observed the Salinans in this area engage in intensive conversations to settle disputes referred to the place as "Pleito." The Pleyto cemetery was moved to a knoll off Cemetery Road before the lake was filled.

At the lake, a marina rents motorboats and pontoon boats primarily for fishing. Groceries, sundries, and prepared food are available. A population of America's most famous symbol, the bald eagle, winters at Lake San Antonio, one of the largest eagle winter habitats in Central California. Beginning around the middle of December hundreds of eagles fly south from Alaska, Canada, and Oregon to winter at warmer inland water locations. Two types of eagles nest at San Antonio. The bald eagle, so named because from a distance its white head feathers make it look bald, constructs enormous nests, some weighing a thousand pounds, in the tall trees around the lake. The regal birds feed on carrion, waterfowl, and fish. Viewers sometimes see the large birds plunge down and grab a fish from the placid waters. Golden eagles, dark brown with a pale golden neck, also nest at the lake. The birds soar above and sweep down to catch rabbits, squirrels, and other small ground animals.

A sixty-person tour boat glides over the quiet waters of Lake San Antonio, close to the nesting sites of the eagles. Eagles often hover above the boat. Tours are held on Fridays and often tandem tours are held on weekends from the December arrival through March, when most of the eagles leave to nest in northern locations. (Some of the golden eagles stay to nest along the Big Sur coast.) On Sundays there's an added morning brunch tour. Enjoy French toast, sausages, and hot chocolate as eagles nab the catch of the day around you. Tours last about two hours and depart on time, rain or shine. A slide lecture, half an hour before the boat sails, offers an overview of the eagles, their migratory patterns, their habitat, and the causes for their threatened status on the endangered species list.

The eagle's success at Lake San Antonio is a tribute to its clean waters and safe environment. The eagle has been on the endangered species list for several decades mainly due to pesticides that enter its system when it feeds on fish in polluted waters. The toxic substances in the pesticides interfere with the bird's calcium metabolism, causing its eggs to be thin-shelled and often infertile.

Each year the number of eagles that winter at Lake San Antonio increases. At the same time more and more people are discovering the tours. Early reservations, through the Monterey County Parks Department, are advised (831/755-4899).

National and international premier biathletes swim, run, and mountain bike at the annual Wildflower Triathlons and Festival, held at the beginning of May. One of the biathlon events is designed for novice and beginner biathletes, from eleven years old to eighty-plus, who swim a quarter mile, hike ten miles, and run two miles, just for the thrill of it. Long course biathletes here are qualifiers for national collegiate championships and international events. When you're not watching the tests of the iron-muscled people, take part in

DIRECTIONS

To return to Highway 101 north, from the stop sign at the Lake Nacimiento Dam turn left, cross the dam, and stay on the highway (G-19) for fifteen miles to the 101 junction at Bradley.

To return to Highway 101 south, from the stop sign at the Lake Nacimiento Dam turn right. Stay on the highway (G-14), following signs to Paso Robles. It is approximately seventeen miles to the 101 junction.

For Cambria, San Simeon, and the southern Big Sur Coast follow the directions above to Highway 101 south, and travel south on it for two miles. Take the exit for Highway 46 west (also marked Hearst Castle) and follow the signs to the coast (and Hearst Castle), about fifty miles.

the festival; it offers music, entertainment, sports-expo exhibits, regional foods, photography competitions, and arts and crafts booths. Through it all the wildflowers reign supreme. This is often touted as the best wildflower show in the western United States (831/755-4899).

Whether you drive, bike, or run along Interlake Road, it connects you with Lake Nacimiento, 12 miles south of Lake San Antonio. After the final turn of rolling grasslands and chaparral you cross the Nacimiento Dam. Towering pine forests of the southern Santa Lucia range frame the glassy blue dragon-shaped lake-of-many-inlets below you. The verdant pine forests that surround Lake Nacimiento are a contrast to the summer-tanned rolling hills and woodland of Lake San Antonio. Nacimiento is sixteen miles long and offers 165 miles of coves and inlets to explore from rented boats. In the winter the waters near the stream inlets at the western reaches of the lake run clear. Golden eagles soar overhead, and fish fill the buckets of line casters.

Ski boats and fishing boats are rented at the marina. In the summer the main section of the lake is filled with zooming power boats. In autumn through spring, especially midweek, four hours on a pontoon boat makes for a restful afternoon and allows time to explore the lake and catch a stringful. The resort staff are very helpful to beginners and the fish are plentiful, according to the smiles of little ones and ageless kids. As at Lake San Antonio the crappie is the popular favorite among eating fish. Nacimiento is the only lake in California stocked with the line-thrilling white bass. The white bass is the center of a controversy because it creates problems for trout if stocked in the same areas—and white-bass lovers sometimes sneak live white bass out of the lake to plant at other fishing holes. Because of this practice the white-bass experiment at Lake Nacimiento is being monitored.

Lake Nacimiento's open, grassy-knoll campsites (for tents and RVs) are full California service, with a nearby country store, restaurant in the summer months, playground, picnic areas, pool, and hot tubs—now that's roughing it. Summer is very crowded at Lake Nacimiento, as it is a favorite getaway from Los Angeles. Make reservations early (805/238-3256). Winter at the lake is peaceful. The rental townhomes overlooking the lake and forest catch beautiful sunsets and little noise.

WHAT ELSE TO SEE AND DO

PARKFIELD

Miles from nowhere, discovered and studied by seismologists, this tiny settlement offers the comfort of the newly built, log-cabin style Parkfield Inn to those who seek the solitude of wide open spaces and a chance to sample the "Old West." Parkfield, "Earthquake Capital of the World," registers an earthquake measuring 6 or greater every twenty-one years. The town is also the site of the First Officially Recognized Scientific Predicted Earthquake in the United States. Since the predicted quake of 1966 lasers, creep meters, and seismographs have been set in the oak studded landscape. The Parkfield Inn offers a twenty thousand acre ranch playground. City cowboys and cowgirls bring their horses or rent local ones to ride the hills and flatlands of the Varian Ranch. Local ranchers gather at the Parkfield Cafe. We bring our telescope for incredibly clear nights.

THE PINNACLES NATIONAL MONUMENT

Take Highway 101 to Soledad, exit on Route 146, and drive eleven miles to West Pinnacles and the Chaparral Visitor's Center. Along the way you can visit the Chalone vineyard, the oldest winery in Monterey County (831/678-1717). Two different routes lead to separate sides of the Pinnacles National Monument. You can hike between the two sides but not drive. East Pinnacles is located south of Hollister via Route 25.

This craggy, rugged area is a spectacular but incomplete formation of volcanic rhyolite that thrusts through the nonvolcanic Gabilan Mountains. The peaks and underlying caves are the remnant of an ancient volcano fifteen miles long, five miles across, and eight thousand feet high that spewed lava some twenty-three million years ago. As evidence of the shifting San Andreas fault and of the shifting plates beneath the earth's surface, the rest of the original volcano is about two hundred miles to the south around Lancaster, California. Constant grinding along the North American and Pacific plates caused a break along the North American stress line. For more than twenty million years the Pinnacles have been hitching a very slow ride astride this northward rift line of the North American plate, which constitutes the San Andreas fault. Wind and water have ground the volcano down to a third of its original size and carved caves within its interior. In spring the peaks and spires of the West Pinnacles rise above fields awash in wildflowers: poppies, wild mustard, lupines, and Indian paintbrush. Every summer and autumn slow-moving tarantulas crawl along roads and open spaces searching for mates in this arid, desertlike environment. They are mostly harmless but should never be touched, for their own protection and yours.

Three walks, including a cave trek, wind through the park. A small stream crosses the West Pinnacles, and tributaries trickle through the caves. The Balconies Flat trail is a four-mile walk to the East Pinnacles. The steep Junipero Canyon walk passes ravines painted with wildflowers in spring and leads to "Top of the Pinnacles" views. Pack at least a quart of water per person and also a flashlight for the caves. The hike to the east side and back takes about five hours.

Junipero Canyon meanders easily through mountain mahogany and juniper before it seduces you to climb higher and higher, past poppies and stone ravines, finally to the breathtaking peaks and spires. Golden eagles and falcons soar above you. You swig your water as turkey vultures circle. The trail descends two miles through chaparral into the interior of the ancient volcano, the Bear Gulch Caves. You can return to the west side by retracing your steps or along the Balconies Flat trail.

Two campgrounds serve the Pinnacles, both on a first-come, first-served basis. A small campground of eighteen sites is available on the west side. Fee is $10 per night. Camping is restricted at various times during the year. Picnic tables, barbecues, and the small Chaparral Visitor's Center are available.

The larger Pinnacles Campground near the east entrance is $6 per person per night. A larger visitor's center serves the east entrance. During summer, parking close in fills up early, and a shuttle bus transports monument guests from parking farther away. No bike riding or pets are allowed in the park. For information call the East Pinnacles main station (831/389-4485).

SAN JUAN BAUTISTA

This town of Old California has as its center a mission plaza where visitors can view influences of Spanish, Mexican, and early California. Mission San Juan Bautista is the only one in California that has been in continuous use from its beginning. It centers on a twelve-block area where some three dozen historic structures can be visited. When the missions were secularized the priest here was allowed to stay. The other missions in California were built very narrow; Mission San Juan Bautista is the largest, with high arched roofs and side aisles. In summer the Cabrillo Music Festival presents concerts in the church because its acoustics are so balanced. Known as the "Mission of Music," its museum features some antique violins and cellos. A statue of the mission's patron, Saint John the Baptist, is the principal piece of a set of five statues and artwork that date to the mission's origin. Of the millions of visitors, the most memorable may be the bear and a coyote that apparently entered the empty edifice while the floor tiles were still drying and left their tracks in the main aisle.

The San Juan Bautista State Historic Park surrounds the mission. One of the focal buildings, the Castro-Breen adobe, contrasts the differing lifestyles of its two previous owners. Two rooms are furnished in the basic wood furniture of the Mexican period, when this served as Joe Castro's adobe. Castro was the military commandant serving San Juan Bautista and Monterey. The Breen family who later lived in the adobe traveled to California with the Donner party. A mural of their journey fills one wall. Their furnishings are ornate Victorian style. On the first Saturday of each month volunteers with the California State Parks Department present reenactments of various periods in the town's history.

San Juan Bautista's streets are like a walk back in time. Wooden sidewalks lead to specialty shops, antique stores, and old-time restaurants. The rarest gem in the world and the state gem of California can be found at Tops rock shop (831/623-4441). Benitoite, the only rock that occurs as a triogonal tripyramidal natural crystalline structure, has only been found at the nearby Blue Diamond Gem mine. Most of the rock was unknowingly shattered during turn-of-the century explosive work for quicksilver (mercury).

The west side of San Juan Bautista, reached by taking the Monterey Street exit from Highway 156, offers the opportunity to visit artisans and craftspeople in their studios and workshops. At San Juan Foothills Pottery (831/623-4305), the owners create functional and one-of-a kind pieces of stoneware.

The passion of San Juan Bautista flows at El Teatro Campesino, 705 Fourth Street (831/623-2444). Local Luis Valdez founded the theater more than two decades ago, and when not on movie location he still directs plays and workshops here. The highlight of the theater offerings is the Christmas pageant at the mission, which alternates each year between the *La Pastorela* and *Our Lady of Guadalupe* plays.

Mission San Juan Bautista

GILROY

Famous for its garlic, Gilroy offers a variety of reasons to visit. It is difficult to be smitten with Gilroy by the looks of its freeway entrances, but a day spent here is worth your while. Shopping, ranch tours, historical and antique tours, winery tours, hot springs, and park recreation are possibilities. Whether you are interested in eco-tourism or historical tours or just want to know more and talk to very friendly people, call the Gilroy Visitors Bureau at 408/842-6436.

Will Rogers joked that Gilroy was the only place you could marinate your steak just by hanging it on the clothesline. To celebrate the local top produce, the annual Garlic Festival in July features garlic foods, entertainment, and tours. This event is very popular, with attendance figures topping the hundred-thousand mark. Garlic, local produce, gourmet items, garlic, souvenir items, Gilroy wines, and more garlic are offered at Garlic World and Garlic Shoppe located south of Gilroy on Highway 101.

With more than 150 factory outlet stores featuring recognized names in apparel, toys, crystal, and china, and more, the Outlets at Gilroy attract bargain seekers from throughout California. The stores are in one center for an easy shopping vacation. Take Highway 101 to the Leavesley exit for easy access. Open Monday through Friday 10 a.m. to 8 p.m., Saturday 9 a.m. to 8 p.m., and Sunday 10 a.m. to 6 p.m. For more information call 408/842-3729.

Gilroy's newest tourist attraction is its oldest: downtown historical Gilroy and its antique shops. Gilroy Historical Museum (408/848-0470) is located in the Carnegie Library at the corner of Fifth and Church Streets. The museum is open between 9 a.m. and 5 p.m. weekdays. You can pick up a self guided tour map of the downtown historic district. Gilroy celebrated its 125th birthday in 1995. The downtown historic district is an unusual blend of early brick commercial buildings, twentieth-century period revivals, the art deco of the 1920s, and the modern style of the 1940s. More than fourteen antique venues, several of which are antique malls with dozens of dealers, dot the downtown. Gilroy Antiques, 7445 Monterey Street, is an elegant shop with an extensive collection of jewelry and a rare collection of antique binoculars. At Monterey Street Antiques, 7511 Monterey, a complete set of leatherbound Louis L'Amour books, cookbooks, and vintage kitchen items are just a few of the special wares.

For one popular Gilroy attraction that's not on the tourist office information list, you will need to make your own arrangements: the historic Gilroy Yamato Hot Springs are again in operation. Directional signs can be seen on Highway 101, but prior arrangements must be made with Gilroy Yamato Hot Springs Kenko Tomonokai group in San Francisco before you visit (415/434-2180).

Twelve family-owned wineries are located in Hecker Pass, Watsonville

Road off Hecker Pass, Highway 101, and farther north in Morgan Hill. Rapazzini Winery (408/842-5649), directly off Highway 101 at Monterey Street, offers wine tastings daily until 5 p.m. Special wines here include the famous Gilroy garlic wine and Aprebella, a smooth apricot and peach wine.

To visit other wineries, parks, and rural destinations: From downtown Gilroy drive Main Street to First Street. Turn right on First Street and follow it for a couple miles until you are out in the rolling hills of the surrounding countryside. While in the country you can wander through fields of gorgeous flowers at Goldsmith Seeds. March through August are the best times to visit. Guided tours are available Monday through Friday and offer a "behind the scenes" look at how a hybrid flower seed is developed. For information and tour arrangements call 408/847-7333.

CHAPTER 8

FROM MONTEREY TO THE SANTA CRUZ BEACH TOWNS

SEASIDE, SAND CITY, MARINA,
BEACHES, ELKHORN SLOUGH,
APTOS, CAPITOLA, AND
BACKROAD JOURNEYS

The forty-mile inner crescent of Monterey Bay curves from the city of Monterey through Santa Cruz, which itself is the focus of the next chapter. From the bay's southern tip to Capitola and the other resort communities just south of Santa Cruz, you can visit Northern California's highest sand dunes, artichoke and strawberry fields, the only national marine estuary in Northern California, historic towns filled with antique shops, artists' studios, newly developed high-volume discount centers, expansive beaches, redwood-forested back roads, and seaside resorts.

GETTING READY

BEST TIMES TO VISIT AND SPECIAL EVENTS

In summer the morning and evening fog can be quite thick from Monterey to Aptos, making visibility a concern for travel at either end of the day. Highway 1 traffic can be extremely heavy especially heading north at the close of three-day weekends. Special-event weekends on the Monterey Peninsula cause heavy traffic from Castroville to near the Route 152 exit north of Moss Landing, where the road widens. Accident-prone sections of the road are designated Highway 1 Safety Corridor Daily Headlight Sections.

From May through November, sun-loving locals and tourists flock to the sunny beaches around Capitola. Local produce ripens from May through November for productive farm-road excursions. Special events north of Monterey include the Castroville Artichoke Festival in September. The Elkhorn Slough populace celebrates National Estuaries Day in September. Moss Landing hosts a popular antique fair in July. The Antique Fly-In soars into the Watsonville Airport in May. Also in May, the Strawberry Dessert Festival sweetens the main street of Watsonville (831/724-3954); at one

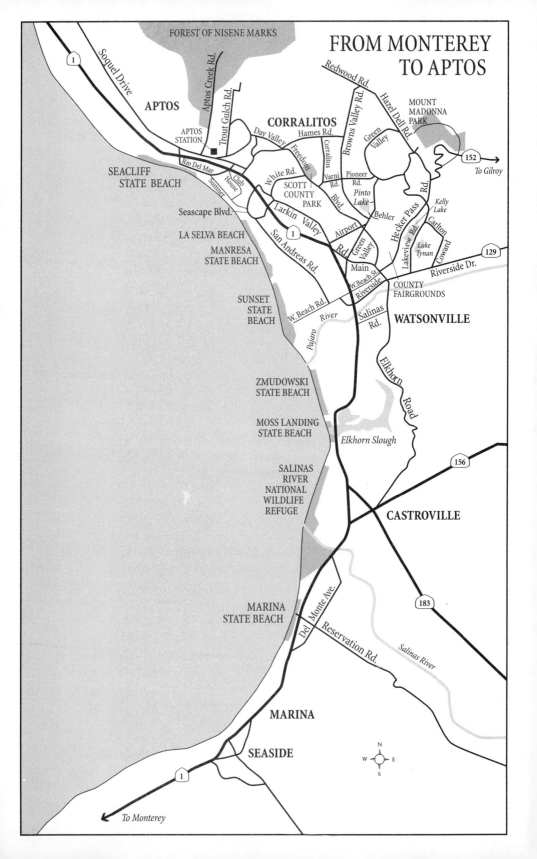

previous festival, participants made the largest strawberry shortcake ever recorded by the *Guinness Book of World Records*. The "World's Shortest" parade—the area's most popular—marches through Aptos on the Fourth of July. Musicians for Music turn Soquel's Main Street into an all-day Music Fest in late spring while raising funds for the town's music programs. In September, during the popular Capitola Begonia Festival, floats decorated with begonias sail down Soquel Creek. As part of a fundraiser to promote education, fireworks brighten the skies above Aptos in October.

CLIMATE AND CLOTHING

Both ends of the bay—the south bend that includes Seaside, Sand City, Marina, and the Capitola-Seacliff areas farther north—are often gloriously sunny while the rest of the bay is cloaked in gray. Elkhorn Slough can be sunny when Moss Landing is covered as if with a dense blanket. Winters are mild but unpredictable. On any day in winter you might witness a raging storm that tosses foamy breakers onto rain pelted beaches. A couple of days later sunbathers might relax among the driftwood on the shore. Winter storms often close the northern Elkhorn Slough Road and the entrance to Salinas River Beach.

Winds can be quite strong along the stretch of beaches between Seaside and Seacliff. Swimming is not advisable at any of the beaches along this route with the exception of Capitola Beach. The water temperature is cold year-round and except for those with the thickest of skins, wet suits are needed for swimming. Rip currents are common at most of the beaches. The Capitola and Seacliff beaches offer the best wading possibilities.

Hills block cooling ocean breezes and trap fog pockets on Fort Ord Public Lands. No water is available on the trails. The layered approach is your best bet. On some days in summer and autumn, just ten miles from the ocean, daily temperatures reach one hundred degrees.

Clothing along this entire route is casual. Capitola is a sunny family resort town as well as a vibrant fun-seekers' mecca of bare chests and bikini tops. Go for comfort but dress for variable temperatures. Pack a sweater and a jacket along with shorts and swimsuit. Bring binoculars and also a camera, for fun-in-the-sun shots, panoramic vistas, surfers' moves, and those shark fins under the oaks at Elkhorn Slough.

TOUR LENGTHS

The drive from Seaside to Capitola takes forty-five minutes nonstop in light traffic. Get an early start for lighter traffic and to enjoy the many places along the way. If the traffic is heavy it is best to visit the ocean side of Moss Landing during a southbound trip, as the absence of overpasses makes crossing the highway difficult. Exploring or sunbathing at beaches can fill many days. Allow at least three to four hours for hiking or kayaking Elkhorn Slough. Antiquing at Moss Landing, Aptos, or Soquel can take a full day. Exploring Fort Ord Public Lands can take weeks or can reward you with beauty and serenity in just fifteen minutes. A county crossroads tour of the strawberry farms, apple orchards, public gardens, and ranches in the area with relaxing drives through bucolic backcountry and redwood groves fills a day and an ice chest. At Nisene Marks State Park a hike or bike ride can span two hours or extend to an overnight backpack camp-in. If you like jazz plan to be at the Whole Enchilada in Moss Landing by 4 p.m. on Sunday or the Capitola Wharf restaurant on weekend afternoons. Capitola, with the beach, river, shops, restaurants, and historic Victorians, is fun for an afternoon, full day, or weekend. To really relax, take advantage of weekly rentals in the northern beach towns of Capitola, Seacliff, and Rio Del Mar.

HIGHLIGHTS FOR KIDS

"Come join the fun! Get your hands dirty!" Throughout the year, a consortium of community groups and organizations coordinate planting days at Fort Ord to reintroduce native plant species and control erosion (831/394-8314).

Kids of all ages get vertical at Sanctuary Rock Gym, 1855 East Avenue, Sand City (831/899-2595). Climb 5,600 square feet of climbing wall and enjoy the large boulder area. Climbing equipment is available and a pro shop answers questions. Special weekend hours are set aside for beginners. Next door, kids enjoy Skate Station (831/899-3291 www.teamadventures.com).

The visitors centers at Elkhorn Slough and Sea Cliff State Beach are interactive and friendly. The hiking isn't too difficult for short strides.

Kids can pick strawberries, climbing berries, and apples. Gizdich Ranch is the largest of the pick-your-own farms. See page 289.

The Chocolate Factory, 1291 Fremont Boulevard, Seaside (831/899-7963) offers weekday tours when the factory is in operation and sells delicious candies daily.

WILDLIFE WISDOM

Oak woodlands, vernal ponds, small lakes, and an incredible range of habitats highlight the 7,211 acres given to the Bureau of Land Management as the Fort Ord Public Lands, an area bounded by the land limits of Monterey, Seaside, Del Rey Oaks, and Marina.

Fort Ord Public Lands are managed by the Bureau of Land Management to protect thirty-five species of rare plants and animals and their native coastal habitats. Wildlife is abundant. Songbirds, vultures, birds of prey, deer, bobcats, rabbits, and silver foxes can be seen year-round. If the animals sense your presence first, their tracks and scat remain as evidence of their habitation. Mountain lions are the top predator here. Rarely seen, they do claim this country. Keep children and dogs in sight while hiking. It's a good idea for a member of your group to carry a big stick. If you have an extremely rare encounter with a mountain lion, pick up small children and don't run. Act big, be noisy, and fight back.

Elkhorn Slough is a bird-watcher's heaven. More than two-hundred fifty species of birds have been observed here, including the endangered brown pelican, golden eagle, and cormorant. You have a great chance of seeing waterfowl, wading birds, and shorebirds from December through March and pelicans from spring through autumn. Egrets roost at Elkhorn Slough in April. Wednesday though Sunday the visitors station at Elkhorn loans out binoculars and bird books to visitors. If you see a fenced-off or meshed area it could well be a protected endangered snowy plover's nest. Look for the tracks of deer, bobcat, fox, and muskrat around the slough. The estuary boasts more than fifty varieties of fish, including several types of sharks, which can be seen feeding in spring and summer. Throughout the slough and Moss Landing area thirty varieties of crabs and shrimp add to thirty-eight species of oysters, clams, and mussels—part of more than four hundred species of invertebrates. No wonder all those seals, otters and sea lions swim through here.

Salinas River National Wildlife Refuge is a favorite of great blue herons, western sandpipers, and waterfowl. Allow yourself time on this trip to get absorbed in the habits or antics of some of the animals you meet along the way.

VISITOR INFORMATION

For information about the communities along this route, refer to the Chamber of Commerce listings in the Resource Guide (pages 343–344). Newspapers that cover Seaside to Moss Landing include the *Monterey County Herald,* the *Californian,* and the free *Coast Weekly.* From Moss Landing to Capitola check for information in the *Santa Cruz Sentinel* and in *Good Times,* free at newsracks.

Here is a list of information sources for some of the officially designated destinations along the bay.

ELKHORN SLOUGH NATIONAL ESTUARINE RESEARCH RESERVE, 1700 Elkhorn Road, Watsonville, CA 95076. 831/728-2822. Open Wednesday to Sunday 9 a.m. to 5 p.m.

THE NORTHERN REGION OF THE ELKHORN SLOUGH PRESERVE: contact the Nature Conservancy Preserve, the Nature Conservancy, P.O. Box 267,

Moss Landing, CA 95039, 831/728-5939. This region is open only by appointment.

CALIFORNIA STATE DEPARTMENT OF FISH AND GAME AND MOSS LANDING WILDLIFE AREA: 831/649-2870.

FORT ORD PUBLIC LANDS: 831/394-8314

MOSS LANDING HARBOR DISTRICT: 831/633-2461.

SALINAS RIVER NATIONAL WILDLIFE REFUGE: U.S. FISH & WILDLIFE SERVICE, 510/792-0222.

SALINAS RIVER STATE BEACH: 831/649-2836.

MOSS LANDING STATE BEACH AND ZMUDOWSKI STATE BEACH: 831/649-2836.

PALM BEACH STATE PARK AND SUNSET STATE BEACH: 831/763-7063.

FOREST OF NISENE MARKS STATE PARK: 831/763-7063.

NEW BRIGHTON STATE PARK: 831/464-6330.

ALTERNATE TRANSPORTATION

A pedestrian and biking trail links Pacific Grove to Seaside and Seaside to Marina, in two separate segments. There are plans for a continuing eighteen mile span to Castroville. You can pick up the trail from Pacific Grove at Lovers Point, Fisherman's Wharf, or any spot along the way. The trail continues to Roberts Lake in Seaside. You can pick up the second segment beginning in Seaside at the end of Del Monte Boulevard; it parallels portions of the freeway and continues to Marina.

PARKING

Where to park is not an issue except at the beach towns neighboring Santa Cruz. On sunny weekends and during summer, get to Rio Del Mar Beach early or don't expect to park. The largest parking lot in Capitola is located on Monterey Avenue near its intersection with Park Avenue.

PLACES TO STAY

SEASIDE AND MARINA

EMBASSY SUITES, 1441 Canyon Del Rey, Seaside. Waterfalls and gardens welcome you in the beautiful lobby. The 225 two-room suites here are categorized according to ocean view, partial ocean view, and non–ocean view. Rooms feature subdued earth tones and the motel's plant-and-seashell motif. The ocean-view balcony rooms above the third floor offer spectacular views. Separate living rooms, microwaves, and coffeemakers. Indoor swimming pool, fitness center, sauna, and whirlpool. AX, MC, V. 831/393-1115. For two—includes complimentary cocktails from 5:30 p.m. to 7:30 p.m. and complimentary full buffet breakfast cooked to order—$146 to $206.

SUPER 8 MOTEL (Reservation Road exit to Dunes Road, Marina). Set back on a highway frontage road, adjacent to Marina State Beach, 141 standard motel units are surrounded by dunes. The more expensive king-bed rooms have ocean views. Some rooms have highway views. This could be the least expensive beachfront motel room in the National Marine Sanctuary area. Heated spa. AX, MC, V; others also accepted. 831/384-1800. For two from $59 to $79.

APTOS, CAPITOLA, SEACLIFF, SEASCAPE, WATSONVILLE BEACH

APPLE LANE INN Bed and Breakfast Inn, 6265 Soquel Drive, Aptos. Flower gardens, still-warm-in-the-shell eggs for breakfast souffles, and a vegetable garden where guests "feel free to fill up a bag to take home" are among the special pleasures found at this old farmhouse. Owners Douglas and Diana Groom were married here and shower this inn with love and attention. The Blossom Room features a Battenburg lace-covered eighteenth-century French canopy bed and skylight. After a hard day of picking that bag of vegetables, relax in the room's clawfoot tub. Each of the five guest rooms is decorated with farmhouse touches from hand-painted stencils to handmade quilts. Three rooms have private in-room baths. 831/475-6868. MC, V, D. For two, includes breakfast, from $85 to $185.

BAYVIEW HOTEL Bed and Breakfast Inn, 8041 Soquel Drive, Aptos (at the entrance to Nisene Marks Park). This three-story landmark Victorian is "the heart of Aptos village." Rooms are beautifully renovated with antiques and

Victorian decor, all with private baths, a few with fireplaces. The casual White Magnolia restaurant offers relaxing dining inside or on the wrap-around porch. 831/688-8654. AX, MC, V. For two, includes breakfast, from $90 to $150.

BEST WESTERN SEACLIFF INN (north of Highway 1, at the Seacliff exit). One-hundred forty comfortable rooms are garden landscaped. Suites with whirlpool available. Pool, whirlpool, putting green, restaurant. Full-bar lounge area featuring local musicians. Close drive or walk to beach and shops. 831/688-7300 or 800/367-2003. MC, V; others also accepted. For two from $79 to $169.

THE INN AT DEPOT HILL, 250 Monterey Avenue, Capitola. An elegant inn, with the highest Mobil-guide rating for a bed and breakfast; each distinctive suite is decorated in exacting detail to present a different place and time. The Delft Room features Dutch indulgence in blue with a huge featherbed draped in linen and lace, a private sitting room, a marble shower, and a private tulip garden with outdoor jacuzzi. The Railroad Baron Suite features a domed ceiling, red and gold fabrics, rich woods, and a large indoor soaking pool under a skylight. Full breakfast, afternoon tea or wine, hors d'oeuvres, and dessert included. VCRs, stereo systems, and fax/modem connections in all rooms. 831/462-DEPO (3376). AX, MC, V. For two, rooms under $200, suites under $275.

K.O.A. CABINS, 1186 San Andreas Road, Watsonville. Newer-construction one- and two-bedroom log cabins, with barbecues, porch swings, and a pastoral setting. They share the full-bath-and-shower facilities of the adjacent two-hundred-plus space K.O.A. campground. One mile to Manresa State Beach. Heated pool, spas, miniature golf, and children's play areas. 831/722-0551. For two $49. Children stay free.

MANGELS HOUSE Bed and Breakfast Inn, 570 Aptos Creek Road, Aptos. Redwoods line the road leading to this classic one-hundred-year-old Italianate Victorian estate. The grand two-story mansion sits in a clearing surrounded by four acres of neatly clipped lawns and gardens. Each room has a unique style ranging from the South African artifacts displayed in Nicolaus's Room to the wicker furniture and English garden setting in the Guest Room. Mangels House borders Nisene Marks State Park, where guests can hike and bike for miles or enjoy picnics under the redwoods. Six rooms, all with private bath—two of which are detached. 831/688-7982, www.innaccess.com/mangles. AX, MC, V. For two from $115 to $150. According to the owner, "Children over twelve will be happy here."

SEASCAPE RESORT AND CONFERENCE CENTER (Seascape Boulevard and Sumner Avenue, Aptos-Seascape). The newest complex in the area has three hundred guest units, studios, and one-bedrooms within a three-phase condominium development. Private balconies, ocean views, beach access by foot or golf carts, a swim and racquet club, golf privileges, childcare, beach bonfires. Summer and special event jazz concerts on the bluffs. Spa, pool, and full-service restaurant. 800/929-7727. AX, MC, V. For two from $165 to $250.

Weekly rentals of private homes and timeshares are commonly arranged for visitors and residents by real estate firms in the area. Three offices that cater to vacation renters are Bob Bailey Real Estate, 831/688-7009, Cheshire Realty, 831/479-1110, and Kendall and Potter, 831/688-3511. Capitola home, cottage, and beach-front motel room rentals are available through Vacations by the Sea, 831/479-9360.

RESTAURANTS

CASTROVILLE, MOSS LANDING, SEASIDE

BING'S DINER, 10961 Merritt Street, Castroville. Stroll up to the counter, choose a cushioned stool, and feel the presence of John Steinbeck in this rescued #960 Oakland streetcar. Dave Bonderenko saved this diner, claimed by researchers to be one of Steinbeck's favorite imbibing spots near the bay, from walls of mud after the flood of 1995. Friendly Crystal Statzer serves popular breakfasts in large portions and shares local stories. The dining room is bright and inviting. On Friday and Saturday evenings, Dave barbecues ribs on his custom-made hand-cranked grill. Deep-fried Castroville artichokes and artichoke chicken breasts are possibilities on the varied menu. Breakfast, lunch. Dinner served Friday and Saturday. 831/633-0400. MC, V; others accepted. Entrees mostly under $12.

CENTRAL TEXAN BARBECUE, 10500 Merritt Street, Castroville. With the three flags of Texas, California, and the United States flying overhead, this barbecue giant of the Central Coast will probably catch your eye before you look for it. Swagger in with your family and enjoy such favorites as smoked ribs, beef brisket, and homemade Chisholm Trail sausage. "The fire never comes close to the meat. The secret is the smoke," twangs proprietor and usual server Don Elkins, who looks and sounds like Willie Nelson. Western regalia ranging from flintlocks to Harley Davidson emblems surrounds diners. Sawdust on the floors, very casual. Lunch, dinner. 831/633-2285. No credit cards. Entrees mostly under $10.

FERDI'S, 740 Broadway, Seaside. Giant portions and the best cajun-style food I've found on the Central Coast. Choose from a small knotty-pine dining room or the popular know-what-you-want takeout counter. The three-sausage poor boy sandwich and the jambalaya are spicy. The Manale, a dozen peppered shrimp cooked in their shells, needs a warning "whoeee spicy hot" label. Lunch only. No credit cards. 831/394-2244. Sandwiches by length, $4 for four inches to $9 for twelve inches. Entrees mostly under $9.

FISHWIFE SEAFOOD DELI & CAFE, 789 Trinity at Fremont, Seaside. Enjoy excellent seafood at either the selfserve area with takeout counter or relax in the cream-and-blue-hued dining room. Lunch, dinner. Closed Sunday. AX, MC, V. 831/394-2027. Entrees mostly under $8.

LA SCUOLA, 10700 Merritt Street, Castroville. An 1860 schoolhouse now serves fine Tuscany cuisine. Specializing in pasta, veal, seafood, homemade gnocchi, and tiramisu. Dinner only. 831/633-3200. MC, V. Entrees mostly under $20.

OYSTER BAY, 413 Moss Landing Road, Moss Landing. In a friendly atmosphere, fresh fish when available, from the Moss Landing harbor vessels. Seafood pastas. Dark, rustic wood with a touch of the nautical. Lunch, dinner. 831/632-0119. AX, MC, V. Entrees mostly under $20.

PHIL'S (at the Island), Moss Landing. Casual indoor or outdoor harbor dining features open-hearth cooking of radio-transmitter-selected fresh-catch fish carried in from the fishing boats that are anchored across the street. Choose your fish or seafood from a large ice table; Phil or friends will prepare it. Specialties include cracked crab, stuffed prawns, creamy chowder, and cioppino in French bread rounds, to eat in or to go. Lunch, dinner. 831/633-2152. No credit cards. Entrees mostly under $10.

THE WHOLE ENCHILADA, Highway 1 and Moss Landing Road, Moss Landing. Authentic Mexican furnishings and art add to a colorful and upbeat atmosphere. Garlic prawns and the "Whole Enchilada," a fresh filet of red snapper wrapped in a corn tortilla with spicy sauce and melted cheese, crown an extensive menu. Beginning in the late afternoon on Sundays, after lunch or before dinner, jazz at the adjoining lounge annex, Moss Landing Inn, packs in listeners. Lunch, dinner. 831/633-3038. AX, MC, V; others also accepted. Entrees from $6 to $16.

RIO DEL MAR, SOQUEL

BITTERSWEET BISTRO, 787 Rio Del Mar Boulevard (at Deer Park Shopping Center), Rio Del Mar. Marge Vinolus greeted me at the entrance to this family-owned restaurant. There is a warm glow of firelight in the larger rooms. In the Angel Room, a multilayered faux finish interpretation of a wall in Pompeii with angel frescos now surrounds diners. Entrees are culinary and artistic delights. A sampling includes Mediterranean Pasta, Herbed Salmon, and pizzettas from the wood-fired oven. Vegetables are fresh, locally grown, and organic when possible. Extensive wine list. Winner of Santa Cruz Mountain Winegrowers Association Award for best selection of wines. Bistro hours 3 to 6 p.m., dinner 5:30 to 10 p.m. 831/662-9799, www. bittersweetbistro.com. AX, MC, V. Entrees from $12 to $20.

CAFE RIO, 131 Esplanade, Rio Del Mar. Across the parking lot from the beach there is fine dining with tropical ambiance. Specializing in fresh seafood, with an oyster bar. Outdoor appetizers and drinks beginning at 3 p.m.; dinner begins at 5 p.m. 831/688-8917. AX, MC, V. Entrees, from $11 to $30.

CARPO'S, 2400 Porter Street, Soquel. Eat inside or outside on the patio, in a lively, family atmosphere. Burgers, pastas, fresh seafood, salad bar. Lunch, dinner. 831/476-6260. No credit cards. Entrees mostly under $10.

DHARMA NATURAL FOODS RESTAURANT, 4250 Capitola Road, Capitola. A casual, vegetarian restaurant, Dharma has a wonderful selection of baked goods, sandwiches, and pastas. Breakfast, lunch, dinner. 831/462-1717. No credit cards. Entrees from $4 to $8.

GAYLE'S BAKERY AND ROSTICCERIA, 504 Bay Avenue, Capitola. The aromas of fresh-baked breads and herbed chickens fill this take-out European style bakery/deli. Outdoor patio dining. Lunch, dinner. 831/462-4747. Delicatessen items mostly under $10.

RED APPLE CAFE (on the upper level at Deer Park Center), Rio Del Mar Boulevard, Rio Del Mar. A cozy breakfast and lunch spot, the Red Apple overlooks a green belt of grass and trees. Homemade scones and omelettes are among breakfast selections. Lunches include pasta, fresh seafood specials, and sandwiches. 831/685-1224. AX, MC, V. Selections from $4 to $9.

SHADOWBROOK RESTAURANT, 1750 Wharf Road, Capitola. Lush gardens cover the hillside above this wood-and-glass romantic hideaway along Soquel Creek. A free funicular railway carries six passengers at a time down the verdant hillside to the restaurant door. Having cocktails on the deck that meets the creek is fun by itself or as a beginning. Pasta, seafood. Reservations suggested. Dinner, Sunday brunch. 831/475-1511. AX, MC, V; others also accepted. Entrees from $14 to $25.

THEO'S, 3101 North Main Street, Soquel. This intimate and romantic restaurant has fourteen tables and "three-hour" comfortable chairs. Impeccable service. Classic French with an eclectic touch. Fresh salmon, house-smoked trout. Surrounding restaurant garden provides the freshest greens and vegetables possible. Lunch, dinner. 831/462-3657. AX, MC, V; others also accepted. Entrees from $12 to $18.

WATSONVILLE AREA

CILANTROS, 1934 Main Street, Watsonville. Serving Michoacan-style Mexican dishes, with a variety of sauces, Cilantros has a bright and lively tropical look. Guajillos Camarones with lingonberries is a tasty favorite. The heaping Cilantro Platter offers a selection of items with a tangy ceviche center. Lunch, dinner, Sunday brunch. 831/761-2161. AX, MC, V. Entrees from $8 to $15.

GREEN VALLEY GRILL, 40 Penny Lane, Watsonville. An indoor cactus garden brings the Southwest to this popular grill located in a small shopping center off Green Valley Road. Pastas complement the grill menu, which includes baby back ribs and grilled shrimp. Lunch and dinner. 831/728-0644. AX, MC, V. Entrees from $5 to $20.

ZUNIGA'S, (at the Watsonville Airport) on Aviation Way, Watsonville. This local favorite moved from the downtown after the earthquake. Lunch, dinner. 831/724-5788. AX, MC, V. Entrees from $5 to $13.

INTRODUCTION WITH HISTORICAL HIGHLIGHTS

Change is the constant for the stretch of coast that follows the crescent-shaped curve of the Monterey Bay from Monterey to Santa Cruz. Buildings, mountains, and trees disappear in front of your eyes in seasonal coastal fog. If you blink long enough or drive three hundred feet farther, bright sunlit sands may make you reach for sunglasses. Green-shrouded coastal dunes burst into color in spring, just before the last notes of migrating songbirds welcome the formations of pelicans that glide in for the summer. The pickle-weed of inner estuarine waters turns bright green in summer and autumn when golden grasses cover surrounding hills. As the pelicans fly south in winter, songbirds and shorebirds return to this section of coast seeking temperate winter homes.

Changes brought by people mirror those that occur in nature. Closest to Monterey cluster the communities of Seaside, Del Rey Oaks, Sand City, and Marina. The closure of the major military facilities at Fort Ord has changed the economic, cultural, and recreation identities of these and surrounding communities. The evolving "old" Fort Ord Lands hold thousands of acres of preserved parkland and wildlife areas, as well as potential for expansion of local university options, of housing, and of the economy.

The very course of the Salinas River that touches the northern border of Fort Ord was altered in 1908 by farmers, who diverted the river from its mouth at Moss Landing to its present outlet, some three miles south at what is now the the Salinas River Wildlife Area. The 170-mile-long Salinas River flows as Demeter's shadow—often submerged in summer and autumn to emerge anew with winter and spring rains. The two- and three-foot depths of water visible at the surface cover a deeper underground stream.

Years before the flow of fresh water from the Salinas River was diverted, the waterways around Moss Landing served as a major Central Coast port. From fishing village to grain harbor, from whaling station to sardine processor, from fishing-fleet harbor to marine research site, the economic focus in Moss Landing changes with the tides of time. A section of the old port town's main-street Victorians now house "antique row."

About ten miles inland the abandoned piers of shipping ports lie silhouetted against the sky in the mudflats of the Elkhorn Slough National Estuarine Reserve. The thousands of acres of slough marshes, creeks, and wetlands keep evolving to adapt to the human imprint. In spring through summer many varieties of coastal fish, including anchovies, herring, and sharks, lay eggs or give birth in the slough and tidal creeks. As salt water levels rise the lower banks of this cradle of marine life are crumbling, causing some to wonder how the

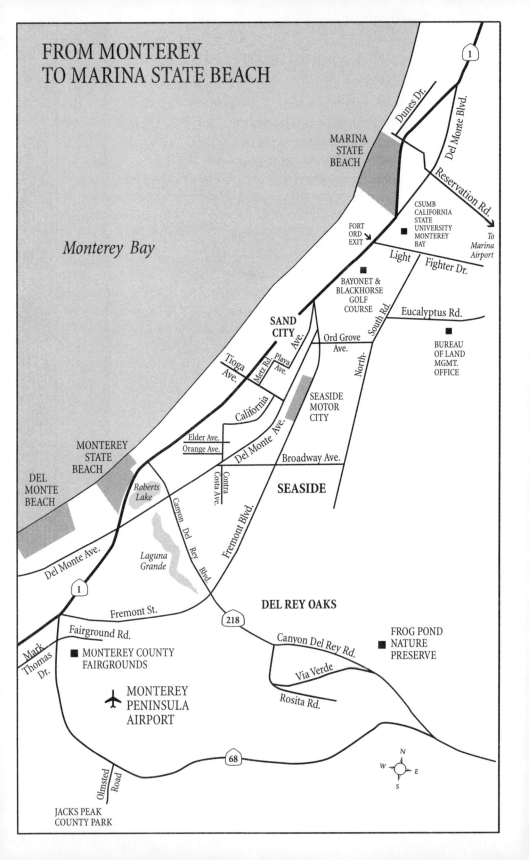

complex ecosystem of Elkhorn Slough will survive until the twenty-first century. The major research facilities at Moss Landing, which include the Moss Landing Marine Laboratory and MBARI, David Packard's nonprofit oceanic research institute, grow in importance.

Beyond Moss Landing, miles of strawberry fields cover hills where thick riparian oak forests and redwood groves grew to the water's edge less than a century ago. In the mid 1800s the lumbering of the redwood forests, which extended miles back to the areas above Santa Cruz, was instrumental in the beginnings of the Santa Cruz County "mill towns" of Aptos and Soquel. La Selva Beach is the first vanguard of beach communities on the Santa Cruz side of the crescent-shaped bay. The sands of Sunset and Manresa beaches meet at the shores of this tiny hamlet. Rio Del Mar, Seacliff, and Capitola are the larger beach communities south of Santa Cruz. Capitola calls itself the oldest seaside resort on the Pacific Coast. Tourists first came to "Camp Capitola" by horsedrawn vehicles. By 1876, the railroad was extended to Capitola and brought pleasure seekers from San Francisco. The railroad's high trestle over Soquel Creek is a town landmark. In September, floats covered with begonias cruise under the trestle to cheers from crowds of adoring fans. Nightclubs, restaurants, shops, and a quintessential California beach attract the fashionable, the fun seekers, and families, who crowd together on sunny weekends.

Aptos and Soquel extend into the forested mountains above the beach communities. The historic village of Aptos is the entry point to the Forest of Nisene Marks State Park. If you hike or bike back farther into the park you can view the epicenter of the 1989 earthquake; a written plaque alerts you to the spot, since the forest itself has covered the physical evidence. Gone are the old post office and village square businesses. As it has since 1870, a three-story Victorian inn marks the center of town. A survivor of two major earthquakes and the changing whims of people, the Bayview Hotel has been restored regally to serve both as a quality bed and breakfast inn and as the sentinel of a century-plus of changes.

TOURS

FROM SEASIDE TO MOSS LANDING

The communities of Seaside, Del Rey Oaks, Sand City, Fort Ord, and Marina lie within fifteen minutes' drive of Monterey, on the opposite side of Highway 1. Although these communities are in a transition period following the military downsizing at Fort Ord, they are basically residential-, educational-, retail-, and industry-based. Some cities are gaining a new focus. In the words of consummate metal artist Tim Botonis, "Artists are receiving unbelievable support from the city government of Sand City. It seems to be a goal and dream of the city to have a strong contingent of artists here." Some residents here even refer to parts of Sand City as a future "SoHo" district.

About two miles south of Monterey, the Canyon Del Rey Boulevard, Highway 218, exit from Highway 1 leads west to the Monterey Beach Hotel and expanses of beach, which rise to low dunes. The skies over the beaches here are often filled with colorful and comical kites, such as a thirty-foot-long pair of very wide jeans.

Across the freeway, east on Highway 218, twelve stories of the Embassy Suites fill the skies above Seaside. The motel is the highest structure on the coast and very visible from all parts of the inner crescent of the bay. Unfortunately, there is no skyview restaurant at the top. If you rent an oceanside room you are treated with a spectacular view.

Seaside tingles with potential. The diversity of the city adds a human cultural treasure unparalleled in the marine sanctuary area. Today Seaside is the population center of Monterey County bayside communities. As is the case in many cities Seaside faces crime problems. With the exception of the Frog Pond Natural Area these tour areas are in parts of the city commonly visited.

The Frog Pond Natural Area, which provides a retreat for naturalists, families, and frog lovers, is reached by traveling east on Canyon Del Rey Boulevard for two miles. You will see the city hall of the residential city of Del Rey Oaks to the right. The entrance to the Frog Pond Natural Area is kitty-corner from the next junction, Via Verde and Canyon Del Rey Boulevard. Look for a small wooden sign marking the path through the willows. Limited parking is available on the side of the road. More parking directions and nature guide books are available at city hall.

The seventeen-acre preserve with pond—actually a marsh—doesn't offer spectacular vistas, but the tranquil wetlands can soothe a family's busy agenda. In the spring, tadpoles line the water's edge. The tonal mating songs of the tiny Pacific tree frogs fill the air of December and January. Less than one inch in size, the tiny frogs may be brown or green, changing in a chameleonlike manner. They share the area with other toads and frogs, wintering wild ducks, and such upper-woodland birds as hawks, Anna's hummingbirds, sparrows, chestnut-backed chickadees, and rufous-sided towhees.

Some signs remain of a self-guided tour, and restoration of the markers is planned. A loop trail leads through dense willows. Until they were cleared for farming in the late 1800s and early part of this century, similar groves of willows were prevalent throughout much of the inland areas of the Monterey Bay and Salinas Valley. Even more historic—rather, prehistoric—are the clumps of *Equisetum*, plants that you will encounter early in your walk and that resemble, and are called, horsetails. From the true Jurassic period, the ancestors of these plants were growing in the age of dinosaurs. Also known as scouring rush, the plants' rough stems and foliage contain silica and were used as scouring pads by early pioneers.

In addition to the pond and willow settings, trails lead through oaks, redwoods, wild roses, and grassy hillsides. If you are hiking with youngsters you may want to visit Del Rey Park before you leave for the day. Located behind the city hall, the park has barbecue pits, play areas, and rest rooms.

Back in Seaside, travel northeast on Del Monte Boulevard to Broadway Avenue. The Seaside–Sand City Chamber of Commerce, 505 Broadway Avenue, is located on the left side of the first block. Maps and information about new studios and businesses are available here. Drive across Del Monte Boulevard on Contra Costa Street to visit an eclectic assortment of Sand City businesses, many of which are housed in warehouses with the products offered at the site of creation. Sweet Elena's Bakery (831/393-2063), 465 Olympia Avenue, uses all-natural ingredients to bake a selection of cakes, pies, biscotti, and granola. Gil's Gourmet Gallery (831/394-3305), 577 Ortiz, features an outlet shop in front of his fine-foods warehouse. According to Gil, "We specialize in special firey foods." You can try before you buy. The wall of flame features one hundred hot sauces from around the world. You can also sample stuffed olives. Try the chardonnay garlic-stuffed olives. Another wall is packed with delectably different sweets like pinot noir chocolate-covered cherries. The outlet store prices all Gil's products below retail prices.

A large metal sculpture visible from Highway 1 heralds the entrance to Big Sur Heavy Metal (831/393-0110), 460 Elder Avenue. Welding, grinding, and shaping metal are the work here. A planned gallery will combine painting and metal sculpture. Furniture and sculpture from here is seen at Post Ranch and the Gregory Hawthorne Gallery in Big Sur. Worley Iron Works (831/394-7552), 337 Olympia Avenue, also excels in metal work. Mary's Angels (831/393-0345), 425 Elder Avenue, offers a beautiful collection of heavenly angels. Couroc Partners (831/899-5479), 501 Ortiz, is a world-famous showroom for inlay wood designs prized by collectors. At A Bent 4 Rent Recumbent Bicycle (831/393-2368), 637 Ortiz, you can rent or purchase a sit-down-peddle-in-front bike and receive information on the northern bike path connections to Santa Cruz as well as the path from here to Monterey. More than a dozen varieties of the "most comfortable bike on the planet" are showcased here. The Three Spirits Gallery (831/393-2787), 361 Orange Avenue, presents "Art and Music Productions for all ages, no smoking, no alcohol." Call for an itinerary of events and classes.

After you leave the "SoHo" venues, proceed north on California Avenue to the "megastore" center of Sand City. For Highway 1 travelers take the Del Monte exit from Highway 1, with a right turn at Fremont Boulevard, to a variety of discount stores. Borders Books & Music (831/899-6643) often features local authors, music, or symposiums. As of yet, it is also the only place in Sand City I can find an espresso.

Continuing on Fremont Boulevard leads to automobile row. Route 66 Collector Car Sales (831/393-9329), 1933 Del Monte Boulevard, is like a museum of classic cars. The owners' willingness to provide cars for special events is appreciated and enjoyed in parades throughout the south bay. Many Monterey area residents love cars and some of their best "oldies" and collector accessories are here for commission resale.

Whether you drive a classic car, a new car, or a van pool continue on Highway 1 to the Fort Ord exit. From this exit tour the new California State University at Monterey Bay (831/582-3330), opened in a dedication ceremony by President Clinton in 1995. Former Presidential Chief of Staff and area Congressional Representative Leon Panetta instructs here and organizes a series of every-seat-taken government symposiums. Panetta was instrumental in winning approval for the university on former Fort Ord Land.

Follow the entrance road to North South Road if you are driving to the two eighteen-hole championship golf courses, Bayonet and Black Horse (831/899-7271). Both courses have been restored by the City of Seaside, their new owner and operator. The course is challenging for even the best of top golfers but welcoming to beginners, especially in afternoon discounted times. Ocean vistas abound.

Parts of Fort Ord still serve the military. The Defense Language Institute houses students on base here. Other sections have become second chance havens for formerly homeless residents of the county.

The gift to all of us from Fort Ord is fifteen thousand acres of open space, encompassing some lands that have been untouched by humans for generations. However, half of the land is off limits due to explosives areas. Do not enter areas with "Danger" signs. Miles of trails ranging from easy to strenuous traverse more than seven thousand accessible acres.

Park at the kiosk area on Gigling Road. To enter pristine oak forest woodlands and areas of breathtaking beauty you will need to walk or mountain bike for about one-half mile. Visit in the spring to walk amid fields of wildflowers and watch clouds move across the surface of vernal ponds. These ponds appear with the spring rains and dry by autumn.

Walk on Gigling Road until you come to Hennekin's Ranch Road. Here you can explore trails to vernal pools, woodland areas, and historical sites. Among the two-hundred- to three-hundred-year-old oaks just east of the Hennekin Road intersection, you will see the foundation, well, and livestock watering trough of the Hennekin family, who arrived on the Peninsula as homesteaders after the Civil War. The family ran cattle in these hills even after they sold the property to the army in 1916. A short path from the

Hennekin Ranch pond leads to "Comanche's Grave." Comanche's owner was a soldier in the U.S. Army's horse calvary.

Roberto Maceira works as a Bureau of Land Management ranger here. The Americorps work in the new park has given a new dimension to his life. "I ran here as a child, and now I help other kids connect with the beauty here. It's breathtaking to watch the egrets, blue herons, and that kestrel on the tree looking at the ducks."

The trails in the park will receive further historical recognition when they join the Juan Bautista de Anza National Historic Trail. De Anza and his band of two hundred determined settlers rode through these trails in 1775 to establish homelands in the then Spanish territory. Other entrances to the park, each with their own beauty, can be reached from Highway 68.

The sandy hills along the continuation of the Highway 1 coastal drive form one of the tallest and most extensive dune systems on the California coast. Brightly colored hang gliders catch the optimum-condition winds off the dunes at fee-free Marina State Beach, which is at the end of Reservation Road off Highway 1. The hang-glider takeoff spot, a model-glider flying area, and snack hut are just inside the park entrance. On sunny weekends when the winds "shear" and hold at twenty to twenty-five miles an hour, the skies might fill with rainbow ribbons as thirty or forty pilots catch waves of air. Gliders can ride the wind waves above the ridge for six miles south, to Sand City. All members of the United States Hang Gliding Association who are rated three or better can register at the Western Hang Gliders' building for ramp use at the hang-gliding area. The association offers lessons for beginning through advanced hang gliders at the beach (831/384-2622).

At the northern end of Marina State Beach a wheelchair-accessible boardwalk leads from the parking lot through living dunes carpeted with native plants, such as the rare Monterey paintbrush and Menzies wallflower. Volunteer groups, neighborhood groups, and schoolchildren are replanting the shifting sands with native dune dwellers. Flowering plants help the dunes withstand pelting rain and driving winter winds. Nature's fragile balance is demonstrated by buckwheat, which roots in the dunes and serves as the food source for the endangered Smith's blue butterfly. Beyond the walkway one of the few remaining sand plants continues to process sand.

The Reservation Road exit is an alternate route to Salinas. To visit the Monterey Sculpture Center, 711 Neeson Road, drive four miles east from Highway 1 and turn left at the entrance to Marina Municipal Airport, formerly Fort Ord Fritchi Field. A view of two watertowers marks the entrance at Imjin Road. Turn left again on Neeson Road. More than four hundred artists bring their original ceramic molds here for bronze casting. Tours provided for individuals and groups show you the entire lost cast-wax casting process. On pouring days, green flames rise from two-thousand-degree molten bronze flowing into ceramic molds. Through viewing windows you can see metal workers welding seams with propane torches. The center is open from 8:30 a.m. to 5 p.m. and tours are presented from 9 a.m. to 4:30 p.m.

The Marina Municipal Airport is home to Skydive Monterey Bay (831/384-3483) which offers a preferred West Coast sky-dive park. Imagine the view.

Return to Highway 1 or continue on Reservation Road to connect with Highway 68 and more access points to the Fort Ord Public Lands. The access points are identified by kiosks and parking areas.

The Salinas River Wildlife Area is reached by the next exit from Highway 1, Del Monte Boulevard. Bring water and binoculars if you visit this birder's paradise. A dirt road (passable in the dry season, too muddy just after a storm) to the parking area traverses agricultural fields. Often muddy trails link the Salinas River, South Marsh, and a sandy beach. The two-mile trail to the beach passes a dune-sheltered brackish lagoon. Just south of the river's mouth at the beach a dune barrier separates the brackish South Marsh from the ocean. Storm-powered waves sometimes breach the barrier.

The barren, sandy beach is the preferred nesting spot of the snowy plover and the site of early morning races. The plovers' nests are nothing more than light depressions in soft sand. Their speckled eggs blend perfectly with the sand. At the crack of dawn the plovers leave their eggs to probe the wet beach for small crustaceans left vulnerable by the early morning receding tides. The plover parents hurry to gobble their daily intake of crustaceans and other tiny sand dwellers before their eggs cool. Meanwhile volunteers, roused by early morning phone calls of plover nest sightings, rush to erect plover-friendly mesh fences before the parents return. The fences shield the eggs from fox attacks and the tread of humans.

The Salinas River flows northwest for one hundred seventy miles from its headwaters in San Luis Obispo County to its mouth at the Salinas River Wildlife Area. The elusive Salinas River is one of the largest submerged rivers in the United States. Gulls, terns, and endangered California brown pelicans forage for food along the lower river. Stilts, avocets, and gadwalls nest on small islands in it. Black-shouldered kites and short-eared owls hunt over the river trail, which leads back through grasslands to your car.

Heading north again on Highway 1 after the last residential developments of Marina, the fertile fields of the Salinas Valley line the road. Many of these fields are still owned by descendants of the Cooper-Vallejo families from Mexican California days.

About three miles past the last Marina exit the road divides between the Highway 1 and Santa Cruz connection and the Highway 156 connection to Highway 101. The Highway 1 route will bypass the town of Castroville for a faster Santa Cruz connection. Backroads travelers who would like to trade inland Elkhorn Slough for coastside Moss Landing may prefer the route on 156, on Castroville Boulevard and then on Elkhorn Road, along the slough. Elkhorn Road north connects with Highway 1 via Salinas Road or, farther along at Watsonville (page 288), via Riverside Drive.

To take the Highway 156 connecting route to Castroville is to be escorted by rows and rows of large bushy plants with club-topped spikes. Take the Highway 183 exit to "Castroville, the Artichoke Center of the World." Turn left, north, at the first street, which is Merritt. If it is early September you may be in time for the tasting, crafts booths, and music of the annual Artichoke Festival. While some claim the artichoke as an indigenous California plant, major growers say this special thistle was brought to the state's Central Coast from Italy during the late 1800s. Commemorating more recent history, Franco's Restaurant at 10639 Merritt Street (831/633-2090) pays homage to the first Artichoke Queen of Castroville, Marilyn Monroe. You might enjoy a Marilyn Monroe hamburger (with Swiss cheese and arti-choke hearts) while enjoying the memorabilia.

For more than forty years a giant light-green replica of an artichoke has welcomed the curious and the avid artichoke fan to the Giant Artichoke, a landmark Castroville restaurant and vegetable stand on Merritt Street just beyond the freeway. In addition to a range of entrees the restaurant offers different chokes for different folks: steamed and marinated artichoke dishes, artichoke pancakes, artichoke soup, artichoke bread, artichoke quiche, and shrimp-stuffed artichokes.

Castroville reconnects with Highway 1 northbound by way of Merritt Street. The drive on Merritt passes through a town poised on a fulcrum even though the floods of 1994 covered sections in more than ten feet of water and slowed development. Across from the Giant Artichoke Restaurant, new shop-ping centers are branching into the historically agriculture-based town. Midway through town the original schoolhouse now opens its doors to patrons of Tuscany-style Italian food, having become La Scuola. Older cot-tages, many with peeling paint and tall grasses in front yards, share the sur-rounding streets with freshly constructed homes and businesses. The black sign that proclaims Castroville the artichoke center of the world spans Merritt Street; just beyond the arch a colorful legitimized-graffiti art wall delivers the same message.

Artichoke plants grow between houses and stretch into fields that escort you to Highway 1, a headlight-required traffic safety corridor where traffic ranges from bumper to bumper on sunny weekends to one slow country truck on the midmornings of winter weekdays. On the west side, the acres and acres of artichokes, broccoli, chard, and other garden vegetables are replaced now and then by fruit and vegetable stands. The Thistle Hut at the corner of Molera Road, Springfield Farms farther up the road, the red barns of Johnny Boy, and the occasional open-bed pickup loaded with sacks and advertised with hand-lettered signs sell a wide variety of local produce, including, of course, artichokes. To turn across the highway can be dangerous; visit these stands on your southbound trips.

Ahead, always in view on sunny days, drifting in and out of the field of vision like an elusive dragon on foggy days, the five-hundred-foot-tall towers of the lighted electric plant emit steam into the air. Built in 1952, it is the second-largest fossil-fuel thermal-electric power plant in the state.

The traffic jam you may be sitting in is not new to this area. Back in the 1860s grain wagons backed up for five miles waiting to be unloaded at Moss Landing. At that time the Salinas River emptied into the slough, making navigation possible. Today visitors are often surprised to learn that no river flows through Moss Landing. The seasonal estuary that surrounds Moss Landing gets fresh water after winter rains through an assortment of creeks. North of the power plant, Highway 1 crosses a wide channel created in 1946, when the Army Corps of Engineers diverted a meandering channel to cut straight through sand dunes. Two harbors, on opposite sides of the Highway 1 bridge, form a T at the mouth of the channel.

Antique stores and restaurants flank the most southern entrance to Moss Landing, at Potrero Road. The outside mural of the Moss Landing Cafe, at the intersection of Potrero Road and Moss Landing Road, depicts the village and harbor that lie ahead. Moss Landing Road travels parallel to Highway 1 and joins it again directly opposite the power plant, at an exit that is marked by a very bright pink landmark building, the Whole Enchilada Mexican Restaurant. *Icpali*—the traditional leather furniture from Mexico—and walls painted in the style of Frida Kahlo's kitchen, plus aromas of Mexican dishes, make the inside of the Whole Enchilada restaurant as lively as the exterior. On Sunday afternoons, sport coats replace motorcycle leathers in the lounge annex as jazz fans from miles around gather here for concerts.

For the historical and antique dealer's section of Moss Landing take the first left turn inland from the Whole Enchilada. You will be on Moss Landing Road. When I walk down the old Victorian main street and look up to the towers of the power plant I feel like a time traveler caught in two centuries at the same time.

Some twenty-five antique stores occupy old Victorians, an old refinery, a railroad car, and new construction that matches the historic buildings. Most of the antique shops in Moss Landing deal in affordable Americana. On the last Sunday in July, the Moss Landing landlubbers show their "catch" at the town's mammoth flea market. More than three hundred dealers and thou-

Moss Landing Ship Yard

sands of antique hunters converge on the town. Come early for a parking place.

If you continue straight from your turn off Highway 1 at the Whole Enchilada, or turn left at the northern end of Moss Landing Road, you will be on Sandholt Road. The harbor master's office and Tom's Sport Fishing office (831/633-2564) will be on your right. A narrow one-lane bridge crosses the Old Salinas River Slough and leads to Moss Landing Island, where the masts and colorful cabins of some four hundred commercial fishing boats, some pleasure craft, and several large research vessels, such as the 140-foot Point Sur, welcome you to the South Harbor. Twenty years ago the boats in the seven hundred berths were almost exclusively for commercial fishing; today only a hundred or so of the boats are regular fishing vessels. Some of the fish nabbed by the fishing boats are whisked across the street to couldn't-get-fresher fish markets.

The road continues to where the Monterey Bay Aquarium Research Institute (MBARI) fills massive buildings, changing the core of the island from commercial to research. Fishing is permitted at the end of the jetty, and people often have fishing tailgate picnics here.

To reach the north side of the channel, return to Highway 1 and continue north. A sign marks the entrance to the Elkhorn Yacht Club, where there are pleasure craft, kayak rentals, and a large public boat ramp. The Moss Landing Wildlife Area, a mile north of Jetty Road along Highway 1, is the

MOSS LANDING & VICINITY

newest access point on the slough. It offers four miles of trails and two wildlife viewing blinds. To reach the ocean end of the slough turn left off Highway 1 for Moss Landing State Beach. Dunes meet ocean and marsh in this location. On the beach side of the dunes anglers surfcast for ling cod and rockfishes. Slat-board walkways lead through native-plant-restored dunes and the picnic tables with barbecues that line the mouth of the harbor. You might spot the large white *Point Sur* research vessel or any of the smaller fishing boats sailing to the harbor.

Before the antiques, before even the harbor, elk roamed the area around present-day Moss Landing. The Ohlone people shared the bounty of the tidal waters; their middens are visible along the banks of Elkhorn Slough, which extends in a branched shape from the harbor ten miles inland. Elkhorn Slough is an estuary; it opens to the ocean but receives fresh water from an inland source. Fresh water and brackish water, marsh, salt ponds, and mudflats cover more than 2,500 acres bordered by oak woodland, strawberry fields, and grasslands. Of these, 1,400 acres are included in the National Estuarine Research Reserve. Another five hundred acres are preserved through the Nature Conservancy. To view the reserve take Dolan Road at the foot of the power plant in Moss Landing east 3.5 miles to Elkhorn Road. Turn left and drive 2.2 miles to the entrance of the visitor's center. As described next the slough can be intimately observed on foot over the many trails, or in kayaks, which can be rented at the harbor and launched at Kirby Creek, above the visitor's center.

The cradles of marine life, estuaries such as Elkhorn Slough are the fish nurseries for a number of species. Elkhorn marine babies get super formula from the offshore Monterey Bay, which sends the slough a constant supply of nutrients that mix with slough decay, such as old pickleweed, and humus from top soil to make "Elkhorn Slough stew." The stew is the first course in a food chain that passes from protozoa to plankton to young fish. Sharks, raptors, seals, otters, and humans share the harvests farther up the chain.

As you turn off Highway 1 for a moment it seems the angle of your drive will take you through the massive power plant. The gray towers that have loomed throughout your trip are just feet from your car. Twisting pipes, large fuel tanks, and megavoltage wires line the beginning of the drive, which then gently curves by cattle ranches and strawberry fields. Wooden windmills dot the land as you view the ribbon of water leading from the power plant to inland tributaries and marshes.

About two miles north of Dolan Road turn left to the slough's visitors center and entrance. Before you even open your car door you might want to roll down your windows and close your eyes. Treble notes, beautiful melodies, and changed-pitch calls from surrounding trees are your invitation to watch thousands of shorebirds probing the marsh flats at low tide, or to scan pine and eucalyptus groves for the nests of the great blue heron and great egret, or to just unwind while watching harbor seals basking on the mudflats.

The visitor's center is open on Wednesday through Sunday and charges a minimal fee. It houses a relief map of the Central Coast inland and ocean region, offers free checkout of binoculars and bird books, and has checklists of birds, flowers, and animal life as viewing aids. Raptors highlight some mounted wildlife displays that aid field observation. Local guide books and wildlife books line shelves in the Elkhorn Slough Foundation gift shop. Before beginning a hike check with the ranger about any recent special slough bird sightings or activities, such as mating or fledging.

At first glance the scenery on a hike may not be breathtaking—no craggy peaks or crashing waves. As your glance lingers, fingers of fog may reach out to you. When beams of sunlight touch the slough, liquid gold surrounds you. A statuesque great egret posed on stilted legs in the mudflats brings you peaceful, deeper breaths. Then, just as you have entered the depths of meditation, the brilliant white wings of a flock of sandpipers flash before you.

The slough trail system begins just west of the visitors center. The Long Valley loop runs .8 mile, the Five-Finger loop, 1.1 miles, and the South Marsh loop, 2.2 miles. Elkhorn Slough docents lead weekend walks at 10 a.m. and 1 p.m. The Five-Fingers loop trail leads to the Parson's Slough Overlook, which is the best place to watch migratory and resident bird populations that peak during the winter. This is the site of the "Big Sit" at which bird-watchers clinched the record for the most bird species seen in a single day in all of North America—116 species, on October 31, 1982.

At the entrance to the South Marsh loop you'll pass the old Elkhorn dairy site. During Estuaries Day in September the barns are scenes of activities ranging from pressing colorful leaves to slough storytelling. Theater members dress as historical figures from the slough's past to tell the stories of the changing tidelands. The Elkhorn farm dairy operated from 1922 until the early 1970s. Rises of marshland in this area were diked and used for pasture. In 1983 the dikes were lowered in an attempt to return more of the slough to wetlands.

You can launch kayaks or hike a wheelchair-accessible trail on the eastern side of the slough at Kirby Park, which is about four miles beyond the visitor's center.

Rejoin Highway 1 via Elkhorn Road to Salinas Road or Riverside Drive west (left).

WATSONVILLE AND PAJARO DUNES

Highway 1 north of Moss Landing eases over miles of rolling agricultural hills shrouded with dark green enclaves of trees. The route from Watsonville to Santa Cruz is approximately the same as the Portola trail of 1769 and the

Camino Real of the mission days. The Pajaro River marks the dividing line between Monterey and Santa Cruz counties. Pajaro, Spanish for "bird," was the name given to this river during the first Portola expedition that searched for Monterey Bay. According to Father Crespi's diary of the expedition, "We saw in this place a bird which the heathen had killed and stuffed with grass. To some of our party it looked like a royal eagle. . . . For this reason the soldiers called the stream Rio del Pajaro." The Portola party rested a day along the Pajaro River before beginning a day's march to the Corralitos region (see What Else to See and Do, page 299).

Just beyond the river the Riverside Drive exit leads inland to Watsonville and Highway 152 or, oceanside, to the Pajaro Dunes Vacation and Conference Center, Palm Beach, and San Andreas Road. This road parallels Highway 1 north to Sunset State Beach and through the community of La Selva Beach and back to Highway 1. Pajaro Dunes, a selection of deluxe private residences, rental homes, and townhomes, is situated at the site of a resort center of the 1930s named Palm Beach by developers who likened it to the style of Palm Beach, Florida. Eucalyptus and oak trees shade picnic areas here, but not a single palm tree is seen anywhere. The wave action at this public beach is gentler than most, and a lifeguard is sometimes on duty. Beachcombing yields large clam shells and sand dollars. Palm Beach melds into Sunset State Beach. This 218-acre park has ninety overnight camping sites on wooded dune bluffs above the beach.

Turn inland on Riverside Drive from Highway 1 to drive to Watsonville, which is known as the "Strawberry Capital of the World" and "Apple City of the West." Strawberries, raspberries, apples, and almost any variety of produce can be picked by you or bought fresh picked at many of the farms that surround Watsonville. You can have your apple and eat your pie too at Gizdich Ranch (831/722-1056). To reach the "Pik Yor Self Berries" part of the ranch turn left from Riverside onto Lakeview. Drive through two miles of apple orchards, berry farms, and other small farms, then turn left at Carlton Road, where signs will direct you to the five-acre picking farm. May through June is strawberry season. Olallieberries, raspberries, and boysenberries are available June through August. Tours through the family-run apple pressing plant are given by appointment at the main ranch headquarters, which is located at the next turn off Carlton at 55 Peckham Road. Picnic tables are spread out in the orchard where you can enjoy fresh pies and fresh-crushed juice. To get a free Country Crossroads map, send a self-addressed envelope to the Santa Cruz County Farm Bureau, 141 Monte Vista Avenue, Watsonville, CA 95076. The map shows where to get everything from kiwi fruit to Paso Fino horses, from fresh eggs to apricots, direct from the farmer or processors in Santa Clara and Santa Cruz counties.

Besides the agricultural attractions, Watsonville boasts many Victorians and historic structures that survived both the 1906 earthquake and the 1989 temblor, which damaged much of the now-rebuilt downtown area. A Walking and Driving Tour Map of Historic Watsonville is available from the Watsonville Chamber of Commerce (831/724-3900).

JUST SOUTH OF SANTA CRUZ

The towns and communities close to Santa Cruz, begin with tiny La Selva Beach, reached by either the Mar Monte Avenue or San Andreas Road turnoffs from Highway 1. After La Selva Beach, the progression to Santa Cruz continues with Seascape, then Rio Del Mar, Seacliff, and Capitola. The general rule is, the closer you get to Santa Cruz the sooner the sun breaks through on foggy days. Aptos is to the east of Highway 1 above Rio Del Mar and melds into Soquel, which is east of Capitola and adjoins Santa Cruz. A visitor may choose to drive the back roads that parallel the freeway to connect the towns or pick and choose from direct freeway exits that are marked with the town's names. Soquel Avenue can be confusing, as it crosses the freeway and traverses Aptos, Soquel, and Santa Cruz—so if you are looking for something on Soquel Avenue, ask for the city name.

LA SELVA BEACH. Mar Monte Avenue and San Andreas Road intersect at La Selva Beach Boulevard. A row of palm trees lines this main entrance to La Selva Beach. The corner business section is anchored by a community market that offers picnic fixings and a local beach shop that offers rentals and advice. La Selva Beach Boulevard curves at a parking area along high bluffs above the bay. Just a few paces from the bluff parking, romantic benches overlook stretches of golden sand beaches and yield views across to Monterey.

MANRESA BEACH. Accessible from San Andreas Road, Manresa Beach is especially popular on sunny weekends. The fee parking lot often fills early. While the parking lot is jammed, miles of sands keep the beach from ever seeming crowded. You can walk north from Manresa to Sand Dollar Beach, where you might find the rounded white "dollar" shells of sea urchins in the sands at wave's edge. Manresa Uplands provides sixty-four campsites.

SEASCAPE. The spacious homes, Aptos Beach Golf Course, and open beaches of Seascape lie between the communities of Rio Del Mar and La Selva Beach. Turn at Seascape Boulevard, which runs only north from San Andreas Road. Seascape Boulevard intersects Sumner Avenue. A large community playground precedes the Seascape Resort and Conference Center on Sumner Avenue. Cement paths lead to easy beach access here. You might want first to pick up picnic items and gourmet fixings, which are available across the street at Bruno's Market in Seascape Village.

RIO DEL MAR. Continue on Sumner with a left turn at Rio Del Mar Boulevard to reach the flatlands of Rio Del Mar Beach, a popular gathering spot for beach lovers. Hot dog vendors or the steak and seafood at Cafe Rio help you play all day. You can walk to Seacliff Beach along a beachfront walkway that crosses Aptos Creek. If you turn right at Rio Del Mar Boulevard you will pass the stylish Deer Park Shopping Center before crossing over Highway 1 to the Aptos area.

SEACLIFF. Seacliff State Beach Park, off Highway 1 at Seacliff, five and a half miles south of Santa Cruz, is popular for day use and offers overnight spots on the beach for twenty-six trailers and campers. The eighty-five-acre park also has more than one hundred one-night "en route" spots available for self-contained vehicles, but they're allocated on a first-come, first-served basis. Ample day parking is usually available above the cliffs, which offer great vistas of surrounding beaches. Look for ancient sea fossils in the cliffs as you walk the hillside staircases.

Seacliff Beach is recognizable for miles around by the long pier that connects to the huge gray concrete ship *Palo Alto*. The cement-hulled ship was built for World War I at a cost of $2 million as part of a "concrete fleet." The war ended before she served on the seas. She was towed to Seacliff, and ballasted to the ocean floor, then hosted a bingo and dance hall for two years as part of a floating amusement park until closing during the Depression. She has since served generations as part of the fishing pier. Winter storm waves crash over the hull of the boat and have untethered her from the pier periodically. You can walk across the main sections of the *Palo Alto*. The ballroom has become the landing spot for sea stars and sea anemones. Red brick and black iron support rods hold the sections together.

A wall of fossil-filled rocks surrounds the visitor center here. On weekends, guided walks explore such topics as "Shipwalk" and "Fossils Found in Cliffs." Walks leave at noon and last about an hour. The museum houses several interactive displays, a tidepool touch tank, a historical room, a video theater, and an eerie sensory corner. One of the most haunting sounds of the marine sanctuary plays on earphones—echoes of the cement ship's movements rising from deep within her hold.

APTOS. Across the freeway roughly from Freedom Boulevard to the Seacliff exit lies the inland area of Aptos. To drive to the historic center of Aptos and entrance to the Forest of Nisene Marks State Park, exit from Highway 1 at Rio Del Mar Boulevard, then turn left at Soquel Drive. Or you can exit the beach flats of Rio Del Mar Beach on Trout Gulch Road for a woodsy drive under the freeway, then turn right at the intersection with Soquel Drive.

The stretch of land on the west side of Highway 1 between Freedom Boulevard and Rio Del Mar Boulevard often seems to be smoking on sunny days. Actually it is the steam rising from the main swampy breeding area of some five hundred of the last of the earth's long-toed salamanders. Plans to widen the freeway at this point were stopped by protests on the salamander's behalf. Cattails were planted, and salamander easements were included in the deeds of neighboring properties.

When you have reached Aptos village via Rio Del Mar Boulevard or Soquel Avenue the restored Bayview Hotel, built in 1870 and shaded by an enormous century-plus-old magnolia tree, will catch your eye as the three-storied center piece. In the late eighteenth century Aptos was the base of a large logging industry and held two railway stations, thirteen taverns, and three hotels. After 1900 apple orchards filled much of the cleared lowlands. A packing plant for the industry was built behind the landmark hotel. The shops that surround the Bayview Hotel are known as Aptos Station.

Across the street from the hotel, wooden sidewalks lead past a variety of shops and the reasonable and locally recommended Cafe Sparrow Restaurant (831/688-6238). The old grocery and post office used to stand where a big gap now divides the business district. The 1989 earthquake spared the hotel but leveled this historic section.

The earthquake was centered in the Forest of Nisene Marks State Park—a sprawling ten-thousand-acre reserve of redwoods—which is directly north of Aptos village. The park entrance is located on Aptos Creek Road, next to Aptos Station. When you cross the train tracks set the "0" mileage marker for the following distances. Continuing into the park, Aptos Creek Road is paved for .8 mile, then changes to dirt. Three miles from the railroad tracks, the dirt road is closed to vehicles at a locked gate. A parking lot and the entrance to the Porter picnic area are located here.

The Aptos Creek fire road past this locked gate is one of the most popular mountain biking areas along the Central Coast. Although the fire road offers an easy hike to a picturesque creek and provides people who have an interest in earthquakes the opportunity to claim they stood at the epicenter of a major one, I find it too frequented by cyclists who kick up too much dust to recommend it as a good walking trail. The sign that identifies your location as close to the epicenter is 1.5 miles beyond the locked gate. Across the creek from the epicenter sign you can pick up the Aptos Creek trail that continues for a half-mile to the true epicenter. Farther on, in a canyon, Aptos Creek trail be comes the Big Slide trail, which climbs to White's Lagoon, a sag pond created during the 1906 earthquake, before it loops back to the fire road about four miles beyond the trailhead for the Aptos Creek trail. Bike racks installed at the West Ridge, Loma Prieta, and Aptos Creek trailheads provide the opportunity for a pleasant combination of hiking and biking. If you do hike or bike the Aptos Creek fire road, look at the cliffs along the way for shelves of seashell fossils, attesting to the time millions of years ago when the collision of the Pacific and North American plates and ensuing earthquakes caused the uplift of the hills from the ocean.

More than thirty miles of trails, some exclusive to hikers, lead off the main fire road to cool redwoods by meandering creeks, hillsides with sweeping views of the bay, and such vestiges of logging days as old mill sites, abandoned railroad trestles, and loggers' cabins. One of the best of these is the Loma Prieta Grade trail (a six-mile round trip), which leads to the ramshackle wooden remains of a turn-of-the-century lumber camp that housed three hundred workers in its heyday. For this trail, walk .4 mile beyond the locked gate to the Loma Prieta Grade trailhead. The trail travels above Aptos Creek for awhile, then continues along the old lumber railway bed for three miles. Your final destination is Hoffman's Historic Site. This was the last section of the park to be logged and offers hikers views of the youngest, most recently regenerated trees in the forest. You can double back on the Loma Prieta trail or take the ridge-connection trail to West Ridge trail, which connects to Aptos Creek Road, just south of the Porter picnic area.

The Forest of Nisene Marks is second-growth redwoods. The entire park was clear cut in a forty-year logging frenzy (1883 to 1923). You will not see here the ancient first-growth trees of huge circumference that have been preserved in Henry Cowell and Big Basin state parks in the Santa Cruz Mountains. The last stand of first-growth redwoods in Aptos was lumbered out in 1923. The logging industry here was then finished. Workers moved on and the narrow railroad was removed. In the 1950s the land was bought by the Marks, a family of Danish ancestry who were active in Salinas Valley farming. In 1963, Herman, Agnes, and Andrew Marks donated the land to the state of California in memory of their mother, with the stipulation that the property be left undeveloped to continue the process of regeneration. An excellent brochure produced by the Santa Cruz Mountains Natural History Association is available by writing the Forest of Nisene Marks State Park, 201 Sunset Beach Road, Watsonville, CA 95076, or calling 831/688-3241.

Soquel Avenue continues south, passes Cabrillo Junior College, and connects with the town of Soquel.

SOQUEL. Majestic oak trees and the white-steepled Congregational "Little White Church in the Vale" mark Soquel. According to Santa Cruz mission and other local legends the original spelling of this community was Shoquel or Osocales, from an Ohlone term meaning "Place of the Willows." If you have visited the Frog Pond area in Del Rey Oaks you can superimpose that area on this landscape to imagine what Soquel looked like two centuries ago. My own most poignant memory of the town dates from the winter of 1982, when Soquel Creek rose over the streets and mud poured through restaurants and shops. Business owners, shopkeepers, and visitors grabbed shovels and wheelbarrows to trudge through the streets and dig out the town. Today the town sparkles like the eight hundred pounds of sugar that was processed here yearly in the 1870s.

More than fourteen antique shops, many with a number of dealers, line Soquel Drive and nearby passageways. Wisteria, at 5870 Soquel Drive (831/462-2900), features furniture, French country antiques, and locally forged iron furniture. Near the heart of the town, across from the steepled church, the Trader's Emporium at 4940 Soquel Drive (831/475-9201) houses twenty-five dealers. After Effects (831/475-5991), next door, features a wide variety of Americana.

After antique browsing, let the cool breezes of Soquel Creek soothe you at one of a selection of restaurants along Main Street. Wine tasting is available at award-winning Bargetto Winery, 3535 North Main Street (831/475-2258), which overlooks the creek and displays old winemaking tools. See page 306.

Park Avenue, for which there is a Highway 1 exit in southern Soquel, leads to New Brighton State Beach, where interpretive nature trails lead through wooded plateaus in the sixty-five acres of parkland. More than a hundred camping sites occupy highlands above a curving beach that is protected from pounding surf by headlands. On clear nights campers are treated to magnificent views of Monterey Bay.

CAPITOLA. The town of Capitola, toward the bay from Soquel, also borders Santa Cruz, the bay's topmost city. Greater Capitola includes a large retail shopping mall at 41st Avenue, a variety of smaller shopping centers, many residential areas, and the still-California-dreaming resort of Capitola village, where a wharf, popular sunny beach, and more than a hundred shops nestle at the mouth of Soquel Creek under rows of Victorians perched on hillside bluffs. My favorite pick for an entrance to Capitola village is the woodsy creekside route along Wharf Road, which is reached by turning south on Robertson Road as you drive toward the bay from Soquel. The entrance sign for the Shadowbrook Restaurant, with its hillside tram, is to your left before Wharf Road drops to the beach area. Parking is most available in the public lot off Monterey Avenue.

CAPITOLA

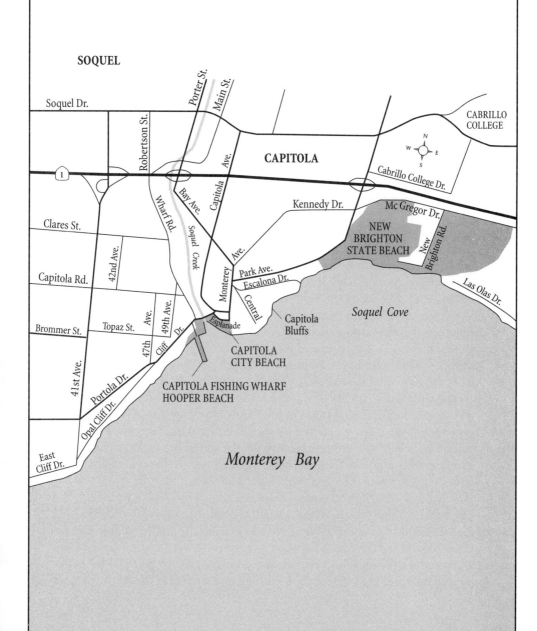

As you drive down Wharf Road during the winter months you will see Soquel Creek rolling along to join the breakers of Capitola Bay. In summer, the outlet is closed with bulldozed sand and the creek becomes a lagoon for rental paddleboats, rubber rafts, and families of mallard ducks. Wharf Road curves by a century-plus-old wooden railway trestle, then meets the colorful stucco units of the circa-1920 Capitola Venetian Hotel (831/476-6471). The Italian-style hotel spans the beachfront at the bottom of Wharf Road from Soquel Creek, in the heart of the village, to the Capitola wharf, which lies on the village's northern beach boundary. From Wharf Road you can veer across the road to the wharf, where limited parking is available, or merge with Opal Cliff Drive, which loops through the heart of Capitola village.

The Capitola Chamber of Commerce recommends making Capitola village your home base: five miles southeast of Santa Cruz, "this charming amalgam of beach, winding streets, restaurants, galleries, and shops is so compact that your car will seem blessedly obsolete during your stay." The Capitola Historical Museum at 410 Capitola Avenue (831/464-0322) traces the town's past through photographs, books, and period clothing and furniture. My favorite time in Capitola begins at twilight on the night before its big event of the year—the Begonia Festival parade. Flashlights and laughter illuminate the banks along Soquel Creek as neighbors, friends, and business groups cover hand-sculpted frames with thousands of begonias. Begonia-covered barges, powered by strong arms, really float down Soquel Creek. Prizes are awarded, to the cheers of onlookers who swarm the banks and block Opal Cliff Drive. Barbecues, sailboard races, and tours of begonia gardens add to the festivities. Antonelli Brothers Begonia Garden (831/475-5222), in northern Capitola at 2545 Capitola Road, displays thousands of begonias and ornamental plants in a ten-thousand-foot display greenhouse. June through October (peak months are August and September) hanging begonias cascade from the roof, lending a slightly pastel glow to the place.

The wide wooden slats of Capitola wharf lead to a fishing supply outlet, a restaurant, and sweeping views of the entire Monterey Bay. The wharf has been rebuilt after being battered by several severe winter storms. From the end of the wharf you can see the curve of the gentle bay to the village built alongside the mouth of Soquel Creek. The cliffs above the village are lined with the picturesque Victorians of Depot Hill. When the tide is low you can walk around the cliff and cement breakwater at the northern edge of Capitola to China Beach, where a small Chinese fishing village flourished in the late 1800s. On sunny days your view extends around Monterey Bay from China Beach and the Seacliff cement boat to the Moss Landing power plant and around to Point Pinos. No cars are permitted on the pier and the commercial ventures are limited, so the fishing and strolls for the views are very

Capitola Venetian Hotel

peaceful compared to the busy Monterey or Santa Cruz commercial wharfs.

Capitola Boat and Bait (831/462-2208) rents poles and boats during the calm months, March to December. On any June day you might get good reports of halibut and rockfish. The Wharf House at the end of the pier serves breakfast, lunch, and dinner, with sweeping bay views from almost every seat. On weekends, longtime resident-musician Don McCaslin and the band Warmth, "the jazz soul of the Santa Cruz Bay," play on the top deck of the restaurant. When we first lived in Santa Cruz, some twenty years ago, Warmth played at a restaurant in the downtown Cooper House, which was originally the city courthouse. After the 1989 earthquake, viewing the rubble that was the Cooper House shocked me to tears. Now, as sailboats bob on their moorings just a skip away, the jazz tradition continues on the wharf with the motion of the ocean.

Sail boarders, surfers, and boogie boarders glide offshore while sun worshippers, sand castle builders, volleyball players, and kite enthusiasts share the sands at popular Capitola Beach. Capitola Bay is relatively calm, as it is protected by headlands. The water is cold, but some diehards swim without wetsuits. Boogie board enthusiasts recommend this as a great beginner's beach. The first building of any importance in Capitola was a storehouse for potatoes built in 1852. If you are a beach potato, the six sand courts of volleyball team competition and the offshore surfing make great spectator sports. Bring your own picnic or simply walk to any number of eateries that offer take-out food around the village.

Above the beach, bathing suits and bare chests are common on the Esplanade, where you can get ice cream cones, slices of pizza, and cooling drinks. The grand 160-room Capitola Hotel stood, from 1895 until it burned to the ground in 1929, where now rest rooms and a grassy area occupy the southern end of the Esplanade. Local artists display their work here on summer Sundays and at the Capitola Art Festival in September. Several restaurants line the upper section of the Esplanade. Mr. Toots Coffee House (831/475-3679) and Margaritaville (831/476-2263), a lively Mexican restaurant and bar, overlook both creek and ocean. The large patio of Zelda's (831/475-4900) virtually extends to the beach.

Besides enjoying the beach and sampling the restaurants, you'll want to browse through some of the unusual clothing and gift shops, arts and crafts galleries, of the village area, which fills several blocks between Monterey Avenue and Capitola Avenue and extends uphill along Capitola Avenue. A row of beach houses and small rental cottages line the beachfront and a lawn area between the shops. A California Registered Historical Landmark plaque identifies the large Victorian that fills the corner of Capitola Avenue and Bay Avenue as the first superintendent's building of the fifteen-acre resort community of Camp Capitola, which was established in 1869. Kickback (831/464-9100), a casual men's and women's clothing store with an emphasis on nostalgia, presently occupies the corner. The Hour Place (831/464-2433) features handmade and unusual clocks. While walking through the village you will pass several California-style women's clothing stores, including Oceania Imports (831/476-6644) at 204 Capitola Avenue and Clothes Garden (831/475-7648) at 131 Monterey Avenue. The Village Mouse (831/476-7566), 201 Capitola Avenue features a world of miniatures, thousands of figurines, and locally handcrafted gifts. Owners Bobbie Moore and Steve Austen have a wealth of information about the area if you have questions. The background music you hear in the store is probably from the tapes of local musicians, such as *Music to a Wild Rose* by Linda Gauthier. The entrance to the Craft Gallery (831/475-4466) is just off Capitola Avenue at 126 San Jose Avenue. Bronze fountains highlight an extensive array of pottery, paintings, and handicrafts, many of which are created by local artists.

You can also grab a cookie at the Mercantile, which is a bright collection of shops on Monterey Avenue.

My personal choice for a Capitola weekend is a watercolor workshop with Sally Bookman (831/464-3838). This workshop is held inside on Saturday for directed instruction; on Sunday even complete stuck-in-fourth-grade-ability artists move outdoors to paint the village. Sally supplies a home-cooked lunch and you take a set of beautiful watercolors away with you. Sally

Bookman Gallery, 109 Capitola, features her watercolors and those of other local artists.

The narrow wedge of streets between Capitola Avenue and Bay Avenue is home to a variety of Victorians and resort homes that are squeezed together on narrow lots. At 202 Cherry a blue plaque awarded by the Santa Cruz County Historical Trust recognizes an 1887 Victorian of distinction, built in Queen Anne and Eastlake styles. Before you leave Capitola village you may want to drive by the row of picturesque Victorians on Depot Hill. You can also make reservations to tour or stay at the Inn at Depot Hill (831/462-DEPO/3376), the turn-of-the-century railroad depot that has been transformed into a four-star Mobil-rated bed and breakfast inn. To reach Depot Hill travel toward Highway 1 on Bay Avenue and turn right on Central Avenue. From Depot Hill you will enjoy a panoramic view of Capitola village north to Santa Cruz.

WHAT ELSE TO SEE AND DO

HIGHWAY 152. Coming to the Monterey Bay from Highway 101, twisty Highway 152, which exits Highway 101 at Gilroy and winds over Hecker Pass, offers you a bird's eye view of Elkhorn Slough, the city of Watsonville, and stretches of coast south to Point Lobos and north to Santa Cruz. Take advantage of the few viewing-area pulloffs, and drive slowly. If you are already at the bay it may well be worth a couple of hours of your time to drive from Watsonville to the summit of Highway 152, enjoy a walk through the redwood groves of Mount Madonna County Park, and wind back down the very curvy road. Mount Madonna County Park also offers many camping possibilities, nature trails, and a small herd of white deer.

BACKROADS FROM WATSONVILLE TO APTOS

The backroads between Watsonville and Aptos, popular with bicyclists and adventurous Highway 1 travelers, pass bucolic hillsides and through vales dappled with apple orchards, turn-of-the-century farmhouses, flower sheds, and occasional vineyards. Redwood groves shade the roads as they wind along the foot of the Santa Cruz Mountains.

One of my favorite routes (a twenty-one-mile excursion from Watsonville to Aptos) begins at the Green Valley Road exit just north of Riverside Drive, Watsonville's main exit. Turn northeast on Green Valley Road. This route can be a pleasant forty-minute drive or a full-day excursion. The road is basically urban and busy until you cross Freedom Boulevard. (If you want a road that parallels Highway 1 and gives you a feel for the countryside but is not so lengthy, turn left—northeast—at Freedom Boulevard.)

Continuing on Green Valley Road, you pass the Watsonville Hospital at the corner of Airport Boulevard. The first entrance to Pinto Lake (831/722-8129), a small lake with wooded shores, is one-half mile north of the hospital. If you miss the first entrance a second one is a little farther up Green Valley Road. You can rent boats, sail, and picnic or barbecue, but no swimming is allowed at this time. Trout are planted twice monthly for anglers. There is a small fee for day use. Overnight parking of trailers and RVs is permitted on the lake shore. In recent years the park has become a mecca for the devoted who come to pray at an oak tree, which they feel holds an image of Mary, mother of Jesus.

As you climb the foothills past Pinto Lake, you view orchards and surrounding small farms that are interspersed with groves of eucalyptus and redwoods. This is a slow, winding country road with an occasional tractor to really compel you to slow down and take it easy. About eight miles past Pinto Lake you enter a thick redwood forest. About a half mile farther Green Valley Road ends at Hazel Dell Road, where you turn left.

A fern-lined stream meanders alongside Hazel Dell Road for part of this stretch, and an occasional sunny dell peeks through the forested road. After about two miles veer left on Browns Valley Road. Deep redwood stands and fern grottos grow along the roadside creek.

Roses of Yesterday and Today, at 802 Browns Valley Road, offers old, rare, and unusual roses for purchase. In May and June the one-acre demonstration garden with close to three hundred varieties from "wide parts of the world" is a mass of colorful blooms and sweet fragrance. Roses in the garden are labeled with introduction or discovery dates. Ancient musk rose and eglantine roses form the beginning of a "Shakespeare corner." The delicate pink blossoms of Cecile Brunner (1894) climb into a backdrop of redwood trees. Maiden's Blush, also called Passionate Nymph's Thigh (1797), entices visitors with the palest of blush pink buds and a sweet fragrance. The public is welcome to walk through the garden and relax on garden benches, seven days a week.

Browns Valley Road leads to the mountain village of Corralitos. People often pack ice chests with the old-fashioned apple-wood smokehouse products available at the Corralitos Market & Sausage Company (831/722-2633), including cheesy Bavarian, Cajun, and fifteen other varieties of sausages, along with smoked salmon, smoked Cornish game hens, beef jerky, and ham. The grocery includes a full-service market. You might be there when a local farmer brings in crates of fresh double-yolk turkey eggs. A picnic spot under the redwoods is located behind the community center, three buildings back on Browns Valley Road.

At the market junction jog right onto Hames Road. In springtime, roll down your windows for the fragrant apple-blossom breezes that surround the

Apple Barn (831/724-8119), one-and-a-half miles past Corralitos at 1765 Hames Road, Aptos. Family owned and operated since 1882, the farm outlet sells eighteen varieties of apples and fresh cider at a large 105-year-old red-wood-planked barn, between August and November. You might be lucky enough to catch the cider mill in operation. The cider is popular; people often call ahead to reserve ten gallons for freezing. Beyond the Apple Barn Hames Road merges briefly with Pleasant Valley Road, then intersects Freedom Boulevard (which continues to Aptos). After you turn onto Freedom Boulevard, an immediate right turn on Day Valley Road leads through softly rounded hills and farms. Merge with Valencia Road; pass the first turn signed "Valencia Road" and continue along until the road just changes names. Valencia Road leads through a thick redwood forest, crosses a bridge, and delivers you to Aptos village.

CHAPTER 9

SANTA CRUZ

THE CITY, THE MOUNTAINS, AND POINTS NORTH

Santa Cruz anchors the northern curve of the Monterey Bay. With a University of California campus and the boardwalk amusement park the city vibrates with energy. Redwood forests line the inland side of this city of many beaches.

GETTING READY

BEST TIMES TO VISIT AND SPECIAL EVENTS

Santa Cruz is beautiful year-round. Summer brings tourists seeking sun and the beach. The weather in spring and fall is just as nice and the crowds are few. Traffic to Santa Cruz is very heavy during weekends in the summer and commute hours year-round. Santa Cruz activities start with waterfront breakfasts and continue into late night.

In January, "Sealabration" (650/879-2025) offers special fundraising tours to off-limits rookery and mating areas at Año Nuevo State Reserve. The birthing of elephant seals begins in December and the excitement continues until March. Make your reservation early for regular weekend tours. The Boardwalk offers crowd pleasing summer weekend concerts. Shakespeare Santa Cruz (831/459-2121) plays in August and in December. On the first Sunday of October, fireworks light up the skies as Santa Cruz celebrates its birthday. In the same month, during Open Studios (831/688-5399) three hundred artists' workplaces are opened for three weekends. In November, Vintners' Passport Weekend (831/479-WINE/9463) mixes wineries, tours, and delectable dining pleasures. Beginning in October and continuing to March, monarch butterflies are thick in Natural Bridges State Park.

WINE TASTING

In the late 1880s vineyards yielded the first wines in the Santa Cruz Mountains. Few of the original wineries, Bargetto being the most famous, survived Prohibition. Forty small wineries, most family-owned, now claim the Santa Cruz Mountain appellation which encompasses the Santa Cruz

Mountain range from Half Moon Bay in the north to Mount Madonna in the south. Many of the wineries' tasting rooms offer the bonus of beautiful forest settings and views. Hand-harvesting is common, and hand-crafting is evident in the area's selection of premium wines. Choosing a designated driver or using a driver service is highly recommended if more than one winery is on your list.

Santa Cruz Mountain Winegrowers (831/479-WINE/9463) sponsors several annual events and publishes a free map to all forty member wineries. In spring, the Santa Cruz Mountains Wine Auction offers the chance to taste all the Santa Cruz Mountain winegrowers at one location. The Vintner's Festival takes place on two weekends in July at wineries and restaurants throughout the area. On selected Saturdays in January, April, July, and November the wineries invite visitors to join the Vintners' Passport Weekend. Passport holders visit wineries not usually open to the public, meet with wine makers, take tours, and receive a special passbook gift.

Grouping wineries by location offers you the opportunity to visit several on a wine tasting tour or as parts of another tour in this book. The listings here include wineries that offer tastings at scheduled hours.

NORTH COAST

BONNY DOON VINEYARDS, 10 Pine Flat Road, Santa Cruz. To reach this "distinctively esoteric" tasting room and winery you can either drive narrow and winding roads through towering redwoods from Highway 9 or drive along the open coast vistas of Highway 1 and then travel three miles inland on gentle curves through redwoods and abandoned orchards. Pierce's disease wiped out the vineyard here in 1995. World-acclaimed winemaker Randall Grahm now selects grapes from a variety of vineyards for more than twenty-two different wines and he also includes French-grown grapes for the new Eurodoon series. Le Cigare Volant and Old Telegram, 100 percent Mourvèdre, are favorites. Even if you don't want to wine taste, you might enjoy the road through the redwoods, a comfortable fire in the redwood room, and a purchase of a Ralph Steadman label hat or sweatshirt. You can also have the virtual experience of visiting this winery by signing up for the Distinctive Esoteric wine network to receive two or three bottles of wine not sold anywhere else. The tasting room is open daily from 11 a.m. to 5 p.m. (831/425-4518, fax 831/425-3856).

SANTA CRUZ

STORRS WINERY, in the Sash Mill, 303 Potrero Street, #35, Santa Cruz. Down the Sash Mill walkway you will find Storrs Winery, the only winery in the Santa Cruz city limits. Winery tours and tastings, highlighted by their award-winning chardonnay, are offered here. You can sample the difference in coopering between domestic and French barrels, and Pamela and Stephen Storrs will share their intimate knowledge of grape growing in Santa Cruz County with you (831/458-5030).

SANTA CRUZ MOUNTAINS

AHLGREN VINEYARD, 20320 Highway 9, Boulder Creek. At this mountain home, vineyard, and winery the weather decides your tasting location. New plantings in the vineyard grow along the hillside. On sunny days you taste on the patio-crushing-slab, under a large umbrella with a spectacular view of the surrounding forest. On rainy days you meet in the cellar, surrounded by winemaking equipment and one hundred fifty barrels of wine. Dexter Ahlgren is the owner and winemaker, and if you come up at the right time during crush, "You can even help us." The handmade approach and low volume of production provides for some of the most renowned cabernet sauvignons and semillons in California. Ahlgren also produces an Italian varietal nebbiolo. This tasting room is open from noon to 4 p.m. on Saturdays (831/338-6071).

BYINGTON WINERY & VINEYARD, 21850 Bear Creek Road, Los Gatos. This grand chateau with a panoramic view is so popular, you need to reserve picnic tables in advance. As you enjoy the ocean view outside a charcoal barbecue is provided for your use. The fireplace and cordial people keep the inside tasting room cozy. Weddings, private parties, and seminars are welcomed. Award-winning chardonnay, cabernet sauvignon, and merlot are poured. Tours are given by appointment. The tasting room is open daily from 11 a.m. to 5 p.m. (408/354-1111).

DAVID BRUCE WINERY, 21439 Bear Creek Road, Los Gatos. The rustic tasting room here overlooks a small vineyard. These partners specialize in chardonnay, zinfandel, and petite syrah, and claim America's most decorated pinot noir. Picnic tables invite you to relax at this idyllic mountain retreat. Tasting daily, noon to 5 p.m. (408/354-4214 or 800/397-9972).

HALLCREST VINEYARDS, 379 Felton Empire Road, Felton. This winery, offering two styles of wine for two different labels, is located in the rolling hills above Felton. The Hallcrest Vineyards estate riesling and cabernet sauvignon sell out early. The Organic Wine Works was the nation's first certified organic wine made without the use of sulfites. Tastes and gold and silver medals prove owner and winemaker John Schumacher's organic wines continue to be leaders in the industry. Award ribbons accent the tasting room, the original redwood laboratory of founder Chafee Hall. On sunny days enjoy the deck and bring a picnic. Mother's Day Bluegrass festival brings upbeat music to enjoy under the shady oaks. The tasting room is open daily from 11 a.m. to 5:30 p.m. Hallcrest Vineyards (831/335-4441); the Organic Wine Works (800/699-9463).

SOQUEL

BARGETTO WINERY, 3535 North Main Street, Soquel. History and warm woods, most notably a carved wood tasting bar, fill this spacious tasting room by Soquel Creek. Third-generation owners are planting the Corralitos hills with grapes indigenous to the Piedmont region of Italy, former home of founders John and Philip Bargetto. Dolcetto and pinot grigio are their Italian varietals. Bargetto is also known for limited-production, barrel-fermented dry gewurztraminer and dessert wines, such as ollaliaberry, from 100 percent pure fruit. The tasting room is open from 9 a.m. to 5 p.m. Monday through Saturday and on Sundays from 11:30 a.m. to 5 p.m. The winery offers art shows and several special events during the year (831/373-4053 or on the web at www.webwinery.com/bargetto).

DEVLIN WINE CELLAR, 3801 Park Avenue, Soquel. From Highway 1, exit on Park Avenue and drive away from the ocean. Follow the signs to the end of Park Avenue. Set in the country, the Devlin estate overlooks redwood forests and the Monterey Bay. The winery excels in its emphasis on premium chardonnays, merlots, and cabernets. Just one and a half miles from the highway, this wonderful ocean view retreat has a lawn area and picnic tables. The tasting room is open from noon to 5 p.m. daily (831/476-7288).

SOQUEL VINEYARDS, 7880 Glen Haven Road, Soquel. At this award-winning boutique winery, instead of separating visitors from winemakes Paul and Peter Bargetto and Jon Morgan with a tasting bar, the emphasis is on bringing the visitors and winemakers together. Wine is tasted under towering redwood trees or, in inclement weather, inside the all-French-oak barrel room. The owners present handmade premium wines. Premium cabernets garner world championship gold medals. The tasting grove and cellar are open on Saturdays from 10:30 a.m. to 3:30 p.m. (831/462-9045).

CLIMATE AND CLOTHING

Santa Cruz is the sunniest city on the bay. Wear fun and casual clothes here. Bring shorts, a hat, a bathing suit, and suntan lotion. Wear comfortable walking shoes for hillside hikes. Fog and winds are common any time of the year. So bring a sweatshirt and jacket. The water is usually cold, so if you plan more of a swim than just a quick dip you will need a wet suit.

TOUR LENGTHS

Plan to spend at least three hours downtown. Adding the boardwalk and beach can fill your whole day. West Cliff Drive takes about an hour to walk and five minutes to drive (not including the time you will want to spend at various stops along it). Try to allocate at least a half-day for the monarch butterflies, tidepools, and lovely beach at Natural Bridges State Park, with time reserved for Long Marine Lab. You can spend all day at the university, especially if special activities are scheduled. Wine tasting is a full-day tour, or pick a few for your itinerary. The drive to Davenport takes about fifteen minutes; to experience a turn-of-the-century farm or enjoy coastal and wooded hikes, stop and experience Wilder Ranch along the way. Elephant seals haul themselves out of the water thirty minutes north of Santa Cruz at Año Nuevo State Reserve. Tours take two and a half hours. You can fill a full week with Santa Cruz tours, shopping, and restaurants.

HIGHLIGHTS FOR KIDS

Santa Cruz has special attractions favored by young fun seekers. The Pacific Edge Indoor Climbing Facility and the Santa Cruz Beach Boardwalk are especially kidworthy. Roaring Camp Railroad offers family train rides and special events, see page 323.

WILDLIFE WISDOM

Seals and sea lions can be seen at many places along the coast, especially along the West Cliff Drive tour. Natural Bridges State Park tidepools are among the best in California. Remember never to turn your back on the ocean. After observing and holding the tidepool creatures, remember to return them to their own pools. Monarch butterflies winter in the eucalyptus groves at Natural Bridges. For information about monarchs see the Pacific Grove chapter, pages 86–87. Schwan Lake, off East Cliff Drive, and Neary Lagoon, a freshwater marsh located near the center of town, attract many birds, such as herons, coots, willets, and mallards. At Waddell Creek Marsh and Bird Sanctuary, gulls, waterfowl, and shorebirds such as willets and sanderlings overwinter on the dunes. Avocets, stilts, herons, and egrets are sighted in the marsh preserve. There is a harbor seal rookery south of the beach. Rockfish, halibut, and salmon frequent the bay. In the mountains you can see deer and squirrels, and raccoons will visit your campsite during the night.

VISITOR INFORMATION

Santa Cruz County Conference and Visitors Council, 701 Front Street (831/425-1234), is very helpful in meeting visitors' needs for information about lodging, restaurants, events, and the general area. The *Good Times* is a free weekly guide to news and entertainment. The *Santa Cruz Sentinel* also provides visitor information about the area. Santa Cruz Walking Tours with Capitola native Ross Gibson (831/423-1932) offer informative introductions to all areas of the county.

PARKING

The beach and boardwalk area gets very congested with cars in the summer. On weekends there is a shuttle bus parking lot at the government center on Ocean Street. Parking at the boardwalk usually costs $5 a day. Downtown, the parking structure at Cedar and Locust charges $.50 an hour. Otherwise, downtown parking is free but is limited to two hours, unless you park farther away on side streets.

ALTERNATE TRANSPORTATION

Santa Cruz Metro Center is located at 920 Pacific Avenue. Buses serve all of Santa Cruz County. Regular fares are $1, and day passes are $3. A free beach bus shuttles between Ocean Street downtown and the beach boardwalk area.

PLACES TO STAY

IN TOWN

BABBLING BROOK INN, 1025 Laurel Street, Santa Cruz. A bed and breakfast inn set under redwoods in town has twelve individually decorated rooms with garden views, private decks, and a lovely old waterwheel. Private baths, fireplaces, jet tubs. 831/427-2437 or 800/866-1131; fax 831/427-2457. AX, MC, V; others also accepted. Two-night minimum for Saturday accommodations. For two from $85 to $150.

CARMELITA GUEST COTTAGES, 431 Main Street. Very clean, very proper, and very friendly. This member of the International Network of Hostels even has an 11 p.m. curfew. Some rooms are reserved for couples and families. The setting is a historic assemblage of whitewashed Victorian cottages. 831/423-8304. No credit cards. For two $30. For families $40. $3 extra charge for nonmembers.

DARLING HOUSE, 314 West Cliff Drive, Santa Cruz. Eight units in an elegant oceanside 1910 mansion have wood-accented interiors with

Chippendale furnishings, Tiffany glass, orchids, and fresh roses. Breakfast included. Private and shaded baths. 831/458-1958. AX, MC, V; others also accepted. For two from $80 to $225.

THE DREAM INN, "On the Beach," 175 West Cliff Drive, Santa Cruz. The Cowell Beach–front hotel has an ocean view for each of the 164 units. Large rooms, decorated with soft pastels. Restaurant, cafe, and lounge on premises. Pool, hot tub, and sauna. In-room coffee and mini-refrigerators. 831/426-4330 or 800/426-0670; fax 831/427-2025. AX, MC, V; others also accepted. For two from $175 to $275.

IN THE MOUNTAINS

BOULDER CREEK LODGE AND CONFERENCE CENTER, 16901 Big Basin Highway, Boulder Creek. Set in the redwoods adjacent to eighteen-hole Boulder Creek Golf Course are forty-three condominiums. All units have fireplace, kitchen, dining room, deck, and daily maid service. Golf, tennis, swimming pools, and restaurant with lounge on premises. 831/338-2111; fax 831/338-7862. AX, MC, V. For two from $96 to $107. Larger units available.

GRIFFINS FERN RIVER RESORT, 5250 Highway 9, Felton. Four acres of redwoods surround these thirteen units. Private river beach. Near Henry Cowell State Park and Roaring Camp Railroad. Some fireplaces, kitchenettes, suites. 831/335-4412. AX, MC, V. For two from $60 to $120.

RESTAURANTS

IN TOWN

ASIAN ROSE, 1547 B Pacific Avenue. Several glass cases display tempting vegetarian Sri Lankan dishes. Orders are taken at the counter for single items or combination platters. Turmeric and cardamom prevail in a variety of selections such as spicy zucchini, garlic lemon mushrooms, and eggplant moja. Casual indoor dining. Courtyard seating is also available. Service is gracious and friendly. Open Monday through Saturday from 11 a.m. to 8:30 p.m. 831/458-3023. No credit cards. Entrees and combination plates from $3.

CASABLANCA RESTAURANT, 101 Main Street. Beautiful bay views and attentive staff enhance the romantic candlelit dining room. Menu selections include grilled salmon with honey mustard glaze, chicken breast with tarragon sauce, and grilled portobello mushroom. Exceptional wine list. 831/426-9063. AX, MC, V; others also accepted. Entrees from $14.95 to $24.

COCONUT GROVE SUN ROOM (at the Santa Cruz Beach Boardwalk). Sunday brunch only is served here. Private parties or public events at other times. The buffet, with a wide selection of items, was recently voted the best in town. Ocean views from the glass-domed sun room. 831/423-2053. AX, MC, V. $14 for adults and $8 for children.

THE CREPE PLACE, 1134 Soquel Avenue, Santa Cruz. Walk through a bar area to a wood-paneled room filled with oak refectory tables. Bob Dylan's music plays in the background; you might feel like the calendar moved back three decades. From spring through autumn, seating in the garden is lovely. Create your own wholesome crepes. Salsa crepes, shrimp creole crepes, dessert crepes, and Tunisian doughnuts, too. Lunch, dinner, and late-night. 831/429-6994. MC, V. Dinner crepes mostly under $10.

CROW'S NEST RESTAURANT (at the Santa Cruz Harbor). Wood-highlighted interior, fresh breezes, and ocean views make a wonderful atmosphere. Deck or indoor dining. Watch the sailboats and small craft while you enjoy fresh seafood, vegetarian, or meat dishes. Lunch, dinner. Upstairs lounge with dancing. 831/476-4560. AX, MC, V; others also accepted. Entrees from $7 to $15.

EL PALOMAR, 1336 Pacific Avenue. This former ballroom of the El Palomar Hotel has cathedral ceilings and one wall is covered with a picturesque mural of a Mexican lake and marketplace. A large marble fireplace adds warmth. Upholstered chairs and comfortable booths. The menu is extensive. Especiales Del Mar include several prawn selections and my favorite, Huachinango Guajillo—fresh charbroiled filet of red snapper lightly basted with a cilantro-garlic butter. An inexpensive burrito bar specializing in huge portions is found in the courtyard. 831/425-7575. AX, MC, V; others also accepted. Entrees from $6 to $15.95.

INDIA JOZE RESTAURANT, 1001 Center Street, Santa Cruz. Watch for this restaurant's events, especially the Squid Festival in August. Voted best in the county for Mediterranean to Middle East, Indian, and Southeast Asian cooking. Art shows by locals give this a living-museum atmosphere. Lunch, dinner. 831/427-3554. MC, V; others also accepted. Lunch, dinner. Entrees from $6 to $13.

O'MEI, 2316 Mission Street. This stellar Pacific Rim restaurant with a strong Szechuan influence, originally located at the university, is now situated in a small shopping center in western Santa Cruz. The food preparation is close to perfection. Dinner begins with a tray of offerings such as sesame-cilantro carrots and drunken mushrooms. Cashew chicken and other old favorites join house specialties such as deep-fried sea bass sautéed with red peppers. Lunch and dinner. Monday through Saturday. 831/425-8458. Reservations suggested on Friday and Saturday. AX, MC, V. Entrees from $7 to $11.

SEABRIGHT BREWERY AND JAVA JUNCTION, 519 Seabright Avenue. The atmosphere is light and bright at both establishments on this beverage corner at the border between Santa Cruz and the unincorporated Seabright. Java Junction offers a juice bar along with coffees. Award-winning beers are brewed at Seabright Brewery. Also enjoy light bistro fare, bagels, and pastries. Lunch, dinner. 831/426-2739. MC, V. Entrees from $6 to $15.

SUNSET DINING ROOM AT CHAMINADE, 1 Chaminade Lane. Panoramic views of the bay enhance casual dining, with a different buffet theme each night, such as Mediterranean or seafood. Breakfast, lunch, and dinner. 831/475-5600. AX, MC, V; others also accepted. Dinner buffets from $16 to $25.

ZOCCOLI'S PASTA HOUSE, 431 Front Street. Lofty beam ceilings, linen tablecloths, and fresh flowers bring elegance to this former Pontiac dealership garage. Try the homemade Genovese pasta and sauces, California seafood ravioli, Gorgonzola lasagna, and southern Italian sauces. Excellent service. Lunch, dinner. 831/423-1717. MC, V. Entrees from $6 to $10.

IN THE MOUNTAINS

SCOPAZZI, 13300 Big Basin Highway, Boulder Creek. Italian-French fare is served outdoors or in a rustic yet semiformal redwood dining room where patrons have gathered since 1912. I admit I crave the Caesar salad. Pastas, veal dishes, and fresh seafood complete the offerings. Lunch, dinner. 831/338-6441. AX, MC, V. Entrees from $11 to $25.

ON THE NORTH COAST

NEW DAVENPORT CASH STORE RESTAURANT (Highway 1 and Davenport Avenue), Davenport. Enjoy soups and hearty California and international dishes in the friendly atmosphere of a large inn. Ocean views. Breakfast, lunch, and dinner. Bed and breakfast available. 831/426-4122. MC, V; others also accepted. Entrees from $8 to $15.

INTRODUCTION TO SANTA CRUZ WITH HISTORICAL HIGHLIGHTS

You can't put Santa Cruz in a capsule. Its spirits are too free, waves too wild, and energy too eclectic. On a walk downtown you'll rub shoulders with those dressed to shock and high-tech highbrows. You can revisit the 1960s and 1970s in the multitude of coffee shops here, where you'll find the most politically correct and artistically knowing conversations around. You can also walk along quiet streets lined with Victorians and spend the day with families at the beach where you can watch timeless waves and their "Surf City" riders.

Ocean Street divides the original section of Branciforte and surrounding residential areas from the government center next to the San Lorenzo River. Across the river you'll find the newly revitalized downtown shopping and business area, which formed the Pacific Garden Mall before the devastating earthquake of 1989. Ocean Street with a turn at Beach Street leads to Santa Cruz Beach Amusement Park, the only one left on the West Coast. You can ride to a superb view at the top of the rollercoaster, a National Landmark, but your adrenalin will probably shut those eyes tight before they can look north to the streets of old Victorians and, farther still, to the University of California at Santa Cruz, set in the northeast section of the city.

If you drive to Santa Cruz on Highway 17, you will pass through the flatlands of Scotts Valley. Up to seven thousand years ago, an immense lake covered this region. The oldest archaeological records here date to ten thousand years when local tribes lived on the abundance of the lakes. Following the drainage of the lake by unknown causes, the people moved toward Santa Cruz with major population centers developing around the San Lorenzo River and Soquel Creek. The windswept waterless highlands of what is now La Selva Beach separated the peoples of this region from the those farther south. In 1769 while searching with Portola, Jose Ortega led a scouting party into this land of several tribes. Although each tribe had a word for the Creator (in Rumsien, *Parataruk*), the people were identified as heathens, baptized, and set up as a labor force for the Santa Cruz mission which was completed in 1794. Their numbers declined so rapidly due to attacks on their safety and health that by 1806 Yokuts from the Central Valley were recruited as a labor force for the mission. The town that prospered in conjunction with the mission was the pueblo of Branciforte, now part of Santa Cruz.

Even before Santa Cruz was officially a city, it was an important port on the Monterey Bay. Potato growers used the first wharf during the "spud rush" of 1852 when potatoes sold for an ounce of gold each. After the spud rush went bust, the lime industry and then lumber mills boomed. While Monterey slumbered as a peaceful village in the late 1880s, Santa Cruz vibrated with industry. Also a center for local ranchos, the city has the longest-operating tannery on the West Coast. Nowadays the city is a resort, residential center for the neighboring high-tech Silicon Valley, and center for higher education as host for the University of California. Although the largest cannery in the city has been converted into the largest indoor recreational climbing facility in the world, light industry continues in the tourists' shadows.

Historian Sandy Lydon likens the spirit of Santa Cruz to a phoenix. Through recurring floods, massive fires, and destructive earthquakes Santa Cruz has risen each time in a somewhat metamorphosized state. A devastating fire in 1894 resulted in a brick-building code for the downtown. Many of these brick structures toppled in the 1906 earthquake and more recently in the 1989 quake. Floods covered the city regularly, most notably by a devastating 1955 flood that resulted in the dredging and present levee design of the lower San Lorenzo River. The 1989 Loma Prieta earthquake devastated the city but has united the community, with the rebuilding of a strong and vital downtown, referred to by Neil Coonerty, Santa Cruz mayor in 1992 and 1993, as a "civic living room." He speaks with warmth and pride of the rebuilt downtown which, a decade ago, consisted mainly of deep holes, trenches, piles of bricks, and tent businesses.

TOURS

The first tour leads through downtown, with a look at buildings and places that were important to the city's past or are important in their own right— just as survivors. Bicycle or walk to fully experience the West Cliff Drive tour that leads past stately Victorians and also to the premier surfing spot for both thrillseekers and thrillwatchers. Dress for tidepools and rock-hiking, since the tour continues to Natural Bridges State Park. The mountain tour is accessed by Highway 9 and leaves the city for ancient redwood forests and small mountain towns. Many of the Santa Cruz County wineries are nestled in the mountains. The north coast tour begins at the western border of Santa Cruz and continues along beaches that, along with spectacular rock formations, hold a recreated Victorian farm park and the old lumber and whaling town of Davenport.

THE DOWNTOWN TOUR

Pacific Avenue is the main street of downtown Santa Cruz. More than two hundred fifty restaurants and retail shops fill the twenty-nine-block business district bordered west to east by Laurel and Water Streets and north to south by Cedar and Front Streets.

Free parking lots are plentiful throughout the area. At most of the lots however, parking is allowed only for two hours, which is the bare minimum you should set aside for the downtown area. If you can walk or take bus connections from your lodging, all the better. On the weekends you can park at the county government center on Ocean Avenue and walk across a footpath and bridge to downtown. You can get directions at a kiosk information booth in the parking lot.

The original downtown once extended no farther than Cooper Street; over the decades it advanced block by block farther south on Pacific Avenue. As a result, one could take a walk southward on Pacific and see the architectural history of Santa Cruz revealed in chronological order. The 1989 earthquake disrupted this "Heritage Walk." Original brick buildings that withstood the 1989 quake, replicated facsimiles of historic structures, new buildings with complementary architecture, and a few vacant excavated lots now fill downtown. The clock tower on Pioneer Plaza is a good place to begin a renewed heritage tour.

Overlooking what was once known as the "American Plaza," the clock tower stands at the northern head of Pacific Avenue, where it intersects Water Street. The tower marks the spot where the downtown was born. In 1848 potato magnate Elihu Anthony built the first building, which was a combination blacksmith shop and general store, as well as the first foundry in California outside of San Francisco.

The clock tower was built into a freestanding tower in 1976 as the city's American Bicentennial project. Look for donors' names in honorary bricks.

Across Water Street from the clock tower, a bronze eagle on a marble pedestal honors World War I veterans and symbolizes the spirit of what was previously known as the Pacific Garden Mall. This downtown area was first saved from blight in the 1960s, through the efforts of photographers Esther and Chuck Abbott. Brick planters and flowering nooks highlighted the outdoor mall.

Don Gardener, a longtime local, reflected about the downtown's present character: "It's newer, cleaner. It seems wider, open, lighter. But in other ways it seems more distant." The sidewalks on the sunny side of the street have been widened. For sidewalk enjoyment, kiosks sell flowers and refreshments such as Mexican ague frescas and Italian calzones.

Zoccoli's Deli, at 1534 Pacific Avenue, is one of the prequake-business survivors. This building, with a 1925 stucco facade, was first built in 1852 as a stagecoach barn.

Across the street at Espresso Royale Cafe, 1545 Pacific Avenue, you can view the unreinforced brick construction that was typical of many prequake buildings. Why this building stayed erect while the neighboring one housing

Bookshop Santa Cruz collapsed is a mystery. The Espresso Royale Cafe is one of some fifteen popular coffeehouses that now fill the cups of what some call the Java Garden Mall. Cafes range from cozy to upbeat, from hippy to upscale. The cafes are a telling sign of the times, as people tend to socialize more in coffeehouses than in bars like the very popular Lulu Carpenters, which used to serve drinks here and was known as the best bar in town.

Cafe Pergolesi, situated in the Victorian-era Dr. Miller's Building on Cedar Street, is a favorite gathering place for students and artists. According to old-timers, you order coffee at what used to be the waiting room of one of the first dentists in Santa Cruz. The Cafe Bene, on the north end of Cedar, is a small, cheery cafe with a scrumptious selection of pastries and coffees. Soft lighting and wooden tables are conducive to conversation at the Java House on Union Street. You'll find people playing board games or conversing after the movies at the Santa Cruz Roasting Company on the southern end of Pacific Avenue. Logos, Gateways, and the Bookshop Santa Cruz have coffee shops or outside bars where you can enjoy your newly acquired book and a favorite cup of coffee.

Nearby the Espresso Royale Cafe, a little walkway called Plaza Lane leads from Pacific Avenue to Cedar Street. One of the businesses along the walkway, Rhythm Fusion (831/423-2048), carries imported and locally crafted percussion instruments including congas, kalimbas, rainsticks, and marimbas.

Behind the Plaza Lane, a courtyard lined with delectable restaurants faces the quake-torn hole that was formerly foundation of Bookshop Santa Cruz. The store operated out of a huge tent for several years following the 1989 quake.

With tens of thousands of books, plush chairs, private alcoves, garden benches, and an adjoining coffee shop, the new Bookshop Santa Cruz, farther south at 1520 Pacific Avenue, now occupies a building with a Saint George Hotel exterior facsimile. A luxury hotel had opened here in 1893 and burned a year later. It was rebuilt and reopened as the Saint George Hotel because Saint George had defeated the fire-breathing dragon, and the owner wanted to emphasize that the hotel was fireproof. It contained the first elevator in town, had a lobby with an Italian mosaic floor, and once housed the offices of the mayor. Its Wisteria Dining Hall had French panel paintings of dancing nymphs in floral bowers and a glass-roofed "tea room" called the Garden Court.

The hotel survived first the 1906 and later the 1989 earthquakes, but the fire dragon prevailed and it burned a year later in 1990. Most of its external features have been incorporated into its new design, and the Garden Court skylight was partially replaced in one of the interior spaces.

The Bookshop Santa Cruz (408/423-0900) is one of several bookstores located downtown. Others feature specialty collections and used-book buyer discounts: Logos, 1117 Pacific Avenue (831/426-2106), features philosophical and used books. Literary Guillotine, 204 Locust (831/457-1195), specializes in rare and out-of-print books. Gateways, 1018 Pacific Avenue (831/429-9600), offers a selection of metaphysical books.

Outside the Bookshop Santa Cruz, flowers usually fill the metal hands of a lively man with a bent saw. Music seems to flow from the metal bow and tapping toe of the likeness of Tom Scribner, to whom this sculpture was dedicated in the late 1970s, before his death in 1982. When Scribner played on the mall, crowds would often gather, just as they do nowadays around exceptionally talented street musicians and performers who frequent Pacific Avenue. However, crowds also move away from some off-key hawkers who also perform on the street. The dilemma of what constitutes art and what constitutes music often is brought to the discussion table at city hall. What constitutes art in downtown Santa Cruz was the basis for an actual civic election that resulted in the selection of the eight sculptures now "living" on Pacific Avenue.

Following the Great Fire of 1894, the rebuilding effort focused on quality architecture inspired by the Renaissance. This effort produced, among others, the 1895 Romanesque Court House, which was known as the Cooper House at the time it was destroyed in the quake of 1989; the 1910 I. D. Building, which is still standing at the north corner of Pacific and Locust Streets; and the 1911 main post office on the upper plaza. The post office's design was modeled after the Foundling Hospital in Florence—the building that began the Italian Renaissance. Across the street from the site of the old Cooper House, at 109 Cooper Street, Annie Glass (831/427-4260) is a beautiful sun filled showroom for a variety of fine handmade glass dinnerware, artisan stemware, fine gifts, and jewelry. The store offers top line and outlet selections of glass designed by local Ann Morhauser, internationally acclaimed artist, whose signature Roman antique dinnerware features textured glass rimmed with a thick band of gold or platinum.

Locust Street offers a snapshot of the many shops and merchants downtown. The spacious Integrand Design (I. D.) Building (831/426-4717) stocks household design items beneath its high, antique tin ceilings. At 103 Locust, Tom Bihn Packs (831/423-5659, www.tombihn.com.) offers about one hundred varieties of made-in the U.S.A. computer packs, day packs, and shoulder bags. Some twenty-five years ago, Tom Bihn designed, sewed, and sold down-filled sleeping bags and jackets while at Aptos Junior High School. Now he has worldwide distribution. Still the individual force in his company, he sews and designs prototype packs here. His bags feature finished seams, durability, and subtle sophistication. People still come inquire here about the Beatles store Imagine that used to be next door but is no longer in business.

A side trip three blocks west on Church Street takes you to the 1937 city hall, a Monterey Colonial–style building designed by C. J. Ryland and built by Hearst Castle's contractor, George Loorz, to duplicate the architecture of a provincial governor's palace from Old California. Here, a Spanish-style garden entreats you to reflect awhile and enjoy year-round fragrances and blooms.

Across the street, the Santa Cruz Civic Auditorium offers concerts. During July the Cabrillo Music Festival offers the public free practice performances before two weeks of memorable concerts. It's a treat to watch a practice, prior to enjoying a concert, with a greater understanding of the hours expended and nature of the preparation.

You can continue on this side tour or come back for dinner at India Joze Restaurant, 1001 Center Street, where the annual Calamari Festival and Fungus Faire are celebrated each year. Actors Theater (831/425-PLAY/7529) is located in the same building and draws large crowds to performances by locals. At receptions and during rehearsal evenings you might meet directors such as Clifford Henderson, who enjoys the opportunity to direct plays featuring strong women's roles for local audiences.

When you continue along Pacific Avenue you have the opportunity to view art and walk through local history at the McPherson Center for Art and History (831/429-1964). The red-brick Octagon Building at the south corner of Pacific Avenue and Cooper Street now houses the museum store (831/454-9986). The Octagon Building was erected in 1882 as the Hall of Records. When the architect asked what sort of design the city wanted, the town fathers handed him a twenty-dollar gold piece featuring a picture of the U.S. Treasury Building. The architect, however, thought that the octagonal shape of the coin was what was wanted (since octagonal construction was experiencing a brief vogue). The building is now a gallery for changing exhibits.

Behind the Octagon Building, the former County Jail building has been converted to the McPherson Center for Art and History. Its history gallery on the second floor has a complete exhibit on Santa Cruz County that will give you a new appreciation for the local places you visit. The museum presents talks, tours, and films. If you visit the rental gallery of fine local art, you can regularly change the artwork in your home or office.

You will find a variety of local artists' work for sale at Artisans (831/423-8183), 1364 Pacific Avenue. Artisans is located along a part of Pacific Avenue that was redeveloped by F. A. Hihn in the 1880s and 1890s. He produced San Francisco Eastlake and Italianate architecture to the point that Santa Cruz was nicknamed "Little San Francisco" in the 1880s.

The building at 1134 Pacific Avenue was once the Bank of Italy. Picnic items and organic goods are now available from the New Leaf market here.

As Rhythm Fusion anchors the music scene on the north end of Pacific Avenue, a local tradition packs in music fans at the southern end. In business for more than thirty years, the Catalyst (831/423-1336) still books top bands in Santa Cruz. Rock and roll, reggae, and occasional country and western music keeps the beat. True to its name, the Catalyst has become the anchor for several music-centered businesses.

You can walk to the Santa Cruz Wharf from the end of Pacific Avenue, but you will be passing empty lots. Extra police patrols have been added to the beach flats area at the time of this writing because of increased need for security.

If the post-quake vision continues, downtown Santa Cruz will extend beyond its present terminus to connect with the wharf and boardwalk area. In the words of Neil Coonerty, "I see Santa Cruz's shops, cafes, bookstores, and neighborhoods close to downtown, keeping it for real. Santa Cruz will continue to evolve."

WEST CLIFF DRIVE TOUR

Architectural treasures, pleasing surf and a surfers' museum, Natural Bridges State Park, and Long Marine Lab are found along the two mile route that begins on West Cliff Drive. An adjoining pathway makes this one of the Central Coast's best city-and-seashore walking tours.

The initial stretch of West Cliff Drive before the lighthouse was once known as Millionaire's Row. Each block was a private estate. The block between Gharkey Street and Santa Cruz Street was owned by Bishop Henry W. Warren, whose estate was called Epworth by the Sea. When he and his wife divided their estate between their children, the daughter received the original house and son William Warren got the horse pasture. On it he constructed the 1905–10 Warren House, designed by William Weeks. In the 1980s the Mission Revival style home was renamed the Darling House and converted to a bed and breakfast.

On the cliff at the end of Pelton Street a statue of a 1930s surfer stands in front of his ten-foot-long surfboard and scans the waves. In 1885 Santa Cruz became the birthplace of mainland surfing. The Hawaiian royal family was visiting Mrs. Lyman Swan, a former chamberlain of the queen, for the summer. Prince David Kwananakoa and his brothers milled the first redwood surfboards and surfed the San Lorenzo river mouth. Supposedly, the fifteen-foot planks weighed one hundred pounds apiece! Their redwood creation and the decline of koa wood generated a fad in Hawaii for redwood surfboards from Santa Cruz.

The original beacon on Lighthouse Point was constructed as a wooden Stickstyle building in 1867. The coast guard installed an automated beacon on a tripod at the point in 1941, and demolished the historic lighthouse in 1948. In the 1960s nationally known photographers Chuck and Esther Abbott lobbied city officials to construct Pacific Garden Mall. In the midst of their triumph, their son was killed in a surfing accident. In memoriam the Abbotts built the Mark Abbott Memorial Lighthouse in 1968.

In the 1980s Lighthouse Museum (831/429-3429) opened as the nation's first surfing museum. Photographs, memorabilia, and a ceiling of surfboards display the prominent Santa Cruz connection in the development of the sport of surfing. When the legislator for a Southern California city introduced a bill to the state legislature in 1993 for the rights to the name "Surf City," there was no contest. The rich heritage of surfing in Santa Cruz convinced lawmakers that no other city could exclusively claim the title Surf City.

The surfer monument stands in front of a stretch of coast called Steamer Lane. Once a busy shipping lane, today it ranks as one of the premier big-wave surfing spots in California. Jack O'Neill invented wet suits in Santa Cruz to block "the cold and ice-cream headaches." The big waves that do roll in here, especially in winter, are for experienced surfers. Waves in the ever-present pile of sea plants you can see from in front of the museum are known as the middle peak and can reach heights of fifteen feet in winter. In the words of local surfer Zach Acker, "You've got to be mentally and physically fit to surf here. When the waves are that big, you run on adrenaline. You just go. Never hesitate. You put your head down and paddle as hard as you can. You feel the wave take you. Aim for the bottom. Make a bottom turn and ride out the wave. When you kick out, you're still shaking 'cause you rode a giant wave. And you go out and do it again."

In summer the waves are from the south, and surfing by the point predominates. You can sometimes see surfers "tube" in the hollow waves of the slot between the cliffs and middle peak. While watching surfers you'll notice those with the shorter boards making quick turns. Watch for the fancy footwork of the smooth-riding longboarders.

Lighthouse Field State Park was originally the large, forested estate of James Duval Phelan and was known as Phelan Park. Phelan's estate was a Bohemian retreat for artists and writers well known in California, such as Jack London, Ambrose Bierce, Gertrude Atherton, Joaquin Miller, and Isadora Duncan.

The historic Eastlake-style mansion and artists' cabins were bulldozed during the planing stage of a 1960s hotel complex of eleven-story Las Vegas–style skyscrapers. This concept drew opposition from a grassroots coalition that wanted to see California's last open headland in a metropolitan area preserved. Citizens voted the complex project down two to one, in favor of making the site a state park.

Small beaches and sheltered coves mark West Cliff Drive. A stretch of cliffs between Lighthouse Beach and Woodrow Street is called Seasculptors because, when the pounding surf hits these crags, the breakers form ephemeral sculptures. The shore along this section has sculpted caves, natural bridges, and figural rock formations. Offshore, sea lions bark commands and share the surfers' spotlight.

NATURAL BRIDGES. At the end of West Cliff Drive you reach Natural Bridges State Park, which can also be reached by car if you exit Highway 1 on Swift Street and follow the signs. There is a state park day-use fee if you bring your vehicle into the park. Plan to spend at least three hours here.

Natural Bridges was named for three natural arches along its seawall. The last of these bridges collapsed after the quake of 1989. This special park has myriad opportunities for the day visitor. Plan to be here for low tide if you want to visit one of the best tidepool areas on the Central Coast. The tidepools are located about a five-minute walk down the beach on a rock ledge. Several rocky outcroppings must be traversed to reach the tidepool area from the beach. Between the beach and tidepools you pass the Secret Lagoon; great blue herons and ducks galore are spotted here.

On calm days this beach is very pleasant, but winds can pick up in the afternoons. You might find yourself heading for the sheltered picnic tables back on the bluffs.

MONARCH BUTTERFLIES. From October through March, in a good year you might see upwards of two hundred thousand monarch butterflies clustering or fluttering in the eucalyptus trees above the beach area. A signed monarch trail begins by the park's small interpretive center. It branches to a self-guided nature trail that ends in a grove of Monterey pines. Docents also lead tours during peak months.

LONG MARINE LABORATORY AND MARINE AQUARIUM. The lab (831/459-2883) is reached by continuing past Natural Bridges State Park to turn right on Swanton Street and left at Delaware Avenue. The University of California, Santa Cruz, which operates it, opens the lab to the public Tuesday through Sunday, 1 to 4 p.m., with ongoing docent tours. This marine research and instructional facility features fascinating tidepool aquariums, touch tanks, the skeleton of an eighty-five-foot blue whale, a dolphinarium, and a glimpse of current research.

THE HIGHWAY 9, INTO THE MOUNTAINS TOUR
Highway 9 leads through redwoods to connect with the mountain towns of

Felton, Ben Lomond, and Boulder Creek. Highway 9 was one of the original stagecoach roads to Santa Cruz. Multilaned Highway 17 now provides the major transit connection and Highway 9 is still the same slow-paced, narrow, winding road.

If you are in downtown Santa Cruz, you can take River Street north until it merges with Highway 9. If you are driving Highway 1, take the Highway 9 exit. South of Felton, Highway 9 winds through dark groves of redwoods and intermittent bright sun. You can also drive Graham Hill Road or Highway 17 to Mount Hermon Road to connect with Highway 9 in Felton. Although these routes appear longer on the map than taking Highway 9 to Felton, their time traveled is less. If you have the time to enjoy a back road through the redwoods, slow down and enjoy all of Highway 9.

Pogonip Park, a relatively new open-space park operated by the city of Santa Cruz, stretches along the lower reaches of Highway 9. Access it by parking at a turnout of Highway 9 just past the railroad tracks. A relatively flat trail leads along four miles of open meadows, redwood groves, oak, and madrone. Incredible ocean views, probably the best, overlook Santa Cruz. A walking-trail map is available at the Santa Cruz City Information Office, 323 Church Street (831/429-3777), Monday to Friday, 9 a.m. to 6 p.m.

Halfway between Santa Cruz and Felton a line of parked cars will lead you to the Garden of Eden, a legendary swimming hole in a bend of the San Lorenzo River. In the late nineteenth century Highway 9 was a toll road. The old Toll House still stands at a bend in the road, just past the Garden of Eden. The Toll House used to be the south entrance to Big Trees Grove.

Other summer swimming holes occur along the length of the San Lorenzo River. After Memorial Day the town of Ben Lomond dams up the river at Ben Lomond Park, and lifeguards are on duty. In Boulder Creek, a popular local swimming hole is found in town at the corner of Middleton and Junction streets; "the dam" is located a half-mile up at Irwin and Middleton.

Heading up 9 you soon approach the southern entrance to Henry Cowell Big Trees State Park. Rising from massive trunks, redwoods grow to be the tallest trees in the world. The Henry Cowell redwoods are some of the few first-growth redwoods preserved in the heavily logged Santa Cruz Mountains and make this park a highly recommended stop on your trip. Some trees here are 285 feet tall. The widest tree has a fifty-two-foot circumference. Henry Cowell Park was preserved as a Victorian showplace of some unusual tree formations that you can still view. Near the ranger kiosk off Highway 9 a type of deciduous redwood, the dawn redwood, has been planted from seeds brought from China, where it was rediscovered in 1944.

Redwoods have the unusual adaptation of being able to sprout new shoots from damaged roots, particularly when they are damaged by fire. Each of these shoots then grows to maturity as an exact clone of the parent tree. The

HIGHWAY 1 NORTH FROM SANTA CRUZ
and
HIGHWAY 9 INTO THE SANTA CRUZ MOUNTAINS

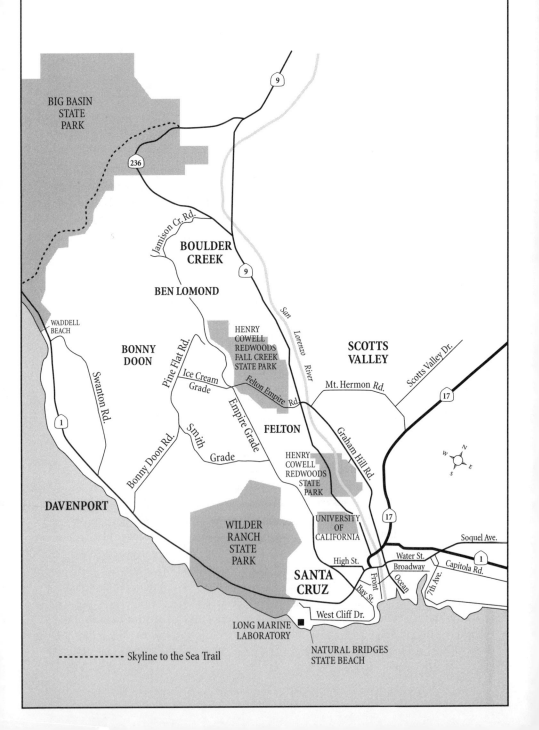

BIG BASIN STATE PARK

236

Jamison Cr. Rd.

BOULDER CREEK

9

BEN LOMOND

WADDELL BEACH

BONNY DOON

HENRY COWELL REDWOODS FALL CREEK STATE PARK

San Lorenzo River

SCOTTS VALLEY

Scotts Valley Dr.

Swanton Rd.

Pine Flat Rd.

Ice Cream Grade

Felton Empire Rd.

Mt. Hermon Rd.

17

1

Bonny Doon Rd.

Smith Grade

Empire Grade

FELTON

Graham Hill Rd.

HENRY COWELL REDWOODS STATE PARK

DAVENPORT

WILDER RANCH STATE PARK

UNIVERSITY OF CALIFORNIA

17

Soquel Ave.

High St.

Water St.

Broadway

Capitola Rd.

1

SANTA CRUZ

Front

Ocean

7th Ave.

Bay St.

West Cliff Dr.

LONG MARINE LABORATORY

NATURAL BRIDGES STATE BEACH

- - - - - - - Skyline to the Sea Trail

Rincon trail, which starts at a parking lot at the southern end of the park, leads to a ring of these cloned trees. When the sun is hidden behind them, rays of light that filter through the shady forest rim them with a luminescence, so it is apropos that this ring of haloed trees is called the Cathedral Redwoods. Throughout redwood country you can see similar rings of young clones growing from a single parent base.

The Redwood Grove is an easy circular hike. If you feel the bark of redwoods you'll see it is soft and fibrous. This fiber is relatively fire-resistant. Trees here have lifespans up to eighteen hundred years. Over their lifetimes these trees have lived through many fires; many have partially burned trunks. Fifty people can fit inside the largest hollow tree in the park. Legend has it that Fremont camped inside this tree on his 1846 expedition. You aren't allowed to sleep in a hollow tree, but you can picnic at grounds overlooking the San Lorenzo River or, if you get your reservations in early enough, you will be able to camp at one of 113 sites.

All aboard! Directly adjacent to Henry Cowell Big Trees is Roaring Camp and Big Trees Narrow Gauge Railroad, on Graham Hill Road (831/335-4400). At this living railroad museum you can ride authentic narrow-gauge locomotives to the top of Bear Mountain, or take the old broad-gauge line through Rincon Gorge for an hour-and-a-quarter trip from Roaring Camp to the Santa Cruz Beach Boardwalk. Along the way conductors comment on the history of railroading along the Central Coast. This train continues as a round trip between the boardwalk and Roaring Camp, allotting time for you to explore before returning. Beach trains are scheduled for two round trips each day. Throughout the year the Roaring Camp schedules events, such as loggers' contests, the Mountain-Men Rendezvous, and Civil War reenactments.

The railroad park was named for the first power sawmill in California. Built near Felton, it was named for the racket it produced. Famous Western writer Bret Harte had a summer home in Santa Cruz in the 1860s and borrowed the mill's name for his first short story, "The Luck of Roaring Camp." Although you can see the railroad's steam billowing and recognize the whistle from Henry Cowell Park, you need to drive Highway 9 to the intersection of Graham Hill Road for access. Travel east on Graham Hill Road. The entrance to Roaring Camp is one-half mile south of the Mount Hermon and Graham Hill roads intersection.

Felton, although it lies at the crossroads between the San Lorenzo Valley to the north and Scott's Valley to the east, has not developed as a tourist center and still has the aura of a logger's town. They still serve logger-size pancakes at Dales Diner, 6560 Highway 9 (831/335-2000). Set in a rambling old house this restaurant consistently wins Best Place for Breakfast contests.

Most people enjoy eating on the porch that encircles the whole house. The Felton Bowl was the greatest draw for crowds before Salawinski Auctions, 6192 Highway 9 (831/335-9000), opened its doors. The antique auctions are favored by collectors and other dealers. Other antique stores are found along Highway 9 through Ben Lomond and Felton. Past Glass and Crafts, 7222 Highway 9, Felton (831/335-7202) specializes in Depression glass, kitchen collectibles, and rhinestone jewelry while the group of cooperatives at Before My Time, 6221 Highway 9, south of Ben Lomond (831/336-9400), offer a gamut of items.

Coming up 9, north from Santa Cruz, if you turn left on Graham Hill Road you will travel a winding sideroad through the redwoods to Fall Creek State Park, Bonny Doon, then descend a grade to Highway 1. (See the Highway 1 North Coast Tour, page 328.) If you turn right on Graham Hill Road you will eventually follow a large bow to Roaring Camp Railway and, continuing, return to Santa Cruz. The Felton Covered Bridge County Park is the first right turn you can make on Graham Hill Road from Felton. There, redwood slats let sunlit reflections of water slip through the cracks. The thirty-five-foot height of the roof, built so high to allow passage of log-filled wagons heading for the mills, makes this the tallest covered bridge in the United States. Nearby, a redwood-sculpted ox strains to pull a giant log. Picnic tables and rest rooms aid mountain travelers.

Farther on this route a side trip up Zayante then Lompico Road will take you to Loch Lomond Reservoir (831/335-7424), open March 1 through September 15, a fishing and boating lake, surrounded by redwoods. In 1992, after being closed to the public through five years of drought, fishing enthusiasts camped overnight at the park entrance to get a spot on opening day at the renewed, rain-swollen lake.

At Loch Lomond, you can rent paddle boats or rowboats for the day and picnic on Cleir Innish Island in the middle of the lake. According to the chief ranger Walt Cacace, while the streams are running, "You can take a boat up the canyon to see Newell Creek and McFarland Creek Falls. The walls are all mossy and the ferns are overgrown. It's like an E ticket ride at Disneyland."

Besides the ones you catch yourself, the freshest trout on the Central Coast are served year-round at the Trout Farm Inn, 7701 East Zayante Road. In season, the trout you enjoy at dinner were caught the same morning. From Memorial Day through Labor Day, kids enjoy using Huck Finn–style bamboo poles with supplied bait to catch trout. Successful anglers pay by the size of the fish; a twelve-inch catch costs $5, plus $1.50 entrance charge, which includes pole and bait. All-day pool swimming also available for hot anglers and day-users (831/335-4317).

Back on Highway 9 you will curve north through the narrow San Lorenzo

Henry Cowell Redwoods

Felton Covered Bridge

Valley. Because of the large number of Scottish settlers, many of the valley's place names are of Scotch origin. North of Felton, you pass through Brackney and Glen Arbor before seeing Highlands Park on the river side. This was a mill site that in 1902 became Highlands Ranch, which included a Scottish-Tudor farmhouse and outbuildings.

If you are traveling with kids Highlands Park might help you out, with a wide expanse of grass, play equipment, nature trails, and a pool with a use fee that opens to the public in summer. Delis and restaurants, antiques and castles, and a motel with an indoor trout stream, are all situated around the town of Ben Lomond.

Around some curves in the road you'll pass Brookdale Lodge (831/338-6433), once a world-famous resort now being lovingly restored. Still existing are the Mermaid Room, which has a window in the wall giving an underwater view of people in the swimming pool, and a brook that flows through the dining room. The Honeymoon Cottage with fireplace and hot tub has been completely restored. Bands play every weekend in the fireside room, where crowds enjoy the large dance floor.

Highway 9 could be called the Dr. Jekyll and Mr. Hyde of roads. In summer, the redwoods dapple or completely carpet the curvy road with shady patterns, the river babbles along, and an occasional deer or squirrel peeps from an opening in the serene forest canopy. In winter storms, shallow-rooted redwoods slide down mud-soaked cliffs, the river roars, and camouflaged creek waterfalls plunge from rocks. Through it all—flood, fire, quake, or hundred-year snowstorm—Highway 9 is Boulder Creek's link to the outside. The redwoods are special, as are the river, wildlife, restaurants, hundred-year-old buildings, shops, artists' studios, creekside cabins, and views, but the real defining core of Boulder Creek is its people, individuals who are survivors and contributors. Probably the most recognized face in town belongs to Craig Barker, whom many consider the community father figure of Boulder Creek. In 1992, he retired after serving for twenty distinguished years as principal first of the town's only kindergarten-through-sixth-grade school and then, during his last two years, of Redwood Elementary (the new school up Highway 9). He helped design Redwood to accommodate the town's one thousand elementary children (up from four hundred when he started in the early sixties). "I have a real warmth for this town. . . . It began when my wife slipped and broke her ankle on the eve of my first teaching assignment. Our kids were five months and two years old at the time and she was in the hospital for a week. The home and school club took care of my kids, cooked, cleaned, you name it . . . that kind of giving stays with you for a long time. . . . A horrendous hundred-year snowstorm closed the schools later that year and roads were so bad, kids and bus drivers were lodged in a combination of each other's homes for up to a week. In 1976 the drought was so bad we couldn't open school on schedule. In 1982 the floods closed the road for over a week. Every time there's trouble the community pulls together. My son Karl's a volunteer fireman in town now, and every time he hears the whistle, he drops what he's doing and he goes."

Boulder Creek was first settled in the mid-1860s. But it was the coming of the railroad that turned it into a boomtown. By 1884 twenty-five lumber mills surrounded the town, making it one of the busiest rail shipping points in California. Today people settle here for many reasons: some to get away from the smog and traffic of Silicon Valley, just over the "hill"; some to live in beauty; some for a back-hills lifestyle that may seem more like the 1890s than the turn of the twenty-first century; and some because it's the last mountain town on the highway. Take a three-block walk down the main street in Boulder Creek and add some side jaunts to visit the bakeries, bookstore, galleries, and other hometown businesses.

With miles of trails and cascading waterfalls, Big Basin Redwoods State Park is a worthwhile camping or day trip. The year 2000 is the one-hundred-year anniversary of Big Basin State Park, California's first state park. The Highway 9 route above Boulder Creek to Big Basin is a narrow, roundabout approach to the park. For a more direct route turn left at the corner past the

Boulder Creek Market, onto Highway 236, and follow it to the park. If you are planning to hike the Big Basin skyline-to-the-sea trail, described next, you might consider taking a Santa Cruz Metropolitan Transit bus (831/425-8600) that drops off hikers at Big Basin and picks them up at Waddell Beach, the end of the trail. If you are driving back to Santa Cruz, Boulder Creek is the turnaround point.

Various trails traverse Big Basin Park. Several begin from the camping sites, which are well spaced under redwoods. The most memorable trail, the eleven mile walk from the skyline to the sea, begins at the center of the park. You will need to first ascend the Opal Creeks Basin trail and cross over several other trails before descending, alongside Kelly Creek, through a shaded, damp section of redwoods. The bright orange banana slug thrives in this cool, moist environment and is often seen along the trails. Four miles from the trailhead you'll hear and then see the cascading waters of Berry Falls. (If you want a shorter hike than the full eleven miles you may want to choose the next waterfall, named Sunset Falls, as your turnaround point, and loop back to where you started.) Next you'll descend through Waddell Valley, a picturesque setting of redwoods, pines, firs, and meadows. When you reach Twin Meadows Camp you'll be a mile and a half from the ocean. Near the end of the trail, land meets water and you'll find a resting place at Waddell Creek Marsh and Bird Sanctuary and Rancho del Oso Visitor Center, see page 332 in the North Coast Tour.

THE NORTH COAST TOUR

North of Santa Cruz ranches, farms, and pristine wilderness stretch to the Santa Cruz County line and into San Mateo County beyond. On the ocean side, shear cliffs and meandering dunes drop to expansive beaches that are swallowed whole by morning and evening mists. White clouds rise from the cement factory in the old whaling and lumber village of Davenport, the last town left along the beach in Santa Cruz County as you head north. Roll down your windows for the strange mix of fresh ocean breezes and pungently sweet Brussels sprout aromas. When the sun shines the beaches along the way glisten and the eery ghost-like mists vanish. Yet Highway 1 remains now a ghost of stretches of California's past.

Four miles north of Santa Cruz an old coastal dairy, Wilder Ranch (831/426-0505), has been preserved as a historic cultural reserve, featuring an 1897 Victorian farmhouse, an 1830s adobe from earlier rancho days, a blacksmith shop, and various farm buildings.

Costumed docents re-create the atmosphere of a working Victorian ranch, with plenty of livestock: goats, cattle, horses, pigs, and chickens. The ranch buildings formed a self-contained community that included its own working blacksmith forge, and innovations abounded. The dairy barn was built over a stream to provide natural air-conditioning. Butter churns were automated by waterwheel power. In the 1890s a waterwheel powered a generator, making the Wilder house the first outside the city limits to have electricity. The house is outfitted with innovative electric gizmos. For example, an electric foot button helped anyone with their arms full unlatch a door. The ranch is open Wednesday through Sunday, 10 a.m. to 5 p.m, with the possibility of winter schedule changes. Demonstrations, such as of Victorian-style baking, pieced-quilt making, and sheep shearing, are presented on Saturdays and Sundays. Docents also lead trail walks; excellent stands of some rare native plants grow at Wilder Beach. Trails traverse the thirty-five-hundred acres that surround the ranch and extend beyond, east of Highway 1. You can take your pick of walks on the beach, on grasslands with ocean-overlook views, and on redwood forest trails. During the summer the trails are open daily from 8 a.m. to sunset.

Two miles north of Wilder Ranch, a red, white, and blue painted mailbox of 1960s vintage marks the entrance to one of several clothing-optional beaches along the coast. Most others are marked by lines of cars parked along fields or bluffs with no one in sight. For a fee, the Red, White, and Blue Beach (831/423-6332) offers day use for families and adults. Volleyball, picnic tables, barbecue areas, rest rooms, and overnight camping facilities are available.

Four miles north of Wilder Ranch and one mile south of Davenport, Bonny Doon County Beach offers picnic facilities for everyone opposite the turnoff to Bonny Doon Road. Known for its geological formations, this sheltered cove includes steep cliffs and natural bridges.

You can take the backroad Bonny Doon route inland through miles of redwoods, by occasional ocean vistas and the exclusive community of Bonny Doon, and on to Felton and Highway 9. This is also the northwest edge of Santa Cruz County wine country. Bonny Doon Vineyard (831/425-4518), located at the Pine Flat Road intersection with Bonny Doon Road, offers tastings and picnic facilities from noon to 5 p.m., Thursdays through Mondays. After passing the close-knit but spread-out community of Bonny Doon you arrive at the intersection of Bonny Doon Road and Empire Grade Road. If you turn left on Empire Grade Road here, you ascend a sinuous back route to Highway 236, which leads to Big Basin Redwoods State Park. Turn right on Felton Empire Grade Road to continue on to Felton, with connections to Highway 9 or Mount Hermon Road. Along the way you pass trailheads for Fall Creek State Park. Limekiln facilities that operated here provided lime for the bricks and cement in the rebuilding of San Francisco after the 1906 earthquake. Trails lead to ruins of the old lime tunnels and brick furnaces. After about an hour's journey from Highway 1 you see the entrance of Hallcrest Vineyards to your right (831/335-4441). The tasting room opens to a redwood deck with views of a half-century-old vineyard and Henry Cowell State Park. The winery also hosts special events featuring a variety of musicians, and you can rent horses here for picnic trail rides.

HIGHWAY 1 NORTH TO DAVENPORT

If you have not detoured into the redwoods and are continuing north on Highway 1 you soon arrive at the town of Davenport, where you may soon be tempted to holler "Thar she blows!" Parks and land trust acquisition of 7,600 acres of old coastal dairies surrounding Davenport makes the town of two hundred and its surroundings a unique treasure on the coast. Loved by artists and second- and third-generation residents, the town is rural; you'll notice the weathered exteriors of some of the homes. The original settlement of Davenport was built around a whaler's cove formed to the north by El Jarro Point and called Davenport Landing. The settlement was named by a Rhode Island sea captain, John P. Davenport, who is credited with establishing the state's first onshore whaling operations.

Besides whaling, the wharf was used for the shipment of lumber by the San Vicente Lumber Company, which logged its purchased rights to the old rancho grant. As the whale populations have somewhat bounced back, Davenport again is a whaler's town, but only for watching. The Davenport cliffs are known as one of the best landside whale watching areas in California.

At 51 Ocean Street you are guaranteed to spot a forty-foot-long sculptured pyracantha whale in front of Bill and Marilyn Fravel's Whale Hedge Studio of fine watercolors (831/458-1959). A garden hose sprays water out its blowhole during the spring Santa Cruz triathalon and to celebrate goals scored by the local soccer team. While at the studio, get a free copy of the Davenport Street Map and Visitors Guide, so you can find your way around. "the Closest Coastal Town to California's Latitudinal Midpoint. . . . The Beautiful California Equator."

Marilyn is a third-generation Davenport resident. The studio carries collector bags of gray-whale migration buttons first developed and distributed by Marilyn's uncle Alvin Gregory in 1971. The thrust of the gray whales' population growth back from near extinction is largely credited to the efforts of schoolchildren, such as their posters, and grassroots movements such as the distribution of these buttons. Marilyn's father, white-haired Mike Demos, who tipped his fighter pilot wings as he buzzed over the town during training days in World War II, now drives a white pickup up and down the coast selling seeds for Brussels sprouts. A favorite coastal crop, Brussels sprouts resemble baby cabbages attached to lances.

Location number 23 on the visitors' map is RMC Cement Plant, described as "the big thing over behind the trees." In 1903, Eastern entrepreneur William Dingee, known as the "Cement King," arrived in Santa Cruz and proposed to build the world's largest cement plant. His plan was rejected by those who wanted to protect tourist and quality-of-life interests. He persevered and moved his dream north. In 1905 he started construction south of Davenport Landing just in time for the great San Francisco earthquake of 1906. A huge demand for Davenport cement and for San Vicente lumber followed the earthquake, and the town of Davenport boomed. Davenport cement was also used in the 1930s to construct the south pier of the Golden Gate Bridge, as well as a fleet of cement boats, such as the one at Seacliff. Dust accompanied the industry. Telephone wires were known to snap from the weight of the dust, and many residents fled south to Santa Cruz. Present-day environmental standards have reduced the dust coatings.

The 1914 Davenport jail was famous for never being used. Prisoners were sent to Santa Cruz instead! Today, the jail is the Davenport Historical Museum (831/429-1964). Call in advance, as it is open by appointment only. Exhibits explore topics such as the local environment and the days of loggers, whalers and rum-runners.

We used to make a yearly trek to Davenport for the annual Big Creek Pottery open house, but a year now seems too long to wait. The pottery is sold along with other wholesome items at the McDougals' New Davenport Cash Store (831/426-4122), which combines a store and restaurant. The store sells collectible imports—toys, clothing, and musical instruments, as well as environmentally friendly posters, puppets, crafts, and, of course, Big Creek Pottery. The New Davenport Bed and Breakfast Inn operates above and adjacent to the store and restaurant.

Artists and craftspeople of exceptional talent seem drawn to Davenport. The Lundberg Studio, 121 Old Coast Road (831/423-2532) displays a selection of blown-glass lampshades, goblets, and paperweights. David Boye Knives Gallery, 111 Marine View Avenue (831/426-6046), opens weekends and selected weekdays. Custom woodwork is sawed at the Davenport Mill, 433 Marine View Avenue (831/425-8577), a veritable museum of antique woodworking tools. If you can haul yourself over to the nearby Aeolus Boat Works (831/423-5681) you might catch owner Bill Grunwald at work hand-crafting a custom-order boat.

Other discoveries in Davenport are close together on Highway 1. Swirls of color lead you into another dimension at Omware Glass Studio, founded by glass artist Joseph Mendelsohn. Now living locally, Loren Gitthens, creator of the *Scream* mask and other Hollywood monster masks, shows his space-creature sculptures here. One of the pleasures of being in this Davenport studio is the opportunity to talk with the representative artists who share the space. You can get sandwiches, homemade cookies, and thick, rich brownies at Whale City Bakery Bar and Grill at the delicatessen to enjoy on the cypress-shaded bluff across the highway. The general Arro's Country Store sells fishing gear. Fishing at this beach is recommended at low tide only. The tides here can catch you unaware. People are frequently stranded on the rocky outcroppings.

Speaking of rocks, the large Greyhound Rock, five miles north of Davenport, has been a popular fishing area for years and is now run by the state as a seventy-acre "Fishing Access." It is named for a rock formation that extends into the ocean, forming a point. There is a paved walkway that leads down to the beach from the parking area. The endless stretch of beaches and the rock formations that meet the sands at Greyhound Rock are well worth every step back up.

This stretch, between Davenport and northern Pescadero, was once known as the Graveyard of Ships, and many points, coves, and rocks were named for the ships that were wrecked here. This was a major shipping route for freighters carrying gold from the 1849 rush, lumber, lime, supplies for the gold camps, and passengers. Pigeon Point was named for the 1853 wreck of the clipper *Carrier Pigeon;* Franklin Point, for the 1865 wreck of the *Sir John Franklin.*

Just north of Greyhound Rock you might see people completing the sky-line-to-the-sea trail. Seventeen-hundred acres of this region known as Rancho del Oso, "Ranch of the Bears" are today a subunit of Big Basin State Park and include the popular skyline-to-the-sea trail. The trail descends 1,200 feet and eleven miles, from park headquarters at Big Basin, or descends thirty miles from Castle Rock State Park at the summit, to the terminus of Waddell Creek at Waddell State Beach. Hikers can catch a Santa Cruz Metro bus back to their cars (see page 341 for more information).

Herons, egrets, and legions of shorebirds welcome the hiker or Highway 1 traveler to Waddell Creek and marsh. The freshwater marsh at the trail's end is a prime stopover for birds on the Pacific flyway. The Theodore J. Hoover Natural Preserve here protects more than two hundred kinds of native and migratory birds. Look for the sign to the Rancho del Oso Visitor Center. A dirt road leads inland to a fireplace-warmed visitor center filled with collections of shells, rocks, bones, preserved animals, and historical relics of the region. In January 1998, Hulda Hoover McLean, daughter of Theodore Hoover and niece of Herbert Hoover, welcomed back a fourteen-foot blue whale rib bone once collected on this beach by her sister Louise, some eighty years before. Resident naturalist Diane West-Bourke leads hikes through the reserve on Sundays at 1 p.m., endeavoring to help people rediscover their "attachment to the land and sea." Rancho del Oso is the northernmost of four natural Monterey Pine forests. Only 15 percent of the trees are expected to survive the present rage of pine pitch canker. There is expected to be a large volunteer effort to plant resistant trees throughout the range of the trees from here to Cambria. The visitor center is open weekends from noon to 4 p.m. and for special events, most notably the annual Valentine's Newt Night when everyone who makes reservations can rock the night away with venerated scientists dressed in newt suits, frog suits, and other amphibian attire.

Beyond Waddell Creek, crumbling cliffs rise like sheer walls near Highway 1. Winter storms used to block wagon travelers along this stretch from their polling places in Santa Cruz County. Now the cliffs form a natural and political separation between Santa Cruz and San Mateo Counties, and between the Central Coast and parts north in California.

Nineteen miles north of Santa Cruz, spine-tingling roars rise from pockets in the dunes. At Año Nuevo State Reserve (650/879-2025, www.anonuevo. org) you are in elephant seal country; see page 43. Sea caves, tidepools, marine terraces, redwood forests, and dune fields are part of the landscape. Elephant seals do not move away from cameras and can move quickly to lunge at someone if they are feeling threatened. Tours come a very close, yet responsible, distance to the animals. During the pupping season, viewing is limited to reserved tours, which take two and a half hours and three miles of walking over sandy, uneven ground. Guided walks over a boardwalk for disabled visitors are available with advance reservation. The first tour is at 8:30 a.m.; the last is at 2:45 p.m. All weekend tours book early. You can try your luck with cancellations. Wear warm layered clothing; the beach area is raw, windy, and cold. "Once you come to this park you fall in love with it," says ranger Kevin Williams. Thousands of gray, brown, and black hulks flip sand; a few bellow belligerently at the day. You are at the westernmost point, as wild as it gets.

WHAT ELSE TO SEE AND DO

SPECIAL SANTA CRUZ ATTRACTIONS

SANTA CRUZ BEACH BOARDWALK (831/423-5590). Whiffs of corn dogs and shrill cries of thrillseekers may be calling you to the Santa Cruz Beach Boardwalk, home to the Big Dipper, a sunny beach with swimming lagoon, and crowds of summer fans. This oceanside park is the only remaining coastal amusement park in California and a registered National Historic Monument.

My favorite time to visit the boardwalk is from October through March. If you are joining the summer crowds, catch the shuttle from the government center on Ocean Street. Parking at the boardwalk is $5 daily. Traffic is slow and hot. Steps lead from the boardwalk to the beach, so dress is as casual as you want. You can put on your better clothes for the Sunday brunch at the Coconut Grove, which also offers special events and weekend concerts.

Fred Swanton brought electricity to Santa Cruz in 1889. In 1903, he laid plans for a Moorish pleasure casino, a tent-city campground, boardwalk attractions, and a river-bend Neptune Park for water carnivals.

The Swanton boardwalk opened in 1904 to great success. Then two years later, after surviving the 1906 earthquake, his casino and a previously built bathhouse burned to the ground. Undaunted, he rebuilt the casino and plunge larger than before, with John Philip Sousa providing music for the opening ceremonies.

Swanton sold the boardwalk in 1915 to the Seaside Company, which has operated it ever since. The brass-ring merry-go-round was created by master designer Adolph Looft, who also designed the Big Dipper Roller Coaster in 1924, with the intent of combining in one ride all the thrill experiences he could think of. The ride after the ascent is powered by the coaster's own momentum.

The old saltwater plunge has today been replaced with a miniature golf attraction and a museum exhibit depicting the history of the boardwalk.

The San Lorenzo River mouth is north of the boardwalk area. In summer the offshore steelheads are frustrated but calm-water swimmers delighted when sand blocks the river's course, which provides a swimming lagoon. The lagoon is sometimes closed to swimming due to high bacteria counts; watch for posted warnings.

Santa Cruz Beach Boardwalk

SANTA CRUZ MUNICIPAL WHARF AND COWELL BEACH (831/429-3628). At the wharf and the beach you can kick back and relax. The half-mile-long wharf is lined with shops, fish markets, and seafood restaurants. Fish off the wharf, spend some time at the "main beach" between the boardwalk and the wharf, get a bite to eat or enjoy a fancy meal, join a charter boat trip with the long-established Stagnaro Family Boat Charters (831/423-1020), or rent your own boat and line at Santa Cruz Boat Rentals (831/423-1739). Parking on the pier is available for seventy-five cents an hour, with twelve-hour meters designated by blue poles. The wharf separates the main beach from the also-public Cowell Beach in front of the Dream Inn. In summer, the Richard Schmit Surf School (831/423-0928) offers the premier surfing lessons on the West Coast. Schmit, one of the world's top big wave riders, has pioneered a unique method in which he rides out to the waves with you, then the two of you catch the waves together. He lifts you up and you are riding on the first day.

KUUMBWA JAZZ CENTER. The nonprofit organization at 320 Cedar Street, Number 2 (831/427-2227), presents jazz concerts by both internationally known and local talent. On weekends an eclectic mix of music adds to the concert series. Theater-style seating and a jazz art gallery add to the concert experience. Seriously, several locals have told me Kuumbwa is the reason they moved to town.

THE LAST SUPPER. The life-size wax figures at 1927 Ocean Street Extension (831/ 426-1601), on the grounds of Santa Cruz Memorial Park, are an interpretation of Leonardo Da Vinci's famous painting.

MISSION SANTA CRUZ. The mission at 196 High Street in Santa Cruz (831/426-5686) was founded in 1791 as the twelfth in California. The original buildings were destroyed in 1857. In 1931 a half-size replica was built about seventy-five yards from the original site, where the Holy Cross Church now stands. Nearby is Casa Adobe, Santa Cruz's oldest building, which is undergoing extensive archaeological research and reconstruction. The mission chapel is open daily, 9 a.m. to 5 p.m.

MYSTERY SPOT. At 465 Mystery Spot Road in Santa Cruz (831/423-8897) balls roll uphill and visitors find themselves leaning at precarious angles in a place where the laws of gravity appear to be reversed. Guides lead thirty-minute free walking tours daily from 9:30 a.m. to 4:30 p.m.

PACIFIC EDGE INDOOR CLIMBING FACILITY. The facility at 105 Bronson Street, Suite 5012 (831/454-9254) is the largest indoor climbing gym in the world. Fifty-foot tall artificial cliffs rise from the floor of a former cannery. Lessons are offered to beginners.

SALZ LEATHERS. On River Street not far inland from its intersection with Highway 1, the old tannery dates back to the 1800s and is still operating. Tours are given (831/423-4470) and fine leather goods can be purchased.

SASH MILL. The diverse businesses found at 303 Potrero Street in buildings that housed the turn-of-the-century Sinkinson Sash Mill are on the other side of the tracks but worth the effort to discover. In summer you can sit on the deck of the Sash Mill Cafe (831/426-7392) and wave to the engineer of the Roaring Camp Suntan Special as the train passes on its way to redwoods or the Boardwalk. Down the Sash Mill walkway you will find Storrs Winery (831/458-5030). The William James Foundation (831/426-2474) is found in the upstairs office space; and visitors can view a small gallery of prison art that is an outgrowth of the foundation's work with artists in prisons. Kayakers at the Sash Mill? For true adventure walk to the back of the mill where Adventure Sports (831/458-3648) uses a large pool to teach kayaking, scuba diving, and other aquatic sports. It also carries the necessary sports equipment and organizes scuba, kayaking, and camping trips. You might end your visit to the Sash Mill with cookies from the retail out of the Pacific Cookie Company (831/429-6905).

SANTA CRUZ CITY MUSEUM. The museum at 1305 East Cliff Drive (831/429-3773) features six rooms of collections and exhibits dedicated to the natural sciences, history, and art of Santa Cruz County. Working exhibits include a beehive and fossil dig. Special tours and lectures, including the popular Spring Garden Tour of Victorian homes, are offered throughout the year. Because Santa Cruz is so rich in natural history and the program is so excellent the museum is planning to expand on a larger lot. The museum is open Tuesday through Saturday, 10 a.m. to 5 p.m., and Sunday, noon to 5 p.m.

UNIVERSITY OF CALIFORNIA AT SANTA CRUZ (UCSC). The campus (831/459-0111) has at present eight colleges with an enrollment of about ten thousand on two thousand acres. Each college is self-contained, with a complex of classrooms and student and faculty lodging. Libraries and laboratories are examples of shared facilities. Each college has its own focus and style. Students have a history of vocal participation in city politics. Several graduates have been elected to the city council. Some permanent residents "off the hill" feel that the transient nature of student voting weakens consistency in local government, while other people enjoy the energy and volunteerism that the students offer to the community.

To reach UCSC, turn inland from Highway 1 (Mission Street) onto Bay Street. Maps and guides are available at an entrance kiosk. The weathered buildings were originally part of the Cowell Ranch. If you visit the campus on a weekday you can hop on and off the campus shuttle bus—the Banana Slug.

When I talked with campus architect Frank Zwark he had just conducted a tour with top Tokyo architects who had traveled to the United States to view the best architecturally designed college campuses—including Harvard, MIT, Stanford, and UCSC. When visitors come to UCSC to see the architecture, Zwark suggests they view Cowell Hall: "For two reasons, one because I graduated from Cowell College, so I have an added pride, and two because it exemplifies what the architecture at UCSC seeks to achieve. It's located at the edge of the forest and fields. You have a sense that the campus and the campus landscape are the same. It's not what you see at UCSC; its what you don't see—the architecture blends with the surrounding landscape. You have views over the fields of the whole city and beyond, to the bay. When the Cowell Foundation donated the college it was with the understanding that this college would be located in a spot where it could see the city and the city see it, to symbolize the interconnectedness of the two." Cowell College is typical of architecture by Wurster, Bernardi, and Emmons, which blends the use of industrial materials with traditional standbys, such as tile roofs and planked timbers.

You are welcome to wander through the campus and in the buildings to appreciate the architecture. While on campus be sure also to visit the science complex, most notably the Earth Science Building completed in 1993 and the Science Library, which was designed by the architectural firm of Esherick, Homsey, Dodge, and Davis—the same architectural firm that designed the Monterey Bay Aquarium. The large bay and corner windows invite the forest inside. The library fits the environment so well that, in the Zwark's words, "It looks like they helicoptered it in among the trees."

The campus forest paths and bookstore areas as well as the coffee shops and restaurants are exploration points for tourists. The campus arboretum, 1156 High Street, (831/427-2998) displays an international selection of plants, especially those of Australia and South America. Open daily. Drought-tolerant plants are sold here Tuesday through Sunday. Docents are usually on hand to answer questions. The UCSC Center for Agroecology (831/459-4140) offers free public tours of its organic gardens. Fresh organic produce and flowers grown on campus are sold to the public every Tuesday and Friday, May through October.

APPENDICES

Resource Guide

EMERGENCY SERVICES

Dial 911 (Police, Fire, Ambulance, Coast Guard)

Monterey County

Community Hospital of the Monterey Peninsula, 831/624-5311.

Salinas

Natividad Medical Center, 831/755-4111.

Doctors on Duty Medical Clinic, 831/372-6700 or 831/649-0770.

TRANSPORTATION

Airports

Monterey Peninsula Airport. On Olmsted Road off Highway 68, four miles from Monterey and 19 miles from Salinas. Served by seven different airlines: Air Alaska, American Eagle, British Airways, Skywest/Delta, Northwest, United, and U.S. Air. Four rental car companies— Avis, Budget, Hertz, and National—are located at the airport.

San Francisco International Airport. Served by all major airlines and regional carriers.

San Jose International Airport. Served by all major airlines and regional carriers.

Ground Transportation

TO AND FROM ALL AIRPORTS

A-1 Chartered Limo and Van Service Inc., 831/899-2707.

ABC Transportation, 3131 Porter Dr., Soquel, 831/464-8893, 800/754-4313.

Adventure Tours Unlimited and Airport Shuttle, 831/375-2409.

American International Transportation Service, 831/649-0240.

Otter-Mobile Tours & Charters, 831/649-4523, http://www.otter-mobile/.com.

Your Maitre d' Limousines, 831/624-1717.

TO SAN FRANCISCO AND SAN JOSE AIRPORTS

Monterey/Salinas Airbus, 800-291-2877, 831/883-2871.

Santa Cruz Airporter, 831/423-1214.

MONTEREY AIRPORT TAXI SERVICE

Joe's Cab/Carmel Taxi/Yellow Cab, 831/626-3333.

HANDICAPPED SERVICE

Lift Line, 236 Santa Cruz Ave., Aptos, 831/688-9663.

LOCAL BUSES

Santa Cruz Metropolitan Transit District, 831/425-8600, http://www.scmtd.com.

Monterey-Salinas Transit, Monterey, 831/899-2555. Salinas, 831/424-7695.

San Luis Obispo County Area Transit (SLOCAT) Buses, 805/541-2277.

RAIL LINE

AMTRAK, 800/872-7245 (USA RAIL).

WEATHER AND ROAD INFORMATION

National Weather Service/Monterey Bay, 831/475-3033.

Weather Information and Surf Report, 831/429-3460. (Service of the Santa Cruz County Beach Lifeguards.) Daily, Memorial Day through Labor Day. Weekends only in spring and fall.

Road Conditions, Caltrans, 800/427-ROAD.

VISITORS CENTERS

Monterey County

Carmel Visitors Center, San Carlos between Fifth and Sixth, P.O. Box 4444, Carmel. 831/624-2522, 800/550-4333.

Monterey County Travel & Tourism Alliance, 137 Crossroads Blvd., Carmel. Open daily, 9:30 a.m. to 5 p.m. 831/626-1424, http://www.GoMonterey.org.

Monterey County Parks Department Tourist Center, 1160 Broadway (in San Lorenzo Park), King City. Open daily, 10:00 a.m. to 4 p.m. 831/385-1484.

Monterey Peninsula Chamber of Commerce and Visitor's and Convention Bureau, 380 Alvarado Street, Monterey. Monday through Friday, 8:30 a.m. to 5 p.m., 831/649-1770.

Monterey Visitors Center, Lake El Estero at Franklin and Camino El Estero, Monterey. Open seven days a week, 9 a.m. to 6 p.m., Monday through Saturday; 9 a.m. to 5 p.m, Sunday.

24-hour phone information service, 831/649-1770.

Santa Cruz County

Santa Cruz County Visitor's Information, Conference, and Visitor's Council. Three locations: 701 Front Street, Santa Cruz, 831/425-1234 or 800/833-3494, http://www.infopoint.com/sc/cvc/. Open seven days a week, all year. Kiosk location in front of county buildings at 701 Ocean St., Santa Cruz open from Memorial Day to Labor Day. Summit Visitor's Center (at the top of Highway 17, by the Summit Inn Garden Restaurant); open seven days a week, all year.

Gilroy

Gilroy Visitor's Bureau, 7780 Monterey Street, Gilroy. 831/842-6436. Information center for areas around Gilroy including Morgan Hill, local wineries, and garlic events. Open daily. In addition, many cities offer visitor's centers in their Chamber of Commerce or business-association offices.

INFORMATION AND ACCOMMODATION RESERVATION SERVICE

Big Sur Reservations, 831/667-2929, http://www.bigsurreservations.com, for Big Sur lodging.

Resort II Me Roomfinders, 800/757-5646, for Monterey Peninsula information.

Time to Coast, 800/555-WAVE (9283), http://www.gocalif.ca.gov, for information and special packages in Monterey and Pacific Grove.

CHAMBERS OF COMMERCE

Monterey County

Big Sur Chamber of Commerce, P.O. Box 87, Big Sur 93920, 831/667-2100.

Carmel Business Association, in the Eastwood Building on San Carlos St. between Fifth and Sixth Ave. or P.O. Box 4444, Carmel 93921, 831/624-2522.

Carmel Valley Chamber of Commerce, 13 West Carmel Valley Rd. or P.O. Box 288, Carmel Valley 93924, 831/659-4000.

Castroville Chamber of Commerce, California Artichoke Advisory Board, P.O. Box 744, Castroville 95012, 831/633-6545.

Del Rey Oaks: contact the Monterey Peninsula Chamber of Commerce.

Gonzales Chamber of Commerce, P.O. Box 216, Gonzales 93926, 831/675-9019.

Greenfield Chamber of Commerce, City Hall, 215 El Camino Real or P.O. Box 333, Greenfield 93927, 831/674-3222.

King City Chamber of Commerce, 203 Broadway, King City 93930, 831/385-3814.

Marina Chamber of Commerce, P.O. Box 425, Marina 93933, 831/384-9155.

Monterey Peninsula Chamber of Commerce, 380 Alvarado Street, Monterey 93940, 831/648-5350 and 648-5360 (Info Center).

Moss Landing Chamber of Commerce, P.O. Box 41, Moss Landing 95039, 831/633-4501.

Pacific Grove Chamber of Commerce, Forest Ave. and Central or P.O. Box 167, Pacific Grove 93950, 831/373-3304.

Salinas Valley Chamber of Commerce, 119 East Alisal or P.O. Box 1170, Salinas 93902, 831/424-7611, http://www.salinaschamber.com.

Seaside–Sand City Chamber of Commerce, 505 Broadway Ave., Seaside 93955, 831/394-6501.

Soledad Mission Chamber of Commerce, City Hall, 248 Main St. or P.O. Box 335, Soledad 93960, 831/678-2278.

Santa Cruz County

Aptos Chamber of Commerce, in Redwood Village, 9099 Soquel Dr., #12, Aptos 95003, 831/688-1467.

Capitola Chamber of Commerce, 621 Capitola Ave., Capitola 95010, 831/475-6522.

Pajaro Valley Chamber of Commerce (Watsonville), P.O. Box 1748, Watsonville 95077, 831/724-3900.

San Lorenzo Chamber of Commerce, serving the cities of Ben Lomond, Felton, and Boulder Creek, P.O. Box 67, Felton 95018. 831/335-2764.

Santa Cruz Area Chamber of Commerce, 1543 Pacific Ave., Santa Cruz 95060. 831/423-1111.

Santa Cruz Downtown Association, 1543 Pacific Ave., Suite 212, Santa Cruz, 95060. 831/429-8433.

Scotts Valley Chamber of Commerce, 4 Camp Evers Lane, Scotts Valley 95066, 831/438-1010.

Cambria and San Simeon

Cambria Chamber of Commerce, 767 Main, Cambria 93428. 805/927-3624.

San Simeon Chamber of Commerce, 9255 Hearst Drive, San Simeon 93452, 805/927-3500.

San Juan Bautista and Gilroy

Gilroy Chamber of Commerce, 7471 Monterey St., Gilroy 95020, 408/842-6437.

San Juan Bautista Chamber of Commerce, 402-A Third St. or P.O. Box 1037, San Juan Bautista 95045, 831/623-2454.

GUIDED TOURS

Ag Venture Tours, Monterey, 831/643-9463.

Otter-Mobile Tours & Charters, 831/649-5423, http://www.otter-mobile/.com.

Robles & Associates, Local history and Steinbeck specialist, P.O. Box 2342, Salinas, 831/751-3666.

Santa Cruz Touring Company, P.O. Box 3508, Santa Cruz, 831/763-0620.

Steinbeck Country Tours, 831/659-0333.

The Tour Center, 131 Center St., Santa Cruz, 831/426-8687.

SPECIALIZED TOURS

Hot Air Balloon Tours

Balloons By-the-Sea, Marina Airport, 831/384-3483.

Kayak Tours: see Water Sports

Walking Tours

Bio-Tours with Todd Bliss, 831/375-5089.

Cannery Row Walking Tours, 831/373-5571.

Monterey State Historic Park Walking Tour, 831/649-7118.

Santa Cruz Touring Company, P.O. Box 3508, Santa Cruz, 831/763-0620.

Santa Cruz Walking Tours with Ross Gibson, 831/423-1932.

The Tour Center, 131 Center St., Santa Cruz, 831/426-8687.

WHALE-WATCHING TOURS, NATURE TOURS, AND FISHING TRIPS

Capitola Boat and Bait, 1400 Wharf Road, Capitola, 831/462-2208. Daily skiff rentals and charter fishing trips.

Chardonnay Sailing Charters, west side of Santa Cruz harbor, FF dock, Santa Cruz, 831/423-1213. Whale watching, sunset, wine tasting, and ecology.

Chris's Fishing Expeditions, 48 Fisherman's Wharf No. 1, Monterey, 831/375-5951. Fishing and whale watching.

Elkhorn Slough Safari/Guided Nature Boat Tour, Moss Landing Harbor, 831/633-5555.

Loch Lomond Recreation Area, 100 Loch Lomond Way, Felton, 831/335-7424. Lake open March 1–September 15. Pedal boats, row boats, and electric motorboat rentals.

Monterey Sport Fishing, 96 Fisherman's Wharf No. 1, Monterey, 831/372-2203. Fishing and whale watching.

Pleasure Point Charters, Gate G-3, Upper Santa Cruz Harbor, Santa Cruz, 831/464-3045, http://www.innaccess.com/PPI/Charters.html.

Randy's Fishing Trips, 66 Fisherman's Wharf No. 1, Monterey, 831/372-7440.

Sam's Fishing Trips, Municipal Wharf No. 1, Monterey, 831/372-0577. Fishing and whale watching.

Santa Cruz Sportfishing, Inc. Upper Santa Cruz Harbor, Dock H, Santa Cruz, 831/426-4690, http://metro.net/~go/Santacrz.html. Fishing and whale watching.

Sea Life Tours, 90 Fisherman's Wharf #1, Monterey, 831/372-7150. Glass-bottom boat tours of Monterey Bay.

Shamrock Charters, 2210 East Cliff Dr., Santa Cruz, 831/476-2648. Fishing, whale watching, and sanctuary tours.

Shearwater Journeys, 831/637-8527. Nature tours and whale watching.

Stagnaro's Fishing Trips, 32 Municipal Wharf, Santa Cruz, 831/427-2334. Fishing, whale watching, and scenic bay tours.

Virg's Landing, William Randolph Hearst State Beach, San Simeon, 805/927-4676.

BREWERIES

Santa Cruz County

Boulder Creek Brewing Company, 13040 Highway 9, Boulder Creek, 831/338-7175 or 338-7882, http://www.hiway9.com/bebrewey.

Santa Cruz Brewing Co. and Front St. Pub, 516 Front St., Santa Cruz, 831/429-8838.

Seabright Brewery, 519 Seabright Ave., #107, Santa Cruz, 831/426-2739.

WINERIES

The wineries offer tours and/or tastings. For complete information about wine tasting on the central coast see the Monterey, Inland Valley, and Santa Cruz chapters. Call in advance for special arrangements, days, and times.

Monterey and Vicinity

A Taste of Monterey, 700 Cannery Row, Monterey 93940, 831/646-5446. Monterey Wine Country visitor's center features Monterey County wines exclusively.

Bargetto Winery, 700 Cannery Row, Monterey 93940, 831/373-4053.

Bernardus, 5 West Carmel Valley Rd., Carmel Valley, 831/659-1900.

Chalone Vineyard, Highway 146, Soledad 93960, 831/678-1717.

Chateau Julien Winery, 8940 Carmel Valley Rd., Carmel Valley 93922, 831/624-2600.

Cloninger Cellars, 1645 River Rd. or P.O. Box 5, Salinas 93902, 831/675-9463.

Galante Vineyards, 1818 Cachuagua Rd., Carmel Valley 93924, 800/GALANTE.

Georis, 4 Pilot Rd., Carmel Valley 93924, 831/659-1050.

Heller Estate Durney Vineyards, 69 West Carmel Valley Rd., Carmel Valley Village 93924, 831/659-6233.

Jekel Vineyards, 40155 Walnut Ave., Greenfield 93927, 831/674-5522.

Joullian Vineyard, P.O. Box 1400, 20300 Cachagua Rd., Carmel Valley 93924, 831/659-2800.

Lockwood Vineyard, Steinbeck Station, P.O. Box 1997, Salinas 93932, 831/753-1424.

The Monterey Vineyard, 850 South Alta St., Gonzales 93926, 831/675-4060.

Paraiso Springs, 38060 Paraiso Springs Rd., Soledad 93960, 831/678-0300.

River Ranch Vineyards, White Oak Grill, 19 E. Carmel Valley Rd., Carmel Valley 93924, 831/659-1525.

Ventana Vineyards, 2999 Monterey/Salinas Highway, Monterey 93940, 831/372-7415.

Santa Cruz and Vicinity

For more information on individual wineries, wine tasting, special events or a winery map, contact Santa Cruz Mountains Winegrowers Association, 7605-A Old Dominion Ct., Aptos 95003, 831/479-WINE, http://www.wines.com/schome.html.

Ahlgren Vineyard, 20320 Highway 9, Boulder Creek 95006, 831/338-6071.

Bargetto Winery, 3535 North Main St., Soquel 95073, 831/475-2258, http://www.bargetto.com.

Bear Creek Vineyard, 21428 Bear Creek Rd., Los Gatos, 95033, 408/395-3718.

Bonny Doon Vineyard, 10 Pine Flat Rd.

or P.O. Box 8376, Santa Cruz 95061, 831/425-4518.

Byington Winery and Vineyard, 21850 Bear Creek Rd., Los Gatos 95033, 408/354-1111, http://www.byington.com.

Crescini Wines, 2621 Old San Jose Rd., Soquel 95073, 831/462-1466.

David Bruce Winery, 21439 Bear Creek Rd., Los Gatos 95033, 408/354-4214.

Devlin Wine Cellars, 3801 Park Ave. or P.O. Box 728, Soquel 95073, 831/476-7288.

Hallcrest Vineyards, 379 Felton Empire Rd., Felton 95018, 831/335-4441.

Nicasio Vineyards, 483 Nicasio Way, Soquel 95073, 831/423-1073.

River Run Vintners, 65 Rogge Lane, Watsonville 95076, 831/726-3112.

Roudon-Smith Vineyards, 2364 Bean Creek Rd., Scotts Valley 95066, 831/438-1244, http://www.Web Winery.com/Roudon-Smith.

Salamandre Cellars, 108 Don Carlos Dr., Aptos 95003, 831/426-0321.

Santa Cruz Mountain Vineyard, 2300 Jarvis Rd., Santa Cruz 95065, 831/426-6209.

Silver Mountain Vineyards, 408/353-2278, P.O. Box 3636, Santa Cruz Mountains 95063 http://www.Web Winery.com/SilverMountain.

Soquel Vineyards, 7880 Glen Haven Rd., Soquel 95073, 831/462-9045.

Storrs Winery, 303 Potrero St., #35, Santa Cruz 95060, 831/458-5030.

Zayante Vineyards, 420 Old Mount Rd., Felton 95018, 831/335-7992.

SHOPPING CENTERS AND DEPARTMENT STORES

Monterey County

American Tin Cannery Outlet Center, 125 Ocean View Boulevard, Pacific Grove, 831/372-1442. Forty factory outlet stores with items ranging from baby clothes to jewelry, from fine china to toys, offer discounts in the spaces of this former cannery.

The Barnyard, 26400 Carmel Rancho Lane, Carmel, 831/624-8886. Beautiful gardens surround barnlike buildings housing a collection of fifty shops including clothing boutiques, a bookstore cafe, art galleries, and restaurants.

Carmel Plaza Associates, Ocean and Junipero, Carmel, 831/624-0137. Fifty stores, including twenty clothing stores, gift shops, a bookstore, and specialty shops, cover a two-block area at the eastern entrance to Carmel.

The Crossroads, 159 Crossroads Boulevard, Carmel, 831/625-4106. Cobblestone walkways lead to eighty specialty stores and restaurants that win many local taste awards. A Safeway and Longs Drugs anchor the collection of shops.

Del Monte Shopping Center, 1410 Del Monte Shopping Center, Monterey, 831/373-2705. Wall murals, gardens, and special events add ambiance to this shopping center with more than one hundred stores in an open mall setting.

Harden Ranch Plaza, 1762B North Main Street, off Highway 101, Salinas, 831/449-6672. This plaza houses thirty-five stores including major department and discount stores.

Northridge Mall, 796 Northridge Mall, off Highway 101, Salinas, 831/449-7226. A hand-carved carousel and more than one hundred forty stores including major department stores, electronics stores, and home furnishing stores line this indoor mall.

Major shopping areas are located in the downtown areas of Carmel, Monterey, Pacific Grove, and Salinas. Cannery Row in Monterey is a shopping mecca with more than one hundred fifty stores and new centers planned. Carmel Valley has shopping at Mid-Valley and Carmel Valley Village. Large discount stores are located in Marina and Sand City. Seaside also offers retail stores. Moss Landing Village includes forty businesses, among them twenty-five antique stores.

Santa Cruz County

Brown Ranch Marketplace, Clares Street, off 41st Avenue, 831/464-3555. The newest shopping center in the Santa Cruz area includes discount gourmet food stores, discount toy stores, and quality clothing stores as well as popular restaurants.

Capitola Mall, 1855 41st Avenue, Capitola, 831/476-9749. More than one hundred fifty stores anchored by major department stores fill this inside mall.

Downtown Santa Cruz includes a major shopping area along Pacific Avenue and adjacent streets. New shopping complexes are centered in Scotts Valley. Shops are also located along Highway 9. Various stores are located in downtown Watsonville, and small shopping centers are located on the outskirts of town.

Cambria and San Simeon

These two enclaves include small town shopping areas as well as a variety of galleries, craft stores, and specialty shops.

Gilroy

The Outlets at Gilroy, 8300 Arroyo Circle, Gilroy, 831/842-3729. More than one hundred factory outlet stores for almost every need cover several acres.

COLLEGES AND UNIVERSITIES

Monterey

California State University Monterey Bay, 100 Campus Center, Seaside, 831/582-3330.

Hartnell Community College, 156 Homestead Avenue, Salinas, 831/755-6721/6700.

Monterey Peninsula College, 980 Fremont Street, Monterey, 831/646-4000.

Monterey Institute of International Studies, 425 Van Buren Street, Monterey, 831/647-4100.

Santa Cruz

Cabrillo College, 6500 Soquel Drive, Aptos, 831/479-6100. A community college.

University of California at Santa Cruz, 1156 High Street, Santa Cruz, 831/459-0111.

MUSEUMS

In addition to these museum listings, many visitor locations such as libraries, missions, wineries, and state parks offer museums on their sites. Monterey and San Juan Bautista State Historic Parks include several museums on their grounds.

Monterey County

Boronda History Center, 333 Boronda Road at Calle de Adobe, Salinas, 831/757-8085.

Center for Photographic Art, in the Sunset Center, San Carlos Street and Ninth Avenue, Carmel, 831/625-5181.

Maritime Museum of Monterey, in the Stanton Center at Custom House Plaza near Fisherman's Wharf, 831/373-2469.

Monterey Peninsula Museum of Art, 559 Pacific Street, Monterey, 831/372-7591. La Mirada addition, 720 Via Mirada, Monterey, 831/372-3689.

Museum of Natural History, 165 Forest Avenue, Pacific Grove, 831/648-3116.

Monterey County Agricultural and Rural Life Museum, 1160 Broadway, in the San Lorenzo Park just outside King City, 831/385-5964.

Tor House and Hawk Tower, 26304 Ocean View Avenue, Carmel, 408/624-1840.

Santa Cruz County

Aptos Museum, 7605 Old Dominion Court, Aptos, 831/688-9514.

Capitola Historical Museum, 410 Capitola Avenue, Capitola, 831/464-0322.

Evergreen Historical Cemetery, Evergreen and Coral Streets, Santa Cruz, 831/429-1964.

Lighthouse Surfing Museum, Mark Abbott Lighthouse, West Cliff Drive, Santa Cruz, 831/429-3429.

Mission Santa Cruz, 126 High Street, Santa Cruz, 831/426-5686.

Museum of Art & History at the McPherson Center, 705 Front Street, Santa Cruz, 831/429-1964.

Ranch Del Oso Nature and History Center, 3600 Highway 1, Davenport, 831/427-2288.

Santa Cruz City Museum of Natural History, 1305 East Cliff Drive, Santa Cruz, 831/429-3773.

Save Our Shores, 2222 East Cliff Drive, #5A, Santa Cruz, 831/462-5660, http://www.human.com/sos/. Marine Sanctuary Center at the Santa Cruz harbor provides an overview and observation areas of the Monterey Bay National Marine Sanctuary.

William Volck Museum, 261 East Beach Street, Watsonville, 831/722-0305.

PERFORMING ARTS

Monterey County

MUSIC AND THEATER FESTIVALS

The following is a list of major annual festivals that have continued for several years.

Carmel Bach Festival, Carmel Sunset Center and the Carmel Mission Basilica, Carmel, 831/624-1521.

Dixieland Monterey, Main Street, downtown Monterey and Fisherman's Wharf, Monterey, 831/649-1770.

Monterey Blues Festival, Monterey Fairgrounds and Exposition Park, 831/649-1770.

Monterey Jazz Festival, Monterey Fairgrounds and Exposition Park, 831/373-3366.

Mozart Monterey, 831/624-8792. Summer concert series at several locations including the Monterey Conference Center.

SYMPHONY ORCHESTRAS

Monterey Bay Symphony, P.O. Box 146, Carmel, 831/372-6276. This symphony offers free outdoor concerts on the lawns of the Naval Postgraduate School on Memorial Day, July Fourth, and Labor Day, as well as an August concert for children at the Del Monte Shopping Center in Monterey.

Monterey County Symphony, P.O. Box 3965, Carmel, 831/624-8511. This symphony offers a series of six concerts from October through May at the Sunset Center in Carmel and at Sherwood Hall in Salinas.

THEATERS

Ongoing musical and performing arts events throughout the year are presented at these locations.

California's First Theatre, Scott and Pacific Streets, Monterey, 831/375-4916.

Carl Cherry Foundation, Guadalupe and Fourth, Carmel, 831/624-7491.

Forest Theater, Mountain View and Santa Rita, Carmel. Indoor and outdoor performances, Children's Experimental Theatre, 831/624-1531.

Golden Bough Theatre, home of the Pacific Repertory Theatre, Monte Verde and Eighth, Carmel, 831/622-0100.

Hidden Valley Music Seminars, Carmel Valley and Ford Roads, Carmel Valley, 831/659-3115.

Monterey Peninsula College Theatre, 980 Fremont Boulevard, Monterey, 831/646-4213.

Sherwood Hall, Salinas Community Center, 940 North Main Street, Salinas, 831/758-7477.

Steinbeck Forum, Monterey Conference Center, 1 Portola Plaza, Monterey, 831/646-3770.

Sunset Center Theater, San Carlos Street between Eighth and Ninth, Carmel, 831/624-3996.

Unicorn Theatre, Hoffman and Lighthouse, Monterey, 831/649-0259.

Western Stage, Hartnell College Performing Arts Center, 156 Homestead Avenue at Alisal Street, Salinas, 831/755-6816.

Wharf Theater, Old Fisherman's Wharf, Monterey, 831/649-2332.

Santa Cruz County

MUSIC AND THEATER FESTIVALS

The following is a list of major annual festivals that have continued for several years.

Cabrillo Music Festival, summer concerts in Santa Cruz and at Mission San Juan Bautista, 831/426-6966.

Dickens Players, Kresge College, University of California at Santa Cruz,

Santa Cruz, 831/459-2103. Year-round performance schedule of high-spirited vignettes culled from the works of Dickens, highlighted by productions in conjunction with summertime Shakespeare Santa Cruz Festival and Dickens Universe conference.

Santa Cruz Baroque Festival, Santa Cruz, 831/476-2313. An annual concert series with a focus on the baroque period and a range of music from medieval through classical and early romantic. Season runs February through May.

Shakespeare Santa Cruz, Performing Arts Complex, University of California at Santa Cruz, Santa Cruz, 831/459-2121. Year-round performance events, highlighted by a six-week summer festival of Shakespeare and contemporary theater masterpieces.

SYMPHONY ORCHESTRA

Santa Cruz County Symphony, 200 Seventh Avenue #225, Santa Cruz, 831/462-0553, tickets 831/429-3444. Year-round concert series featuring symphonic classics and world premieres of contemporary compositions. Performances are held at the Santa Cruz Civic Auditorium and the Mello Center in Watsonville.

THEATERS

The Cultural Council of Santa Cruz County, 831/688-5399, http://www.ccscc.org, offers information about performing arts groups and presentations. Ongoing musical and performing arts events throughout the year take place at the following locations.

Actors' Theatre, 1001 Center Street, Santa Cruz, 831/425-PLAY(7529). A year-round production company offering dramatic and musical performances, as well as a play-reading series held one Wednesday each month. Call for performance and ticket information.

Atelier, 320 Cedar Street, Santa Cruz, 831/429-9005. Performance work and art is designated to supported the showcase project "For the Seventh Generation," a one-mile mural project for ocean protection.

Hallcrest Vineyards, 379 Felton Empire Road, Felton, 831/335-4441.

Henry J. Mello Center for the Performing Arts, E. Beach and Lincoln Streets, Watsonville, 831/763-4047. One of the most exciting new performing arts facilities on the Central Coast.

Kuumbwa Jazz Center, 320-2 Cedar Street, Santa Cruz, 831/427-2227, http://www.jazznet.com/KUUMBWA/. Santa Cruz County's premier jazz venue.

Mountain Community Theater, 1000 Alba Road, Ben Lomond, 831/336-2278. Regular season of live family-oriented theater.

Santa Cruz Civic Auditorium, 307 Church Street, Santa Cruz, 831/429-3444.

UCSC Performing Arts Concert Hall, University of California at Santa Cruz, Santa Cruz, 831/459-2787, http://events.ucsc.edu. Offers a wide range of performing arts events, from classical to ethnic music, from drama to ballet, as well as lectures.

Cambria and San Simeon

Pewter Plough Playhouse, 824 Main Street, Cambria, 805/927-3877.

San Juan Bautista and Gilroy

El Teatro Campesino, 705 Fourth Street, San Juan Bautista, 831/623-2444.

Gavilan College Theatre, 5056 Santa Teresa Boulevard at Mesa Road, Gilroy, 831/848-4860.

BEACHES

The Monterey Bay, from Monterey north to Santa Cruz, has wide expanses of sandy beaches. Along the northern and southern ends of the bay and open ocean there are rockier shores, some of which hide coves, interspersed with wide beaches. Most beaches are known to have rip currents and undertows. Ask rangers and lifeguards about surf conditions. Large, erratic waves are common along many of the beaches. There is camping at some beaches in Santa Cruz County and along Big Sur. The following list includes the major beaches, as there are hundreds of small intimate beaches in this area.

South of Carmel

Andrew Molera State Park Beach. On Highway 1, twenty-one miles south of Carmel. Primitive walk-in meadow campsites (no showers). 4,786 acres of beach and woodland hiking and riding trails. 831/667-2315.

Garrapata State Beach. On Highway 1, 6.7 miles south of Carmel (eighteen miles north of Big Sur). 3,000 acres. Activities include fishing and hiking. 831/667-2315.

Julia Pfeiffer State Beach. From Highway 1, one mile south of Pfeiffer Big Sur State Park, turn right toward the coast on Sycamore Canyon Road. Part of Pfeiffer

Big Sur State Park. Beautiful, windy beach. 831/667-2315.

Limekiln Creek Beach, Limekiln State Park. On Highway 1, fifty-three miles south of Carmel at the Limekiln Creek Campground. Some campsites here are on the sands. In the summer, waders dip their feet in pleasant Limekiln Creek and kayakers glide over the waves in the cove. 831/667-2403.

Monastery Beach. On Highway 1, one mile south of Carmel. Strong undertow; be careful near the water at this beach. Great view of Point Lobos State Reserve and the Carmelite Monastery.

San Simeon State Park and Beach. On Highway 1, five miles south of William Randolph Hearst State Beach. One hundred thirty campsites are located on an inland expanse of grass. Walking trails lead from the campground and from turnoffs along Highway 1 to sandy stretches interspersed with tidepools. Farther south, San Simeon State Beach merges with Leffingwell Landing State Beach and then Moonstone State Beach, where quartz agates can be gathered after large tides. 805/927-2035, For reservations call 800/444-4445.

William Randolph Hearst State Beach. At San Simeon Landing, near the entrance road to William Randolph Hearst Castle. Usually sunny, this sheltered beach, with a fishing pier and a creek for wading, is a Central Coast favorite. San Simeon Landing (805/927-2037), a fishing and whale-watching business, operates near the parking lot. 805/927-4676.

Monterey and Vicinity

Asilomar State Beach and Conference

Center. Along Asilomar Avenue, Pacific Grove. 105 acres. Conference grounds are available. Rocky shoreline surrounds a wide expanse of beach. 831/372-4076.

Carmel River State Beach. From Highway 1 in Carmel, take Ocean Avenue and Scenic Road. 106 acres. Wetlands and sandy beach. Strong undertow.

Lovers Point Beach. Along Ocean View Boulevard, Pacific Grove. A man-made cove with two sheltered beaches, picnic areas, kayak rentals, diving access, and snack vendor.

Marina State Beach. At the foot of Reservation Road in Marina, ten miles north of Monterey. High dunes; windsurfing and sailing areas. Strong rip currents. 831/384-7695.

Monterey State Beach. In Monterey, take Del Monte Avenue and Camino Aguajito. A long stretch of beach; two sections interspersed with city beaches. Continues to wharf area. 831/384-7695.

Mid–Monterey Bay

Moss Landing State Beach. From Highway 1 in Moss Landing take Jetty Road. Within close view of the PG&E plant. Picnic tables along a jetty, a sandy dune beach; en route camping for self-contained vehicles. 831/384-7695.

Salinas River State Beach. From Highway 1, one mile south of Moss Landing, take Potrero Road. Remote sandy beach that stretches south to a National Wetlands. Strong rip currents. 831/384-7695.

Zmudowski State Beach. From Highway 1, one mile north of Moss Landing, take Struve Road. 220 acres. Coastal dunes and sandy beach, primitive parking, chemical toilets. Strong currents. Fishing and bring-your-own horse riding. 831/384-7695.

Santa Cruz and Vicinity

These organizations are primarily responsible for the beaches in the county.

California Department of Parks and Recreation (state parks), 600 Ocean Street, Santa Cruz, 831/429-2850.

Santa Cruz County Parks, Open Space and Cultural Services, Soquel Avenue, Suite 101, Santa Cruz, 831/462-8300.

Santa Cruz Parks and Recreation Department, 323 Church Street, Santa Cruz, 831/429-3777.

Watsonville Parks and Recreation Department, 30 Maple Street, Watsonville, 831/ 728-6081.

Capitola State Beach. Beside Capitola Wharf and the Esplanade. Shops and restaurants border this sunny, popular beach. Volleyball, restrooms, lifeguards.

Cowell Beach and the Main Santa Cruz Beach. Along the Dream Inn and Boardwalk. A sandy stretch of beach; volleyball, surfing, lifeguards. Cowell Beach has gentle waves. In the summer, the mouth of the San Lorenzo River is blocked by sand walls here to create a swimming lagoon.

Davenport Landing. Off Highway 1 some ten miles north of Santa Cruz. No lifeguards or amenities. Whale watching area. Be aware of the tides so as not to get stranded here. Experienced windsurfing area.

East Cliff Coastal Access Points

Greyhound Rock. At Swanton Road and Highway 1, some fifteen miles north of Santa Cruz. A paved walkway leads downhill to a scenic beach and popular fishing access.

Manresa State Beach. From Highway 1 north of Watsonville take Mar Monte from the exit with that name, then San Andreas Road. At La Selva Beach the first parking lot is a day-use area. Manresa Uplands, with sixty-four walk-in tent campsites, is located a half mile north of the day use area. Turn toward the coast on Sand Dollar Drive. Both sections offer wide expanses of beach with breathtaking cliff views, frequent morning fogs.

Moran Lake Beach. Along East Cliff Drive at 26th Avenue in Live Oak, an unincorporated section of Santa Cruz County, just south of the city of Santa Cruz. A cove beach, popular with surfers.

Natural Bridges State Beach. At the end of West Cliff Drive in Santa Cruz. Picnic areas, marshes, hiking trails, a monarch butterfly grove, interpretive center, and rocky tide pools. Docents lead interpretive walks. 831/423-4609.

New Brighton State Beach. Off Park Avenue in Capitola. Camping on wooded bluffs above sandy beach. 831/464-6330.

Pleasure Point. Along East Cliff Drive, near 41st Avenue in Live Oak. Popular with surfers.

Red, White, and Blue Beach. Along Highway 1 (at red, white, and blue mailbox), some six miles north of Santa Cruz. Private Beach. Swimsuit optional;

admission fee. Camping available.
831/423-6332.

Rio Del Mar Beach, Rio Del Mar
Boulevard, Aptos. A very popular wide
strip of sand and a jetty. Restaurant
patios and shops line the adjoining street.
Dogs allowed on beaches. 831/429-2850.

San Lorenzo Point/Castle Beach. Along
East Cliff Drive between the San Lorenzo
River and the Yacht Harbor in Santa
Cruz. Summer lifeguards, rest rooms; less
populated than the main Santa Cruz
beach.

Seacliff State Beach. Off Highway 1 at
the Seacliff exit in Aptos. Popular sandy
beach and fishing pier, home of World
War I cement boat. Picnic areas, hiking
trails, fishing, RV, and trailer camping
only. 831/685-6442.

Sunset State Beach. From Highway 1
north of Watsonville take Mar Monte
from the exit with that name, then San
Andreas Road south about three miles to
a brown sign at Sunset Beach Road,
Watsonville. Large dunes, camping.
831/763-7062.

Twin Lakes Beach. Along East Cliff
Drive, east of the Yacht Harbor. A sunny
crescent beach with fire pits. Rest rooms,
nature walks across the street at Schwann
Lagoon, and bird refuge.

Waddell Creek Beach. On Highway 1
just south of the San Mateo County line.
Sea to Skyline trail from Big Basin Park
connects near the marsh on the inland
side of Highway 1. The marsh is a popular bird refuge, while the offshore waters
are frequented by large-winged, mam-
malian windsurfers.

CAMPING

Big Sur

STATE PARKS

Andrew Molera State Beach, 831/667-
2315. Walk-in, primitive campsites only.

Pfeiffer Big Sur State Park, Big Sur,
831/667-2315.

Julia Pfeiffer Burns State Park, 831/667-
2315. Four walk-in campsites.

LOS PADRES NATIONAL FOREST
CAMPGROUNDS

Five Big Sur Campgrounds and several
back country camps are under this juris-
diction, 831/667-2315. The campgrounds with water are Kirk Creek and
Plaskett. Ponderosa and Nacimiento
campgrounds are set on the eastern side.
The private concession at Bottchers
Camp provides water on request.

Riverside Campgrounds and Cabins, Big
Sur, 831/667-2414.

Ventana Campgrounds, Big Sur,
831/667-2331.

Carmel Valley

PRIVATE PARKS

Carmel by the River RV Park, Schulte
Road, Carmel Valley, 831/624-9329.

Saddle Mountain Recreation Park,
Schulte Road, Carmel Valley, 831/624-
1617.

Ventana Wilderness Ranch, Tassajara
Road, Carmel Valley, 831/625-8664.

MARINA

Marina Dunes RV Park, 3330 Dunes
Drive, Marina, 831/384-6914.

Monterey and Vicinity

Cypress Tree Inn RV Park, 2227 N. Fremont Street, Monterey, 831/372-7586. Motel amenities for RV campers.

Monterey County Park at Laguna Seca Recreation Area, 1025 Monterey Road, Salinas, 831/755-4899.

Veterans Memorial Park (municipal), Jefferson Street and Skyline Drive, Monterey, 831/646-3865.

SOUTHERN MONTEREY COUNTY

Camping is available near King City at San Lorenzo Park and at Lake San Antonio with the Monterey County Parks, 831/755-4899. Camping is also available at Lake Nacimiento 805/238-3256.

Santa Cruz and Vicinity

STATE PARKS

Big Basin State Park, 21600 Big Basin Way, off Highway 9 north of Boulder Creek, 831/338-8860, 800/444-7275 reservations, 800/874-8368 tent cabin reservations. 147 camping sites, 36 tent cabins; nature trails, natural history museum. Hiking trails, redwoods-to-ocean hike with bus transportation available for return.

Castle Rock State Park, 15000 Skyline Blvd., 2.5 miles southeast of Saratoga, Los Gatos, 408/867-2951. Primitive campsites, 2.8 miles from parking lot. 23 backpack sites. More than 3,600 acres with spectacular views, waterfalls, and lush forests.

Forest of Nisene Marks State Park, Aptos Creek Road, Aptos, 831/763-7063. Backcountry camping only. No water available.

Henry Cowell Redwoods State Park, Highway 9, Felton, 831/335-4598, 800/444-7275 reservations. 105 developed campsites; hiking trails and nature walks along the San Lorenzo River. 4,000 acres of redwoods and other plant communities.

Manresa State Beach, the uplands. Sand Dollar Drive. From Highway 1 north of Watsonville take Mar Monte exit, then San Andreas Road. 831/761-1795, 800/444-7275 reservations. 63 walk-in campsites for tent camping only.

New Brighton State Beach, 1500 Park Avenue, Capitola, 831/464-6330, 800/444-7275. 115 campsites on bluffs overlooking beach and meadow. Some sites are scenic, most are crowded, but the location is a favored beach access.

Rancho del Oso State Park, Highway 1, Davenport, 831/425-1218. Six horse camping facilities with beach and trail access.

Seacliff State Beach, 235 Santa Cruz Avenue, Aptos, 831/685-6442, 800/444-7275 reservations. Recreational vehicle camping only. Beach sites. Fishing. Site of the *Palo Alto* cement boat, see page 291. Reservations needed.

Sunset State Beach Park, 201 Sunset Beach Blvd., Watsonville, 831/763-7062, 800/444-7275 reservations. Beautiful beaches and sand dunes. 90 beach sites. No RV hook-ups. Group campsite available.

PRIVATE PARKS

Carbonero Creek Travel Park, 4556 Scotts Valley Drive, Scotts Valley, 831/438-1288, 800/546-1288. Daily, weekly, monthly rates.

Cotillion Gardens RV Park, 300 Old Big Trees Road, Felton, 831/335-7669. RV park located in the redwoods bordering the San Lorenzo River.

K.O.A. Campground, 1186 San Andreas Road, Watsonville, 831/722-0551, 800/562-7701. This family resort is located one mile from beach. Pool, hot tubs, tennis courts, mini golf, and laundry.

Pinto Lake, 757 Green Valley Road, Watsonville, 831/722-8129. 34 developed RV campsites.

Santa Cruz Harbor RV Park, 135 5th Avenue, Santa Cruz, 831/475-6161. Enjoy the beautiful harbor. Seven hookup spaces; five non-hook-ups.

Smithwoods RV Park, Highway 9, Felton, 831/335-4321. Located in the redwoods along the San Lorenzo River.

San Simeon

San Simeon State Park, located on Highway 1 just south of San Simeon, 805/927-2035.

San Juan Bautista

Fremont Peak State Park, at the top of San Juan Canyon Road, 12 miles south of Highway 156, 831/623-4255.

SPORTS AND RECREATION

This section is divided into aviation, land, and water recreation; see page 359.

AVIATION RECREATION

Balloons-by-the-Sea, Marina Airport, Marina, 831/384-3483.

Monterey Bay Aero Sportsplex, Marina Airport, Marina, 831/384-3483.

Soar Hollister, Hollister Municipal Airport, Hollister 888/467-6276 (GO-SOAR N), http://www.soarhollister.com.

Skydiving

Sky Dive Monterey Bay, Marina Airport, 831/384-3483.

LAND SPORTS

Bicycle Rentals

MONTEREY

A Bent 4 Rent Recumbent Bicycles, 637 Ortiz Avenue, Sand City, 831/393-2368 (BENT), http://www.abent4rent.com.

Adventures by the Sea, 299 Cannery Row, Monterey, 831/372-1807.

Bay Bikes, 640 Wave Street, Monterey, 831/646-9090. Also on Lincoln between Fifth and Sixth, Carmel, 831/625-2453 (BIKE).

Monterey Moped Adventures, 1250 Del Monte Avenue, Monterey, 831/373-2696.

SANTA CRUZ

The Bicycle Rental and Tour Center, 131 Center Street, Santa Cruz, 831/426-8687.

Santa Cruz County Cycling Club, 248 N Pacific Avenue, Santa Cruz, 831/423-0829.

CAMBRIA

Coast to Coast Hardware, 1266 Tamson Drive, Cambria 93428, 805/927-9930.

Bowling

MONTEREY COUNTY

Lincoln Lanes, 2161 North Fremont Street, Monterey 831/373-1553.

Valley Center Bowl, 1081 S Main Street, Salinas, 831/422-9031.

SANTA CRUZ COUNTY

Surf Bowl, 115 Cliff Street, Santa Cruz, 831/426-3324. Twenty-six lanes.

Climbing

MONTEREY COUNTY

Sanctuary Rock Gym, 1855-A East Avenue, Sand City 831/899-2595, http://www.rockgym.com.

SANTA CRUZ

Pacific Edge, 104 Bronson Street, #12, Santa Cruz, 831/454-9254. Indoor climbing experiences for all ages and abilities. One of the largest rock gyms in the world.

Golf

MONTEREY COUNTY

Carmel Valley Ranch, One Old Ranch Road, Carmel, 831/625-9500.

Del Monte Golf Course, 1300 Sylvan Road, Monterey, 831/373-2700.

Golf Course at Quail Lodge, 8205 Valley Greens Drive, Carmel, 831/624-2770.

Laguna Seca Golf Club, 10520 York Road, Monterey, 831/373-3701.

The Links at Spanish Bay, Inn at Spanish Bay, 17 Mile Drive, Pebble Beach, 800/654-9300.

Pebble Beach Golf Links, 17 Mile Drive, Pebble Beach, 800/654-9300.

Peter Hay Par Three, 17 Mile Drive, Pebble Beach, 831/624-3811.

Rancho Canada Golf Club, Carmel Valley Road, Carmel, 831/624-0111, www.carmel-golf.com.

Spyglass Golf Course, Spyglass Hill Road and Stevenson Drive, Pebble Beach 800/654-9300.

SANTA CRUZ COUNTY

Boulder Creek Golf and Country Club Golf Shop, 16901 Big Basin Highway, Boulder Creek, 831/338-2111.

De Laveaga Golf Course and Lodge. De Laveaga Park. Golf reservations, 831/423-7212, http://www.birdie. com/delav. A two-story, lighted driving range is also available.

Pajaro Valley Golf Club, 967 Salinas Road, Watsonville, 831/724-3851.

Pasatiempo Golf Club, 555 Highway 17 (take Pasatiempo exit off Highway 17), 831/459-9155, http://www.infopoint. com/sc/sports/pasatiempo.html.

Scotts Valley Course (same as Valley Gardens Golf Course), 263 Mount Hermon Road, Scotts Valley, 831/438-3058.

Seascape Golf Course, 610 Clubhouse Drive, Aptos, 831/688-3213.

Spring Hills Golf Course, 31 Smith Road, Watsonville, 831/724-1404.

CAMBRIA AND SAN SIMEON

Cambria Adult Recreation Golf Association, 805/995-0911.

Horseback Riding and Trail Rides

MONTEREY COUNTY

Barlocker's Rustling Oak Ranch, 25252 Limekiln Road, Salinas, 831/675-9121.

Carmel Valley Ranch Trailrides, 1 Old Ranch Road, Carmel Valley, 831/625-9500, Ext. 306.

The Holman Ranch, Carmel Valley, 831/659-6054.

Molera Trail Rides, Andrew Molera State Park, Highway 1, Big Sur, 831/625-5486.

Monterey Bay Equestrian Center, 19805 Pesante Road, Salinas, 831/663-5712.

Pebble Beach Equestrian Center, Portola Road and Alva Lane, Pebble Beach, 831/624-2756.

Ventana Wilderness Ranch, Tassajara Road, Carmel Valley, 831/625-8664, http://www.nativeguides.com.

SANTA CRUZ COUNTY

Redwood Riding Adventures, 5423 Highway 9, Felton, 831/335-1334.

Motor Sports

MONTEREY COUNTY

Laguna Seca Raceway (SCRAMP), Highway 68, Monterey, 800/327-7322 (SECA).

SANTA CRUZ COUNTY

NASCAR Stock Car Racing/Watsonville Speedway, Santa Cruz County

Fairgrounds, 2601 E. Lake Boulevard, Watsonville, 831/462-6101. NASCAR stock-car races Friday nights at the speedway. Open April–September.

Skating

SANTA CRUZ COUNTY

Go Skate, 601 Beach Street, Santa Cruz, 831/425-8578. Rentals, sales, service, and repair of skateboards, in-line skates, surfboards, boogie boards, wetsuits, and snowboards.

Sports Center

Monterey Sports Center, 401 East Franklin, Monterey, 831/646-3700.

Tennis

MONTEREY

Carmel Valley Racquet and Health Club, 27300 Rancho San Carols Road, Carmel Valley, 831/624-2737.

John Gardiner's Tennis Ranch, 114 Carmel Valley Road, P.O. Box 228 Carmel Valley 93924, 831/659-2207. Elegant accommodations for weekend or weekly emersion tennis.

King City Park Tennis Courts, South Vanderhurst Avenue (next to golf course). 401 Division Street. King City, 831/385-3575.

Hyatt Hotels, 1 Old Golf Course Road, Monterey, 831/372-1234.

City of Pacific Grove Tennis Courts, 515 Junipero Avenue, Pacific Grove, 831/648-3129.

Sherwood Tennis Center, 930 North Main Street, Salinas, 831/758-7318.

SANTA CRUZ

Aptos High, 7301 Freedom Boulevard, Aptos, 831/688-6565.

Cabrillo College, 6500 Soquel Drive, Aptos, 831/479-6266. Nine unlit courts open to the public.

Cabrillo Courthouse, 6200 Soquel Drive, Aptos, 831/475-5979.

Harbor High, 300 LaFonda, Santa Cruz. Near Soquel and Capitola Roads.

Jade Street Park, 4400 Jade Street, Capitola, 831/475-5935. Four courts available. Lights come on at sunset.

Mike Fox Tennis Park & Roller Hockey Court, Riverside Avenue at San Lorenzo Boulevard, Santa Cruz, 831/429-3663.

Neary Lagoon Park, Bay and California Streets.

Santa Cruz High School, 415 Walnut Avenue, Santa Cruz.

CAMBRIA AND SAN SIMEON

Cambria Tennis Club, Cambria, 805/927-1041.

WATER AND BEACH SPORTS

Boating and Sailing

MONTEREY COUNTY

Carrera Sailing, 66 Fisherman's Wharf, Monterey, 831/375-0648.

El Estero Boating, Lake El Estero, Monterey, 831/375-1484. Pedal boats for paddling around lake.

Lake San Antonio Resort, South Shore, 831/472-2313. Jet skis, fishing boats, and pontoon boats.

Otter Cove Ocean Sports, 32 Cannery Row, Monterey, 831/647-0147. Zodiac and kayak rental.

SANTA CRUZ COUNTY

Capitola Bay Marina, 1400 Wharf Road, Capitola, 831/462-2208. Public mooring rentals daily, weekly, monthly, and seasonally.

Chardonnay Sailing Charters, Santa Cruz, 831/423-1213. Monterey, 831/373-8664. Sail Monterey Bay aboard a 70-foot luxury sailing yacht.

Harbor Water Taxi, 135 5th Avenue, Santa Cruz, 831/475-6161. Free inner-harbor taxi stops at four locations from May to September.

Loch Lomond Reservoir for boating, fishing, exploring, Felton, 831/335-7424.

O'Neill Yachts/Yacht Charters, 222 East Cliff Drive, Santa Cruz, 831/476-5200, http://www.oneillnet.com. 65-foot catamaran sails on summer afternoons.

Pinto Lake Park for boating, Watsonville 831/722-8129.

UCSC Office of P.E., Recreation & Sports, Santa Cruz Harbor, Santa Cruz, 831/459-2531. http://www.ucsc.edu/ucsc/opers/index.html. During the summer, sailing and boating courses are open to the public.

Diving

MONTEREY

Aquarius Dive Shop, 2240 Del Monte Boulevard, Monterey, 831/375-1933.

Bamboo Reef, 614 Lighthouse Avenue, Monterey, 831/372-1685.

Extreme Adventures, Campbell, 408/871-3111, http://www.extreme-adventures.com.

Monterey Bay Dive Center,225 Cannery Row, Cannery Row, Monterey 831/656-0454.

Adventure Sports, 303 Potrero Street, #15, Santa Cruz, 831/458-3648, http//www.asudoit.com.

Aqua Safaris Scuba Center, 231 Evergreen Street, Santa Cruz, 831/426-8084.

Kayaking

Adventures by the Sea, 299 Cannery Row, Monterey, as well as Lovers Point, Pacific Grove, 831/372-1807.

Adventure Sports, 303 Potrero Street, #15, Santa Cruz, 831/458-3648, http://www.asudoit.com.

Kayak Connection, 413 Lake Avenue, Santa Cruz, 831/479-1121. Moss Landing, 831/724-5692.

Monterey Bay Kayaks, 693 Del Monte Avenue, Monterey, 831/373-5357 (KELP).

Otter Cove Ocean Sports, 32 Cannery Row, Monterey, 831/647-0147.

Venture Quest Kayaking, 125 Beach Street, Santa Cruz, 831/427-2267.

Parasailing and Hang Gliding

Pacific Parasail, Santa Cruz, 58 Municipal Wharf, Santa Cruz, 831/423-3545.

Western Hang Gliders, Reservation Road and Highway 1, Marina, 831/384-2622.

Surfing and Windsurfing

MONTEREY

Adventures by the Sea, 299 Cannery Row, Monterey, 831/372-1807.

On the Beach Surf Shop, 693 Lighthouse Avenue, Monterey, 831/646-9283 (WAVE). Also at Ocean and Mission, Carmel, 831/624-7282.

Sunshine Freestyle, 443 Lighthouse Avenue, Monterey, 831/375-5015.

SANTA CRUZ

City of Santa Cruz Beach Rentals, Main Beach, Santa Cruz, 831/429-3110.

Club Ed Surf Schools, Rentals and Surf Camps, located on Cowell Beach in front of Dream Inn Santa Cruz, 831/459-9283. Lessons, rentals, and surf camps available.

Cowell's Surf Shop, 109 Beach Street, Santa Cruz, 831/427-2355. Beach rentals and surf lessons.

O'Neill's, 1149 41st Avenue, Santa Cruz, 831/475-4151.

CALENDAR OF EVENTS

Exact dates may change. Check local papers and visitor's guides for a complete event listing. Call the appropriate Chambers of Commerce for additional information.

JANUARY

Gray whales migrate to lagoons in Baja. You can watch them from overlooks along the coast and on whale-watching expeditions. Good viewing days also in December and February. Elephant seals birth and breed at Año Nuevo State Reserve, along the Big Sur Coast, and north of San Simeon.

Guided Elephant Seal Walks at Año Nuevo State Reserve, 800/444-7275. Reservations are usually necessary to join guided naturalist-led walks of elephant seal birthing, breeding, and nursery areas. Tours are ongoing until March 31.

Usually in the First Two Weeks:

January 1. Rio Resolution Run, Carmel, 831/644-2427. A cross-country run on trails, beaches, and roads surrounding Carmel. Proceeds benefit the Family Resource Center.

Fungus Festival and Fungus Fair, presented by the Santa Cruz Natural History Museum, 831/429-3773, and Santa Cruz India Joze Restaurant, 831/427-3554. Features mushroom identification and tastings, too.

Often Later in the Month:

AT&T Pro-Am Golf Tournament, Pebble Beach, 800/541-9091. First week in February, sometimes in last week of January. Well-known professionals are paired with celebrities and amateurs for this crowd-pleasing event.

Monterey SwingFest, Monterey, 805/937-1574. Four days of dancing and dance workshops.

Sealabration, Año Nuevo State Reserve, 800/444-7275. Docent naturalists lead groups to off-the-regular-tour locations to view elephant seals.

Whalefest, Monterey, 831/644-7588. Art exhibits, special whale-watching outings, family whale celebration activities.

FEBRUARY

Millions of ladybugs are hatching in the sun-speckled valleys of the Santa Lucia Mountains. Canadian geese trim the greens at Pebble Beach.

Usually in the First Two Weeks:

Chocolate Extravaganza, Monterey Museum of Art, 831/372-5477. Mounds of chocolate and caloric relief dancing for Valentine's Day.

Masters of Food and Wine, Carmel Highlands Inn, 831/624-3801. International star chefs and vintners present cooking classes and tastings.

Migration Festival, Natural Bridges State Beach Park, Santa Cruz, 831/423-4609. Information booths, slide shows, and talks about the migrating animals of the Central Coast.

Often Later in the Month:

February 27. Annual John Steinbeck Birthday Party, Monterey, 831/372-8512. Music, play excerpts, readings, and impersonations celebrate John Steinbeck's birthday.

Clam Chowder Cook-off and Great Chowder Chase, Santa Cruz, 831/429-3477. Taste the best chowders on the Central Coast on Saturday. On Sunday, run off all the calories you ate the day before.

MARCH

Wildflowers begin painting hillsides. Peak viewing may be next month or in May. Songbirds fill gardens and glens with their calls and melodies.

Usually in the First Two Weeks:

Beans and Jeans Jamboree, Cambria, 805/927-3624. Chili cook-off and square dancing event.

Dixieland Monterey, Monterey, 831/443-5260. A selection of the nation's finest Dixieland bands parade and play in cabaret locations throughout downtown Monterey and Fisherman's Wharf.

Colton Hall Birthday, Monterey, 831/646-5640. Celebrate Monterey's birthday with historic plays, free birthday cake, and punch.

Often Later in the Month:

California Chocolate Abalone Dive, Monterey, 831/375-1933. Divers search for chocolate abalone in the bay to benefit the Pacific Grove Marine Rescue Unit and Divers Alert Network.

Sea Otter Classic, Laguna Seca, 650/306-1414, http://www.seaotter.org. Complete sports festival and exposition featuring mountain bike racing, BMX racing, and in-line skating.

APRIL

Harbor seals give birth and snowy plovers nest on selected beaches.

Usually in the First Two Weeks:

Garden Affair, the Barnyard, Carmel. Visits with gardening and floral experts, garden displays, hors d'oeuvres, and music. 831/624-8886.

Good Old Days Celebration, Pacific Grove, 831/373-3304. A celebration of a bygone era. Events include a parade, arts and crafts fair, and annual quilt show.

Monterey Wine Festival, Monterey, 831/656-9463 (WINE). The festival features tastings of more than eight hundred wines from two hundred wineries, gourmet luncheons, and seminars.

Often Later in the Month:

AMA National Superbike Championship, Laguna Seca, 800/327-7322 (SECA). This race series showcases the top American motorcycle riders in several riding classes.

Rhododendron Show, Antonelli Brothers Begonia Garden, Capitola, 831/475-5222. Hundreds of trusses of rhododendrons in colorful display.

Annual Adobe Tour, Monterey, 831/372-2608. Local guides dressed in period costume escort you through Monterey history in twenty-five adobes and gardens.

Big Sur Jazzfest, Big Sur, 831/667-2654. Weekend of top jazz performances in various Big Sur venues.

Big Sur International Marathon, Big Sur, 831/625-6226. One of the most beautiful and challenging foot races along the coastline of the Pacific Ocean. Walking and shorter running courses are also offered.

Book Festival, Monterey County Fairgrounds, 831/375-1855. Meet Pulitzer Prize– and Newberry Award–winning authors, and other fine Central Coast authors. Music, poetry reading, storytelling, and the chance to browse the large selection of new, used, and anti-quarian books.

British Car Meet, Pacific Grove, 831/373-3304. Car tour and viewing of fine British vehicles.

Springtime at La Mirada, Monterey, 831/372-3689. Afternoon tea and tour of the historic home and gardens of La Mirada as well as other beautiful gardens of the Monterey Peninsula.

Wildflower Festival and Triathalons, Lake San Antonio, 831/755-4899. A weekend festival combining the county's most extensive wildflower exhibits with entertainment, an arts and crafts fair, and two world-class triathalons.

Wildflower Show, Pacific Grove Museum of Natural History, 831/648-3116. View 600 Central California species of wild-flowers—all in one place.

Winegrowers Spring Festival, Casa de Fruta, 1003 Pacheco Pass Highway, 800/548-3813. Award wining wines, dinner, and music.

MAY

Pelicans fly in formation and dive-bomb submerged fish from above. They are commonly viewed through early autumn.

Ongoing through October. Wednesday Night Sailboat Races at the Santa Cruz harbor, 831/425-0690. Colorful boats depart Santa Cruz harbor around 6 p.m. and return by 8 p.m.

Usually in the First Two Weeks:

Bluegrass Art and Wine Festival, Hallcrest Vineyards, Felton, 831/335-4441. On Mother's Day, bluegrass music fills the air at the beautiful Hallcrest Vineyards.

Del Monte Kennel Club Dog Show, Lodge at Pebble Beach, 831/624-3811. Very prestigious show of canine friends.

Living History Day, Wilder Ranch State Park, Santa Cruz, 831/426-0505. Turn-of-the-century ranch life is re-created. Demonstrations include steam-driven tractors, horse-drawn equipment, soap making, blacksmithing, and quilting.

Robinson Jeffers Tor House Garden Party, 831/624-1813, Carmel. An inti-mate party in the English-style garden, hawk tower, and residence of poet Robinson Jeffers.

Spring Fair, Downtown, Santa Cruz, 831/425-1234. Arts and crafts booths and entertainment bring a festive atmos-phere to the park.

Monster Truck Race/Tractor Pull, Salinas, 831/757-2951. Major tractors and monster trucks go head to head.

Often Later in the Month:

Cooper-Molera Garden Day and Plant Sale, Monterey, 831/649-7118. Enjoy the beauty of plants typical before 1865. Seeds and plants from the garden are on sale.

Salinas Valley Fair, King City, 831/424-7611. A celebration of local farming and agriculture. Carnival, live entertainment, 4-H exhibits, and more.

Strawberry Dessert Festival, Downtown, Watsonville, 831/724-3954. Strawberry dessert contests, entertainment, and crafts.

International Extravaganza, Seaside, 831/394-6501. More than fifteen cultures are represented in dance, song and food. Headline blues performers and craft booths.

Memorial Day Weekend:

Blues Festival, Aptos Village Park, Aptos. Two days of premier blues performances, staged in a grass amphitheater. All ages enjoy this musical event.

Boulder Creek Art and Wine Festival, Boulder Creek, 831/335-2764. Fourteen area wineries share tastings amid food and crafts booths. Designated drivers recommended.

The Great Monterey Squid Festival, Monterey, 831/649-6544. A one-of-a kind event featuring squid every which way. Entertainment, arts and crafts, cooking demonstrations, and more.

West Coast Antique Fly-In Air Show, Watsonville Municipal Airport, Watsonville, 831/496-9559.

Felton Remembers Parade and Fair, downtown Felton, 831/335-2764.

Annual Civil War Memorial, Roaring Camp, Felton, 831/335-4484. Costumed Union and Confederate soldiers re-enact the parades and conflict of the Civil War.

JUNE

Sharks swim up Elkhorn Slough to pup. Does emerge with young fawns in Pacific Grove, Pebble Beach, and mountain areas. Strawberries and raspberries are ripening on rural vines.

Usually in the First Two Weeks:

Burrito Bash, Ramsey Park, Watsonville, 831/728-6083. Cast your vote for the best burrito and enjoy a fiesta of music, art, family fun, and food.

Northern California Volley Tournament, main beach, Santa Cruz, 831/429-3665.

Monterey's Birthday Party, Monterey, 831/655-8070. A celebration of Monterey's birthday sponsored by the Old Monterey Business Association. A parade and a four-block fair along historic Alvarado Street featuring more than a hundred booths.

Redwood Mountain Faire, Highlands Park, Ben Lomond, 831/336-8551. A gathering of local vintners, arts and crafts booths, and entertainment—all to benefit nonprofit organizations.

Vintner's Festival, Santa Cruz County, 831/479-9463. Annual festival at local wineries and restaurants.

Often Later in the Month:

Monterey Bay Theaterfest, Monterey, 831/646-3866. An arts and crafts fair begins a summer series of free performances that feature fairy tale theater, comic opera, Shakespeare, musicians, and arts and crafts.

California Golf Association Amateur Championship, Pebble Beach and Monterey, 831/625-4653. The top amateurs in California play Pebble Beach Golf Links.

Santa Cruz Japanese Cultural Fair, Mission Park Plaza, Santa Cruz, 831/429-3778. Martial arts exhibitions, rice pounding, flower arranging, the tea ceremony, and Japanese dancing are featured.

Monterey Bay Blues Festival, Monterey, 831/649-6544. This festival celebrates the best of blues music amid the lawn and oak trees of the Monterey Fairgrounds.

Surf City Classic: Woodies on the Wharf, 831/429-3477. Cars from the '50s and '60s along with surf, music, and food enliven the Santa Cruz Wharf.

Father's Day Weekend:

Father's Day Special Rail Enthusiast Day, Roaring Camp, Felton, 831/335-4484. Free engineer hat for Dad, BBQ, model railroad displays, and railroad movies.

Pops for Pops Annual Free Concert, Henry Cowell State Redwood Park, Felton, 831/462-0553. The Santa Cruz Symphony Orchestra honors fathers with classical pops in the park.

JULY

Coastal fog lingers as inland valleys heat up. Halibut and salmon swim along the coast.

Summer programs begin at local parks. At Wilder Ranch State Park, two miles north of Santa Cruz, 831/426-0505, docents dressed in Victorian attire present crafts and farming demonstrations of yesteryear. Rangers and docents lead guided walks and share their knowledge of natural wonders and local history at Seacliff State Beach, 831/685-6444; Big Basin Redwoods State Park, 831/338-8861; and Big Sur State Park, 831/667-2315.

Friday Nights Free Concert Series begins at the Santa Cruz and continues through late August, 831/423-5590. Free concerts feature great bands of the '50s, '60s and '70s.

Some Fourth of July Celebrations:

World's Shortest Parade, Rancho Del Mar to Aptos Village, Aptos, 831/688-1467.

Celebration and Firecracker 10K, Harvey West Park, Santa Cruz, 831/429-3665.

Fireworks over Christmas Hill Park, Gilroy, 831/842-6437.

Granite Rock's Independence Day Concert, Quarry Road, Aromas, 831/768-2300. The Monterey and Santa Cruz County symphonies and local rock bands accompany firecrackers over a lake in the area's largest quarry.

Hometown activities in the park and fireworks galore at Cambria, 805/927-3624.

Parade and City Celebration, Monterey, 831/646-3866. A hometown flag-raising parade down Alvarado Street features marching bands, clowns, jugglers, military units, and more.

Usually in the First Two Weeks:

Handcar Races and Steam Festival, Roaring Camp, Felton, 831/335-4484.

July 10. Sloat Landing Ceremony, Monterey, 831/649-7118. Commemorates anniversary of Commodore Sloat's landing with the laying of wreaths, military band performances, and a gun salute.

California Rodeo, Salinas, 800/771-8807. America's best cowboys compete for world championship points on the wildest broncos and bulls in the country. Also trick riders, horse races, and horse show competitions.

Beach Street Revival, Watsonville, 831/724-3900. Nostalgic car show and festival with live entertainment, car races. "Twilight Time Cruise," car auction, contests, kids' activities, and a variety of food and special interest booths.

Obon Festival, Monterey Peninsula Buddhist Temple, Seaside, 831/394-0119. Music, food, and celebration.

Often Later in the Month:

Carmel Bach Festival, Carmel, 831/624-1521. A three-week celebration of classical music, highlighting J. S. Bach. Includes concerts, recitals, educational events, children's concerts, and a candlelight concert at the Carmel Mission Basilica.

Gilroy Garlic Festival, Gilroy, 831/842-1625. The garlic capital of the world celebrates with three days of food and fun.

Moss Landing Annual Antique and Flea Market, Moss Landing, 831/633-4501. Vendors from all over the West Coast display and sell their treasures.

Musical Saw Players Festival, Roaring Camp, Felton, 831/335-4484. Unique saw instrument musical festival.

Wharf to Wharf Race, Santa Cruz to Capitola, 831/429-3665. A 10K race for true athletes and fun runners including bands, bird callers, and six-foot-tall squid.

Wineries Passport Program, 831/479-9463. Tours of and tastings from a variety of Santa Cruz wineries. Special restaurant presentations.

AUGUST

Poison oak turns fiery red along paths and up the trunks of trees. Be extra careful with fire this time of year.

Carmel Shakespeare Festival comes alive in August and continues to October, 831/622-0100. Performances are presented at the historic outdoor Forest Theater.

Shakespeare Santa Cruz, Performing Arts Complex, University of California, Santa Cruz, 831/459-2121. This month-long outdoor theater festival enjoys a reputation for innovative interpretations of Shakespeare productions.

Usually in the First Two Weeks:

The Annual San Juan Bautista Flea Market and Antique and Collectible Show. 831/623-2454. For over thirty years this show has presented some of the best collections in California.

Cabrillo Music Festival, Civic Auditorium, Santa Cruz, 831/426-6966. The Santa Cruz Symphony presents classic and modern themes in a week of concerts that include a children's concert in the park and concerts in Mission San Juan Bautista. Includes an arts and foods festival.

Calamari Festival, India Joze, Santa Cruz, 831/427-3554. Contest for best squid art, squid tasting, and squid review entertainment.

Carmel Valley Fiesta Days, Carmel Valley, 831/659-4000. A weekend celebration featuring food, games, music, parades, entertainment, arts, crafts, and a Saturday night street dance.

Dickens Universe, Kresge College, University of California, Santa Cruz, 831/459-2103. A gathering of Dickens lovers—students, scholars, and members of the public.

Monterey Scottish Festival & Highland Games, Monterey, 831/648-5360. This traditional gathering of Scottish clans and families includes a parade, live bagpipe music, Highland and country dancing, Scottish food, and athletic competitions.

Russian-American Festival, Harvey West Park Clubhouse, Santa Cruz, 831/439-3778. Russian and Ukrainian arts, crafts, food, music, and dancing.

Often Later in the Month:

Aloha Outrigger Races and Polynesian Festival, Municipal Wharf, Santa Cruz, 831/429-3477. Outrigger competitions, novice races, and Polynesian cultural event with food, dance, music, and more.

Antique Tractor Pull, Casa de Fruta, 10031 Pacheco Pass Highway, Hollister, 408/842-9316.

Monterey County Fair, Monterey, 831/372-5863. Carnival rides, agricultural displays, livestock exhibits, and home arts are the hallmarks of this county fair.

Pro Volleyball Tournament, main beach, Santa Cruz, 831/429-3665.

Annual Monterey Historic Automobile Races, Monterey, 831/648-5100 or 800/327-SECA (7322).

Concours Italiano, Quail Lodge, Carmel Valley, 831/624-1581 or 425/688-1903. The finest Italian automobiles and Italian products are showcased on this lawns of this elegant resort.

Pebble Beach Concours d'Elegance and Christie's Auction, Pebble Beach, 831/659-0663. Considered the world's most prestigious Concours, the Pebble Beach event showcases more than a hundred of the world's finest classic automobiles. Auction proceeds benefit local charities.

SEPTEMBER

Sycamore leaves turn golden. Round pods hang from the bare branches of buckeye trees. Summer fog retreats and clear days prevail.

Usually in the First Two Weeks:

Greenfield Broccoli Festival, Greenfield, 831/674-3222. Enjoy more than thirty arts and crafts booths, entertainment, and a variety of broccoli delicacies.

Santa Cruz County Fair, Santa Cruz County Fairgrounds, 831/724-5671. Carnival rides, local agriculture, displays by artists.

Annual Greek Festivals, Monterey, 831/424-4434, Santa Cruz, 831/429-6500. Festivals feature authentic Greek food, live music, traditional dancing, and crafts.

Begonia Festival, Capitola Village, 831/476-3566. Two-week festival; the high point is a parade of begonia-covered floats down the San Lorenzo River.

Fiesta Italia, Santa Rosalia Festival, Monterey, 831/649-6544. An all-day Italian event includes an outdoor mass, parade, procession down Main Street to Custom House Plaza, blessing of the fishing fleet, food, and entertainment.

Often Later in the Month:

Monterey Jazz Festival, Monterey, 831/373-3366. The oldest continuous jazz festival in the United States, starring some of the greatest jazz performers in the country. Music, clothing, and food booths. Outdoors during the day and under the stars to the morning hours.

Castroville Artichoke Festival, 831/633-2465. At the artichoke capital of the world, this festival provides entertainment, a crafts fair, a parade, and food.

Capitola Art and Wine Festival, Capitola Village, 831/475-6522. Art in the park and a long beach promenade. Tastings of local vintners' wines.

Monterey Bay 10K Run for the Beacon, Monterey, 831/372-2334. A 10K race along the coastline, including a Kids' Fun Run. All proceeds benefit the Beacon House, a drug-and-alcohol rehabilitation program.

Ohlone Day, Henry Cowell State Park, 831/335-3174. Ohlone stories, music, food, and crafts under the redwoods.

San Juan Arts & Crafts Show, San Juan Bautista, 831/623-2454. More than 300 vendors, live entertainment, specialty foods, family fun.

Shark Festival and Feeding Frenzy, Municipal Wharf, Santa Cruz 831/429-3477. Entertainment, educational shark information, and live pup tank above the ocean on the Santa Cruz Wharf.

OCTOBER

Monarchs fly in for the winter. Look for them at Pacific Grove and at Natural Bridges and Andrew Molera state parks.

Usually in the First Two Weeks:

California International Airshow, Salinas, 831/754-1983. Top civilian and military acrobatic performers take to the sky to benefit local charities.

Carmel Performing Arts Festival, Carmel, 831/644-8383. Music, dance, and theater in a variety of Carmel locations.

Cherry's Jubilee, Monterey, 831/759-1836. Antique cars, automobile regalia, music, and fun fill this weekend.

Salinas Valley International Mariachi Festival & Conference, Salinas, 831/424-7611. Spectacular concerts, educational music workshops, and family festival.

Fireworks Spectacular, Municipal Wharf, Santa Cruz, 831/429-3477. The city of Santa Cruz celebrates its anniversary with a grand display of fireworks.

Indy Car World Series at Laguna Seca Raceway, Monterey, 408/648-5100 or 800/327-SECA. The final stop on the 1993 PPG/INDY car world series, featuring some great race stars.

Jewish Food Festival & Crafts Fair, Carmel Valley, 831/624-2015. Family festival with delicious food.

Loch Lomond Highland Games, Highland Park, Ben Lomond, 831/338-1722. Traditional Scottish game competitions, bagpipes, harps, and Celtic arts and crafts.

Open Studios, Santa Cruz, north county, 831/688-5399. Arts and Crafts studios open their doors to display their work. Meet local artists, visit studios, and purchase one-of-a-kind pieces, for two weekends.

Butterfly Parade, Pacific Grove, 831/646-6520. Elementary school children parade in butterfly costumes and different themes to welcome the return of the Monarch butterfly.

Pacific Grove Victorian Home Tour, 831/373-3304. Visit impeccably restored Victorians often featuring artwork of owners and antique furnishings.

Welcome Back Monarchs Day, Natural Bridges State Beach, Santa Cruz, 831/423-4609. Educational booths, music, merriment and munchies, and the superheroes Monarch man and Monarch woman welcome the return of the monarch butterflies to Santa Cruz county.

Gorda Jade Festival, Gorda, 805/927-5574. The largest gathering of jade artists in the country.

October 13. California Constitution Day, Monterey, 831/649-7118. Festivities celebrate the signing of California's Constitution in Colton Hall.

Often Later in the Month:

Apple Butter Festival, Gizdich Ranch, Watsonville, 831/722-1056. Traditional copper-kettle cooking, canning of apple butter, hay rides, pumpkin patch, and apple juice bottling.

Big Sur River Run, Big Sur, 831/667-2100. A 10K Run through the redwoods and oak groves of beautiful Pfeiffer Big Sur State Park.

Harvest Festival and Draft horse Days, Wilder Ranch State Park, Santa Cruz, 831/426-0505. Experience the farming techniques of the past as a variety of draft horses, farmers, and volunteers provide demonstrations.

NOVEMBER

Shorebirds and waterfowl flock to Elkhorn Slough. The first of the migrating gray whales are spotted off the coast.

Usually in the First Two Weeks:

Pacific Grove Band Review, 831/646-6520. High school bands from throughout Northern California compete in marching and performance competitions.

November 13. Robert Louis Stevenson's "Unbirthday," Monterey, 831/649-7118. Join young and old alike to wish Robert Louis Stevenson a "Happy Unbirthday", see pages 12–13.

Rosemary Festival, Cambria, 800/266-HERB(4372). Festival celebrates rosemary and other herbs.

Often Later in the Month:

Christmas Craft & Gift Fair, Cocoanut Grove, Santa Cruz, 831/423-5590.

DECEMBER

Christmas tree lighting ceremonies and holiday festivals brighten the coast from Cambria to Santa Cruz. Northern storms send gifts of large waves to beaches. Eagle tours begin at Lake San Antonio.

Usually in the First Two Weeks:

Festival of Trees, Monterey, 831/372-5477. View lovely Christmas trees at the Museum of Art, each uniquely decorated with handcrafted ornaments.

December 10. La Posada, Monterey, 831/646-3866. A traditional Christmas candlelight parade led by carolers in Spanish and English. A piñata party follows the parade.

Lighted Boat Parade, Santa Cruz Yacht Harbor, 831/425-0690. Features boats with yule lights and holiday themes.

Christmas in the Adobes, Monterey, 831/649-7118. Monterey's historic buildings are candlelit and enhanced by period Christmas decorations, musical entertainment, and the presence of costumed volunteers.

Christmas at the Inns, Pacific Grove, 831/373-3304. Victorian bed and breakfast inns decorated for the holidays hold open house.

New Year's Eve

First Night Monterey, 831/373-4778, and Santa Cruz, 831/425-7277. Each community celebrates New Year's Eve with grand community family-oriented festivals of visual art, dramatics, performing arts, and music.

BIBLIOGRAPHY

Ansel Adams. *Ansel Adams: An Autobiography.* Boston: Little Brown and Company, 1985.

California Coastal Commission. *California Coastal Access Guide.* San Francisco: University of California, 1997.

Clark, Donald Thomas. *Monterey County Place Names: A Geographical Dictionary.* Carmel Valley, Calif.: Kestrel Press, 1991.

Dana, Richard Henry. *Two Years Before the Mast.* New York: Penguin Books, 1981.

Fink, Augusta. *Monterey County: The Dramatic Story of Its Past.* Santa Cruz: Western Tanager Press/Valley Publishers, 1972.

Gilliam, Harold, and Ann Gilliam. *Creating Carmel: The Enduring Vision.* Salt Lake City: Peregrine Smith, 1992.

Gordon, Burton L. *Monterey Bay Area: Natural History and Cultural Imprints.* Pacific Grove, Calif.: The Boxwood Press, 1977.

Gordon, David, and Alan Baldridge. *Gray Whale.* Monterey, Calif.: Monterey Bay Aquarium, 1991.

Hensen, Paul and Usner, Donald J. *The Natural History of Big Sur.* Berkeley and Los Angeles: University of California Press, 1993.

Howard, Donald M. *Early Man of the Monterey Peninsula.* Carmel, Calif.: Antiquities Research Publication, 1978.

Koch, Margaret. *Santa Cruz County: Parade of the Past.* Fresno, Calif.: Valley Publishers, 1973.

Lydon, Sandy. *Chinese Gold: The Chinese in the Monterey Bay Region.* Capitola, Calif.: Capitola Book Company, 1985.

Margolin, Malcolm. *The Ohlone Way: Indian Life in the San Francisco Monterey Bay.* Berkeley, Calif.: Heyday Books, 1978.

McLane, Lucy Neely. *A Piney Paradise: A Pictorial Story of the Monterey Peninsula.* Monterey, Calif.: Herald Printers, 1975.

Miller, Henry. *Big Sur and the Oranges of Hieronymus Bosch.* New York: New Directions, 1957.

Monterey Bay Aquarium. *A Natural History of the Monterey Bay National Marine Sanctuary.* Monterey, Calif.: Monterey Bay Aquarium Foundation, 1997.

Monterey Peninsula Japanese American Citizens League. *The Japanese of the Monterey Peninsula:Their History & Legacy 1895-1995.* Monterey, Calif.: Monterey Peninsula Japanese American Citizens League, 1995.

Muir, John, and J. R. Fitch. *Picturesque California: The Rocky Mountains and the Pacific Slope.* San Francisco and New York: J. Dewing Company, 1887.

Schaffer, Jeffrey P. *Hiking the Big Sur Country*. Berkeley, Calif.: Wilderness Press, 1995.

Silberstein, Mark, and Eileen Campbell. *Elkhorn Slough*. Monterey, Calif.: Monterey Bay Aquarium Foundation, 1989.

Steinbeck, John. *Cannery Row*. New York: Bantam Books, 1945.

Steinbeck, John. *East of Eden*. New York: Viking Press, 1952.

Young, Stanley. *Paradise Found, the Beautiful Retreats and Sanctuaries of California and the Southwest*. San Francisco: Chronicle Books, 1995.

INDEX